ABINGDON PREACHER'S ANNUAL 1994

ABINGDON PREACHER'S ANNUAL 1994

COMPILED AND EDITED BY

John K. Bergland

ABINGDON PRESS

Nashville

For Barbara
A faithful ally, dear friend, strong encourager, and devoted wife.

She provides space when I need it, does the worrying when I'm careless, and stays in touch.

When long days have become long nights, and the work is still not done, she brings bread for the desert (sandwiches) and wine for the journey (black coffee).

For forty years we've been a family, and the end is not yet.

CONTENTS

□

7

CONTENTS

8

CONTENTS

CONTENTS

SECTION II
SERMON RESOURCES

11

PREFACE

□

The *Abingdon Preacher's Annual* for 1994 is a resource for preachers who want to know what the Sunday lessons are and what they are about. The new Revised Common Lectionary, Cycle B, determines the scripture lessons that are addressed in this book. The texts, textual comments, and reflections that will help the preacher get started, or as Halford Luccock used to say "prime the pump," are provided for each Sunday of 1994. There is also a complete sermon based on one of the Sunday lessons.

Dr. Robert Cushman, a distinguished theologian and the former dean of Duke Divinity School, had preached a sermon in a morning chapel service. I found it very helpful. When I expressed my gratitude for such a good word, I referred to his sermon as "true biblical preaching." His terse response was, "If I didn't have the Bible, I wouldn't have anything to say."

If that is the case for a gifted, scholarly, and insightful preacher and teacher such as Dr. Cushman (one who has read and remembered more good books and current literature than even the most zealous readers among us), it is surely true for us. Without the Bible to inform Christian preaching, we have nothing to say. George Buttrick, for many years the preacher at Harvard, felt so strongly about this that he wrote, "There is no true preaching except biblical preaching." (*The Interpreter's One Volume Commentary on the Bible* [Nashville: Abingdon, 1971], "The Bible and Preaching," p. 1255.)

Use of the lectionary does not ensure that preaching will be biblical. A sermon can begin with a text, illustrate with biblical sermons, and proof text every point and still not be biblical. For a full discussion of the ways to measure and test true biblical preaching, read Tom Long's recent book, The Witness of Preaching (Atlanta: John Knox Press, 1989). Dr. Long, who teaches preaching at Princeton, has also provided helpful suggestions for guiding the biblical preacher in the move from text to sermon.

Use of the lectionary does provide a helpful beginning place for ministers who address the same congregation week after week. One does not need to search for a subject and look for a text. The lectionary text finds you.

13

Dr. Wallace Fisher, pastor emeritus of The Lutheran Church of the Holy Trinity, in making the case for biblical preaching, observed that "biblical preaching is not reserved for an intellectual elite. . . . The task is within the reach of any committed person who, possessed of emotional resilience and intellectual curiosity, accepts God's authority, honors his demands, claims his promises, and works at preaching" (*Preaching and Parish Renewal*). Dr. Fisher has contributed the Christmas sermon for this annual.

For every Sunday of the church year, this book provides:

1. The Old Testament, Epistle, and Gospel lessons assigned to each Sunday.
2. A brief summary of the contents of each lesson.
3. Reflections related to the text that are intended as sermon idea starters.
4. Two prayers for the day.
5. Suggested hymns.
6. The psalm or other act of praise assigned for each Sunday.
7. A responsive call to worship that is based on Scripture.
8. A complete sermon related to one of the lectionary texts.

The ministers who have written the sermons for the *Abingdon Preacher's Annual* represent varying theological positions. They are broadly based, both geographically and denominationally. The sermons have not surfaced from any competition or comparison. These sermons are the witnesses of men and women who are alert, responsive, and committed to the lasting authority of the Bible and the Word. They reflect the unique and differing gifts of persons whom God has called to preach. One thing is the same for all of them—they want an increase of faith and love in church and in the whole world.

Some of the sermon contributors are well known and widely heard. Others preach in more obscure, but not less important, places. (There are no small churches, only churches of small membership.) The sermons of bishops, homiletics professors, chaplains, media preachers, and modern-day prophets will be found in this book, along with the sermons of parish pastors and parish priests.

Now we offer our work as a beginning place and resource for yours. Use it confidently, preach boldly, and be assured that the word of God will not return empty.

The preachers of the New Testament and prophets of the Old Testament have something in common. They were reluctant and anxious about their role. They simply did not want to be that lonely voice proclaiming the Word of God. Jonah tried to run away from the call. Moses argued that others were better suited for the task. Elijah despaired of it all and hid in a cave. Amos preferred being a shepherd. Paul kicked against it, and Peter claimed to be unworthy.

In his book *Freedom and Destiny* (New York: W. W. Norton Company, 1981) Rollo May names such a response as being one of "the anxious prophet." He suggests that one can distinguish between true and false prophets by the sense of anxiety they have about their role. True prophets dread the responsibility. Pretenders welcome the chance to do it. "Authentic ones do not want to be prophets; they do their best to decline the role. They would escape if they could because of the dizziness and dread such great freedom entails" (p. 193). Noting that freedom and anxiety are two sides of the same coin, he points out that *angst* (anxiety that dreads) is a part of the possibility and risk of a new idea or vision.

We encourage you not to let the anxiety of the prophet cause you to trust the witness of somebody else more than you trust your own. Texts are larger than any preacher or any single sermon. Texts yield many insights for many preachers. Choose and use freely the commentary, sermon ideas, and illustrations found in this book, but do not stop there. Let us join together in work and prayer so that biblical sermons—prompted by the text, shaped by the text, and judged by the text—will be heard in the church.

As editor, I have compiled the sermons and prayers found here. I have outlined the Sunday lessons, written brief descriptions of each text, added some comments, and have authored the reflections, or sermon starters. But this is not my book as much as it is our book. I am indebted to the preachers who have contributed sermons. Jill Reddig, an Abingdon editor, has provided general oversight and helpful guidance. Marcia Moritz has typed large parts of the manuscript.

PREFACE

This is an ongoing series. On the last page of this book there is a form you may use to subscribe to subsequent issues of the *Abingdon Preacher's Annual*. You will automatically receive each new volume as it is published annually.

John Bergland
Pentecost, 1992

SECTION I

□

FIFTY-TWO WEEKS OF SUNDAY SERMONS

JANUARY 2, 1994

☐

Epiphany

The call goes out to all people in every nation—"Your light has come. Come and worship."

The Sunday Lessons

Isaiah 60:1-6: "Arise, shine; for your light has come" (v. 1) are words spoken for the new Jerusalem. The light of the Holy City is contrasted with the darkness that covers the other nations. "Nations shall come to your light, and kings to the brightness of your dawn" (v. 3). A camel caravan will come from Midian, Ephah, and Sheba. "They shall bring gold and frankincense" (v. 6).

Ephesians 3:1-12: Paul the apostle to the Gentiles writes about God's revelation, "the Gentiles have become fellow heirs, members of the same body, and sharers in the promise" (v. 6). The apostle's ministry was "to bring to the Gentiles the news of the boundless riches of Christ" (v. 8). He encouraged them to be confident in their access to God through faith.

Matthew 2:1-12: "Wise men from the East came to Jerusalem, asking, 'Where is the child who has been born king of the Jews' " (vv. 1-2). Herod was troubled and wanted the child dead. The Jews were indifferent. Magi (men wise about sacred things) came from afar to worship the child. Matthew employs Micah's words (Mic. 5:1-2) to lift up the Davidic line and the Isaiah 60:7 passage to recall traditions of frankincense and gold. The gifts, frankincense and myrrh, were vegetable resins from southern Arabia, quite scarce and very costly. They, along with gold, were worthy gifts for a king.

Reflections

A rabbi had expressed his worry about an ambitious evangelistic and missionary outreach program that The United Methodist

19

Church called Key 73. His worry was that such an effort did not respect his faith and that it threatened religious freedom.

A Christian pastor responded with D. T. Niles's familiar words—"One beggar telling another beggar where to find bread"—and assured his Jewish friend that the program was intended to share good news. The rabbi's terse response was, "I have bread. I don't need yours."

Two assumptions are apparent in the dialogue. The first is that clearer light, a new revelation, a new savior has come to offer new bread. The second is that there are outsiders in darkness who eagerly seek the light and who will, upon invitation, follow the Bethlehem star.

The words of the English poet Ben Jonson portray another point of view.

> But make my strengths, such as they are,
> Here in my bosom, and at home.

Some folks do not want to go anywhere to find new light, and would just as soon be left alone.

The phrase "rich in mercy" (Eph. 2:4) must never be forgotten by the church. Paul says it again and again. God is rich in mercy. "Grace was given . . . through grace given." The apostle sees it to be the beginning of everything important. In a pagan world filled with fear, he offered good news to challenge the fates, the follies, and the harsh realities of life itself—good news about love for and trust in a God of mercy. The magi came bearing gifts. Christian missionaries are sent bearing the gift. (JKB)

A ROAD MAP TO BETHLEHEM

Matthew 2:1-12

A SERMON BY MICHAEL B. BROWN

Every year about this time you expect me to trot out the customary wise men's sermon—you know, the old three-point outline on gold, frankincense, and myrrh, or the traditional "Going Home by Another Way." In fact, often that sermon comes earlier.

We don't even wait for Epiphany. If we sing it as a Christmas carol, then, by golly, let's preach it in December! (It's kind of like pizza. What the heck if it's an American dish! It looks Italian; it smells Italian; it tastes Italian; let's call it Italian!)

Well, according to the calendar of the Christian year, today is the day for the sermon. I hope you won't be too disappointed if I part with tradition a bit this morning and skip the part about how the wise men went home by another way. For our purposes today, let us spend a few minutes thinking instead about how they got to Bethlehem in the first place.

You recall the story—how they followed a star as far as the palace in Jerusalem. Why follow it all the way to Bethlehem? Kings aren't born in out-of-the-way places like Bethlehem; they are born in capitals like Jerusalem. Kings aren't born in mangers; they are born in palaces. So, the Zoroastrian priests went to the palace and asked Herod: "Where is the child who has been born king of the Jews" (Matt. 2:2)? Herod, who felt there was only room in his kingdom for one king, found their question troubling. So he gathered his advisors (his own wise men) and posed to them the question that had been posed to him. One of his advisors knew the answer: He will be born "In Bethlehem of Judea, for so it has been written by the prophet [and then he quoted that famous passage from Micah]: 'And you, Bethlehem, in the land of Judah, are by no means least among the rulers of Judah; for from you shall come a ruler who is to shepherd my people, Israel' " (Matt. 2:5-6). The wise men listened carefully and followed those directions to Bethlehem where the star came to rest over a house. And in that house they found the Savior.

When visitors from the East came asking how to find Jesus, this story says they ultimately located him because someone in Herod's palace had read the Bible. You will find him in "Bethlehem of Judea: for so it has been written by the prophet" (Matt. 2:5). They found him by looking to the scriptures.

One of my colleagues in ministry directs the program of Evangelism and Church Growth for the Virginia Annual Conference. Recently, we were together in a meeting at Lake Junaluska. While there, he shared the story of getting to know a man from Malaysia who presides over the work of The Methodist Church in his country. This man felt called a few years ago to go into the Malaysian bush country (the jungle area) to win converts to the

faith. Friends and family members warned him not to go. Too
many villagers had disappeared into the bush country never to
be seen again. But he felt compelled to "go into all the world
making disciples," and he could not be dissuaded. All went well
for a while. In fact, he established churches among several tribes
and baptized a fair number of first-time believers. One day he
was driving his Jeep back home a bit later than usual. Ordinarily,
he tried to be home before sunset, but this time darkness fell
while he was still in the bush. Rounding a corner on a dirt road,
he was stopped by a dozen men, two of whom were carrying
guns. He recognized immediately that they were pirates, infa-
mous in the region for robbing travelers by night. They searched
him and his car and found little of value—with one exception.
He happened to be carrying an English translation of the Bible.
The leader of the pack was impressed. He wanted to learn English in order to seize advantage over the increasing number of
English-speaking travelers who passed that way. Thus, he
informed the minister that from that moment on, he would be
the property of the pirates. They took him to their campsite at
gunpoint and kept him there for six full months. By night they
would do their work of thievery. By day they would sit and listen
as he read them stories from the "English book." (What they did
not know, of course, was that every English lesson was also a lesson in biblical studies.)

At the end of six months, he was awakened early one morning
by the gang's leader. "Pack your things," he ordered. That took
only a moment, as he had hardly anything with him. Outside the
hut were the other eleven pirates, all crammed into the four-
seater. "We're going home with you," the leader announced, "so
you can teach us more of this man named Jesus whose stories are
in your book." And so they did. The man and his eleven kidnap-
pers returned to the village (where all had long since assumed his
death; they had even performed his funeral). The pirates moved
into his home, ate from his table, slept beneath his roof, and listened to his stories. Then came the morning when the leader
again made an announcement: "We will be baptized and join
your church."

Today those former pirates are residents of the village. And
each morning they rise early, dress, put Bibles under their arms,
and walk into the bush country. For they know where the other

pirates live. Daily they go to those people, risking their lives, to tell them of the Christ whom they found in the Book.

"Where is the child who has been born king of the Jews?" The wise men found their King because someone had read the scriptures and knew how to tell them where to look. You shall find him "In Bethlehem of Judea, for so it is written by the prophet."

Most of us are indebted to our own version of the court advisor or the Malaysian evangelist. Few of us simply awoke one morning and decided: "Today I will purchase a Bible, skim through it, and see if I can discover a Messiah." Not at all. Most of us were introduced to Jesus by someone who had already met him—a spouse, a parent, a coach, or a Sunday school teacher, a friend in the dorm, or a pastor. Someone was able to point us to Christ by pointing us to the Book.

And, like those Malaysian pirates, when we open the Bible, we do not just find Jesus. We also find ourselves. Prior to reading the Bible, those twelve men lived only to steal. Afterward, they lived instead to give themselves away for God and neighbor—flesh and blood examples of Christ's words: "Whosoever shall lose his life for my sake and the gospel's, the same shall find it." They read the Bible and found a sense of meaning and purpose for life.

Why did Schweitzer remain in Lambaréné? Why does Mother Teresa continue her work on the streets of Calcutta? Why do third-world missionaries endure stress, deprivation, and danger? Why do people with Masters degrees shun the white-collar office and work for little more than minimum wage staffing clothing closets and soup kitchens? I suspect it is not because of innate altruism. Rather, I would wager, somewhere along the line they read the Book. And in that Book they met Jesus. And in that meeting they heard a call to take up the cross and follow.

I was intrigued to read an account of Terry Waite upon his release from five years of captivity in Lebanon. Apparently, he had been warned by the terrorists that if he returned to the Mideast he would be taken captive. However, in spite of their warnings, return he did. And they made good on their threats. It is reported that one night one of the captors asked him: "Did you not understand our threats?" "I understood," he answered. "Did you not believe them?" "I believed." "Then why did you come back?" "I came back," he answered, "because my mission was not over. They were hostages whom I thought I could help. They were worth the risk."

Probably, for most of us, our sense of mission will not be quite so dramatic as Schweitzer's or Mother Teresa's or Terry Waite's. But still we are called to serve. For some, it means working with youths. For others, it means teaching church school or singing in choirs. Perhaps, it is to write notes to the sick, phone the lonely, visit the homebound, or offer a listening ear to those who hurt. Whatever our avenue of service may be, we are all called to touch lives and mend wounds and spread faith. Life remains empty and unsatisfying until we hear and answer the call. And we hear it only when we read the Book and catch within it the voice of the Savior.

Suggestions for Worship

Call to Worship (Ps. 72:1-3):

LEADER: Endow the king with your justice, O God.

PEOPLE: The royal son with your righteousness.

LEADER: He will judge your people in righteousness.

PEOPLE: Your afflicted ones with justice.

LEADER: The mountains will bring prosperity to the people.

PEOPLE: The hills the fruit of righteousness.

Act of Praise: Psalm 72:1-7, 10-14.

Suggested Hymns: "We Three Kings"; "Go, Tell It on the Mountain"; "Lead, Kindly Light."

Opening Prayer: We gather, O God, as people on a journey. We are men and women in search of truth. Guide us along right paths that lead to your presence. And having found you, make our lives guideposts that point others in your direction. Amen.

Pastoral Prayer: Gracious Lord, author of life that matters, we offer you thanks for all that we have been given. You have provided to us unconditional love, unearned opportunity, and undeserved forgiveness. *Thanks* is so small a word—not even minimally adequate for all we feel. And yet we have no other word that will do.

Perhaps, O God, it is not so much in speaking that our gratitude is expressed, for no words are sufficient. Instead, this day we offer other treasures upon your altar. Here we place our possessions to be fully at your disposal. Here we place our egos to be shaped and edited by your truth. Here we place our deeds to be transformed into Christ-like selflessness. Here we place our loves that you might make them pure. Here we place our dreams that they may be in harmony with your will. Here we place our professional lives that wherever we labor and in whatever capacity, we may see ourselves as ministers for you. Here we place our churches that they may not simply have the form of religion, but the essence as well. Take all these gifts, O God, and look upon them as our offerings of thanks.

In the name of him known as the way, the truth, and the life, we pray. Amen.

JANUARY 9, 1994

□

First Sunday After Epiphany

The presence of the Spirit is evident in these lessons that center on the baptism of Christ.

The Sunday Lessons

Genesis 1:1-5: The creation story begins "darkness covered the face of the deep, while a wind from God swept over the face of the waters" (v. 2). God said, "'Let there be light'; and there was light" (v. 3). Light, firmament, earth and vegetation, moon and stars, birds and fish, animals and man are products of the six days of creation. A recurring verse speaks of God's pleasure with it all. "And God saw that it was good" (v. 10).

Acts 19:1-7: When Paul came to Ephesus he found some disciples who had been baptized and asked, "Did you receive the Holy Spirit when you became believers" (v. 2)? The text distinguishes between the baptism of John the Baptist, a purification rite associated with repentance, and Paul's baptism in the name of the Lord Jesus. There were about twelve who received Paul's blessing. "The Holy Spirit came upon them" (v. 6).

Mark 1:4-11: During Advent these verses were read to focus attention on the mission of John as forerunner. Christ's baptism is the traditional emphasis for the First Sunday After Epiphany and is the first manifestation of his glory. "He saw the heavens torn apart and the Spirit descending like a dove on him. And a voice came from heaven, 'You are my Son, the Beloved'" (vv. 10-11). The presence of the Spirit, the beginning of Christ's mission, and God's delight in him are evident in the text.

Reflections

Hugh Anderson's commentary on Mark notes, " 'The Spirit descending upon him like a dove,' does not denote that Jesus is uniquely possessed inwardly of the Spirit . . . the evangelist

26

intends the descent of the Spirit upon Jesus to indicate that the days of Spirit-famine are ended and that the Spirit is potently active in this new and last epoch."

These lessons provide the preacher an opportunity to speak about the gift of the Spirit and the manifestation of its power in cosmic and universal terms. Sometimes, teachings regarding the Holy Spirit are set in personal and individual frameworks in ways that shortchange the biblical teaching.

The Son of God is the central figure who is to be remembered and honored on this Sunday. We are well acquainted with his virtues that have caused persons in every age to adore him: His kindness, wisdom, and strength; his humility, gentleness, and patience; his courage, confidence, and obedience to the highest; his insight, joy, and vision; his sacrificial suffering, forgiveness, and death for others. But these virtues have been present in others, and yet lacked power to save anyone or anything.

Poured out Spirit is the key to understanding him and knowing him. If you liken it to a discouraged team that suddenly changes from losing to winning—same players but a new spirit—you may begin to see the way of it. It is too small of an idea, however. Not even a discouraged and disillusioned nation transformed by new spirit, or a lukewarm and insipid church reborn, or even darkness and void being displaced by light and order—all of it good—can fully express the power of God's Spirit. It is before all, above all, beyond all. Rejoice when heaven opens.

THOUGHTS ON DAY AND NIGHT

Genesis 1:1-5

A SERMON BY MICHAEL B. BROWN

A newspaper article referred to a certain school system where a furor had arisen. The article dealt with Darwinism revisited. A parent, browsing through his daughter's elementary school science text, wondered why creationism had not at least been mentioned as a possible explanation of how things came to be. It was not so much that he agreed or disagreed with the theory. He simply felt that a well-educated person should be exposed to all the various philosophies of the origin of life. So, innocently enough it seems, he mentioned his concern to a neighbor who happened to attend a rather fundamentalist church. Within weeks, the neighbor had organized a group of concerned parents from his church to storm a meeting of the school board. At that point, the war was on. In any event, the well-thought-out article made an important observation. It said that the final issue at stake had little or nothing to do with the original concern expressed by that dad. He was interested in education; the final issue had become politics. He was interested in his daughter's science text; the final issue had been a battle for power. He was interested in thinking about how the world came to be; the final issue was one of church caucuses versus school boards. And somewhere along the line, said that article, the entire question of "How did we all get here?" was lost.

It is interesting, isn't it, that the Bible (our definitive text) never really argues the issue of creationism versus evolution. It never argues; it simply believes: "In the beginning . . . God created the heavens and the earth" (Gen. 1:1). That's it. Then comes a lengthy roll call of all that God made: waters, land, and air; day and night; sun and moon; trees and fruits; fish; then animals; and finally us—"male and female he created them" (v. 27). Genesis chapter 1 is a beautiful unfolding—an *evolution* of creation, if you will, one step followed by another and another. And the issue at stake is so much more important than science or politics. The issue at stake is faith. "In the beginning God created the heavens and the earth"—in God's own way by God's own method.

You want to argue that Darwin was a fool? That God created it all in six days and that we really do not have any distant cousins at the state zoo? Fine. You can use the first chapter of Genesis to make that argument rather emphatically. Or do you want to argue the "Big Bang" theory? Fine. How's this? And "God said, 'Let there be light'; and there was light." Bang! Just like that. That, also, is from Genesis chapter 1. The fact is, whenever we begin arguing the how of creation, we have missed the point of the Bible. The Bible is not interested in "the how." The Bible concentrates on "the *who*" of creation. How God made the world is God's business. That God made the world is the business of faith.

Okay, enough about that. If we can simply accept the fact, as scripture does, that God made the world and all within it, then we can move on to listen to this text for a personal word. And you know where I hear that word? I hear it in the words *night* and *day, darkness* and *light.* Listen with me.

Darkness covered the face of the deep, while a wind from God swept over the face of the waters. Then God said, "Let there be light"; and there was light. And God saw that the light was good; and God separated the light from the darkness. God called the light Day, and the darkness he called Night. (Gen. 1:2*b*-5*a*)

Perhaps in hearing those words you, as I, sense metaphors for work and rest (laboring by day and sleeping by night). I was riding down Interstate 85 recently with a colleague in ministry. He serves a large congregation in Alabama, one of the fastest growing churches in America. Additionally, he has a wide-scale and time-consuming television ministry, oversees a congregation with well over one hundred active program agencies, and serves his denomination in various administrative posts. A person gets tired just looking at his calendar. "How do you do it all?" I asked. "How in the world do you bear up under the weight of your responsibilities?" He answered: "I don't take a day off. But I do take some time off every day." That's the secret. He is a man with burdens to shoulder and obligations to fulfill. His work demands constant attention. But he realizes that to take proper care of his work he must also take proper care of himself. So many of us fail to achieve that balance and thus fail to accomplish what otherwise we could have. There is a biblical principle involved here. "And God separated the light from the darkness" (v. 4*b*). There is a time for attempting, acquiring, achieving, accomplishing. There is also a time for resting, relaxing, recreating, refueling. The last without the first is laziness. But the first without the last is craziness. All work and no play not only makes Jack dull; in time, it makes Jack dead.

Some time ago I was complaining about my schedule to a man from Oklahoma. He is a devoted, highly skilled, hard-working pastor of a seventy-four-hundred member church . . . a man who knows about managing a busy calendar. I complained to him that I had a growing hatred of highways and airports, that I was beginning to resent my schedule and the fact I was so rarely at home and my children were growing up without me. He said: "Michael, you'll resent your schedule less if you learn how to manage it. Block out segments of time on your calendar every week for your family. Then, if someone asks for that period of time, just answer honestly, 'I'm sorry. I have a prior commitment.'"

Do you remember the old song, "Work for the Night Is Coming?" In our busy, professional lives, perhaps the opposite is also good advice. Rest, at least occasionally, for the day is coming when work is once more at hand. I cannot take care of my responsibilities effectively unless I take care of myself effectively.

I also hear day and night as metaphors for joy and sorrow. "Darkness covered the face of the deep . . . Then God said [amid the darkness], 'Let there be light'; and there was light. And God saw that the light was good" (vv. 2-4).

Since our earliest recollections were first put to parchment, we have been telling the same story of the same experience: how life sometimes feels like "a formless void, and darkness cover[s] the face of the deep" (v. 2). There are seasons of shadows in everyone's life, times when we feel abandoned and alone, hopeless and helpless. And since history's earliest days, we have been testifying that when things were at their worst, "God separated the light from the darkness" (v. 4). In other words, God is present with us—whatever the place or situation—and has the power to turn the nighttime of the soul into day.

Statistics tell us that the nighttime of the soul is a very real phenomenon in our culture and age. Almost 30 percent of us are living under significant stress. Thirteen million of us will worry intensely for at least ninety minutes today. Twenty-seven percent of us claim never to have a genuinely peaceful day. Twenty-two million Americans live alone, and just over 70 percent of us confess to feeling lonely.* We deal with anger, rejection, grief, fear, economic stress, isolation, guilt, divorce, abusive relationships, chemical dependency, depression . . . and the list goes on. And most of all, we fear that there is no way out—that we are abandoned to our pain—that night has fallen, and dawn will never come, and we are desperately alone. To those fears our morning lesson says: "Darkness covered the face of the deep, while a wind from God swept. . . . Then God said, 'Let there be light.'; and there was light" (vv. 2-3). In other words, in our loneliness, we are not alone. The Spirit of God is present and moving. In our

---

*Statistics taken from *American Demographics, MD Magazine* and the *U.S. Census Bureau*.

darkness, there is the promise of light. In our struggles, there is the unfailing love and nearness of one who is greater than whatever the world can throw our way.

In the beautiful North Carolina mountains there is a host of stories about the Native Americans indigenous to our region. I have always loved the one about the ritual of initiation for Cherokee boys who were crossing into manhood. Around age ten or eleven, the youngster would be taken by his father deep into the Pisgah forest. Dad would give his son a bow and one arrow. As darkness descended, the father would leave his son alone in the forest to prove his bravery by facing the frightening sounds of the night. Most of the young boys did not sleep much. Every hoot of an owl sounded like a threatening voice. Every cracking twig conjured up images of a bear or bobcat on the prowl. Every rush of wind sounded like whispers of the enemy in the forest. However, when daylight began to break, the young brave would spot another Cherokee off in the distance beside a tree. It would be his father, who had been there all night long, sitting silently nearby, watching, making certain that his child never actually had to face the darkness alone.

So it is with us. However dark and desperate things may feel, God is near—always watching, always caring, always protecting us from facing the darkness alone—and always promising that in due time God will separate the darkness from the light, and the dawn of joy and peace will break upon our weary souls again. It will happen for you, however much you may doubt it. God has not abandoned you to the nighttime. It will happen. The voice will sound: "Let there be light!" And in time your shadows will disappear.

Suggestions for Worship

Call to Worship (Ps. 29:1-2,11):

LEADER: Ascribe to the LORD, O mighty ones, ascribe to the LORD glory and strength.

PEOPLE: Ascribe to the LORD the glory due his name;

LEADER: Worship the LORD in the splendor of his holiness.

PEOPLE: The LORD gives strength to his people; and blesses his people with peace.

Act of Praise: Psalm 29.

Suggested Hymns: "Love Divine, All Loves Excelling"; "Hope of the World"; "Nothing But the Blood."

Opening Prayer: How wonderful, O Lord, are your tender mercies. The remembrance of them fills our hearts with joy and hope. You are to us a loving parent who nurtures each child, whispering the gentle reminders of your presence. Come again into our troubled world with peace. Come again into our waiting lives with love that will not let us go. Amen.

Pastoral Prayer: O God, creator of life, we turn to you for guidance and strength. We trust in your presence, even when we cannot feel it. We believe in your love, even when we feel unlovely. We are assured of your grace, even when we labor under guilt. We stand firm in your power, even when we have no power to stand ourselves.

Ours can be a frightening world: wars and rumors of wars, hatred and slander, poverty and illness, deprivation and want, rejection and guilt, grief and solitude. Too many shoulders are never wet with another's tears. Too many ears fail to listen when we cry out for help. But you, O God, are always there for us— loving, forgiving, encouraging, empowering us to cope and, in time, to overcome. For this we are grateful.

We realize, O Lord, that as you do for us, we are called to do for others. There are lonely people whom we can befriend. There are frightened people whom we can encourage. There are hungry people whom we can feed. There are homeless people to whom we can offer shelter from the storms. There are people who have never been told of your saving love. We are, O God, stewards of that message. In all these things keep us faithful. As you reach into our lives with hope and gladness, inspire us to reach into others' lives with the truth that sets us free. These things we ask in Jesus' name. Amen.

JANUARY 16, 1994

☐

Second Sunday After Epiphany

The call to discipleship is lifted up in the Old Testament and Gospel lessons. The Epistle teaches that body and soul belong to Christ.

The Sunday Lessons

I Samuel 3:1-10 (11-20): Three times Samuel heard someone calling his name. He thought it was the blind Eli, whom he served, that was calling. The old priest counseled the youth, "If he calls you, you shall say, 'Speak, LORD, for your servant is listening'" (v. 9). Samuel was called to be priest and prophet. The books of Samuel and Kings emphasize his prophetic character rather than his priestly role.

I Corinthians 6:12-20: There were some members of the Corinthian church who claimed to be special leaders. In moral teaching and sexual conduct, they misinterpreted Christian freedom as license. "All things are lawful" (v. 12). Paul teaches that appetites of the body must be controlled, "The body is meant not for fornication but for the Lord . . . your body is a temple of the Holy Spirit within you . . . therefore glorify God in your body" (vv. 12-20).

John 1:43-51: Andrew and another disciple of John the Baptist (possibly the author himself) heard him say, "Look, here is the Lamb of God" (v. 36), and began to follow Jesus. The next day Philip and Nathanael were called. Nathanael, questioning if anything good could come from Nazareth, was told, "Come and see" (v. 46). Complete confidence and faith does not precede their following. It comes to them in small signs (like knowing Nathanael before meeting him), greater signs, and in seeing heaven's doors wide open.

Reflections

The absence of leadership is a frequent complaint of this generation. We want Congress to lead, civic authorities to lead, bishops to lead, pastors to lead, but most of all we want a leader whom all can follow. I want a Messiah whom I can trust with my whole life. Don't you? Military commanders are usually the image employed for great leaders. Soldiers follow to their deaths. Any study of military history will show, however, that there has always been waste, confusion, and goldbricking in military life, from Greece to Rome to twentieth-century armies.

Business and industry continue to analyze leadership. Prentice writes in an article, "Understanding Leadership," "Attempts to analyze leadership tend to fail . . . he misconceives his task . . . he studies popularity, power, showmanship, or wisdom in long-range planning . . . they are not the essence of leadership." He goes on to observe that "human beings are not machines with a single set of push buttons."

When being introduced to a secular leader, we are told about his or her talents and achievements. When our loyalty is solicited, we are told about how good it will be for us. (Some choose the latter style to recruit followers for Christ.) True leadership has an innate power to attract followers. No image makers, power brokers, or coalitions are needed.

There were no promises and no assurances (or threats) for those first disciples; instead, simple words such as *look* and *see*. John the Baptist simply said "Here is the Lamb of God who takes away the sin of the world" (John 1:29). Philip's only encouragement to follow him was "Come and see" (v. 46).

The call of God is so gentle and retiring that it is seemingly shy. One asks, "Who called?" Yet, for those who stop to hear, turn aside to see, and begin to believe apart from any mighty works—the power of his presence and the glory of his vision will claim unending devotion. And they will follow. And they will see. (JKB)

CALLED TO PREACH, NOT YELL

I Samuel 3:1-10, I Corinthians 6:12-20, John 1:43-51

A SERMON BY KENNETH W. CHALKER

Not long ago a woman of about seventy-three came to see me. Having no money for bus fare, she had walked a long distance.

This woman had been spending a number of days walking around Cleveland going from social agency to social agency seeking help for her situation.

Exhausted and tearful, this woman told me that her Social Security check was a month late. The folks at Social Security had made a mistake in her file. So her livelihood was stopped as a result of a record-keeping snafu. Instead of her regular check for a little more than five hundred dollars for the month, they issued her an emergency disbursement check for two hundred dollars, a letter asking her landlord to give her extra time in paying the monthly rent, and the assurance that all would be cleared up by the next monthly pay period.

But after four weeks, the two hundred emergency dollars had run out. The promised check had not come. Other than a can of tomato soup, she had not eaten in several days. She did not even have money for the bus in order to get to our meal program at First Church. There was no phone in her apartment to call for any help, she had no family left, she would not beg—she had worked all her life—so as a last ditch effort she had decided to walk the three miles from her apartment to downtown Cleveland to see if the folks at Social Security could help her.

There was nothing they could do except assure her that the check would be coming in another two weeks. The paperwork had taken longer than they had expected, and "No, we cannot issue another two hundred dollar check because that is all we are permitted to issue to one person in such a situation." With no other options known to her, she came to see me.

Reverend, I am hungry. I am tired. It is late, and I don't want to walk home in the dark. Could you lend me some money 'till my check comes? I need to get a bus pass, some food, and a can of insecticide." The last request came because the landlord was refusing to do anything about the roaches. She said they were so bad at night she had been sleeping on four metal chairs because "the roaches don't climb up on them as much as they do my bed."

Now, as you might suspect, we hear a good many stories such as this from people who come into the downtown churches through the week. Much of the time, while the need is there, the stories about *why* there is the need are not true. But this woman was telling all the truth. And the more I worked with the folks who could provide some long-term assistance for her, the more I discovered that things were harder for her than she was even telling.

Perhaps it was the thought of this seventy-three-year-old woman who had worked her entire life, a woman with dignity and self-respect reduced to sleeping on metal chairs and being hungry that did it, I am not sure. But as I talked with her I just could not help it. My eyes filled with tears.

I was not particularly prepared for what happened next. This woman saw the tears in my eyes and said, "Don't be pathetic with me! Don't look at me with those sad eyes because then I'll cry." I told her that I just could not help it, and asked her what she wanted me to do. She said, "I want you to yell at me and tell me that I'm to blame for all of this. If you yell at me it will make me stronger. It will make me feel guilty, and I won't let it happen again." I told her that I could help her with money for food, the bus, the bug killer, and even work to try and find her a better place to live, but I could not yell at her and condemn her or judge her for the condition of her life.

I relate this incident to you this morning because it raises for me, and perhaps for you, the whole issue of yelling at people as a way to motivate them to do better with their lives. I relate it to you because it touches me at the very center of my understanding of the role of preaching within the church as a motivation for discipleship. Indeed, is the purpose of preaching to call down fire and brimstone and threaten everybody as a result of the way we are thought to behave? Is the role of the church in society to be the source from which guilt and judgment is inflicted as an explanation for and treatment of the bugs that exist in our world and lives?

The texts for this morning suggest something of the wide range of ways in which God motivates discipleship in difficult times. Nowhere is there evidence that people are being yelled at, threatened with hellfire, or manipulated with guilt in order to achieve a conversion in an individual or society.

As little Samuel lies on his bed in the Temple, it is a time when the word of the Lord is rare and no vision is evident. This is not unlike the present American scene when our apathy for the future and for public leadership is so great. Paul is preaching centuries later to a community where the pluralism in social conduct and religious belief has made evangelism for any view difficult. People are emotionally shut down with the pervasive idea that "everybody is entitled to do his own thing as long as it doesn't bother me."

In such a context, God is not revealed in damning fire and smoke, but in a voice to the least likely. Into Samuel's consciousness comes a call so unusual that it is not clear who it is that is calling. Finally, Samuel discovers that it might be God. "Speak LORD, for your servant is listening" (I Sam. 3:9).

Paul does not damn, on God's behalf, everybody and everything around him. He reveals no new method for manipulating the deity or guaranteeing financial success like some hysterical, contemporary television hellfire evangelist. Paul, filled with the Spirit, excitingly reveals that each human being is not a replaceable part of a greater whole, but a temple of the living God, a holy space and place. Out of a sense of wonder and amazement that God might actually be a part of an individual life, people are encouraged to act in ways that are consistent with their role as holy architecture.

Have you ever wondered what it was about Jesus that caused people like Nathanael to leave the life they knew to follow Jesus? Was it fear, threat, guilt? I don't believe it was any of those. What caused people by the thousands to come to hear Jesus speak? What was it about him that could motivate people to risk walking away from their daily chores—chores that when left would threaten their livelihood—gather up their families or friends and walk to some hillside, city, or lakeshore just to see him, touch him, or maybe be touched by him?

Think about it. How many places in the remembered utterances of Jesus did he ever yell at, condemn or judge a person, either for what they were or for what they were not? Clearly, there were people with whom he took issue, but did he ever seek to alter a person's life by threatening damnation, inflicting guilt, or laying blame? Rather, Jesus awakened in people a sense of the divine power that was within themselves; a power available—but often ignored or repressed—for making life choices.

Jesus never once gave a stewardship sermon, for instance, that focused on asking people to give money to the synagogue. There was never a sermon from Christ saying you should feel guilty about your willingness to buy a new camel, or throw big parties, or buy things for yourselves when the synagogue cannot meet its budget.

Instead, Jesus was able to invite people to be heirs of the kingdom of God, present with us already, which is like a pearl of great price or a treasure buried in a field. And people, fascinated by such an engaging mystery, would reexamine their priorities with the result that giving a tithe or all that they had would not be enough. But the giving came from awakened gratitude, and not from a coerced, begrudged spirit under threat.

Jesus never condemned people for adultery, stealing, lying, or cheating. While he was a rigorous proponent of the Ten Commandments, his care for people was directed in such a way as to help people see how breaking those commandments hurt another person and led to the death of one's own soul. In Jesus' presence, one's soul was so alive that the sordid things of life had no power. Indeed, it was by awakening the power within that Jesus enabled people to take responsibility for a dynamic new direction in living.

Jesus never once inflicted a penalty for missing confession. He never told people they would go to hell for missing church and going to chariot races instead. He did not condemn parties, games, or having fun. Instead, Jesus was often the life of the party and the provider of the best wine. What Jesus *did* say was that to live in selfishness, to avoid the true worship of God with others, to think one's life and income to be the measure of one's own skill and never be grateful, or to be so self-centered and self-absorbed as to confuse a pig's life-style and food as a good life is to set a course for becoming a prodigal child.

With the exception of Pharisees and Sadducees, who believed they spoke for God in condemning others, Jesus did not yell at or condemn people. He invited them to see in themselves something that the world tries to take away from us every day: a sense that there is in each of us a divine power, which when recognized and nurtured, transforms the world in which we live.

Jesus knew that a person could go to church and never worship. He knew that we could meet, pray, sing, and never experience the spirit of God in our lives.

Jesus knew that a person could be married according to the law and never be committed to a spouse in heart or spirit.

Jesus knew that a person could do all the right things for the wrong reasons.

Jesus knew that people could condemn quickly the sexual behavior of some, the sexual orientation of others; that they could condemn alcohol and tobacco and all manner of vice and never once, never once represent the Good News that awakens the power within to overcome the forces that lead to aberration and addiction.

I suspect this is why, instead of fire and brimstone, instead of long phylacteries, and outward badges for religious achievement, Jesus said, "Follow me" (John 1:43). I suspect it is why Jesus said that the greatest law of life besides loving God is to love oneself so that caring about a neighbor is spiritually possible. And I suspect that it is why Jesus could see a man under a tree who only had a dim understanding of what it might mean to be alive and be a disciple and say, "You will see greater things than these. . . . You will see heaven opened and the angels of God ascending and descending upon the Son of Man" (John 1:50-51). Then and now, that is an offer we must not refuse.

Suggestions for Worship

Call to Worship (Ps. 139:1-4, 17):

LEADER: O LORD, you have searched me and you know me.

PEOPLE: You know when I sit and when I rise; you perceive my thoughts from afar.

LEADER: You discern my going out and my lying down; you are familiar with all my ways.

PEOPLE: Before a word is on my tongue you know it completely, O LORD.

LEADER: How precious to me are your thoughts, O God!

PEOPLE: How vast is the sum of them!

Act of Praise: Psalm 139:1-6, 13-18.

Suggested Hymns: "We've a Story to Tell to the Nations"; "Behold a Broken World"; "Dear Jesus, in Whose Life I See."

Opening Prayer: O God, who speaks in creative words and exciting deeds, we give you thanks for the ways in which you put content into our lives. Open our senses that we may perceive you and our minds that we may discern you as we follow in your way.

Pastoral Prayer: O God, we give you thanks for the exciting challenge of discipleship. We give you praise that you speak to us in uncommon ways and present dynamic challenges to us. Help us to have the courage to follow the way of your Son—the way that leads to abundant life. Amen.

JANUARY 23, 1994

□

Third Sunday After Epiphany

The lessons speak of repentance and change. Disciples left their nets to become fishers of men.

The Sunday Lessons

Jonah 3:1–5, 10: Nineveh was a large pagan city that symbolized enmity with God. Jonah, a narrow-minded, nationalistic prophet, wanted nothing to do with such foreigners. Nevertheless, he obeyed the second call and preached among them. "Forty days more and Nineveh will be overthrown!" (v. 4). The city repented. "And the people of Nineveh believed God" (v. 5).
I Corinthians 7:29-31: "The present form of this world is passing away" (v. 31). The subject Paul addresses is marriage and virginity. His teachings were based on his belief that Christ would come very soon and that it was expedient to get things right. He suggested that whatever marital state one was in should be continued. Let those who deal with the world live as though they had no dealings with it.
Mark 1:14-20: Jesus came into Galilee preaching, "The kingdom of God has come near; repent, and believe in the good news" (v. 15). This is Mark's account of the call of the disciples. By the Sea of Galilee Jesus said to Simon and Andrew, "Follow me and I will make you fish for people" (v. 17). Farther on he called James and John. They left their nets and followed.

Reflections

Repent in New Testament terms means more than "forsake your disobedience and obey." It means "believe the gospel and follow Christ." Find a new controlling direction for your life.

The phrase, "the time is fulfilled," suggests the eschatological nature of this lesson. There is no need to wait for anything or

41

anyone any longer. For that matter, the only waiting now is for
the final stop at the end. Now is the time to get on board.
There is an urgency in these lessons that should not be over-
looked. The apostle Paul seems to be in a hurry. He knows that
time is running out. Nineveh was given a grace period. Just ten
days more than a month. In forty days Nineveh will be destroyed.
The disciples left their nets and immediately followed.

In this sales-oriented society of ours, we are well acquainted
with ways in which we are urged to decide now. "Someone else
was just looking at this house and may buy it before tomorrow."
"This offer is good only until February 15th." "The supply is limited. Don't delay."

Sometimes urgency is employed in manipulative ways, but
sometimes it is absolutely sovereign. "This is not a *watch*. It is a
hurricane warning, and persons must evacuate this island immediately." "We cannot wait any longer. We go to surgery now."

The message of repentance is set in a context of time fulfilled.
Individuals and nations should not delay a reordering of their
lives—their values, their life-styles, their final allegiance. (JKB)

SPITTING FROM THE CLOSET

Jonah 3:1-5, 10

A SERMON BY KENNETH W. CHALKER

Several springs ago, accompanied by three excited family
members, I drove home from the Animal Protective League ken-
nel in Cuyahoga County, Ohio. We had just adopted a forty
pound, eleven-month-old dog. As the dog took up space all over
my delighted son's body, I knew she was destined to take up permanent residence in our home along with four red-bellied newts,
a frog, several fish, a gerbil, a rabbit, and an obnoxious cat.

Since that day the dog, now more or less answering to the
name Ebony, has become an important part of our family life. An
affectionate animal, she has quickly been accepted into our home
by nearly all the creatures who live there. There has been and
continues to be only one recalcitrant, annoying glitch in the
process.

The obnoxious cat that lives among us has taken great offense to Ebony. As a protest, the cat has determined to live its life in seclusion. It has moved into our bedroom closet. Even though my wife, Grace, and the kids try to pet the cat into contentment, it comes out only at nature's urging. Other than that, the cat is spendings its days in storage with empty shoes.

What is amazing to watch in all this, however, is the dog and the cat when they encounter each other. Ebony tries to be friendly. She wags away at the closet door, invites the cat to play, even lies down inviting the cat to check her out and be friends. But the cat simply stands in the closet with its fur on end hissing and spitting at the dog in the larger world beyond the closet door.

Now, I know that there are some of you who probably feel sorry for the cat. You are probably thinking that it has a right to be upset. It had no say in the decision to get the dog. But so what? I didn't either. Besides, sympathizing with such an attitude is a bit like siding with the child who cannot accept the guidance of parents and who says, "Hey, I didn't ask to be born," as if their lack of choice over birth entitles them to unchallenged choices now.

But all of that aside, we have this cat living in the closet of familiar, safe, well-worn things, hissing and spitting at the dog in the changed world outside.

As I watched our cat spitting at the dog from the closet, it occurred to me that here, in a small way, is one of the greatest problems in the world. The world changes. New lives come into it, new events, new challenges, and new opportunities to love and be loved while a great many times we respond by holing up in the closets of what hangs familiarly around us while we hiss and spit at what is new.

There can be no clearer example of such a person as this than Jonah. This irascible prophet is so committed to one way of believing and one way of thinking that when an international mission opportunity is placed before him, Jonah is not interested. In fact, he is scandalized that God would even operate outside of accepted tribal theology. God pushes. Jonah runs. He would rather be dead than caught involved in the redemption of people he has learned to hate.

Jonah has lots of followers. There are many folks in each generation who would rather fight than be converted, seek common affirmations, think globally, or recognize that being a neighbor has nothing to do with geography. I suspect that this is also why Jesus referred to Jonah as the applicable sign for his ministry. Recalcitrant Jonahs were the ones voting for the cross and cheering for familiar Barabbas.

This is what so often hurts the church. We are like Jonah when it comes to Nineveh or anything foreign. It is this attitude that drives so many people away from what has unfortunately been labeled as *organized religion*. Organized religion relies on structure, rules, accepted procedures, familiar forms and processes, and even on the oxymoron of an organized method of conveying to people the message that God is a free spirit who blows generously on people when and where God wills!

Organization is important, but with vital faith there is truth in the idea conveyed in the signs that read: "God bless this mess!" Such thoughts give me hope. Sometimes, when I observe that First Church has its share of disorganization, rather than feel guilty, I can thank God for the gift! I figure that it is no accident that scandals like the S&L failures are carefully planned while great discoveries and revelations come most often quite by accident and surprise. Evil, on the other hand, is organized. It is an ancient plot.

This is why Jesus calls us to disorganized religion. We experience it in part by rejecting the atittude of Jonah and embracing people who are not familiar, accepting people whose clothes are not like the ones we see in our closets, and checking out people who want to be loved who are new—whose experiences are a different world from our own.

But so often church people are like well-petted cats who hiss and spit from the familiar closets of their sanctuaries: well meaning, self-righteously condemning the world outside for not being like the one they know. It is important to remember in this context that they were religious cats living in familiar, organized closets who called Jesus a dirty dog and crucified him because he stood at the door of a temple-turned-closet and knocked. No one let him in or came out to meet him.

One does not need to look any farther than today's world headlines to see the critical results of organized living in familiar closets.

It was not long ago that Saddam Hussein, with a million soldiers under arms, was using chemical weapons on his own Iraqi people who were racially different from the majority. Is this not hissing and spitting from the closet of familiar views while condemning all who are different? Predictably, the world hisses and spits right back. We are lined up, as we so often are, for another cat fight. How have we come to this? How is it that the Saddam Husseins of the world come to power?

Is the Middle East not in conflict because organized religion is continually infatuated by its familiar, cherished rules and willingness to crucify people in order to keep the law? It is the sign of Jonah. It is everywhere. Sunni fundamentalism, Shiite extremism, the Christian right, the ultra-Orthodox Jew, the dogmatic Marxist—it is all closet living while hissing and spitting at a world of differences.

I do not believe the Jonahs in every culture would be as numerous as they are today if centuries ago we had begun, as Jesus asked, to accept people not like us as equals, as brothers and sisters, as children of God with as much of the spark of the Divine in them as we claim to have found in ourselves. Instead, we continue to value the things in our closets more than the people who produce them. So the value of gasoline rises, wars are made good for business, a lot of our sons and daughters never make it home for any holiday observance of any kind. This is the world of organized religion. It is the sign of Jonah, and it leads to the inevitable cross.

This is why it is so important to believe in and follow Jesus, to proclaim and live out his world-changing message. In a world of organized evil that knows nuclear bombs and chemical warfare, he calls you and me to exciting adventures, to walk on troubled waters by faith, to cultivate the liberal heart and examine the mind that does not fear differences, to come out of the closets and live in the light. This is why it is the spirit of Christ and not the personality of Jonah that saves the world from itself.

It is hard for us to understand why God loves the whole world. It is hard because human beings are so adept at thinking their space is the fairest of them all. For God to love the whole world seems like such a waste of divine affection when so many believe, like Jonah, that some portions of the world are more worthy to be loved than others. But God does love the *whole* world. And it is a good thing. Because if God can have an interest in saving places like Nineveh, then surely there is hope for the spaces occupied by you and me.

Suggestions for Worship

Call to Worship (Ps. 111):

LEADER: Great are the works of the LORD;

PEOPLE: They are praised by all who delight in them.

LEADER: Glorious and majestic are his deeds,

PEOPLE: And his righteousness endures forever.

LEADER: The works of his hands are faithful and just;
            They are steadfast for ever and ever,

**PEOPLE: The fear of the LORD is the beginning of wisdom;
            To him belongs eternal praise.**

Act of Praise: Psalm 62:5-12.

Suggested Hymns: "All Praise to Thee, for Thou, O King Divine"; "Jesus Calls Us"; "Ye Servants of God."

Opening Prayer: O God, in this time of worship help us to see ourselves as world citizens. Help us to understand in fresh ways that Christ is for the world. Amen.

Pastoral Prayer: O God, who sent Christ, not for condemnation but that the world might be saved, strengthen us to believe in these prejudiced and polarized times that this witness is sure and true. Amen.

JANUARY 30, 1994

□

Fourth Sunday After Epiphany

True authority is above and beyond the influence of traditions,
demons, kings, judges, and does not depend on a majority vote.

The Sunday Lessons

Deuteronomy 18:15-20: Pagan nations sought the counsel of
sorcery, but Moses describes the role of the prophet. "The Lord
your God will raise up for you a prophet like me from among
your own people" (v. 15). Such a prophet will not simply offer his
own ideas. "I will put my words in the mouth of the prophet, who
shall speak to them everything that I command" (v. 18).

I Corinthians 8:1-13: Concerning food offered to idols, the
gnostics—an elite group of intellectuals—claimed knowledge
that freed them from compelling superstitions. Paul agrees
"there may be so-called gods . . . yet for us there is one God . . .
for whom we exist" (vv. 5-6). But the apostle goes on to call for
community responsibility above individual freedom. "If food is a
cause of their falling, I will never eat meat" (v. 13).

Mark 1:21-28: "He taught them as one having authority, and
not as the scribes" (v. 22). Jesus' teaching in the synagogue in
Capernaum is linked with an account of an exorcism. A demo-
niac, not allowed to be in the synagogue, but there nonetheless,
cries out against Jesus, who then casts out the demon. "He commands even the unclean spirits, and they obey him" (v. 27).

Reflections

"What's his quality?" someone asked. Another answered, "He's
his own man." He had qualities of boldness and freedom that set
him apart from others, freed him from stifling traditions, insu-
lated him from praise or blame, and seemed to get him beyond
the compelling words, "you must," that prompt the responses of
most of us.

47

Have you ever watched a young colt—full of himself and unaware of any boundaries—run free? But no colt goes very far before encountering fences. No young person, enthusiastic and independent, lives very long without encountering life's limitations. No one, employed by the system, can ever escape the "must" of it.

That's why they were astonished by Jesus' teaching, and amazed by his power over evil. Taught that there are some things that should not be thought and must never be said, and aware of the things one can only accept, they suddenly realized that the ultimate authority, the final word, the Holy God was among them.

All authority belongs to God. Some of it is given to apostles, and a bit to kings and judges. So reads the New Testament. Now we have come to believe in a democracy where the last word belongs to the vote of the people. John Wesley and his Tory Methodist preachers did not believe that authority should ever be given to the public (i.e., the vote of the common man). Today, left with his structures of government in The United Methodist Church, we are conflicted. We can indeed outvote the bishop. Authority and power do reside in majority rule. But we are foolish if we try to challenge the gentle rule and sovereign grace of God. You cannot vote on it. (JKB)

CHRIST'S POWER

Mark 1:21-28

A SERMON BY DAVID W. RICHARDSON

Jesus taught with authority. He acted with power. Authority and power were one in Jesus. Then, as now, preachers and teachers cite authors, or authorities. Jesus' authority was from God and in him in a new kind of teaching.

Authority and power are not always coexistent. For example, let us imagine that a preacher was leading the congregation in worship. He or she has the authority to do that. If one or more people enter to rob the worshipers, they would have power but not authority.

In our scripture, Jesus is in the synagogue at Capernaum on the Sabbath. Synagogues did not have regular preachers as most churches have. They had a person known as the Ruler, who was responsible for administration and arrangements for services. Imagine the shock of having a man shout "What have you to do with us, Jesus of Nazareth? Have you come to destroy us? I know who you are, the Holy One of God" (v. 24). We would give such a person a questioning look at best. Then Jesus cast out the unclean spirit.

We can be thankful we do not live in such a terror-filled world. The late William Barclay informs us that some people believed there were seven and one-half million demons. It was said that every man (and presumably woman and child) had ten thousand on the left hand and ten thousand on the right hand. There were specific demons of leprosy, blindness, and heart disease. People were afraid to open their mouths because a demon might come in and make them sick.

If these people thought they had a demon, they would need to hear Jesus cast them out. Do demons possess us today? Some doctors today have patients who swear they have ailments, and so the doctors prescribe placebos. The madness of Nazi Germany and Stalin's Soviet Union are not far behind us. In fact, that madness is a rising force in the world.

The timeless question is "Is Christ's authority and power relevant today?" The *St. Louis Post-Dispatch* had some heated letters to the editor comparing the merits of Christianity and atheism. I had the feeling that both sides overstated their case, and more pertinent, neither side conceded the faults of their adherents. Isn't it interesting that atheists point out such things as witch trials and slavery— that are a century or more past—without being so bold as to say, "We have had until recently three officially atheist countries: the Soviet Union, China, and Cuba. We regret the oppression and murders that were done in these officially atheist countries."

Look at the neo-Nazis who have sprung up in America. An unnamed Los Angeles detective declared, "They are a threat to the moral fiber of our society." In the 1980s these people were thought to be responsible for over 300 assaults, over 300 cross burnings, and over 120 murders. These people and the Ku Klux Klan say they are Christians, but they actually reject Jesus' authority.

We tend to think of the demonic as the cocaine user, the robber, or the killer. But evil exists among those who know the proper wine to order and the proper fork to use. A man took over one of the leading magazines. He also wrote an autobiography. His recollection of what he did in WWII, his college degree, his pro-football experience, and many other facts were imaginary. Yet, asked what was the most important thing about him, he declares, "More important than anything else is that my word is my bond."

One day I chanced to watch a panel of teachers and a well-known television preacher. Somehow, the word *psychology* was introduced. That riled the preacher, who said something to the effect that if someone brought a book on psychology he would throw it out the window.

Have you ever known someone good enough or smart enough to win or be successful without cheating, but who cheats just to be cheating? A Californian in his early 20s persuaded investors to give him $10 million. He invested, but in a $2 million home for himself and $5 million in paintings. One person said, "The really sad thing is David could have made that honestly. I'd like to know what was going on inside his head." This young man chose to put a quotation from F. Scott Fitzgerald's *The Rich Boy* beside his picture in the yearbook: "We are all queer fish, queerer behind our faces and voices than we want anyone to know or that we know ourselves."

Do not these people need deliverance? Who among us is perfect in love? So we all need Christ's transforming power.

Let us remember, let us celebrate Christ's power. We do not know what happened to the man Jesus helped in the synagogue, but we do know of others: Simon Peter, Paul, Augustine, Luther, Calvin, Wesley, and all contemporary Christians—lay and clergy. We have realized that Christ's authority and his power—while not making us perfect—have changed our lives.

I saw an interview that illustrates what Christ's power can do. A couple was not able to have children, but was given a child by its father. Having kept the child a long while, the couple decided to adopt the child just at the point that the biological mother wanted her child returned. The court ordered that the biological mother receive the child. This man was at his office when his wife called with the bad news. He said that he planned to have the child's mother killed. Then he said, "Last Monday night I met the Lord." Tears came to his eyes and he said, "I met the Lord for the first time. Now I wouldn't anymore wish her harm [the child's mother] than I would you [the television news reporter]." A man was changed from wanting to murder someone because he had met the Lord. Can we deny Christ's power?

On January 5, 1988, Pete Maravich, one of the all-time great basketball players died at forty. He died playing basketball in a church, which was more fitting than many realized. Pete played at LSU and in forty-minute games over three years he averaged 44.2 points a game. Then he went to the NBA where he signed a $1.9 million contract and then a $3 million contract with the New Orleans Jazz. Over ten years, he led the league in scoring one year and made the all-star team five years.

Pete seemed to have everything that some of us envied. Pete became an alcoholic. In fact, Pete told of a girl sticking a pistol in his mouth and saying, "You're going to die, Pistol Pete." He said to himself, "Yeah, kill me, at least I'll have some peace." That explains why Pete said he used to laugh inside at the fame he had in the 60s, the wealth he had later on, and the way people idolized him. So he tried yoga, TM, Hinduism. Pete said, "My life had no meaning at all. With everything I tried, I found only brief interludes of satisfaction." Does that describe you? Then, in 1982, Maravich simply prayed, "Lord, I got nowhere else to go. If you don't save me, I won't last another two days." He was saved and his life changed. Not knowing that he had but six years to live, Maravich said, "My life has never been the same. I don't have much time left, but the time I do have I'm going to dedicate to the Lord." What do you suppose Pistol Pete Maravich would say if he could speak to us today? I think he would ask us, "Are you seeking those things that only briefly give satisfaction, or are you seeking the living Christ?" Pete only found fulfillment in Christ, and only in Christ's authority and power will we find fulfillment.

Suggestions for Worship

Call to Worship (Ps. 111:1-4):

> LEADER: I will give thanks to the LORD with my whole heart,

PEOPLE: **Great are the works of the LORD;**

LEADER: Full of honor and majesty is his work, and his righteousness endures forever.

PEOPLE: **He has gained renown by his wonderful deeds.**

Act of Praise: Psalm 111.

Suggested Hymns: "The Battle Hymn of the Republic"; "Blessed Assurance"; "Pass Me Not, O Gentle Savior."

Opening Prayer: God of grace and God of glory, forgive us for being dazzled by material things. Help us to be amazed by your Son's life, which was neither long nor bogged down with material things. As we testify that Jesus truly lived the abundant life, we remember that we are to find our meaning in you, not in the abundance of things. We pray in the name of him who gave up everything for us. Amen.

Pastoral Prayer: Our mighty God, forgive those of us who have handled your truths and spoken your name so often that we have become deadened to your presence and deaf to your contemporary word. Help us regain the excitement and the joy that would come if we were at the end of our emotional resources and stumbled into this place and heard the powerful words of the Good News.

Let us be joyous in our worship. Yet, let us be mindful of those who are unemployed and underemployed. We pray your blessings on those who grieve this day, for all who are lonely, for those who are hospitalized or confined, for all who travel this day, and for all who lack joy. We pray in the joy that comes from the assurance that our sins are forgiven and that our life is eternal in the name of him who is both our Crucified Savior and Risen Lord.

FEBRUARY 6, 1994

□

Fifth Sunday After Epiphany

These lessons present the healing ministry of the Christ.

The Sunday Lessons

Isaiah 40:21-31: Jerusalem had been destroyed. Its leaders and promising youths had been deported by Babylon, a world power that controlled everyone and everything. In that context, the prophet Isaiah speaks words of comfort and hope. His God, enthroned above the earth, sees its people as grasshoppers and its rulers as nothing. Those who hope in God will renew their strength and fly like eagles.

I Corinthians 9:16-23: Paul, who had every right to claim the pay and privileges given apostles, took none of them. "I have made no use of any of these rights" (v. 15). His motivation is in his call to preach. "Woe to me if I do not proclaim the gospel" (v. 16). His style is to identify with all persons. "To the weak I became weak" (v. 22).

Mark 1:29-39: Simon's mother-in-law, sick with a fever, was healed. The sick and possessed gathered at the door of Simon's house and many were healed. Jesus' fame and popularity grew rapidly, but "he got up and went out to a deserted place, and there he prayed" (v. 35). When found and told, "Everyone is searching for you" (v. 37), Jesus did not return to accept their praise, but went on to the next town to preach there.

Reflections

Some things are ordinary. Everyone who has skin knows that sooner or later it will grow old and wrinkled. Everyone who has a heart knows that one day it will fail. All strength finally gives way to weakness, and even in the midst of life we are inclined to death. Job reflects the condition of all human existence. Our lot will be sickness and suffering.

53

Some things are extraordinary. Failing hearts are repaired and replaced. Broken bones are reset and, when weak, are pinned or braced. Folks gather at the doors of heart surgeons and orthopedic surgeons who offer wonderful help and healing. On some rare occasions, when medical doctors reach their limits, faith healers offer miracles. Sometimes they claim too much.

No one remembering the ministry of Christ would deny his concern for suffering and sickness and his ministry of healing and wholeness. Some of us who serve in his name claim too little.

Mark's Gospel tells the stories of healing in the context of heaven and earth—between mud and stars. An ordinary town, an ordinary house, where ordinary illness is met by supernatural power that contests supernatural demons.

Are we then to expect and seek the supernatural such as miraculous healing? Are miracles the main thing? No, the Gospel lesson teaches that Christ saw the healings to be less important than his call to discipleship.

Mark's Gospel offers a Christ not only with healing in his hands, but also a Christ with nail prints in his hands. We will be forever weak if we reach only for his healing hand and never lend the strength of our hands to help carry the cross—to help, to heal, to restore.

"Not for profit!" "Not for fame." These are the clear messages that one must discern in the ministry of Jesus and the ministry of Paul. They rebuke the shallow and self-serving style of both our search and our service. (JKB)

HEALED? READY TO HELP?

Mark 1:29-39

A SERMON BY DAVID W. RICHARDSON

Centuries before Jesus, the Jewish people complained that God did not know their troubles or care if they suffered injustice. We know that from Isaiah 40. But does God care? A contemporary rock song has these lyrics, "He don't care who all gets hurt. . . ." Why would a person say God does not care who gets hurt? What basis do we have that God does care?

We could cite the great words of Exodus 3, "I have observed the misery . . . I have heard their cry . . . I know their sufferings" (v. 7). But it is too narrow a view merely to know that God cares about us. Unfortunately, too many Christians have this narrow view.

For a proper understanding, let us recall what Mark tells us. He tells us that Simon Peter's mother-in-law had a fever. Barclay tells us of the way the Talmud stated a fever should be treated. A knife solely of iron was tied to a thorn bush by a braid of hair. Then on three successive days were read Exodus 3:2, 3, then Exodus 3:4, and finally Exodus 3:5. Then a magic formula was pronounced and the cure was supposedly effected. In this case a lady needed healing, Jesus healed her, then, "she began to serve them" (v. 31).

Being healed presupposed a brokenness. Call it inauthentic. Call it sin. The church has declared we all have it. Do we forget, dressed as we are in our Sunday clothes, the truth of this?

We must look deeper than the outside to see us as we really are. Once, in St. Louis, I pulled into a parking space next to a Lincoln that was about four years old. A quick glance at the paint and the interior told me this owner had spent time maintaining its appearance. However, a broken radiator hose was causing very rusty looking antifreeze to leak onto the pavement. I went into the only nearby store and asked if anyone owned a black Lincoln. With pride a man stepped forward to say that it was his. He thought his car was in great condition and perhaps thirty minutes before I might have mistakenly agreed with him. I told him his antifreeze was leaking out. We went outside and I asked him when he had last changed his antifreeze. He did not know that he needed to change antifreeze. It needs to be changed every two years, so although his car looked great on the outside, inside there was corrosion.

We may think that we are not weak, but we all are at some point. We may think we are strong enough that we help others but do not need help. Let me tell you something I saw on an icy February day. While stopped at a red light, I saw a young woman come out with what may have been her grandmother. The younger woman said something like this, "I'll take your arm so you won't slip and fall." As I watched, can you imagine what happened? Yes, the younger woman slipped and the older woman had to save her from falling.

Somehow, some way, we need healing or help. Notice that the New Testament tells of Jesus coming to people who are in difficult situations and helping them. We have listened to the radio or watched television when we hear, "We interrupt this program to bring you news." It is almost always bad news. The church has declared that in Christ, God has interrupted history to bring us Good News.

The ancient world was not ready for Jesus as an infant or an adult. Some of us could testify that we were unprepared for Jesus to change our lives. In the life of a real woman named Beatrice, something unexpectedly happened. She was an alcoholic, but did not want to admit it. Some people from AA came to stay with her and finally she attended an AA meeting. She said she thought that she was supposed to have a spiritual experience, but admitted that she had not yet had one. Then she said, "My name is Beatrice. I am an alcoholic." The group loudly responded, "Hello, Beatrice." Tears came to Beatrice's eyes as she said, "I think I just had my spiritual experience."

Todd Marinovich was a quarterback on the Southern Cal football team. Those who remember his story know that Todd's father so wanted him to be a superb athlete that he was not allowed to eat red meat or such things as snack cakes. Perhaps it is not surprising that on January 21, 1991, Todd Marinovich was arrested for possessing cocaine and marijuana. His father would not come to see him in jail. He left jail with his mother saying, "I have just blown my life away." His maternal grandmother said, "And he wept all the way home." Remember what I said about Jesus coming to people in difficult situations and helping them. Todd said, "I wish I could go somewhere else and be someone else. I don't want to be Todd Marinovich." Somehow, I hope Todd has heard about a Simon Peter who failed three times, about a mistaken persecutor named Saul. Todd Marinovich could become a new person. So could we all.

Perhaps William Rockefeller felt overwhelmed by having John D. as a brother. In 1922, William Rockefeller was going to spend $250,000 erecting a magnificent tomb for himself. *Forbes* magazine, which prides itself of being for capitalism, nonetheless declared, "Few men of his wealth and opportunities have more completely failed to build for themselves a worthy place in the hearts of their fellow men." Thus, the difficult situation we might be in is that we are so filled with ourselves that there is no room for Christ to enter. How do we block out Christ? Aleksandr Solzhenitsyn declared, "Only those who decline to scramble up the career ladder are interesting as human beings. Nothing is more boring than a man [person] with a career." Walter Lippmann stated, "I learned from Frank Cobb . . . that more newspapermen [surely that includes television] were ruined by self-importance than by liquor."

God wants to help us to be our best, but being our best includes reaching out to others. Remember that Simon's mother-in-law served. Remember that the good Samaritan was ready to reach out and touch someone, someone with blood stains. If we feel we have been healed and helped, we are called to help others.

Frances Farmer was a well-known actress in the 1930s, but after a 1936 picture she made many enemies. Her story was made into a movie. She was so disliked that the people of "This Is Your Life" sought to relive her life and had to give up the project because they could not find one person willing to be on the show. How tragic!

Jesus has come to help us to be our best, but we must cooperate willingly. To what extent are we loving of those beyond our families? A cartoon showed two obviously successful men, but one man is very unhappy. The man is unhappy because he says, "Treat people as equals and the first thing you know they believe they are." The woman who says sarcastically to her niece after worship, "You'd better sign the guest book because you are so rarely at worship," has not learned to help.

Are we ready to help? Someone has suggested that there are three categories of people: those who make things happen, those who watch what happens, and those who wonder what happened. I could add another: those who did not know that anything happened. What of this category: those who do not care what happens as long as it happens to someone else?

Let us begin here at worship. The least you can do is to speak to someone before you leave. Do not wait until you are a member. Once, a man complained to me that those in his pew did not speak to him. I checked the attendance register and found that he, a visitor, was sitting between visitors. Let us heed the story of the prospective maid who said, "I can serve both ways." This astonished the wife who asked, "What do you mean 'both ways'?" "I can serve so they will want to come back, but I can also serve so they won't want to come back." How you act in worship and afterward will in some measure cause members and visitors to return or not want to return.

On Christmas of 1987, a nine-year-old boy from Quincy, Illinois, Patrick Stevenson, was really happy. He has cerebral palsy. That would not seem to make him happy. Patrick and his family and friends had gathered enough aluminum cans and donations to buy a $9,500 high-tech wheelchair that would not only move about, but also turn on lights and answer the phone.

What is worth remembering is that the Stevenson family decided to keep on collecting aluminum cans even though Patrick had his wheelchair. His mother, Sheila, said, "This is about the only way we can repay the kindness shown us."

Patrick had celebral palsy, others broke into his difficult situation with cans and donations, then his family responded by deciding to help others as they had been helped. They are committed to helping. So should we be!

Suggestions for Worship

Call to Worship (Ps. 147:1-11):

> LEADER: How good it is to sing praises to our God,
>
> **PEOPLE: How pleasant and fitting to praise him!**
>
> LEADER: Great is our LORD and mighty in power;
>
> **PEOPLE: His understanding has no limit.**
>
> LEADER: The LORD delights in those who fear him,
>
> **PEOPLE: Who put their hope in his unfailing love.**

Act of Praise: Psalm 147:1-11, 20c.

Suggested Hymns: "God of Love and God of Power"; "Jesus! the Name High over All"; "Only Trust Him."

Opening Prayer: Our God, for the assurance of your love, for the freshness of your mercy today, for your patience with us, we give thanks. May we hear your word in the spoken and written word so that we may worthily worship you. In Christ's name. Amen.

Pastoral Prayer: Eternal God, grant us an awareness of the greatness of worship today. Help us to realize that we join all the company of heaven in worshiping you. More, help us to realize that we do not have to come to you, because you have already come to us.

While we are different in our backgrounds, grant us to see that we have a unity in the needs you have fulfilled. We want to be loved, and you have loved us. We want to be able to grow, not to be bound by what we are. We acknowledge that you love us as we are, but you also love us so that you will not let us stay as we are.

Thus, we yield our minds and our hearts to Christ, who loved even those who crucified him. In his precious name, we pray. Amen.

FEBRUARY 13, 1994

□

Last Sunday After Epiphany
(The Transfiguration of the Lord)

That the glory of the Lord shall be revealed is the promise.
Can our poor eyes see and our finite minds understand?

The Sunday Lessons

II Kings 2:1-12a: Elijah made his last journey accompanied by
Elisha to Gilgal, Bethel, Jericho, and across the Jordan. Elijah
says, "Tarry here, for the LORD has sent me as far as . . ." (v. 2).
Elisha will not leave his master, and his final request is, "Please
let me inherit a double share of your spirit" (v. 9). Elijah answers,
"If you see me as I am being taken from you, it will be granted
you" (v. 10).
II Corinthians 4:3-6: Sophists who were skillful in devious
argument are contrasted with Paul's less interesting and heavy
method of preaching. If our message is veiled, Paul responds, it is
only veiled to those blinded by the world. We do not preach ourselves (i.e., employ sophisticated rhetoric like the Sophists), but
we preach Jesus Christ as Lord. The light of his glory has shown
in our hearts.
Mark 9:2-9: Peter, James, and John were with Jesus on a high
mountain when he was transfigured. Elijah, the greatest prophet,
was there. Moses, the great lawgiver, was there. In fear and confusion, Peter wants to build three booths and once again fails to
understand. The voice from heaven articulates the most grand
epiphany of all, "This is my Son, the Beloved" (v. 7).

Reflections

In late summer 1978, pilgrims began to come to the town of
Turin in northwest Italy. For six weeks they came, more than
three million, to view a piece of linen cloth that bears the image
of a man who was crucified. The shroud of Turin had been

brought out for public display for the first time in four centuries. Many believe the cloth is a postfiguration of the crucified Christ. The public exposition ended on Sunday evening, October 8, 1978. Then for five days scientists, employing technology that has photographed Mars, studied the shroud in the splendor of a crystal-hung hall often used to receive kings and queens. The ancient relic was removed from its nitrogen-filled case, and with the most modern microscopes, ultraviolet radiation, X-rays and infrared photography, scholars sought to verify its authenticity.

Newspapers still carry the stories. Some thinking men and women, impressed with scientific proof, find in the shroud a reason for faith. (*National Geographic,* June 1980, provides a full discussion.)

The Gospel lesson for today is cherished by the church as a prefiguration of Christ's resurrection glory. On Transfiguration Sunday, Christians around the world will remember, "His garments became glistening, intensely white, as no fuller on earth could bleach them" (Mark 9:3).

What are the manifestations that prompt us to call him Lord? The epiphany of all epiphanies was on a high mountain. A voice from heaven spoke of a poor carpenter from Nazareth who was going to a cross, saying, "This is the one, the only one in all of history who has it right." "This is my Son, the Beloved, listen to him" (v. 7)! (JKB)

I STILL DON'T UNDERSTAND

Mark 9:2-9

A SERMON BY GAYLE CARLTON FELTON

A name is Peter—Simon Peter. You may have heard of me; I'm sort of the captain of Jesus' disciples. Until a few years ago I made my living as a fisherman, but then Jesus appeared and changed everything. He called me to come and work with him, telling me that I would catch people instead of fish! I didn't understand what he meant, but he had such a wonderful appeal that I followed him and I have not been sorry. In the months since then I've seen a lot of unbelievable things happen. But recently I had the strangest experience of all—an experience that I still don't understand! Let me tell you about it!

A couple of weeks ago, Jesus told James and John and me to come with him, to leave the other guys behind—the rest of the disciples. I was really surprised, especially because Jesus and I were . . . well, not on such good terms. The truth is that the week before we had almost had a fight! At the least, we surely had a fuss! It happened in Caesarea Philippi as we were all walking together along the road. Jesus asked us—the whole group of disciples—he suddenly asked us, "Who do people say that I am?" The other guys told him some of the gossip that was floating around: that he was John the Baptist with his head put back on, or Elijah come back down from heaven, or some other prophet. Then he directed the question straight at us: "But who do you say that I am?" I popped up quickly because I was sure that I knew the right answer: "You are the Messiah, the Christ."

Jesus didn't dispute me, but he ordered us all sternly not to let anybody else know who he was. You won't believe what he said next! He started telling us very soberly all kinds of foolish things. He insisted that he was going to be rejected, undergo suffering, even be killed, and rise from the dead in three days! It was weird; it was ridiculous. Our prophets had promised for centuries that God would send a Savior, a Deliverer who would triumph over our enemies, a King who would destroy evil and establish God's rule on earth. This Christ could not be defeated, could not be executed. So, as soon as I got the chance I pulled Jesus away from the others and told him so. I argued with him vehemently, explaining as clearly as I could that he had it all wrong. Jesus really jumped on me! He was mad! He laid me out, called me "Satan" and said that I was not on God's side. I was hurt and confused . . . I still don't understand.

And then, like I said before, less than a week later, Jesus called me, along with James and John, away from everybody else, to climb a mountain with him. By the time we got to the top it was getting late in the day and beginning to turn dark. We sat down and prayed . . . or at least Jesus did. I admit I was too busy trying to figure out what we were doing up there. It had been a tough climb and the view was not that impressive. Suddenly, I realized that something was happening! Jesus' appearance was changing right before my eyes! There was light so brilliant that his very clothing looked pure, shiny white. But strangely, the light was not shining on him from the outside; it was shining out of him; it was coming from inside. Then he was no longer alone: Two other men were there talking with Jesus. I recognized them, or at least I knew who they were; I am not sure how I knew it. They were two people that I had heard marvelous stories about since I was a very young child—Elijah and Moses. Elijah—the great prophet who had been taken up into heaven in the chariot and horses of fire and whose return to the earth all good Jews anticipate. And Moses—who led our people in the Exodus from slavery in Egypt and gave us God's law on Mt. Sinai. I could tell when I glanced at James and John that they were as overwhelmed as I was. My own friend, Jesus, deep in conversation with these two heros who had done God's work in our past! It was clear that Elijah and Moses were recognizng Jesus as the one through whom that work would be fulfilled. Deep inside of me I knew that in Jesus the prophecy of Elijah and the other prophets was fulfilled. I realized in a flash that all the law of God given through Moses was summed up in the command to love God and other persons as Jesus loved.

I was really freaked out! I had seen some pretty impressive things in my time with Jesus, true, but never anything like this. The truth is that I was scared. And when I'm scared, I talk too much. I could hear myself babbling something about building booths; I wanted some kind of monument constructed to this glorious experience. I don't think that I ever finished my sentence, because even more astounding things began to happen. A sudden cloud cast its shadow over us all. It was not like a cloud threatening rain; it was a cloud promising presence. Through my mind flashed recollections of the cloud that led our ancestors through the wilderness, which hung above Mt. Sinai for six days when Moses received the law, which covered the Tabernacle when Moses met with God. And then the most amazing thing of all: the voice. It was not Jesus or Elijah or Moses speaking. It was the very voice of God . . . and it was speaking to us: "This is my Son, the Beloved, listen to him!" For once in my life, even I could say nothing.

I remembered that Elijah had heard the voice of God at the cave where he had fled; that Moses had so often talked with Yahweh. I remembered Jesus telling us about the voice he had heard at his baptism that had declared he was God's beloved Son. In

63

the presence of these awesome sights and sounds, with the help of these memories, I realized who Jesus really is. I had said the words before, but had not grasped their meaning. Jesus is the long-waited Messiah, the one whom God has promised to send to save us. He is the Christ—God's chosen one. He is the divine self in human flesh, God's self-revelation of who God is. In seeing the light radiating from him, we were seeing glimpses of that divinity shining through the curtain of flesh. Oh, don't misunderstand me. Jesus is a real person, a human being. Nobody knows that better than I do after living and working with him for so long. But he is also much more. The greatest wonder is not the momentary radiance we were seeing on the mountaintop, but that his divinity is concealed so much of the time. But now I've seen it . . . and heard God's voice confirm it. I'll never again doubt who he is. I'll never again question what he says.

The cloud faded away; Elijah and Moses disappeared; and Jesus led us back down the mountain. Although James and John and I were still stunned into silence, our minds were busy planning how we would describe what we had experienced to the other disciples. Jesus changed those plans when he instructed us clearly to tell no one about what we had seen until after his resurrection from death. Only then could the meaning of his Messiahship be understood.

I still don't understand. It's been a couple of weeks now and I have been able to think of little else. I keep seeing that brilliant light and hearing those voices . . . especially that voice—the voice of Yahweh. We have been traveling through Galilee and Jesus is healing the sick and teaching the crowds. I know now without a doubt that Jesus is God's revelation—if we want to know what God is like, we look at Jesus. I have the assurance of that because I have seen the divine glory emanating from him like rays of light might escape when you lift the corner of a veil that covers their source. And yet, I'm worried and really quite apprehensive. Jesus has told us that we are now going toward Jerusalem. I know that he has many enemies in the capital city, strong enemies who want to destroy him.

Many of the religious and political leaders believe that Jesus is a threat, that the good news he is proclaiming is dangerous, and that his popularity with the people is making them think in new and disturbing ways. Actually, they are right! Jesus is so different from any person that I have ever known, and after our experience on the mountaintop, I know why. I am awestruck now as I walk alongside him on the dusty roads. I find myself looking at him more intently and listening to him more passionately than I ever did before he was transfigured. I know now that my dear friend Jesus is not simply a great teacher and kind healer. I know that when I look at him, I see all of God that our human minds are capable of comprehending. When I listen to him, I hear the will of God for human lives. But I have heard him say more than once that he must suffer, die, and rise from death to manifest these truths to the world. I don't understand. Why would he need to suffer, much less to die, since he is who he is? Why can't he just announce himself and do something dramatic to show God's power? Why can't he just tell everyone who he is and then, after he's gotten their attention, explain to them what God is like? Why can't he overthrow the tyrannical power of the Roman government and reestablish the kingdom of David?

Maybe he knows there is a better way—a way that will make clear that God, who created us for loving relationship with God, is willing to go to any length to save us, a way that will show beyond all doubt how much God loves us. I wonder what lies ahead in the next few weeks. What's going to happen? I still don't understand.

Suggestions for Worship

Call to Worship (Ps. 50):

LEADER: The LORD speaks and summons the earth from the rising of the sun to the place where it sets.

PEOPLE: **Our God comes and will not be silent;**

LEADER: Gather to me my consecrated ones, who made a covenant with me.

PEOPLE: **The heavens proclaim his righteousness, for God himself is judge.**

Act of Praise: Psalm 50:1-6.

Suggested Hymns: "Immortal, Invisible God Only Wise"; "We Would See Jesus"; "Be Thou My Vision."

Collect: O loving God, who sent Jesus to show us who you are, jolt us out of our complacency and routine. Enable us to see marvelous sights and to hear the wonder of your voice speaking to us. May the light of your presence in Jesus Christ transfigure us, making us into channels of your grace at work in this world.

Pastoral Prayer: Holy God, whose nature and ways are far beyond our understanding, we thank you for the great gift of Jesus Christ. In him, we see you and learn that you are a God of love. In him, we see ourselves as you would have us be and as your power is able to make us. We pray for the transfiguring light of your presence to illumine our littleness and to purify our allegiances. We pray for the clear sound of your voice speaking to us the truth that we are often unwilling to hear. Make us want to be changed, suddenly and dramatically, gradually and daily, into the people you have created us to be.

We pray for the pain of this broken world and for those who suffer alienation, sickness, grief, and injustice. We pray for those—too often including ourselves—who are the instruments of oppression rather than the vehicles of reconciliation. Renew within the church the commitment and the compassion that we see in Jesus, our Savior, for we are aware that often we do so little because we care so little.

On this Sunday when we celebrate the Transfiguration of our Lord, give to us a more profound recognition of who he is and who, through him, you call us to be. Knowing that you are God too large for our understanding, we praise you that you are God large enough for all our needs.

FEBRUARY 20, 1994

□

First Sunday in Lent

The struggle with all that destroys is the theme of the first lenten lessons. The forty days of Lent are days when we recall the passion of our Lord in his struggle with evil. The Gospel lesson tells of the forty days in the haunts of destruction, of the wilderness, and that Christ was victorious.

The Sunday Lessons

Genesis 9:8-17: After the flood waters, God made a covenant with Noah. "Never again shall all flesh be cut off by the waters of a flood, and never again shall there be a flood to destroy the earth" (v. 11). The rainbow is the sign. The covenant, made with all the race, shows God's desire to save rather than to destroy.

I Peter 3:18-22: The lesson is a part of a baptismal sermon that recalls Noah and the eight persons "saved through water" (v. 20). The struggle against evil, evident in the persecutions faced by Peter's readers, is led by the Christ, "the righteous for the unrighteous" (v. 18), who "made a proclamation to the spirits in prison" (v. 19). Christians are identified with Christ's resurrection by rising from the waters of baptism.

Mark 1:9-15: After his baptism and the word from heaven, "You are my Son, the Beloved" (v. 11), Jesus is tempted in the wilderness. Wilderness for the Hebrew mind was the haunt of demons. Mark's account of the temptation is very brief. "Forty days . . . tempted by Satan . . . with the wild beasts . . . angels waited on him" (v. 13). The Gospel writer is interested in one thing. Jesus met evil in its own domain and was victorious over it.

Reflections

Baptism and penance are the historic themes of Lent. These lessons reflect both the waters of baptism, and the times of trial.

Unless one takes seriously the powers of evil—that Martin Luther described as "the flood of mortal ills prevailing"—one cannot experience the power of the cross and the victory of the resurrection. The rest of Luther's hymn is noteworthy: "For still our ancient foe / Doth seek to work us woe; / His craft and power are great, / And, armed with cruel hate, / On earth is not his equal."

In times when the church does not take seriously the destructive powers with which we contend, other programs in our society are teaching discipline and deprivation in order to help people wrestle with all that limits them.

Consider Outward Bound as an example. Participants will spend as much as twenty-six days facing challenges and obstacles that at first seem impossible. One does not compete against other persons, but against the boundaries and confining fears that are so much a part of all of us. The final forty-eight or seventy-two hours of the experience are spent alone in a wilderness place. There are no companions. One has nothing to read, no radio to hear, and nothing to eat. One is alone with some water to drink, the wildness of nature, and the quietness of solitude. The benefit of such an experience is a clearer identity, greater confidence, and new freedom.

Personal growth and spiritual formation require that one face both fears and failures in contending with the structures of evil.

Lent may be—in a variety of ways—forty days in the very haunts of wickedness. "And though this world, with devils filled / Should threaten to undo us, / We will not fear for God hath willed / His truth to triumph through us." (JKB)

WHEN GOD'S DREAM COMES TRUE

Mark 1:9-15

A SERMON BY JOSEPH B. BETHEA

After Jesus was baptized by John in the Jordan and tempted by Satan in the wilderness, and after John was put in prison, "Jesus came to Galilee, proclaiming the good news of God, and saying, 'The time is fulfilled, and the kingdom of God has come near; repent and believe in the good news' " (vv. 14-15).

The gospel that was preached by Jesus and the apostles, the theme of preaching in the New Testament and at its best throughout church history, is God's good news of God's rule and reign in the hearts and lives of God's people. It was the subject of the first sermon Jesus preached and the theme of every parable Jesus taught. In parable after parable, Jesus tried to help us understand what it means when God's dream comes true. Some parables suggest that God's dream has already come true, while other parables suggest that God's dream is like the mustard seed—growing and developing. Still other parables suggest that God's dream is not now a reality, but will come true in God's own time and in God's own way.

Christians live amid all these hopes expressed by Jesus in the parables. Christians live in the world as if God's dream has already come true. Christians involve themselves in the ministries of God and of the church to bring God's dream a bit closer. Christians hope! We look for the time when God and God alone will make the dream come true. In the life and work of Jesus Christ, God's dream broke into the world. In all the years since the life and death and resurrection of Jesus Christ, the church has been and continues to be the vanguard, the spearhead, the promise, the foretaste of God's dream.

During the first four years of my service as bishop of South Carolina, I tried to be intentional about getting to know the people through a series of meetings with clergy and laity where we could be in dialogue with sisters and brothers. In almost every meeting, I was asked about my hopes for our church during my episcopate. Among many hopes expressed is always the one that, when my work is done, the church and the world will be a bit closer to God's dream for the church and the world.

The church and the world moves a bit closer to God's dream when we repent, that is, turn around and believe—really believe—in righteousness and peace with justice and love. God's dream embraces all humankind; it transcends every barrier and breaks down every wall that separates persons from one another. In God's dream there is no distinction between Greek and Hebrew, Jew and Gentile, foreign or savage, male or female, white, black, brown, yellow, or red; all are one in Christ who calls us to righteousness, to love one another, and to live together in peace with justice.

In a world that raises walls and barriers because of class, race, sex, age, and physical conditions, God dreams of peace and justice and equality of access and opportunity. In a world that trusts in military strength and power to ensure peace and the absence of war, God dreams of peace based on love and respect for human dignity and freedom.

That great missionary of the church, E. Stanley Jones, once wrote: "All of life is converging on one thing: the kingdom of God is the way to live. It's the way for nations to live together in the world; it's the way for races to live together in the nation; it's the way for families to live together in the home; it's the way for Christians to live together in the Church and in the world." It is God's dream for the church, the home, the nation, and the world.

The church and the world moves a bit closer to God's dream when we repent, that is turn around and believe—really believe—in God's rule and will. The sum of all the preaching and teachings of Jesus Christ, the apostles, and the church is the kingdom of God. The word *kingdom* is defined as a territorial unit or an organized unit with a monarchical form of government, having a person who rules and reigns as queen or king. Again, Christians are the vanguard and the spearhead, the promise and the foretaste of the territory, the unit where God rules. We live in this world under the rule of God, and we look for the time when the kingdoms of this world will be the kingdom of God and Christ forever.

It is a constant struggle against our human tendency to rebel against God and to have our own selfish way. It is a constant struggle against Satan, who keeps telling us to do our own thing, that we can be our own God. We try and we fail. We will continue to try, and we will continue to fail until by the grace of God, we turn around and let God's will rule in our hearts and every other aspect of our existence.

The National Black Family Summit is an annual event held in Columbia and sponsored by the Columbia Urban League and the School of Social Work of the University of South Carolina. I believe it was the 1990 Summit that was climaxed with a presentation of the musical *Don't Give Up Your Dream*, that was written and presented by a theatrical group from the Phyllis Wheatley Center in Greenville. It told the story of a young man's struggle to achieve a worthwhile goal against the temptation to take the easy and glamorous—but low—road offered by the drug lord in the community. He would have succumbed but for the constant prodding of a girlfriend, who kept pointing him toward the high road.

When "Jesus came to Galilee, proclaiming the good news of God, and saying, 'The time is fulfilled, and the kingdom of God has come near; repent, and believe in the good news,' " Jesus was calling us to turn from our rugged selfish way and believe in God's dream of righteousness and peace with justice and love. Jesus was saying what the true soul knows: God's dream will come true. You can count on it.

Suggestions for Worship

Call to Worship (Ps. 25:1-2, 4)

LEADER: To you, O LORD, I lift up my soul.

PEOPLE: O my God, in you I trust; do not let me be put to shame. . . .

LEADER: Make me to know your ways, O LORD; teach me your paths.

PEOPLE: Lead me in your truth, and teach me, for you are the God of my salvation; for you I wait all day long.

Act of Praise: Psalm 25:1-10.

Suggested Hymns: "Guide Me, O Thou Great Jehovah"; "I Am Thine, O Lord"; "It Is Well with My Soul."

Opening Prayer: Almighty God, you created us in your image. Give us the grace we need to seek your kingdom and to do your will so that as your dream comes true, we may be found faithful; through Jesus Christ, our Lord. Amen.

Pastoral Prayer: God of the universe, who, of your tender mercy toward all people, sent our Savior, Jesus Christ, to take upon our flesh, to be tempted as we are, and to suffer death upon the cross for our sin: We give you thanks for these and every other expression of your love. We thank you that in every situation and circumstance, your grace is sufficient and that nothing in all creation can separate us from your love. We confess that in many ways we separate ourselves from your love— disobedient to your will and alienated from sisters and brothers you gave us to live with. Forgive our sin; forgive our preoccupation with our own will and way. Give us the assurance that comes through Jesus Christ, our hope and dream. Amen.

FEBRUARY 27, 1994

☐

Second Sunday in Lent

These lessons reveal a God who is willing to surrender to suffering and death. The cross confronts us as a compelling witness to the wondrous ways of God's promises and love. God spares nothing in his mighty reach for a right relationship with us—the righteousness of faith.

The Sunday Lessons

Genesis 17:1-7, 15-16: The God of the Mountain, El Shaddai, made a covenant with Abram promising that he (Abram) would become the father of "a multitude of nations" (v. 4). Abram became Abraham, meaning "the [divine] Father is exalted." Sarai's name was changed to Sarah, meaning *princess,* with the promise that kings of people would come from her. Covenants are established by the one in authority stating the way it shall be—and always will be—with those who have less power or no power to define.

Romans 4:13-25: The promise to Abraham was not earned through obedience to the law, but through the "righteousness of faith" (v. 13). Not even his age (about a hundred), nor his weakness, nor Sarah's barrenness caused him to doubt the promise. He was "fully convinced that God was able to do what he had promised" (v. 21). Our confidence is in "Jesus our Lord, who was put to death for our trespasses and raised for our justification (v. 25)."

Mark 8:31-38: Peter and the other disciples could not conceive of a crucified God. When the one he had just called *Messiah* said, "The Son of Man must undergo great suffering and be rejected . . . and be killed" (v. 31), Peter began to rebuke him. Jesus rebuked Peter, "Get behind me, Satan! For you are setting your mind not on divine things but on human things" (v. 33). Five sayings regarding the disciplines of discipleship follow. The second is, "For those who want to save their life will lose it" (v. 35).

Reflections

An evangelist, illustrating the importance of the cross, told of a seventeen-year-old boy who was sentenced to die before a firing squad. As he was led to the wall, a good man stepped forward and took his place. "Imagine the surprise, the joy, the deep gratitude in the heart of that young man," the evangelist said.

Such graphic stories of one dying for another have often been employed to interpret the cross. Careful evaluation of such stories reveals the shoddy response that they suggest. What kind of person could find joy in the knowledge that an innocent person suffered and died so that he or she could go free? In Mark's Gospel, there is a cross for everyone. Yet, the willingness of one to bear the suffering and death of another is love in action. It is the kind of love evidenced by a young father who stood by the bedside of his ten-year-old son. A neurosurgeon had just removed a malignant tumor from the boy's brain. Through his tears, the father said, "I wish it could be me."

Surely no father worthy of the name would intentionally will the death of his son for anything or anyone. Yet, God is known as a father who "did not spare his own." That concept moved a young girl in Sunday school to say, "I love Jesus, but I hate God!" She had come to see God only as ruthless power. To be sure, the cross is God's mighty act. However, any interpretation that distorts the grace and mercy of God is not good enough. Dostoyevsky wrote, "Love in practice is a harsh and terrible thing compared with love in dreams."

We and our children live and die for profit and economic gain. We will live and die for space exploration, technological advance, national security, and political victories. Some who follow the cross will live and die for the ways of God. (JKB)

THE COST OF DELIVERANCE
AND DISCIPLESHIP

Mark 8:31-38

A SERMON BY JOSEPH B. BETHEA

It was at the apex of the Gospel According to Mark, and at the height of the popularity of Jesus, that Jesus began to teach his disciples and the multitude the cost of our deliverance and the cost of our discipleship. Jesus had gone through cities and villages preaching the good news of God's dream and healing many diverse diseases, infirmities, and evil spirits. Great crowds gathered around Jesus. The Pharisees thought that he was important enough to check his credentials. Jesus had fed about four-thousand people with seven loaves of bread and a few small fish. Jesus gave sight to the blind man at Bethsaida and was on the way with his disciples to Caesarea Philippi when he asked his disciples, "Who do people say that I am?" (v. 27). They responded that given the way he preached, taught, healed, and tended to their needs, the people thought that he was "John the Baptist; and others, Elijah; and still others, one of the prophets" (v. 28). Jesus put the question directly to the disciples: "But who do you say that I am?" (v. 29). Peter answered for all of them: "You are the Messiah" (v. 29).

After exhorting the disciples not to tell anyone about him, Jesus went on to tell the disciples, and us, what deliverance and discipleship involves. He taught the cost of our deliverance and the cost of our discipleship.

What is the cost of our deliverance from sin and death? "He began to teach them that the Son of Man must undergo great suffering, and be rejected by the elders, the chief priests, and the scribes, and be killed, and after three days rise again. He said all this quite openly" (vv. 31-32). The Son of Man must suffer and die. It is God's way in the world.

Professor William Barclay, commenting on this text, wrote that Jesus connected messiahship with suffering and death and that the disciples did not understand. It was incredible and incomprehensible to them. They had been taught and they hoped that the Messiah would come as an irresistible conqueror. Now they are told the Messiah will suffer and die. A suffering Messiah—messiahship and suffering do not go together. At least they should not. So Peter took Jesus aside and told Jesus he could not be serious. Peter began to rebuke Jesus. But Jesus rebuked Peter. "Get behind me, Satan! For you are setting your mind not on divine things but on human things" (v. 33). I am thinking and talking about the ways of God. The world thinks in terms of irresistible power and might. How to overcome the world? Recruit the largest army; build the biggest bomb; develop the most sophisticated missile system. The way of the

world is irresistible conquest; but the way of God is irresistible
love: love that suffers, love that dies. That's the way God is. The
cross is the ultimate expression of the grace, the unlimited love
of God. It tells us that God's love will never let us go. It was the
cross that convinced Paul that nothing "in all creation will be
able to separate us from the love of God in Christ Jesus our
Lord" (Rom. 8:39*b*). We may separate ourselves, as we often do!
But God keeps on loving; God keeps on dying. The Son of Man
must suffer . . . and die . . . it is the way God is and the cost of
our discipleship.

In the text, Jesus went on to teach the cost of our discipleship.
"If any want to become my followers, let them deny themselves
and take up their crosses and follow me" (v. 34). That is the cost!
If we would follow Christ, we must disregard all thought of self
and give preeminence to our relationship to God; we must seek
God's dream and God's will first. It is more than making certain
selected sacrifices; it is more than giving up particular interest or
possessions, some of which we do not need and deserve in the
first place. It is total self-denial, unqualified obedience, and radical reorientation of life from self as center to Christ.

When Jesus said "If any want to become my followers . . ." he
was suggesting that we may choose not to follow Christ. If we
choose to follow, the cross is the cost. Dietrich Bonhoeffer died a
martyr's death because he resisted an evil dictatorship in the
name of Christ. Before he died, Bonhoeffer wrote a meditation
on the Sermon on the Mount. In the book he wrote about cheap
grace and costly grace. He also wrote that classic line: "When
Christ calls a man, he bids him come and die." The title of that
book is *The Cost of Discipleship*. If we follow Christ long enough
and close enough to be his disciple, we are going to *the* cross and
there is no way to avoid it.

We live in a Good Friday world, a world so bent on having its
way, that Christians are crucified with Christ. We are always losing.
If you must win all the time, you do not want to be a Christian disciple. Disciples lose! Christ lost! He said "For those who want to
save their life will lose it; and those who lose their life for my sake,
and for the sake of the gospel, will save it" (v. 35). The person was
right who said Christians are a bunch of losers. He or she based
this claim on the standard set by this world—a Good Friday world
that rejects and crucifies the best. It is the cost of discipleship.

There is another world and another word. This world, with all its power and glamour, does not have the last word. God's dream comes true! When we lose our life for Christ's sake and for the sake of the gospel, God will save it.

In his book, *Holy Company*, Elliott Wright writes of a conversation that Tertullian had with a man whose occupation was in conflict sometimes with his Christian principles. "What can I do?" asked the man. "What can I do? I must live!" Tertullian replied: "Must you?"

Suggestions for Worship

Call to Worship (Ps. 22, paraphrased):

LEADER: You who fear the LORD, praise him!

PEOPLE: All you who have faith in God, honor him!

LEADER: For he has not despised or disdained the suffering of the afflicted one;

PEOPLE: He has not hidden his face from us but has listened to our cries for help.

LEADER: From the LORD our God comes the theme of our praise;

PEOPLE: They who seek the LORD will praise him! May hearts of praise live forever!

Act of Praise: Psalm 22:23-31.

Suggested Hymns: "The Old Rugged Cross"; "Are Ye Able"; "When I Survey the Wondrous Cross."

Opening Prayer: Almighty God, you sent your Christ to suffer death on the cross for our deliverance. Grant us grace to follow his example in our discipleship in the assurance that, as we share the sufferings, we share the resurrection; through the same Jesus Christ our Lord. Amen.

Pastoral Prayer: O God of grace and God of love, we praise your holy name. You reclaimed us through the willingness of your Son to pay the cost of our deliverance. May his name be hallowed. We confess that though we know the cost of our deliverance, we have not always been willing to pay our portion and have been even less willing to pay the price. Through the power of your Holy Spirit, give us the faith that will allow us to take up the cross of Jesus and to follow him no matter the cost. Amen.

MARCH 6, 1994

□

Third Sunday in Lent

The law, sacrifices, signs, and wisdom are all surpassed by the weakness and foolishness of God. Final authority and power belong to Christ. Self-examination and confession prepare those who would know his presence.

The Sunday Lessons

Exodus 20:1-17: This is the priestly account of the Ten Commandments, the ten laws of God. The Deuteronomic enumeration of the laws is found in Deuteronomy 5. The church has given the Decalogue a central place in the ethical teachings of catechisms and has used them for self-examination in Lent, before baptism, and before Communion. The first four commandments relate to one's duty to God, the last six to one's duty to neighbor.

I Corinthians 1:18-25: "Jews demand signs, and Greeks desire wisdom" (v. 22). Paul preaches Christ crucified and finds in the cross more power *(dynamis)* than will ever be found in miracles or insight. For Paul, "Christ crucified" (v. 23) includes the Resurrection and the gift of the Spirit.

John 2:13-22: Oxen, sheep, and doves were being sold in the Temple for Passover sacrifices. "Making a whip of cords, he drove all of them out . . . he also poured out the coins of the money changers" (v. 15). The early church saw the happening as the displacement of the old covenant—centered in law and Temple sacrifice—with a new worship centered in Jesus.

Reflections

"Jesus on his part would not entrust himself to them, because he knew all people" (John 2:24). These words refer to persons, like ourselves, men and women who believed in him. And still God knows who we really are.

79

Knowing our hearts, will Christ honor our worship today? Our ethical teachings do little to shape our lives and change our society. Our cathedrals with chiseled stone and stained-glass windows house lovely appointments for worship, the evidence of our stewardship, yet we cherish our temples mostly for ourselves. The power of our faith is directed toward signs and miracles, and the insights of our teachings are offered as wisdom.

With what assumptions do we come to worship? We are fairly good people. Our friends are fairly good people. We are on God's side, and God will bless us. There are some bad people, but they belong to other nations, religions, and races.

With what assumptions do we address our whole life? Are they like this? Humanity, which is essentially good, intends to live responsibly in the universe and will, therefore, protect and improve the environment; distribute fairly the yield of field and factory; maintain freedom and dignity for all races; desire beauty, truth, and goodness; make kindness and justice flow down like water.

Bewitched by human achievement and blinded by our near-sighted vision, we may yet fail to see the might and right of the crucified Christ. Power is not centered in missiles and bombs. Wisdom is not found in the sciences. Righteousness is not achieved through law and order. Blessings are not numbered through money counting. (JKB)

PLAYING IN THE MINEFIELD

Exodus 20:1-17

A SERMON BY CHARLES M. COOK

The Boeing 707 chartered by the U. S. Army from Trans-International Airlines (I had never heard of that company) had just made a brief stop at Saigon, with me inside. As we circled over our next stop, preparing to land at the airstrip that would be my new home, my knuckles were white from gripping the seat in front of me. I noticed off the end of the runway a thousand little three-foot-wide depressions that I assumed to be craters caused by shelling. From a thousand feet up, it looked as though the earth had smallpox.

"Is that a minefield?" I asked.

"Don't worry, rookie," said the senior NCO seated beside me. He had been here for four tours of duty already and knew the neighborhood. "Those holes weren't caused by mines. They're graves."

"Graves?" I shouted over the engine whine. "But they're round."

"Right," he said. "The Vietnamese Buddhists break the legs of their dead so that they can bury them sitting upright in the lotus position. Their graves are round."

Hearing the mechanical scrape as the landing gear deployed, I looked down upon my new home.

"There's your minefield, over off to the left," he pointed.

It certainly was not what I expected. What I saw looked like a beautiful soccer field. All around our compound were the flattest and most verdant fields I had ever seen. They were as green and flat as the top of a pool table, having been smoothed and manicured, courtesy of two seasons' flooding and a company of combat engineers. Their moist greenness begged to be massaged by bare toes, to be played on, to be marked off for a game of football. The only problem was that they were deadly fields. These inviting fields were killing fields. These were the minefields.

I remember one afternoon not long after, seeing a group of kids playing the southeast Asian equivalent of stickball right in the middle of one of those minefields. The MP's who were supposed to be watching the field went colorless, then started yelling, screaming, and waving their arms at these kids, who did not understand a word of English. It would have been funny, had it not been so dangerous. One sweating MP quickly found a map of the field that gave the location of the mines, and his squad beat a carefully circuitous route to the children. Grabbing the children, who were writhing and screaming in terror, they carefully began to retrace their steps back to the edge of the minefield. At about the same time, the children's parents arrived to see their kids flailing insanely and being hauled off by a squad of hefty GI's. I could only wonder at the terror of these children and their mothers, who were gesticulating in helpless anguish. Immediately, the parents tried to run toward the children, but they were held back at the edge of the minefield by another squad of MP's. These mothers, I am sure, believed their children were being killed. Actually, exactly the opposite was happening. They could not realize that the MP's prohibition was infinitely more merciful than a thoughtless permission would have been. Finally, after several tense minutes, the MP's handed the children, still kicking and screaming, but now safe and well, back to the parents. I am glad I did not understand their language, but I believe that those mothers loaded those MP's with enough curses to last them and their families well into the afterlife.

That night as I lay on my cot I could not help reflecting on words I had heard from a pastor years before, "God's law is God's love." As an adolescent, I had not understood precisely what that pastor meant, but there in the green darkness it began to make sense. I lay there wondering what would have happened if, in the name of a shallow and indulgent love, the company commander had listened to the cries of those children? I tried to imagine his saying, "Oh, I'm sorry. We really did not mean to inconvenience you. Go ahead and finish your game of stickball." Would it have been loving for the commander to relax the prohibition against playing in the minefield? Obviously not. As I lay awake on my cot that night, listening to anonymous explosions in the distance, I could not help wondering if the God of the Ten Commandments is less interested in spoiling his children's fun than in telling them that they are in a minefield.

Here at the end of the twentieth century it is easy to believe that when we relax the prohibitions of Exodus 20, that we are somehow being more loving than other Christians who are less enlightened than we are. "After all," we say, "let's be more loving. People are going to be people and it does no good to insist on celebacy in singleness and fidelity in marriage. Let's just relax this prohibition for our young people." Thus, in the name of realism and love, we pretend that *that* part of the minefield is not quite so dangerous as Exodus 20 suggests. Similarly, we say in one way or another, "People can't be expected to take seriously all that stuff about covetousness in a capitalistic economy. The word *covetousness* is so old-fashioned. We cannot be so unloving as to impose our standards on them. It's just not realistic." Thus we, in the name of a shallow and indulgent love, agree that it is really not so bad if we or our brothers and sisters wander out into that part of the minefield. Or if we do try to prevent them, we quickly yield to their shrieks and let them continue playing stickball. We argue with ourselves, "No one really keeps the Ten Commandments anymore. How realistic is it to insist on keeping these outdated 'Thou shalt nots' in today's enlightened world?"

If God's law is God's love, it seems surprisingly easy to persuade ourselves otherwise. How tempting it is simply to soften the warnings of Exodus 20, and in doing so think that one is being as loving as Jesus was! Yet, it is most interesting to note how our Lord dealt with the law. He did not soften its demands, rather he intensified them! Without question, if someone today magnified the laws demands, as our loving Lord did, he or she would be universally criticized as being rigid, unloving, and insensitive to those whose special needs require special indulgence. Nevertheless, the record seems clear. Where the Ten Commandments outlaw adultery, Jesus outlaws even the thought of adultery. Where the Ten Commandments outlaw murder, Jesus outlaws even the hateful intent. Where the rabbis allowed for certain exclusions to the law, Jesus insisted that every jot and tittle would be fulfilled. Jesus amplifies the law, suggesting that its violation affect not only society, but also the soul.

Jesus appears to behave something like the father of the famous basketball player, Michael Jordan. Mr. Jordan would not allow his small son to play basketball with a regulation-size hoop like everybody else. No, he required young Michael to play with a hoop two inches *smaller* than normal. Jesus, like Mr. Jordan, seems even more exacting than the rules require. Is this loving? It hardly seems so. Such demands might be understood if one wanted to make extraordinarily talented basketball players or extraordinarily moral saints, and, of course, there are many who believe that God gave the law merely to make us more moral people. That may be partly true. However, Jesus seems to have something more in mind. He goes even farther still. Not only does he intensify the law (make the basket smaller, if you will), he goes so far as to say that you must shoot 100 percent from the free-throw line! "Unless your righteousness exceeds that of the scribes and Pharisees, you will never enter the kingdom of heaven . . . You, therefore, must be perfect, as your heavenly Father is perfect . . . Love your enemies . . . If someone asks for your shirt, give them your coat too . . . Forgive seventy times seven" (Matt. 5), and so on. Rather than relaxing the law, Jesus intensifies it to the point where any honest person must despair completely of ever fulfilling it. And so the terrible predicament in which we find ourselves is that we are children born in the middle of a cosmic minefield; we have not the least clue about how to get out, and Christ comes and places upon us the inexorable, intensified demand that we must, somehow or other, do precisely that. And the more intense his command, the more hopeless we feel.

That hopelessness is precisely the paradox of grace. Jesus does not relax the law. He applies it with an unequaled rigor. He not only tells us that we are in the minefield, but also insists that it is an infinitely more dangerous environment even than Exodus 20 said that it is. And he does this for one reason—namely, to drive us to the point of hopelessness in our own ability to extricate ourselves. It is then, and only then—when we reach this point of desperation, when we reach this flash point of grace—that we become willing to throw ourselves on the mercy of the Rescuer who we had believed was trying to tyrannize us with his prohibitions. It is only after we have reached this flash point of grace that we understand why it was necessary for Jesus not to relax the demands of the law, but to radicalize them: To be saved from something less than real sin is to be given something less than real salvation. Our self-abandonment to divine grace is absolutely necessary, for to enter into the new life of Christ without first passing through a kind of death *to* and *through* the law is to concoct a resurrection without a true crucifixion. Such was impossible for Jesus, and it is impossible for us.

If Christ's church would be loving *as Jesus was loving*, it must not relax the demands of the law. Rather, the church must press them with a painful intensity that seems harsh to some. The church must insist on the frightening reality of the danger of playing in the minefield for ourselves and others. For it is only when we recognize the very real dangers of the explosive environment mapped out for us in Exodus 20 and intensified by Jesus that we, the children playing in the minefield, will stop our kicking and screaming, and quietly submit to allowing ourselves to be rescued. And when Christ has rescued us and brought us to the edge of the minefield in safety and peace, when he hands us over to be grasped by the everlasting arms of the Parent whose love is boundless, then—and only then—will we truly know in the depths of our souls that God's law is God's love.

Suggestions for Worship

Call to Worship (Ps: 19:7-11):

LEADER: The law of the LORD is perfect, reviving the soul.

PEOPLE: **The statutes of the LORD are trustworthy, making wise the simple.**

LEADER: The precepts of the LORD are right, giving joy to the heart.

PEOPLE: **The commands of the LORD are radiant, giving light to the eyes.**

LEADER: The fear of the LORD is pure, enduring forever.

PEOPLE: **The ordinances of the LORD are sure and altogether righteous.**

LEADER: By them is your servant warned;

PEOPLE: **In keeping them there is great reward.**

Act of Praise: Psalm 19.

Suggested Hymns: "Trust and Obey"; "For the Healing of the Nations"; "O Master, Let Me Walk with Thee."

Opening Prayer: O Holy Redeemer, you rescue us when we cannot rescue ourselves: Give us eyes to see that your law is your love, and that your judgment is your grace, so that we may rest serene and secure in your salvation; through Jesus Christ, your Son, our Lord, who lives and reigns with you in the unity of the Holy Spirit, one God, now and for ever. Amen.

Pastoral Prayer: Holy God, we come into your presence with our eyes averted, for you are too holy to look upon; yet you invite us, and so we come with joy and thanksgiving.

How amazing your love is, Holy Lord! When we do not seek you, you seek us; when we seek to avoid you, you endure in your polite persistence; when we suspect your grace, you always find ways of overcoming our suspicion. How long will it take us to learn that you, who spared not your Son, will not withhold any good gift?

Help us, good and loving God, to continue in your friendship, so that we may know again that in your marvelous grace, what you command, you also provide. Through Christ our Lord, we pray. Amen.

March 13, 1994

□

Fourth Sunday in Lent

The stakes are high. It is a life or death kind of transaction. But you do not have to bring anything except a receptive heart. God provided all that is needed when he gave his only begotten Son.

The Sunday Lessons

Numbers 21:4-9: The Israelites complained about hunger and thirst. "Then the LORD sent poisonous serpents among the people" (v. 6). The serpents were interpreted as God's judgment on their rebellious spirit. Moses lifted up a bronze serpent in the wilderness. Those who looked to it would live.

Ephesians 2:1-10: "We were by nature children of wrath, like everyone else" (v. 3). The passage incorporates an ancient hymn that reflects the kerygma. "But God, who is rich in mercy . . . even when we were dead through our trespasses, made us alive together with Christ . . . By grace, you have been saved through faith . . . it is the gift of God" (vv. 4-8).

John 3:14-21: "As Moses lifted up the serpent in the wilderness, so must the Son of Man be lifted up" (v. 14). As persons who looked on the brazen serpent were saved from the bite of vipers, so those who contemplate the cross of Christ will be saved. Both grace and judgment are evident in the passage. Yet, only those who believe and so receive and return his love are saved. For those who do not believe, that very love becomes judgment.

Reflections

Varieties of images and thought forms have been used to interpret the atonement. Each of these has been shaped by the cultural practices of a particular age in history. In times and places where the sacrificial systems of Judaism prevailed, the "lamb of God" and "blood of Christ" images were significant. When the cruelty and death of slavery were evident, the "ransom for many" idea was rich in meaning.

The atonement image suggested in this passage (i.e., contemplation of the cross and God's love) is reflected in the moral influence theory that is often associated with Abelard. Simply stated the theory is: (1) The cross shows the love of God; (2) such love calls forth an answering love in our hearts; (3) this answering love has power to change one's direction and initiate a return to God; and (4) the revealed love of God assures one of his or her acceptance.

Abelard's insights are shaped by his own love story. In the year 1115, Peter Abelard was appointed as one of the priests in Notre Dame Cathedral. Soon, crowds from all of Paris came to hear his sermons. He fell in love with the beautiful and devoted Heloise, the niece of another canon of the cathedral. A child was born to them, and they were secretly married. Then the uncle, Canon Fulbert, had Abelard ambushed and emasculated. Mutilation was followed by scandal, disbarment from the church, and separation from Heloise, who then lived in a nunnery. Their letters, preserved from medieval times, are among the loveliest letters in history. Both Abelard and Heloise were overwhelmed by tragedy, but nourished by love. They knew the crushing weight of evil and condemnation. They also knew the saving power of steadfast love. (JKB)

A PROBLEM OF FAMILIARITY

John 3:16

A SERMON BY NORMAN M. PRITCHARD

We have all known the words of John 3:16 since our earliest Christian days, and loved them, too, I am sure. However, they may be so well known that there is a danger that we will not really hear them. The words may have become devalued through familiarity—worn thin by overuse—and their startling message may fail to penetrate our jaded minds. We may well have a problem of familiarity with these words.

If that is, or has ever been, a problem for us, it may help to remember that the words were first spoken to deal with a problem of familiarity.

Nicodemus had the problem of familiarity. He was secure in his position as a leader of the Jews. He was a Pharisee, and therefore a person of expertise in religion. He begins to interview Jesus with a confidence born of his familiarity with the things of God: "Rabbi, we know that you are a teacher who has come from God" (v. 2). His confidence is shaken, however, as Jesus leads him into unfamiliar territory with talk of a birth of water and Spirit. When this leaves Nicodemus wondering, "How can these things be?" (v. 9), Jesus goes on to identify himself as the one who has come from heaven to reveal, through his being lifted up on the cross, the truth that God so loved the world that he gave his only son.

The expression Jesus uses, "lifted up," is significant. Today's Old Testament reading supplies the background. The people whom God had rescued from slavery in Egypt have come to wonder what they have let themselves in for. The going is tough, so they start whining. They regret that they ever left Egypt. They complain about the food and water that they do not have, and (typical human touch, this!) they complain also about the food they *do* have, the manna: "We detest this miserable food" (Exod. 21:5). The pain of Egpyt is forgotten, and the brutal slavery. The excitement of the Exodus is glossed over, as well as the privilege of covenant with God. They want to call the whole deal off.

Then comes the plague of serpents, which they interpret as a punishment from God. Crisis! Moses is told to act in a most significant way. He tells the people that those who have been bitten by a serpent will be healed if they look at the symbolic serpent that he will lift up in the camp. As we read, we wonder what he is doing. Why a serpent, the cause of the people's suffering and death? It cannot heal the people. That is precisely the point— only God can. And God will—it is his will to heal them, using the very symbol of their sin.

The point is clear and profound: Even in the midst of the people's sin, God is still present. Even when they fail to trust, and thus forget all God's benefits, God does not forget or abandon them. God is still their God, his love is still with them, and his purpose for them undiminished still. The serpent, symbolic reminder of their sin, embodies the healing and forgiving love of God for the people.

So Jesus uses the Old Testament story in which God's people experienced the love that would not let them go to illustrate the meaning of his life and work—the embodiment, the incarnation, of the very love of God.

If the serpent that was lifted up expressed human rebellion against God, how much more the cross! It, too, is an expression of rejection of God and of God's determination to love us.

Much that is wrong in human life had a part to play in Christ's death: the hatred of enemies, the injustice of oppressors, the maneuvers of power-brokers, the carelessness of the indifferent crowd, and the failure of nerve on the part of those who had promised much, but found themselves unable to deliver. All that is bad enough! But much that is good in human life was also caught up and compromised: religion, politics, law, even a democratic vote—each in some way found wanting, each implicated at least in part.

That is not the way we like to think about the cross! That is a truth we had rather not be made to face. Much more familiar, because much easier to accept and much less threatening to our peace of mind, is the cross of institutionalized religion—cleaned up and smoothed of all its roughness by the mellow clichés of our long familiarity. We dress that cross up in generalities about love and sacrifice to make it suitable to decorate our churches. Such a cross as that will not offend; but such a cross as that will not redeem us, either! It is only when we see how vile the cross can be, and how expressive of our human sin, that we can feel the wonder of its truth—that God was active in the cross, working for our reconciliation, in all God's costly, sacrificial love.

No matter how well we think we know what happened, we must never let familiarity with the story dull our perception of its reality or weaken our hold on its truth. God so loved the world that he gave his only Son . . . unless we plumb the depths of meaning that the cross contains, we will not be able to rejoice with wonder at the greatness of the love the cross reveals, the love that will not let us go—no matter what.

Familiarity can breed, if not contempt, at least indifference in our hearts and lives. It is all too easy to allow familiarity with the great truths and deep realities our faith contains to blunt their impact on our lives. That is true of faith, of prayer, of Christian living, and of worship. Here is an example of what I mean, taken from an experience of worship. A missionary wrote to the biographer of hymn writer George Matheson to tell of a dull service that he had attended in March, 1904. He wrote, "To me it was all lifeless, formal, uneventful, messageless, comfortless." The last hymn was announced as being Matheson's great hymn, "O Love That Wilt Not Let Me Go" and the writer noticed, casually, that there was a change of organist for this hymn.

Suddenly, also, a change of atmosphere—as the congregation began to sing, the organist gave the music much more power. The atmosphere became charged with emotion. "The organist seemed in third heaven. Here and there he made pauses not in the book. He sang and played and carried us along irresistibly . . . he poured out his very soul . . . When we reached the last verse, I for one wished blind Matheson had provided us with more. And yet we might not have been able to bear it."

After the service was over, the writer went forward to find the reason for the change in atmosphere. It turned out that the organist was a distinguished musician visiting the church. Two years previously his wife, who was his equal in musical talent, had lain dying. As death approached she had asked her husband to sing to her the hymn "O Love That Wilt Not Let Me Go." He had done so and they had shared its powerful message of faith and comfort together. He had not dared to play it again until that morning in that church service. (D. Macmillan, *The Life of George Matheson* [London: Hodder and Stoughton, 1908, 194ff.])

That was the explanation for the transformed atmosphere in the service—it was the burning truth of the words, reflecting the organist's own, deeply personal experience, which had made the difference. The faith that the music expressed—faith that we often sing or affirm without too much thought—is the faith summed up in the text we have been considering: "For God so loved the world that he gave his only Son, so that everyone who believes in him may not perish but may have eternal life."

Everyone. That word is important. We see one aspect of its truth in the death of Jesus and its glorious sequel. The disciples who had forsaken him and fled were not themselves forsaken. The risen Christ returned to forgive, restore, and reinstate them in his service. God so loved them that their failure, fear, and fair-weather following were not allowed to be the final word. Forgiveness was, and then the new beginning made possible by the mercy, grace, and love of God.

God so loved them—and you—and me that he gave his only Son, so that everyone who believes in him may not perish but may have eternal life. That is the heart of the Christian faith, and we must never let our familiarity with it dull its meaning or rob us of the joy and wonder that its truth imparts. God wants this truth to live in all our hearts, so that faith in Jesus Christ may live in all our lives.

Suggestions for Worship

Call to Worship (Ps. 107:1-3, 17-22):

> LEADER: Give thanks to the LORD, for he is good;
>
> **PEOPLE: His love endures forever.**
>
> LEADER: Let us give thanks to the LORD for his unfailing love and his wonderful deeds for men.
>
> **PEOPLE: Let us sacrifice thank offerings and tell of his works with songs of joy.**

Act of Praise: Psalm 107:1-3, 17-22.

Suggested Hymns: "Come, Thou Fount of Every Blessing"; "My Faith Looks Up to Thee"; "How Firm a Foundation."

Opening Prayer: Eternal God, whose love is revealed in Jesus Christ, and supremely in the glory of his cross, grant us your grace in our rebellion and your truth in all our seeking, that we may believe in Jesus Christ and receive your gift of eternal life; through Jesus Christ, our Lord. Amen.

Pastoral Prayer: Father, thank you for all the blessings that flow from the life and ministry of Jesus Christ our Lord. Thank you for the way he understands our weaknesses and intercedes for us.

Lord, our lives are enriched by those who live as Jesus lived, and in his name we thank you for: the tenacity of those who struggle in the face of difficulty; the faithfulness of those who carry on when others give in or give up; the thoughtfulness of those who remember when others forget; and the love of those who turn the other cheek or go the second mile, in loyalty to Jesus Christ.

For all your blessings in our lives, we praise and bless your name, through Jesus Christ our Lord. Amen.

MARCH 20, 1994

☐

Fifth Sunday in Lent

The cross is more than the revelation of God's love. It is also a perfect obedience that will not compromise or yield in spite of all the power of evil.

The Sunday Lessons

Jeremiah 31:31-34: Jeremiah likens the "covenant that I made with their ancestors" (v. 32) to a marriage contract "that they broke" (v. 32). Israel, held captive in Babylon, is promised a new covenant. It will be more intimate and compelling. "I will put my law within them . . . write it on their hearts; and I will be their God, and they shall be my people" (v. 33).

Hebrews 5:5-10: Every high priest is chosen of God, and is also one who can sympathize with the weak. Christ is shown as one who in Gethsemane, "learned obedience through what he suffered; and having been made perfect, he became the source of eternal salvation" (vv. 8-9). Being perfect means fulfilling every requirement necessary to become the great high priest who enables others to approach God.

John 12:20-33: John's Gospel is addressed to the Greeks, but this is the first time they appear. "Sir, we wish to see Jesus" (v. 21). They cannot see him until he is glorified in the same way that "a grain of wheat falls into the earth and dies" and so "bears much fruit" (vv. 23-24). The Johannine Gethsemane prayer follows, "And what should I say—'Father save me from this hour'? No, it is for this reason that I have come to this hour" (v. 27). Jesus' death will be the final act of an obedient life. Complete obedience reveals and glorifies God.

Reflections

Twenty years ago I wrote on the blank page of Bailey's *Diary of Private Prayer* the following words: "There's a deep inadequacy in my life. It results primarily from my willingness to compromise. I long for a life that is true and pure. I desperately want to be shaped by loyalty and devotion that will not cower from conflict or pain. But such perfect obedience I cannot yet claim. Like Judas, I sometimes betray the best that I know. Like Peter, I deny my dearest friend. Like the others, I flee when I'm faced with the cross."

It is such inadequacy and longing that has caused me to honor the man or woman who perfectly obeys—who in the words of Kierkegaard, "wills one thing." There is a strange tugging at our hearts when we see another who will bear the suffering, pay the price, and die if need be because of a singular devotion. Socrates drinking the hemlock; Latimer facing the fires of martyrdom; Martin Luther facing the council alone saying, "Here I stand; I can do no other"; Abraham Lincoln enduring civil war; Mother Teresa serving the poor. The willingness to engage any adversary and never give up makes us want to live in finer and truer ways.

Jesus draws all people to himself. His perfect obedience to God is the key. Most of all this obedience touches us in his death. It is there we see the wonder of his Spirit. His whole life has been obedient to the will of God, but his death is the climax of it all. It is a life lived and a death died in the purest obedience in all of human history. (JKB)

THE TRIUMPH OF THE CROSS

John 12:20-33

A SERMON BY BERNARD H. LIEVING, JR.

It must have been late September or early October, 1990, because it was one of my early trips into the Saudi Arabian desert to visit United States Army Chaplains. The Sergeant Major and I left our home base just after dawn and by mid-morning it was hot—probably 105 degrees. There was a slight breeze blowing out of the desert.

We turned off the highway at what we hoped was the correct trail, headed into the desert and started to navigate our way about ten miles into the trackless sand. We were fifteen minutes into our off-road trek when we smelled it.

There was no mistaking that odor—the stench of death! It was that sickening sweet smell of rotting, decaying flesh. We drove another ten minutes and the odor became stronger. Tying bandanas around our faces did not help. The smell persisted. Then we topped a small sand dune and we could see the cause. About two hundred meters off the trail was a beduoin animal disposal yard. It must have been three or four acres of what at one time had been sheep, camels, and other animals. There were two or three bloated, not-dead-very long, fly-covered camel bodies and several stacks of dead sheep. And there were bones, some still in reasonable definition of sheep or camel structure and others strewn about by the ravages of the wild dogs and bleached pure white by the relentless sun. The sight was bad enough, but it was the smell of death that was absolutely overpowering.

Throughout this twelfth chapter of John there is also the heavy smell of death. Everything that happens points toward the impending end. It begins with the anointing at Bethany, a beautiful description of love for Jesus that took place within his circle of close friends. John ends that incident with plans being made to kill Jesus and Lazarus. He then closes the triumphal entry account with the increased anger of the Pharisees. "See, this is getting us nowhere. Look how the whole world has gone after him!" (v. 19 NIV).

Finally, John gives us Jesus' words in response to Andrew and John telling Jesus there were some Greeks who had told Philip, "we would like to see Jesus" (v. 21 NIV). This desire of the Greeks triggered in Jesus the reality that the time of his death was near; the hour had come for him to be glorified by his willing suffering. He would be exalted by his being lifted up to death on a cross and so would draw all to himself.

Here is the smell of death: " 'Unless a kernel of wheat falls to the ground and dies, it remains only a single seed. But if it dies, it produces many seeds. The man who loves his life will lose it . . . Now my heart is troubled, and what shall I say? 'Father, save me from this hour'? No, it was for this very reason that I came to this hour. Father, glorify Your name! . . . But I, when I am lifted up from the earth, will draw all men to myself.' He said this to show the kind of death he was going to die" (vv. 24-33 NIV).

Sooner or later in our Lenten journey with Jesus we come to the stark reality of his cross. We cannot forever sit at his feet and listen to his words; we cannot continue to travel the roads with him and marvel at the unique way he touches at the very heart of the deepest need of the life of each individual who comes to him. Jesus' journey on this road less traveled led to the hill of the skull where, as Garnett M. Wilder, a United Methodist minister, wrote "men's bodies were torn apart and their souls shredded by unbearable shafts of pain and the horrifying rifts of sheer terror." Here is the smell of death.

In the face of what he knew must come, John's Christ does not writhe in agony, does not struggle in Gethsemane, does not offer up a cry of dereliction. Instead, he accepts the "very reason I came to this hour. Father, glorify your name!" (vv. 27-28 NIV). And a voice from heaven confirms and affirms his choice, "I have glorified it, and will glorify it again . . . The crowd that was there and heard it said it had thundered; others said an angel had spoken to him" (vv. 28-29 NIV).

The world was neither forever changed by Jesus words, nor was it made whole by his healing touch. Yet, the world has been brought to a halt—and sometimes turned around—by an awesome confrontation with the cross of Christ, that instrument of death by which he was lifted up from the earth. Here is a Messiah who, "although he was a son, he learned obedience from what he suffered and, once made perfect, he became the source of eternal salvation for all who obey him" (Heb. 5:8-9 NIV).

He died for us. They lifted him up between heaven and earth and he died there on the cross, the most agonizing death known to humankind. In that moment our sins—mine and yours—were picked up and laid on Christ. He was made to be sin for us. He who had no sin of his own became guilty of our sins. He took our sins on that cross. In that cross is the power to change people, to transform the world, to change our lives—to forgive our sins, make us new creations, and start us in totally new directions for living.

The smell of death is still there on that hill of the skull. But in a strange way, the odor is overpowered by the sense of triumph and victory, the assurance of hope and life. It is overpowered by the reality that as Christ was lifted up from the earth on the cross, he became the power of God to draw me and you to the glory of God.

Suggestions for Worship

Call to Worship (Ps: 51:1-12):

LEADER: Have mercy on me, O God, according to your unfailing love;

PEOPLE: According to your great compassion, blot out my transgressions.

LEADER: Wash away all my iniquity and cleanse me from my sin.

PEOPLE: Cleanse me with hyssop, and I will be clean; wash me, and I will be whiter than snow.

LEADER: Create in me a pure heart, O God,

PEOPLE: And renew a steadfast spirit within me.

Act of Praise: Psalm 51:1-12.

Suggested Hymns: "Lift High the Cross"; "Jesus, Keep Me Near the Cross"; "To Mock Your Reign, O Dearest Lord."

Opening Prayer: O Holy God, give us we pray, a hunger and thirst for righteousness; give us true sorrow for our sins and a longing for your forgiveness. Give us such confidence in thy love and grace that we may hear your saving word, and know the salvation that is in the Lord Jesus Christ, in whose name we pray. Amen. (JKB)

Pastoral Prayer: Eternal and loving God, we would see Jesus. We would see him—he who was lifted up to draw us to himself, to show us the Father so that we might worship and praise you.

We would see Jesus so that we could confess anew that we love this life and that we do not want to change. We prefer those thoughts, attitudes, words, and actions that are better suited for serving self than others. Confront us with the cross and convict us of our need of your salvation in Christ.

We would see Jesus that we might glorify your name as we follow and serve him. Empower us to show and tell your love to those who turn to us in search of you. Give us the zeal that would help us show others a vision of your glory. Help us to hold high the cross of Christ before this world, that lives might be changed and your name exalted. In Jesus' name. Amen.

MARCH 27, 1994

□

Palm/Passion Sunday

The triumphal entry (Mark 11:1-11), often used as a processional reading on tihs day, announces the beginning of the passion and humiliation of Christ the King. The passion narrative
(Mark 14–15) recalls the obedient suffering of the Son of God.

The Sunday Lessons

Isaiah 50:4-9a: The third servant song tells of a servant whose
witness was given to him as "the tongue of a teacher" (v. 4). He
became an obedient sufferer offering his back to the smiters, and
setting his face like a flint. "Who are my adversaries? . . . the
Lord God helps me" (vv. 8-9).

Philippians 2:5-11: An early hymn of the church praises the Christ
"who, though he was in the form of God, did not regard equality
with God as something to be exploited" (v. 6). Obedient unto death,
even death on the cross, he is given a name above every name.
"Every tongue should confess that Jesus Christ is Lord" (v. 11).

Mark 14:1–15:47: The passion narrative begins with the anointing of Jesus at Bethany and the question, "Why was the ointment
wasted in this way?" (v. 4). The last supper, the agony in Gethsemane, the betrayal and arrest, the trial before Caiaphas, Peter's
denial, Pontius Pilate's offer to release Jesus or Barabbas, the
crown of thorns, the cross, the death, the tomb are all part of the
story of the crucifixion of "the King." This servant-King rules in
the midst of mockery and mistreatment. "Truly this man was
God's Son!" (v. 39).

Reflections

The self-serving and self-saving ways of humanity are especially evident at the crucifixion of Christ. The scribes and Pharisees post bounty for the arrest of the one who upset their money
tables. The profiteering Judas sells his teacher for thirty pieces of

silver. Peter, unwilling to risk any confrontation, denies that he ever knew him. Pilate surrenders justice and gives an innocent life to silence a clamoring mob. Soldiers roll dice for his robe, passing strangers delight in his suffering, and dying thieves mockingly ask to be saved. The selfish and self-centered ways of sin are garishly apparent.

Who, if anyone, has rightful claim on preference and privilege? Is it not the president, the royal families, the high priests, the aristocracy, the kings? It would seem so when we recall the splendor of inaugurations, coronations, and royal weddings. That is what makes the entry and enthronement of God's own son, who is the King of kings, so incongruous.

When he entered the royal city, it was in a haphazard parade marching to the sound of children's voices. When he was presented to the crowds, they cried, "Crucify him." When he was crowned, it was with thorns. When he was lifted up, it was on a cross. "Behold your King!"

Teresa of Avila was an ordinary nun who went about her daily offices routinely. She recalls that it was with empty formality and in a coldly familiar way, that she passed the crucifix on hundreds of occasions to enter the chapel every few hours for scheduled prayers. Then one day she saw with clear eyes the crucifix and through it the cross of Christ. She really saw her Lord's passion. The selfless surrender, the awful loneliness, the agony, the bloody sweat, the uncalculating love that pays any price—the sacrifice of heaven's very best. Falling to her knees, she dedicated herself then and there, holding nothing back, to the service of this crucified King. She became a saint, going deeper and yet deeper in service to her brothers and sisters, in communion with God, in companionship with Christ. Behold your King! (JKB)

A DIFFERENT DESIGN

Mark 14:1–15:47

A SERMON BY HEATHER MURRAY-ELKINS

Palm/Passion Sunday. Here we sit, a how-to drawing spread across our knees as we try to follow directions. "Bend the palm first to the left and. . . ." Such a curious custom, making crosses out of palms. Perhaps only those of us who repeatedly fail Christian Art 101 are the only ones who resist the smooth transition of palms to crosses. Somewhere in the mangling of the palm and the merging of the texts, we ask ourselves, "Why should this seem natural?" It's like using origami to build an electric chair out of a bulletin.

Palm/Passion Sunday. To walk the way of the cross in hymns and scripture is an annual rite of passage. We know where we are on the journey. This is the place where palms become crosses. The distance from Isaiah to Mark is a well-traveled road. If we insist on standing in the crossroads and asking for alternate directions, we risk getting lost. Who can remember when the suffering of Jesus seemed anything but obvious, anything but what happens next?

It had been quite a hike, helping a toddler up an overgrown trail of North Carolina sticks and stones. The deserted monastery had been intentionally set apart from the highway traffic. The years of disuse had heightened its cloistered walls of isolation. We, a family of three, had driven as far as possible, then parked and traveled on foot like pilgrims to a shrine.

We had been tempted on this journey by an offer of relics. The long-abandoned retreat center was scheduled for a corporate takeover. The architect had offered its garden-variety statues to anyone who managed to move them before the dozers reduced them to rubble. Bill and I packed up one child and a picnic and went in search of religion and art.

The magnitude of our mistake was obvious once we reached the monastery's grounds. The classic forms would require the strength of cranes, not the rescue efforts of two adults, one child, and an old VW. No amount of Protestant good will could protect these larger than life saints from the same iconoclastic fate as their 16th-century counterparts. My pragmatic partner shrugged off the loss and prepared to fix lunch. Daniel, our four-year-old and I joined forces and went exploring. What we discovered continues to surprise me.

In the center of the garden, stood a crucifix. Even in its abandoned state, it dominated the scene. I eyed its height and sighed a dismissal. Too big. Too bad. I lifted Daniel for our retreat.

The stiffness of the child stopped my turn. He had turned to stone. His eyes were like X-rays, restlessly scanning the body.

From the shock on his face, I realized that he had never seen one of *these* before. Every cross he had ever seen had been empty. This one was not empty. This one was filled with the dying agony of a good strong man.

"Jesus?" he questioned, eyes on the form. "Jesus," I answered, turning away from the scene. Suddenly, my child exploded in action and sound. "Take him down!," he shouted. He began pushing against my shoulder, to move me, to move himself. "Take him down. Take him down!" Take him down? When had I learned to take this posture of Jesus for granted? Who taught me to see the text of the suffering servant as naturally etched in blood?

"Take him down!" Against my useless, "I can't take him down," his lament traveled higher, refusing control. I collided with his dad, exploding out of the bushes, prepared to defend his son against danger. We took turns trying to comfort, to carry, to explain. But the load was heavier than we expected.

How do we learn to cover our ears against the shattering cry of "My God, my God"? Can our familiarity with the classic forms of Christian life breed contempt? Can it deafen us to the sounds of humanly-inflicted suffering? We need to have our ears opened. If the sag of death's gravity only appears like a curve in the stone, then where do we go to have our eyesight corrected?

One of the dangers of a ritualized narrative is the way its edges become smooth. There is a hypnotic naturalness to the old, old story. This is the way things are done, this is how it has always been. Jesus, in truly human likeness, humbled himself and we persist in holding him up so that the scandal of the cross cannot come into contact with our everyday lives.

"Take him down!" should be a natural response. When we take Jesus' posture on the cross for granted, its salvific power has been drained away. When human-to-human violence becomes a mere matter of record, society's nerves are paralyzed. As individuals, we are gradually deadened to pain. We cannot feel for our neighbors, our strangers, ourselves. Instead of a childlike cry of "Take him down," we join the jaded taunts of the spectators, "Let the Messiah, the King of Israel, come down from the cross now, so that we may see and believe."

The importance of Mark's narrative of a Messiah who dies quoting a psalm is the stimulus it sends to our hearts. The yearly procession from palms to crosses must not become routine. It is not sufficient to simply read the words and sing the psalms. We must catch their undertones.

If we regularize the gospel journey at this crossroad it will lead us to a dangerous deadend where suffering is seen as normative for relationship with God. The *why* of the cross demands more than an answer from all who hear it. This *why* does not allow us to sacramentalize the violence of our lives. We dare not obscure the perplexing silence and articulated anguish of the one named Jesus. This is no easy ending, no reassurance that we can leave Jesus meekly hanging Sunday after Sunday.

We must remember not to underestimate a dominant narrative that can exclude or render all other voices inarticulate. The documented connections between Good Friday services with their traditional reading of the gospel of John, and the programs in Europe should warn us against the telling of the old, old story in such a way that new victims are created.

In the Black Forest during the war, a village was overrun by the enemy forces. After the troops moved on, the survivors searched the forest for their missing families. Forty years later, those survivors recounted the scene they could not forget to Susan Brownmiller, author of *Against Our Will: Men, Women and Rape*.

A young Jewish girl had been raped to death. Rarely do crimes like this impress an image on an entire community's consciousness. What marked their memories like a burn? An old, old story told in a terrible new way. The soldiers had cut off her breasts when they had finished and nailed her, Christ-like, to a tree.

What does it take to break our paralysis of feeling? One vision of the shape of human evil and the sound of human suffering. All it takes is that one shattering of our insulation against pain, and we know in our hearts, in our guts, and in our bones that the one who creates us has a different ending in mind. "Take them down!" God commands. "Take my children down!"

Morning by morning, may our ears be opened by the God who teaches. Morning by morning, let our hearts be instructed to seek justice and resist evil. Morning by morning, with the confidence of the children of God, we will sing with the psalmist, "Let your face shine upon your servant; save me in your steadfast love" (Ps. 31:16).

When we teach our children to weave palms into crosses, let us remind them that God intends to reverse our design. Crosses will turn again to palms and be lifted in the children's hands.

Suggestions for Worship

Call to Worship (Ps. 31:14-16):

LEADER: We trust in you, O LORD;

PEOPLE: I say, "You are my God."

LEADER: Our times are in your hands; deliver us from our enemies and from those who pursue us.

PEOPLE: Let your face shine on your servants; save us in your unfailing love.

Act of Praise: Psalm 31:9-16.

Suggested Hymns: "Ask Ye What Great Thing I Know"; "O Sacred Head, Now Wounded"; "Alas! and Did My Saviour Bleed."

Opening Prayer: Almighty and everlasting God, in your great love for us, you have sent your Son, our Savior Jesus Christ, to take upon him our humanity, to suffer death upon the cross, to offer forgiveness to all who have sinned. Grant that we may follow the way of his cross and be made partakers of his salvation. Amen.

Pastoral Prayer: Holy One, morning by morning we awaken from the silence of sleep to the stirring of day. Thanks for the night. Alleluia for life! Open our ears as we open our eyes so that we may hear as those who are taught. Open our minds to the soundness of your teachings. Give us this day our daily bread and a taste for your truth. Give us this day our daily bread and the sense of your call. Teach us how to sustain with a word those who are weary of the nonsense of their lives. Teach us how to sustain with our hands those who are weary and heavily laden. Teach us how to sustain with our means those who are weary of poverty's weight. Sustain us lest we grow weary. Spare us from the time of trial, but when it comes, may we hear you speak in our defense, for the sake of our brother, Jesus. Amen.

APRIL 3, 1994

□

Easter Day

The presence of the risen Christ faith is known to us through word and sacrament. The Word recorded in these lessons prompts resurrection faith, true hope, and great joy.

The Sunday Lessons

Acts 10:34-43: At Caesarea, with Cornelius, the first Gentile convert standing nearby, Peter declares that God has no favorites. The risen Christ appeared to some who were chosen (not all), so that they might preach Christ, who was ordained of God to be "judge of the living and the dead" (v. 42). Everyone who believes receives forgiveness of sins.

I Corinthians 15:1-11: Paul, writing to the Corinthian church, reminds them of the gospel message he preached among them. "I handed on to you as of first importance what I in turn had received: that Christ died for our sins . . . that he was raised on the third day" (vv. 3-4). Contending against the Corinthians' gnostic view that there is no resurrection, he recalls the appearances of the risen Christ. "As to one untimely born, he appeared also to me" (v. 8).

John 20:1-18: The two evidences of the resurrection (empty tomb and appearances) that the early traditions employ are brought together in John's Gospel. Mary Magdalene visited the tomb early and, finding it empty, went to tell Peter and the disciple whom Jesus loved (John). Together they ran to the tomb. Later, Mary was greeted by the risen Christ. "Woman, why are you weeping? Whom are you looking for?" (v. 15). Mary told the disciples, "I have seen the Lord" (v. 18).

Mark 16:1-8: Early in the morning on the first Easter Day, three women came to the tomb with spices. They intended to complete the rites of burial. A heavenly messenger (dressed in white) addressed their overwhelming awe and fear with the words, "Do not be alarmed. . . . He has been raised; he is not here. Look, there is the place they laid him" (v. 6).

HEATHER MURRAY-ELKINS

Reflections

There are some things that one must do all alone. No one else can do them for you. Your birth is your own. You must breathe for yourself, eat for yourself, sleep for yourself. And one must die alone. Your believing is like your dying. One does that all alone, too.

Consider, then, the individual and somewhat solitary encounters with the Resurrection that the Gospel of John records. This Gospel tells that Mary came to the tomb alone—while it was still dark. Finding the stone rolled back and the grave empty, she ran to tell others. Peter and John started running together, but they reached the tomb separately. Alone, each looked into the grave. Each one entered alone, saw alone, believed alone.

Mary stayed at the empty tomb and heard with her own ears the words, "Woman, why are you weeping? Whom are you looking for?" Thinking it was the gardener, she said, "Sir, if you have carried him away, tell me where you have laid him, and I will take him away" (John 20:15). Then Jesus called her by name, "Mary!" (v. 15).

I wish that the Lord God would call me by name on Easter morning. Don't you? The widow who weeps alone, the one in prison alone, the one who bears sickness alone, the orphan left alone, the Thomas who doubts alone, and the one who dies alone will surely, like Mary, turn when she hears her name.

The poet Rilke observed that love, which is difficult, is beyond the young. They are beginners at everything and have to learn love. "With their whole being, with all their forces gathered close about their timid upward-beating heart they must learn to love." The learning time is "long secluded time."

Life, especially life that is greater than death and cannot be shut up in a tomb, is like that. But when one has lived enough and lost enough to know that every human relationship is temporary and that union with God and communion with the risen Christ is no easy merger, they may have come to that place where they turn to say like Mary, "Rabboni! My teacher! My teacher!"

The whole church of Christ is singing alleluia today. We join ten thousand voices in nature to praise the God who gives life. I, too, would find my voice and make my witness, "I have seen the Lord." (JKB)

107

THE BEGINNING OF THE END

Mark 16:1-8

A SERMON BY HEATHER MURRAY-ELKINS

Between the fragrance of the lilies
    and the left-over aroma of Easter Sunrise breakfast . . .
Between the rustling of new clothes
    and the bustle of baskets with candy and eggs . . .
Between the glorious greeting
    and exuberant Amen . . .
there's some unfinished business.

There is enough going on any Sunday of the year, let alone Easter, that it is no surprise if we overlook this "unfinishedness." It seems out of place, unseasonal, at odds with the mood of Easter. Within the hour, the choir will deservingly sigh, "It is finished." After the final handshake at the door, those newly confirmed will conclude, "It is finished." As the last car departs the parking lot, even the pastor—especially the pastor—will sigh, "It is finished."

But the Gospel of Mark rubs against the finished grain of Easter Sunday. The Gospel of Mark, with its unfinished ending, insists that it isn't over till it is over. If it is any consolation, we can remind ourselves that the early church had the same problem with this earliest of gospels. The questionable ending of Mark was one attempt to deal with this unfinished business. Most ancient authorities bring the Gospel to a conclusion at verse 8. In most authorities, verses 9-20—with the shorthand version of three resurrection appearances—follow immediately, although they are often marked as being doubtful.

In a Gospel filled with the miracles and mystery of the Son of God, we are left with missing-the-action men and women too frightened to talk. Listen to the triumphant certainty of the opening, "The beginning of the good news of Jesus Christ, the Son of God" (Mark 1:1). Now *that* is decisive language. Why does such a strong beginning have such a strange conclusion? Is there a missing ending? Who would interrupt this drama of salvation with such a hasty exit?

A preacher's natural resistance to the unfinishedness of Mark is increased on Easter. It is hard enough to resist the temptation of trying to raise the dead. It is hard enough to try to hold your own with the lilies of the field and chancel that proclaim so clearly, "Christ is risen!" Surely, the high drama of the Gospel of Mark is more suitable for an Easter text. Why publicly struggle with a gospel that has no sense of an ending? Pronounce "It is finished" and let us all depart in peace.

But what if this refusal to satisfy our all-American hunger for a happy ending *is* the gospel truth? What if history is more of a mystery of transfiguration than anyone can write, preach, or sing? What if we, like Mark's disciples, have followed so long and so wrongly? We come to the tomb every Easter, ready to decorate with eggs and anthems, expecting to find the risen Christ at home. Instead of the expected Host, there is an angelic intruder with the disturbing news that Jesus of Nazareth is not here and is not coming back.

He is not here. What an un-Easter message. It makes me nervous in the same way that a single sentence of Yeats makes me nervous. "Pull up your chair to the edge of the chasm, and I will tell you a story." This Gospel has no safe telling, no firm ending. It threatens us and our need for protection. It draws us to the edge of our projections. He is not here.

But Christ is not here if here means what we expect. He is not in the place where we laid him. Christ is not here, if here only means there and then. "But go, tell his disciples and Peter that he is going ahead of you to Galilee; there you will see him, just as he told you" (v. 7). Galilee. Where is Galilee? Where (or is it when) can we find Galilee on this unfinished map in this never-ending story? Can we get there from here? Mark draws us to the edge of the chasm between our ways and God's ways. This far and no further. An angel bars our way.

We cannot go around. We have to go back. We cannot go around. We have to go on. Like the ancient church, we circle back to the beginning. "The beginning of the good news of Jesus Christ, the Son of God." We read it again. We start at the beginning. "Now after John was arrested, Jesus came to Galilee, proclaiming the good news of God, and saying, 'The time is fulfilled, and the kingdom of God has come near; repent, and believe in the good news' " (Mark 1:14-15). We go back to the beginning. We go on to the end. It is not over till it is over.

There is a silence to be broken. We have to loosen the inner gags and ignore the outer controls in order to speak with the glorious liberty of the daughters and sons of God. We have been commanded to tell the truth. The consequence of silence threatens all the muted, marginal voices in the human community and in creation. The power to speak the living Word has been given to all who share in the baptism, death, and resurrection of Jesus of Nazareth. Ordination is incidental to proclamation. The whole of creation is groaning in labor pains as the Spirit intercedes with sighs too deep for words. We are commanded to articulate these pains, translate the sighs, witness with our language to the power of the Word living in us. It is not over till it is over.

There is a presence to account for. The mournful accusation, "Were you there?" deserves an honest answer of *No*. "No, we can't be counted on to be there when ungodly power slaughters the lambs." But because of the one who cried, "Eloi, Eloi, lema sabachthani" (Mark 15:34), we can keep showing up better late than never. Christ has gone before us. We will learn to travel light, looking for the signs of the Spirit, tracking the way of the one who is our truth and our life. It is not over till it is over.

There is a promise to be kept by someone who is waiting out on the horizon. Unlike the beloved ghosts of our past, who hover out of reach and reason, Christ will meet us as he promised. We cannot overtake our saints. All those who have gone before remain out of sight, just beyond our hearing. The endless dramas of the gifted child play to an empty house. We come, laden with grief and spices to bury the dead, and are told that they are gone. Any hope of reunion lies in the one who has promised to meet us—not in the tomb, but in any place where love's redeeming work is done.

Unfinished business. A presence calls us into the future, and we circle back to the past in order to find our way. The unfinishedness keeps us going. Knapsack Annie showed me this. We had picked her up somewhere between Texas and home. Her roadweary smell made us kids wrinkle our noses and whisper loud complaints from our backseat of privilege. We were ignored.

My parents had outdated customs of travel. Pick up people on the way. In her case, take them home as well. She was an ugly woman, with a face that matched her sack. But mile after mile she enchanted us with stories of the road, stories of adventure. She understood the lure of the horizon.

We rose one morning to find her gone. She left no explanation. But years later, after we were grown, a card arrived after Easter. She was somewhere. On Easter, she had remembered us, and straightening her clothes, had gone to find a church. An usher had stopped her at the door. She wished us well. Perhaps she would meet us on the road sometime.

Unfinished business. I look for her each Easter. I hope we will let her in, but my guess is she will be waiting. Waiting somewhere on the road. Waiting with the one named Jesus. Waiting for us to find our voice and head for the horizon. Enough said. This is the gospel of the Son of the Blessed One. It has no proper end.

Suggestions for Worship

Call to Worship (Ps. 118:14-24):

LEADER: The LORD is my strength and my song;

PEOPLE: He has become my salvation.

LEADER: The Lord's right hand is lifted high; the Lord's right hand has done mighty things!

PEOPLE: I will not die but live, and will proclaim what the LORD has done.

LEADER: This is the day the LORD has made;

PEOPLE: Let us rejoice and be glad in it.

Act of Praise: Psalm 118:1-2, 14-24.

Suggested Hymns: "Christ the Lord Is Risen Today"; "Up from the Grave He Arose"; "The Day of Resurrection."

Opening Prayer: Almighty God, you have shown your great power in the resurrection of your Son, our Lord Jesus Christ. You have revealed our salvation in his victory over sin and death. Now we join our voices with thousands of voices of nature in songs of life and life eternal. Amen.

Pastoral Prayer: God of all pity and power,
your word removes our doubting.
Christ is risen from the dead,
trampling down death by death,
and bestowing life on those in the tombs.
Alleluia!
God of all pity and power,
down into the grave, your beloved one went,
then you struck down the power of Hell,
and lifted your child into life.
You are sufficient for all our grief,
all our need, all our undone living.
Let the myrrh-bearing women rejoice.
Breathe peace, perfect peace, to the hidden disciples.
May all who have stumbled and fallen
find in you their resurrection.
Help us fight free of the shroud that binds us.
Let darkness and chaos and death flee from the face of light.
Let us hear and believe and live what all the angels are saying,
"Do not be afraid. Christ is risen!"
Amen.

APRIL 10, 1994

□

Second Sunday of Easter

Doubt and questioning disbelief are the issues addressed by these lessons on this low Sunday of Easter.

The Sunday Lessons

Acts 4:32-35: The believers were of one heart and soul. They shared their possessions so that there was not a needy person among them. The apostles, with great power, witnessed to Christ's resurrection.

I John 1:1–2:2: The first letter of John is about life and light. He begins, "This life was revealed, and we have seen it and testify to it, and declare to you the eternal life that as with the Father" (v. 2). Contending against the gnostic heresy that denied flesh-and-blood realities and sin, John acknowledges sin and proclaims, "We have an advocate with the Father . . . he is the atoning sacrifice for our sins" (I John 2:1-2).

John 20:19-31: This traditional reading for the second Sunday of Easter recounts two appearances. The first is to the disciples who hid behind locked doors. Thomas, who was not present when the others saw the risen Lord, said, "Unless I see the mark of the nails in his hands . . . I will not believe" (v. 25). Eight days later, Jesus again stood among them and said to Thomas, "Put your finger here, and see my hands. . . . Blessed are those who have not seen and yet believe" (vv. 27-29).

Reflections

A gospel song, sung often in Eastertide, asks the question, "You ask me how I know he lives?" and then boldly answers, "He lives within my heart." The question lifted up by the song is the compelling question of the low Sunday of Easter—How can one know and believe that Christ is risen? The Gospel story of Thomas' questioning unbelief is the traditional lesson for this Sunday.

To be sure, the questions do not go away. Can we believe it all over again this week, when the lilies begin to lose their bloom, the crowds are smaller, and the alleluias are somewhat faint? Indeed, how can anyone in this modern day believe that Christ lives and that because he lives we shall live also?

I want to know it like I know 2+2=4. I want to trust it like I trust sunset and sunrise.

In this moment of history, strongly influenced and perhaps controlled by science and reason, rational inquiry is trusted more than religious teaching. Time was when the pronouncement of the church, ex-cathedra, was the unquestioned foundation for belief. After the Reformation, the Scriptures were available to all; anyone kindly disposed to the Word of God was considered capable of teaching true doctrine.

The personality cults are thriving now. Television personalities, popular preachers, respected theologians, and even movie stars and sports heroes are trusted for giving the "word of truth." "Johnny Cash says . . . " may not receive the same reverence as "The Bible says. . . ." But in some circles, it likely gets more attention in matters of religious belief.

Insipid Sunday-school class discussions are likely to conclude, "Well you can't know. You just have to believe. You know. Believe it in your heart. You know. Just like the song says, 'He lives within my heart!' " But we do not know, and that is what makes the lesson so vitally important year after year.

These are the important points. The insistent quest and question—"I won't believe unless." The personal encounter with truth—"Reach out your hand." And the importance of the witnesses. We are still dependent on the first witnesses of the resurrection and the Gospel record for our Resurrection faith. "Blessed are those who have not seen and yet have come to believe." (JKB)

IS THE DOOR SHUT?

John 20:19, 26-31

A SERMON BY ROBERT E. FANNIN

It was still Easter day, Jesus had revealed himself to his followers some four times. First to Mary Magdalene, the other women, to Peter, and in his fourth appearance, to the two disciples on the road to Emmaus. Our text brings into focus the fifth appearance of Jesus on Easter day. Ten of the disciples had gathered in an upper room with doors shut for fear of the Jews. Trembling there in fear, can you not hear one of them say, "Are you sure the door is shut, bolted, locked?" The reply comes, "Yes, I have checked it twice."

Hardly a day goes by that someone does not say to me, "Well, I wanted to do so and so but the door was shut." Or on the other side, "I know that is what God wanted me to do for every door was open." We must confess, at sometime in our life we have used that kind of testing or thinking. But on this day, Jesus brings us into focus with reality. We must often go in even if the door is shut. Even if it seems that we should stop, we know what we have to do; it is our calling. The door was shut, but Jesus came and stood among them and said, "Peace be with you."

The door was shut! They were in fear of those who had crucified their Christ. They had huddled into a little room hiding in great fear, as we so often do in our lives. I am sure that because of experiences in your own life you can relate to them and their feelings. The sound of unexpected footsteps or the rattling of a doorknob, and suddenly your heart is pounding. Fear can control our lives—fear that comes from within and the fear that comes from an external stimulus. However, both are controlled by our experiences and internal response. Two people are walking down the street when suddenly a large dog starts barking. One jumps back, while the other holds out their hand to pet it.

I was reading an ad not too long ago for a fear clinic sponsored by a school of dentistry. I am sure the clinic would help, but I am afraid once you slipped into that chair some old brain cells would suddenly take over and the fear would flood your soul, or at least mine.

However, there are deeper fears, those that come from the very center of our existence: The fear stemming from guilt, the fear of not doing what you should have done, the fear of a life unfulfilled, the dream left empty. The disciples had shut the door, but the strongest footsteps they feared were from within, not without. Oh, how we want to shut the door and say "it never happened," or "it just won't work"; "oh, if I had just been a different age," or "if the person only knew me better," or "if this had only been a different time." Emerson reminds us, "Do the thing you fear and the death of fear is certain." In shutting the door the disciples forgot, as we often forget, the one who had called us to leave it open, to let the fresh air flow, to allow the Spirit to prepare the way for opportunities and expressions as we mature together.

He was there when good friends of mine lost their baby, just as he has walked with many that have crossed your path and mine in the shadow of death. He was there the day someone heard the hard words, "It is malignant, you have only a few weeks." He was there when the feelings had gone from a partner and they said, "I no longer want to share this relationship." He was there when someone said, "Your heart is bad, you will have to retire." We must always remember that even when we are in the midst of our fear the door must never be totally shut, for we close the way for ourselves and others.

Even though the door was closed, Christ persisted until they saw life. "Eight days later his disciples were again in the house, and Thomas was with them. The doors were shut, but Jesus came and stood among them and said, 'Peace be with you.' " A greeting that stood for more than hello. It can be translated, "May God give you every good thing."

He wanted to make sure that each one, including the doubting Thomas, fully understood the impact of the Resurrection. It was in the context of the Easter event that he reminded them of life. What a challenge to us today, to enter the closed doors, as well as the opened ones. Right after college I was called into the military service. Following my training I was sent to Korea and served near Freedom Bridge for well over a year. When we arrived they told us not to sing in the showers and I soon realized why. The water in the showers was pumped from slimy green ponds around the base. There was a young man from Tennessee who had the job of filling the water truck and then taking the water up to the showers where it was fed by gravity. One day in a conversation with him, seated by one of those ponds, he told me that his wife had written him a letter. I immediately replied, "I thought she wrote you a 'Dear John' letter when we first arrived?" I remembered that she had found another person and had asked for a divorce. He said that was true and that she had a baby by this other man. At that point he pulled out a picture of his ex-

wife and her baby. I said "What are you going to do?" He replied
with tears in his eyes, "I am going to go home and marry her and
adopt the baby." My mind said, "Boy are you stupid. She left you
for another person when you were serving your country. You had
better think this out." He looked at me and said, "I am going to
do it because I love her. She needs a husband and that baby
needs a father." I want to tell you that day, that moment I felt the
presence of God as never before. He had knocked down the shut
door of "What is expected," and allowed love to flow. Thus, we
reestablish the I-Thou relationship with Christ, the conversation
level of experience.

Christ is saying to us that when we think the door is shut, rattle
the doorknob, knock even harder, kick it a few times, even throw
your weight against it, then determine if it is open or closed. Do
you think for a moment that the feeding of the five thousand was
to merely show that God could take a little and feed many? Was
the walking on the water by Christ to show that He could do
what seemed impossible in a physical sense? Was the healing of
the sick to show that He could control nature? No, not totally.
These miracles were called forth to reveal to people of all times
that there must be the expectation that all things are possible.
We must, therefore, see that anything that is in accordance with
the love of God is possible.

Christ came through the closed door into that room and the
disciples and all who followed entered life at a new and higher
realm. "Then he said to Thomas, 'Put your finger here and see
my hands. Reach out your hand and put it in my side. Do not
doubt, but believe.' Thomas answered him, 'My Lord and my
God!' " Thomas had moved from the world of fear to the world of
faith and openness.

One of the great privileges that I have had in my ministry was
to develop a close relationship with the family of Eric Liddell. If
you saw the film *Chariots of Fire*, you will remember Eric as
Scotland's greatest athlete. Because of his faith he had refused to
run on Sunday in the 1924 Olympic Games in Paris. The door
had apparently been shut and he would lose his chance to be an
Olympic star. He later won the gold medal and created a world
record in the 400 meters race. Out of his faithfulness, he
achieved even greater glory for his country as a prisoner of war.
One of his fellow prisoners writes these words, "Eric Liddell

stood out among the eighteen-hundred people in our internment camp . . . His gentle face and warm smile, even as he taught us games . . . showed us how much he loved the children." What was his secret? He talked with God every day and studied the scripture. He had a living relationship.

James Stewart writes, "Lord here am I. I really want to let you in, but I have so little faith. I have forgotten how to pray. I am just an ordinary, unspiritual creature. I have tried to open the door but Lord there is the rust, the accumulated rust of years upon the bolts. You must do it for me, break through! Smash that rusty lock, batter my heart three personed God."

The door is shut only because we have decided to close it. With Easter still fresh in our minds, let us open wide our lives and allow the living Christ to become the power for our daily living as each moment becomes a Resurrection message.

Suggestions for Worship

Call to Worship (I John 1:1-2):

> LEADER: That which was from the beginning, which we have heard, this we proclaim concerning the Word of life.
>
> **PEOPLE: The life appeared; we testify to it.**
>
> LEADER: We proclaim to you the eternal life.
>
> **PEOPLE: Which was with the Father and has appeared to us.**
>
> LEADER: If we confess our sins, he is faithful and just and will forgive us our sins,
>
> **PEOPLE: And purify us from all unrighteousness.**

Act of Praise: Psalm 133.

Suggested Hymns: "God of the Ages"; "Christ Is Alive"; "Come, Sinners, to the Gospel Feast."

Opening Prayer: O God, who raised Jesus Christ and made him Lord of all time, forgive us for the ways we have treated the time given to us. We act as if there is time unlimited, not responding to the opportunities of discipleship that come to us each day. We ask for forgiveness as we often wish for our life to pass by faster and forget it is precious. You are the Lord of the past, present, and future. We give thanks, that in the light of the Resurrection, we have hope for what is seen and what is unseen. Forgive us for our past sins, and give us the strength we need to go forward with the message of eternal hope. We pray in the name of Jesus Christ. Amen.

Pastoral Prayer: O loving God, we thank you for this Sabbath day of worship. We come having experienced the power of Easter. Now in the season of Eastertide we still celebrate the Resurrection. As a community of believers, we pray that we might reveal to the world the power of the Easter event. May we go forth and respond to the need that surrounds us on every side, so as to allow all persons to have a quality life and a personal relationship with Christ. We confess our sins, those that no one knows and those that are seen by all. We remember the sacrifices made by others in preparing the way for our opportunity for service. For those experiencing times of suffering and grief, we ask that they feel your love and our love. We dedicate this church, and all of its gifts and graces, to the building of your kingdom here in this place. In the name of Jesus Christ our Lord and Savior. Amen.

APRIL 17, 1994

□

Third Sunday of Easter

The words from John's letter, "we saw it and proclaim it," suggest a unifying theme for this day. The church, from the beginning, has been called to bear witness to the Resurrection. We, too, are sent forth to witness.

The Sunday Lessons

Acts 3:12-19: Peter, preaching in the temple area, recalls how Jesus was rejected and crucified. "But you rejected the Holy and Righteous Ones . . . and you killed the Author of life, whom God raised from the dead" (vv. 14-15). That denial was made in ignorance. Now Peter asks his hearers, who now know the truth, to "repent therefore, and turn to God . . . so that times of refreshing may come from the presence of the Lord" (vv. 19-20).

I John 3:1-7: "We are God's children now; what we will be has not yet been revealed" (v. 2). To be named and known as children of God is evidence of the love of the Father. Obedience and righteousness are evidence that one abides in him.

Luke 24:36b-48: In the final appearance story recorded in Luke, Jesus came to his disciples saying, "Why are you frightened, and why do doubts arise in your hearts? . . . touch me and see" (vv. 38-39). Luke emphasized the bodily reality of the risen Christ, "A ghost does not have flesh and bones" (v. 39), and goes beyond the invitation to touch to tell of a shared meal. "Have you anything here to eat?" (v. 41). They gave him a piece of broiled fish, and he ate it before them. The great commission follows, "You are witnesses of these things" (v. 48).

Reflections

In our courts of law, hearsay is disallowed. Witnesses are not asked to tell what they have heard others say, but what they themselves have seen and heard. Yet, the jury's verdict rests on the testimony of witnesses—on what they hear told by others.

That light is better than darkness, that sight is better than blindness, that the hierarchy of the senses (sight, sound, touch, taste, smell) rules in matters of knowledge, that experience is better than descriptions—all seem to be principles of the first order in deciding for truth. Yet, they have not displaced the need for witnesses. Indeed, the silencing of witness is a grave omen for any civilization and always marks the decline of faith.

Consider further the difficult task of being a faithful witness. To be set apart by simple yet singular experience ("we gave him broiled fish and he ate it"), to be sent from some solitary place of solemn commission, to try to witness to crowds that do not want to hear, to be questioned and cross-examined and believed or doubted—these are the sobering realities of witness.

An earnest believer who wanted with his whole heart to be a faithful witness for the risen Christ lamented, "It's not that I'm unwilling to speak," he said, "It is that I am so uncertain about what to say." In desert places or on the lonely shore of Galilee, the message may seem clear enough, but in the clamor and affairs of the whole world, the story becomes a hodge podge of confusion and conflict. One tries to remember the commission from the holy mountain, but is persuaded too much by the arguments heard on sectarian hills.

The preacher-poet John Donne spoke of being in consort and concert with God's truth. Give thanks that we are still blessed by some witnesses who have stayed in those places, sufficiently solitary, where God and a good soul meet. (JKB)

IT'S STILL AROUND

I John 3:3-7

A SERMON BY ROBERT E. FANNIN

Several years ago, Karl Menninger wrote a book entitled *Whatever Became of Sin?* I think that the answer is very clear in the world of pain, suffering, and brokenness that surrounds us— it's still around.

The apostle Paul reminds us in Romans 6:23, "For the wages of sin is death, but the free gift of God is eternal life in Christ Jesus our Lord." There is no doubt that the cost of everything is going up. Clerks are apologizing for what they have to charge. Coffee is not only grown on mountains, but it seems that the price is decided at that elevation as well. I stopped in a restaurant on the highway and ordered a cup of coffee to stay awake. When the waitress told me it would be a dollar, I got so upset that I stayed awake all the way. There is no question the price of sin has always been great, as a friend of mine said, "It's the high cost of low living."

Our text reminds us, "Everyone who commits sin is guilty of lawlessness." Sin, what is it? If a person comes up to you and says that someone you know has been sinning, what do you think? I asked a number of people that question. Their first reaction was to say, "They are stealing money, having an affair outside of their marriage, drinking too much, etc." Sin for most of us is doing, or over-doing, the traditional "no-no's." For many people, that is where sin begins and ends. Now there is no question if these things separate us from the love of God or cause us to hurt one another, they are sins. But the reason these actions would be classified as such would vary widely in definition. Are they sins because they have always been sins through tradition, or because people in the past referred to them as sins, or because they show a lack of responsibility?

Reilly, the psychiatrist in T. S. Eliot's play *The Cocktail Party*, asks Celia, a young society leader, this question, "Tell me what you mean by a sense of sin?" Having had a rather rocky life she was now at a time in her life when she wanted to change. She replied, "Having a normal life I was taught not to believe in sin. Oh, I don't mean it was never mentioned; but anything wrong from our point of view was either bad form or was psychological." To many, sin has become bad form or indicates something wrong with society. It is something that others do, not me. Yet, when one begins to examine the definition of sin in terms of the Old and New Testaments, it begins to take on a broadness that encompasses all of us; it is an estrangement from God. The reality is that humankind is unable to find wholeness or fulfillment without a divine-human relationship.

You will often hear people say, "I don't go to church for I am basically a good person and all they talk about is that people are sinners." There are a lot of good people in the world, but we are all sinners striving to better ourselves. Unless one is ready to say that they have arrived and can do no better, they are in need of a strong relationship with God and other persons.

Lance Webb wrote, "Sin is not just 'missing the mark' as the root meaning of the New Testament word for sin describes it. Though it is true, as psychologists point out, that the average person realizes only one-twentieth of their capacity. Neither is sin immaturity—the inability to handle the negative emotions or anger and fear, and their kindred feelings. Nor is sin the destructiveness causing us to hurt ourselves and others. Nor again is sin the disobedience to the Law as the Pharisees taught. These are not sin but the results of sin, the symptoms of the disease itself. Sin is that within us which causes us to miss the mark, even when we see it; that keeps us immature even though wanting maturity; that keeps us impotent and destructive even though we desire to be potent and productive." Sin is everybody's disease. Sin is that thin line between living for God and living for self.

Karl Menninger, in his book, listed the traditional seven deadly sins. He then went on to list some of the modern twentieth century sins as well such as: affluence, cheating, stealing, lying, psychological cruelty, raping the environment, cruelty to animals, abuse—and the list goes on. I think there are several more to be added to the list that reflect the 1990s that, as you would expect, are at the feeling level.

Lucy had set up her "Psychiatric Help Booth" and Charlie Brown came seeking some advice. After paying the counseling fee of five cents he says, "And so I can't help it, I feel lonely, depressed." "This is ridiculous," Lucy shouts back, "You should be ashamed of yourself Charlie Brown. You've got the whole world to live in, there's beauty all around you; there are things to do . . . great things to be accomplished; no man trods this earth alone; we are all together; one generation taking up where the other generation left off!" Charlie Brown answers with a smile on his face, "You're right Lucy, You're right! You've made me see things differently . . . I realize now that I am part of the world . . . I'm not alone . . . I have friends!" Lucy looks at him and says, "Name one!" I would say that Charlie Brown's feelings are reflective of a lot of people today. One of the new sins of our time is *emptiness,* even though we have all experienced these feelings temporarily. I say this because I believe when a person allows their emptiness, or loneliness, to take over their whole being, they have denied the principle that God loves them, thereby limiting their relationship with God. It goes beyond the poor-me syndrome into a deep sense that life is empty without any hope of being filled. It is found in marriages, family relationships, personal goals and desires—my goal and your goals—rather than "What does God want *us* to do?" This sin is growing daily due to a society that emphasizes production over the individual. It seems to find momentum in a "high tech—no touch" syndrome. It is clothed in the darkness of more and more for me.

Another sin for our day is *not believing in oneself*—ones ideas, feelings, and possibilities. The sin of not having a God-given sense of self-esteem. We limit ourselves and, therefore, cannot fulfill our relationship with God. Robert Raines talks about this struggle within ourselves to believe in what we can do. He says, "Lord make me graceful, within limits let me be at ease with my own direction, and sensitive to that of others, respectful of customs and procedures, patient towards my own unfolding, trusting where I cannot manage, believing where I cannot see."

It is capturing the power of the eighth Psalm in speaking of humankind, "Yet you have made them a little lower than God, and crowned them with glory and honor" (v. 5). In a world that seems to be pulled more and more toward separation rather than togetherness, there is hope as our text reminds us, "Little children, let no one deceive you. Everyone who does what is right is righteous, just as he is righteous." Believing in oneself allows that person to understand with new clarity the love of God.

Psychologists tell us that one must have a secure sense of self-esteem before they can reach that universal stage of life, the point at which they are able to give meaningfully to others. One must express a sense of life that calls others to maturity, a fullness that will not allow them to do less than the gifts and graces they possess, thereby becoming a force of change in the world, creating life where death once existed.

A minister friend of mine was traveling, when suddenly he saw a man staggering on and off the road. Cars were weaving around him blowing their horns, saying words that were derogatory. My friend stopped and helped the man, who was drunk, off the road and into his car. He then went back and changed the man's flat tire. Realizing that he was unable to drive, my friend took the man back to the church and waited until he had sobered enough to continue on his way. While they were together he talked to the man about the strong need for him to realize that he was a child of God, and had value and should not waste his life. A few weeks later the man came knocking at the minister's door. He was sober and had a smile on his face. "I thought a lot about what you said and I want to do something with my life. I want to serve a master that has a minister like you, who would help an old drunk like me change his tire and care for him." The man returned to college, studied, and became a minister of the gospel. Oh, he knows who he is and his limitations, but because he started believing in himself and God, he found the strength to answer God's call.

Yes, sin is still around—emptiness, lack of self-esteem, or others you could name, unique to your being. Whatever label we want to put on them—bad form, or psychological terms—if they separate us from God and keep us from being all that we were meant to be, they are sins nonetheless. But regardless of where we find ourselves, we must be ready to accept the free gift of forgiveness that comes to us in these days following Easter.

I was in the Holy Land standing at the location of the Garden Tomb. The view of the proposed site of Golgotha connected to that tomb could be seen from a high point in the garden. As I looked at that craggy rock, I was immediately drawn to the smell of diesel fumes and the sounds of people loading on buses with their bundles in hand. Right below the place of crucifixion was the city bus terminal. At first I was very upset to see such a busy, smelly activity in the midst of that holy place. Then it suddenly hit me, that is exactly where it should be! Jesus came to meet us in the midst of our daily struggles in the emptiness, the pain, and the brokenness. My mind traveled back to that day filled with tumult and loudness, people shouted, the streets were filled, guards pushed the crowds back and grabbed one, Simon of Cyrene, to help carry the cross. The women in the traditional Eastern manner were wailing and crying. Two criminals were to be crucified with Jesus, one on the right and one on the left. Jesus looked over the crowd and said, "Father, forgive them; for they do not know what they are doing" (Luke 23:34). As they were being mocked, one criminal said, "Are you not the Messiah? Save yourself and us!" (Luke 23:39). The other criminal knew he was the Messiah and said, "'Jesus, remember me when you come into your kingdom.' He [Jesus] replied, 'Truly I tell you, today you will be with me in Paradise'" (Luke 23:39-43). Today your sins are forgiven.

I say to you in the name of Christ, if you only ask, "Your sins are forgiven," go and sin no more so that others might know the fullness of God's love.

Suggestions for Worship

Call to Worship (Ps. 4):

> LEADER: Answer us when we call to you, O righteous God.

> **PEOPLE:**   **Give us relief from our distress; be merciful to us and hear our prayer.**

> LEADER: Know that the LORD has set apart the godly for himself;

> **PEOPLE:**   **The LORD will hear when we call to him.**

Act of Praise: Psalm 4.

Suggested Hymns: "All Hail the Power of Jesus' Name"; "Fairest Lord Jesus"; "O Young and Fearless Prophet."

Opening Prayer: O gracious God, we come to you on this morning confessing that we at times do not have any charity to share, or prayers to offer or forgiveness to give. We come with contrite hearts, bringing our times of failure, our disappointments, our unfulfilled dreams, and our times of dryness. We know that you can supply all needs and quench the thirsting of our souls. Help us, O Lord, to be your people.

Pastoral Prayer: We gather, O Lord, as your people with praise and thanksgiving for your presence here in this place. As a community of faith, we feel the power of your spirit, knowing that so often we fail to be all that we are capable of being. Give us the strength we need. Our hearts are heavy for those who are suffering through grief in this hour; fill their souls with a sense of knowing the promise of eternal life. In this season of Easter, let us become a sign of life by embracing our neighbor, empowering the powerless, and sharing the resources that come from your creation. We often fall short and miss the mark of your love, forgive us of our many transgressions. Let the negative pulse in our life be replaced by a vision of where this church and all of your family should be in the coming days. Bless the families, homes, institutions, and businesses of our community both here and around the world. May we through your spirit know right from wrong and follow the teaching of the Holy Word. In Jesus' name. Amen.

APRIL 24, 1994

□

Fourth Sunday of Easter

Knowing and being known is one of the great themes of resurrection faith. In the Gospel lessons, it is set in the context of a shepherd who knows his sheep.

The Sunday Lessons

Acts 4:5-12: Peter and John had been arrested and were being questioned. "By what power or by what name did you do this?" (v. 7). Peter answered, "Let it be known to all of you . . . that this man is standing before you in good health by the name of Jesus Christ of Nazareth, whom you crucified, whom God raised from the dead. . . . There is salvation in no one else, for there is no other name under heaven given among mortals by which we must be saved" (vv. 10-12).

I John 3:16-24: The passage speaks of word and deed, hearts that condemn, confidence before God, belief and love. Love for one another is the final test of our devotion to Christ and evidence that we are his obedient children.

John 10:11-18: A passage from the good shepherd chapter of John is read on this Sunday each year in the lectionary cycle. The dominant idea in each is, "The good shepherd lays down his life for the sheep" (v. 11). This lesson also emphasizes a personal relationship. I know my own and my own know me.

Reflections

"Ask him if he knows me?" she said, recalling a place of meeting and previous association. Then she added, "I doubt that he'll remember. He meets so many people." All of us like to be known. We especially like to be known by persons who have power and influence. But the lament, "Nobody knows the trouble I've seen," is too often our plaintive cry. The Gospel lesson proclaims that the risen Christ knows his own, and they know him.

The lessons of this Eastertide tell of a woman who did not recognize the risen Christ until he called her name. "Mary," he said, and she knew him. "My Teacher," she answered.

An absent and then doubting disciple complained that he had not seen and could not know until he was personally involved. Thomas needed a personal touch before he could say, "My Lord and my God."

When the disciple who swore, "I never knew him," met the risen Christ by Galilee, he was called by name—" 'Simon son of John, do you love me?' He said to him, 'Yes, Lord; you know that I love you' " (John 21:16).

The first-century church cherished these stories of intimate and immediate relationships with the risen Christ. The good shepherd metaphor was cherished as a portrayal of a sovereignty (King David risked his life for the flock) and a sovereign grace that called each sheep by name. Yet, the oneness suggested by this mutual knowing did not deny the distinction between shepherd and sheep, between savior and the saved. As C. K. Barrett notes, "Man is not deified but delivered."

The obvious question follows. How may one know that he or she is known? The evidence is neither simply mystical experience, nor is the relationship made visible by pietistic practice. The knowing referred to by John is a moral relationship marked by love and demonstrated in obedience (see I John 3:10). (JKB)

COPYRIGHT INFRINGEMENT NO LONGER PROHIBITED

Acts 4:5-12

A SERMON BY DAVID Z. RING III

Most Americans today watch videotapes, especially of recent popular movies. Have you ever noticed one thing that is common to virtually every videotape you rent or buy? Right at the beginning of each tape, assuming you don't fast-forward past it, is a very serious and sober *warning*—a warning against copying that tape. Copying a videotape made by someone else is against the law. The same applies to musical recordings, to books, to records, and to many other similar items. The rights to copy and distribute creative material—such as movie videotapes—are reserved to the authors and producers thereof, or their agents. That's what the word *copyright* means. And copyright infringement is strictly prohibited.

The ancient Jews had received a series of dramatic revelations of the nature of God during the time of Moses. God had repeatedly shown them, in awesome and unmistakable ways, his grace, love, and mercy. For centuries thereafter, God had occasionally spoken to them through prophets and other inspired teachers. They had dutifully written down God's revelations to them, entrusting these writings to a special group of men, called priests, to pass on to future generations.

God's special outpourings of grace and his revelations to the Jews gradually became fewer and fewer until, four centuries prior to the time of Jesus, they had ceased altogether. Because there were no more new revelations, the existing, past revelations of God to the Jews became more and more precious. As their value increased, the Jewish priests—who guarded, copied, and transmitted the written record of these former revelations— gained increased authority and power through their handling of these rare, sacred materials. By the time of Jesus, the temple priests of Jerusalem and their appointed agents, called scribes, had assumed exclusive rights to manage the very sacred word of God. God's revelations had become a limited resource, reserved to and carefully conserved by the high Jewish religious authorities. In short, they held the copyright on God's word.

Holding this copyright gave the religious leaders of the Jews exclusive power to dole out knowledge of the word, and the will, of God to whomever they wished, whenever they wished. Or they could withhold it. And that was that.

Then along came a man named Jesus, from Nazareth. He claimed that God's revelations to the Jews had not ceased. Further, he even dared to claim that he was a new revelation of God—and not only to the Jews, but to all humanity. He spoke and the common people heard—many of them for the first time—and openly and spontaneously proclaimed the word of God. This was exciting!

But it was also, from the point of view of the Jewish religious leaders, illegal. Jesus was infringing on their copyright. Revelations from God were their exclusive property. Pronouncements of divine wisdom could only come from them or their authorized agents. So they went to Jesus and asked, point blank, "Who gave you the right to say and do these things?"

I have always wondered what kind of answer they expected. Perhaps if Jesus had said, "Well, I studied under Senior Rabbi Zaran for five years, and I have here a notarized letter, with a raised wax seal, from High Priest Amal," they would have said okay and left Jesus alone.

But Jesus did not give them the answers they wanted. I do not know exactly what the legal penalty is for copying videotapes in this country today, but to the Jewish leaders of Jesus' time, the penalty for copyright infringement was death. Jesus was illegally distributing godly materials—like mercy, forgiveness, and love. So they killed him.

It is pretty hard to imagine a more radical solution to a problem than murdering the one causing it. Can you imagine the frustration the Jewish leaders experienced when, just a few months later, word was brought to them that the same problem had arisen again; and this time, there were ten or more copyright violators? A whole group of men, calling themselves apostles, were publicly proclaiming that God cared for, and was freely available to, the common riffraff on the streets of Jerusalem! And, worse yet, they claimed that God had raised up, from the dead, the man named Jesus whom they had killed for the same crime!

Our text today tells us that the Jewish leaders acted exactly as they had with Jesus. They arrested the two most prominent leaders of this new group, Peter and John, brought them before themselves, and asked them virtually the same question they had posed to Jesus: "By what power or by what name did you do this?" (v. 7b). In other words, "Who gave you the right to trespass in our territory? We've got the originals of everything God ever said, and so we have exclusive authority to speak on God's behalf. You're infringing on our copyright."

Peter's reply to these Jewish leaders is classic:

"Rulers of the people and elders, if we are questioned today because of a good deed done to someone who was sick and are asked how this man has been healed, let it be known to all of you, and to all the people of Israel, that this man is standing before you in good health by the name of Jesus Christ of Nazareth, whom you crucified, whom God raised from the dead. This Jesus is 'the stone that was rejected by you, the builders; it has become the cornerstone.' There is salvation in no one else, for there is no other name under heaven given among mortals by which we must be saved." (vv. 8b-12)

Peter's response was a verbal sword that cut straight to the heart of the entire matter. For centuries, these religious leaders had monopolized, and virtually sealed away, the mercies of Almighty God. Because the apostles had dared to openly proclaim God's love, and to demonstrate it in tangible ways—as in releasing God's healing power for a crippled man—they were being put on trial. It was ludicrous—ridiculous.

And, Peter added, because of the miserly way the Jewish authorities had hoarded the things of God, their copyright was voided—by its true owner, Almighty God. The great Creator had just revoked their presumed right to limit his creativity. God had raised up Jesus from the dead, and, from henceforth, Jesus, not they, would hold the copyright on Godly revelation. And further still, Jesus would freely allow the love, mercy, and grace of God to be openly distributed to any and all who might desire it.

What does all this mean to us today, almost two millennia removed from the time of Jesus, Peter, John, and the Jewish authorities? As followers of Jesus, the Christ, we are his agents, entrusted with the copyright that he now holds on God's behalf. We are most certainly not to be like the Jewish priests of old and limit its distribution, either by intention or by inaction. Instead, we are encouraged to spread the revelations of God—his love, his mercy, his wonderful grace—far and wide. We have blanket permission to *use* the copyright.

Whenever permission is granted to use someone else's copyright, there is one obvious condition that goes along with the permission. You must acknowledge—give credit to—the one from whom the permission was received. And so it is with this. We have permission to reveal and proclaim the love of God, to any and all, in the *name of Jesus*. When we announce the good news of God's salvation made available to all humanity, we *must* do so in the name of Jesus, for it is from him that we have received this blessed right. As Peter said to the Jewish authorities so long ago, "there is no other name under heaven given among mortals by which we must be saved."

Beloved people of God: Tell the good news. Spread the wonderful word of salvation. Reveal the mercies of God to all. You have full authority to use God's copyright—in the name of Jesus. Amen.

Suggestions for Worship

Call to Worship (Ps. 23):

LEADER: The LORD is my shepherd, I shall not be in want.

PEOPLE: He makes me lie down in green pastures, he leads me beside quiet waters;

LEADER: Surely goodness and love will follow me all the days of my life.

PEOPLE: And I will dwell in the house of the LORD forever.

Act of Praise: Psalm 23.

Suggested Hymns: "Crown Him with Many Crowns"; "Jesus Loves Me"; "He Is Lord"; "The Lord's My Shepherd, I'll Not Want."

Opening Prayer: O Lord, as we continue to bask in your light of life and resurrection unto eternal life, grant us the additional blessing of your presence in the time ahead. Reveal your glory, receive our praises, and send into each heart the flame of the Spirit of our risen Lord, Jesus the Christ. Amen.

Pastoral Prayer: Lord, as we come before you in prayer this morning, three weeks have elapsed since we commemorated the glorious resurrection of Jesus on Easter Day. That is a very brief time by godly reckoning, but in human terms it is long enough for us to have begun to forget.

Help us, O God, on this fourth Sunday of Easter, to remember. Help us to recapture the reality of Easter, and to renew its celebration. Just as Jesus rose from death, never to die again, aid us in living a resurrection faith from this day forward. Let us never again be content to merely accept this world's ups and downs, for—through Jesus' great victory—we have been granted a permanent, eternal up. We praise you for that incomparable blessing, and we entreat your strength to help us share it, until the entire world be blessed as we have been with that same, wonderful knowledge of life eternal, available through Christ Jesus our Lord. Amen.

MAY 1, 1994

⊔

Fifth Sunday of Easter

The presence of the risen Christ is sometimes a future expectation. "I will come and take you to myself." In these lessons the presence of Christ is shown to be immediate and abiding. "Abide in me and I in you."

The Sunday Lessons

Acts 8:26-40: Phillip met an Ethiopian eunuch on the road reading Isaiah. The apostle asked, "Do you understand what you are reading?" (v. 30). Phillip then told him the good news of Jesus and baptized him.

I John 4:7-21: The Gnostics claimed a special knowledge of God. The epistle offers the final test for all who would say, "We are of God." It is this: Those who love know God. Those who do not love do not know God.

John 15:1-8: "I am the true vine, and my Father is the vinegrower" (v. 1). With these abrupt words, John introduces another symbol for our understanding of Christ and Christian disciples. The allegory reveals Christ as the vine, and believers as the fruit-bearing branches that are cut away and burned by the judgment of God.

Reflections

At first it sounds so promising and helpful. That one can constantly abide in a source of life and strength is good news indeed. But what is the shape of this abiding presence and power? The vine and the branches are clear symbols. What do they mean?

I can visualize being constantly with someone in a physical way (stay with me and you will be safe). I can imagine sustained relationships that are more than simply being together. Or relationships marked by a sincere emotional presence (weep with those who weep, rejoice with those who rejoice). I have witnessed a type of holiness that seeks to abide constantly in spiritual relationships through prayer and contemplation.

Whether the relationship is physical, emotional, or spiritual, there comes a time when one needs to be apart. Is there anyone in whose physical presence you want always to stay? Is there any emotion, high or low, that you would want to have last forever? The sentimentality and shallow piety of those who claim to walk every step with Jesus is not attractive either.

But the meaning of "I am the vine" is not centered in the consciousness of Christ's presence, but rather in the reality of it. The response to the Word then is not striving to be more conscious of his presence. It is acknowledgment of our dependency. A man whose life reflected an abiding presence often prayed, "O Lord, our God, we are constantly in need of thee and always dependent upon thee."

The psalmist prays, "Every day will I bless thee, and praise thy name for ever and ever" (Ps. 145:2). (JKB)

SQUEEZING GRAPEFRUITS, TAPPING WATERMELONS

John 15:1-8

A SERMON BY DAVID Z. RING III

My wife has a habit that I am sure has raised an eyebrow or two among supermarket produce managers. She is a very demanding shopper for fruits at the produce counter. Grapefruits, oranges, lemons, and the like are always given a good squeeze or two before Fran puts them in her bag. Cherries and grapes are hand selected, one by one, prior to purchase. Watermelons and cantaloupes are always tapped sharply a few times as she listens for the quality of resonance produced.

Some time back, while we were on a trip visiting my parents, we stopped at a local food store looking to buy a watermelon. I just walked up to what appeared to be the biggest one, and hefted it onto my shoulder. But Fran, after tapping here and there on the available melons, picked a smaller one and said, "Put that big one down. This one's a better buy." And she was right. The melon Fran selected turned out to be one of the sweetest watermelons I had ever eaten. My wife's a tough inspector when it comes to selecting fruit, but her grapefruit squeezing and watermelon thumping pays off.

One of the favorite analogies used to talk about human lives in the New Testament, employed by Jesus, Paul, and others, was the topic of fruit and fruit-bearing. The climate of the Holy Land is quite similar to parts of the American Southwest; thus, with irrigation, the people of Jesus' time and locale were able to grow a broad assortment of fruits. The Bible repeatedly mentions such fruits as figs, plums, apples, grapes, melons of several kinds, pomegranates, olives, and pears. So when Jesus and his early followers in and around Israel talked about fruit and fruit-bearing, they were easily understood.

The people of Israel of that day knew, for example, that if a fig tree failed to bear figs for three straight years, as in Jesus' parable of the unfruitful fig tree, it was unlikely to ever do so again. Thus, it should be cut down, and something more promising planted in its place. They understood how olive branches of various types could be grafted onto a single host plant, and that sometimes the grafts held and succeeded, and sometimes they did not. So when the apostle Paul spoke of grafting a variety of wild olive—the Gentiles—onto the Jews' special covenant with God, they quickly picked up on the idea being presented, and the implications thereof. They could inspect the trunk of an apple tree even in the dead of winter and predict from its appearance whether the tree was likely to produce wholesome or diseased fruit in its proper season—again, a practice from which Jesus derived a teaching of spiritual principle.

As Jesus and his early followers told fruit stories, the people to whom they spoke had little problem making the obvious translation of these teachings—moving from fig trees, or grape vines, to human lives. They knew that Jesus was not offering a course in botany when he spoke about non-productive fruit plants, but he was really concerned that persons' lives produce something of value in God's sight.

In today's text, Jesus speaks of himself as a vine and of his followers as branches. In doing this, he was inviting his hearers to graft themselves onto, and to tap into, the boundless life-energy his Spirit—the Spirit of the Living God—wished to supply to all who believed in him. And when Jesus stressed the need for those who claimed to believe in him to remain and bear fruit, he obviously was not talking about growing watermelons.

There is little that is hidden, or mysterious, about today's text, or about any of the fruit stories in the New Testament. Fruit production was an ordinary, commonplace activity for the people of Jesus' day and time. Thus, in using fruit analogies, the Christ met them on their own terms, in the ordinary activity of their daily lives. It's simple. "You want to call yourself my follower?" asks Jesus. "Fine—then bear fruit!"

The problem today with the common, the ordinary, and the obvious, such as the New Testament's fruit teachings, is that many contemporary people are more interested in the extraordinary, the unusual, and the uncommon. I know that is true for me. Cliff diving certainly sounds more exciting than office work. Flying to Europe is a lot more interesting than cleaning the house.

Today, even though most of us still lead fairly common, ordinary lives most of the time, we can always easily escape to the realm of the exciting and unusual through books, magazines, and, most especially, through that one-eyed door to the land of make-believe—the television. How easy it has become to vicariously live through three marriages, five affairs, adopt and raise seven special-needs children, and be chased twice around the world by evil drug-runners—all in the timespan of a ninety-minute made-for-TV movie! Western culture today is so hooked on the unusual that the simple, commonsense appeal of the gospel is no longer as common, nor as appealing, as it once was. If something does not rock us and sock us, it is not worthwhile.

Notwithstanding, let us dare to consider in more detail, for a few moments, Jesus' simple fruit story in today's text. "I am the true vine, and my Father is the vinegrower. He removes every branch in me that bears no fruit. Every branch that bears fruit he prunes to make it bear more fruit . . . . I am the vine, you are the branches . . . . My Father is glorified by this, that you bear much fruit and become my disciples."

One of the reasons I have chosen to be part of the United Methodist branch of Christ's great Church is that Methodists do not preach salvation as the end of the Christian life of faith. Certainly, personal salvation through belief in Jesus Christ is the indispensable beginning of the Christian life for any who would be called followers of Jesus. But when I go into churches where all that is ever preached, week in and week out, is "Get saved . . . get saved . . . get saved!" I feel like shouting, "I am saved! Now, what do I *do*?"

After one is saved, there is work to be done for our Lord. And there is fruit to be borne, lest we lose the meaning of our salvation. "He removes every branch in me that bears no fruit. Every branch that bears fruit he prunes to make it bear more fruit."

And what, specifically, is the fruit that we are to bear for Christ our Lord? The apostle Paul, in Galatians 5, lists nine fruits of the Spirit—love, joy, peace, patience, kindness, generosity, faithfulness, gentleness, and self-control. But in the verses immediately following today's text, which are really the concluding portion of this particular lesson, our Lord Jesus emphasizes only one particular fruit: love. With John 15:17, Jesus completes his teachings on the vine and the branches thereof by saying, "I am giving you these commands so that you may love one another." Love is the fruit we are to bear.

"Just love? Oh, well, that's simple enough. Good sermon, preacher. I'll go home and kiss my spouse, hug my kids, and pet my cat. Thanks for reminding me."

Wait a minute! Yes, love is the fruit we are to bear, but it's not an ordinary, garden variety sort of love. If you really want something unusual, exciting, and extraordinary from Christianity, listen more carefully to our Lord's command, which is also stated, with amplification, in John 15:12. "This is my commandment, that you love one another as I have loved you." Love one another *as I have loved you.*

That is a different kind of orange, folks. That kind of love involves much more than sentimentality, smiles, and kisses. Jesus' kind of love incorporates all of Paul's list of other fruits—patience, kindness, generosity and so forth—into itself. Our Lord's kind of love involves risk. It is a costly kind of love; it includes sacrifice. It may cost us a dollar or two. It may cost us a friend or two. It may even cost us our lives. After all, that's what it cost Jesus.

I have an unusual personal image of the Judgment Day to share with you in drawing this message toward closure. It is a bit fanciful, but I think it is a reasonable extrapolation of today's text. I see myself pushing a wheelbarrow loaded with fruits, of many varieties, up to God's throne. And I imagine God inspecting that fruit, carefully examining the apples for worms or bad spots, taking a test bite of a grape, squeezing the oranges, thumping the melons.

Let us conclude our message with prayer: "Lord, I pray that all our fruits may be found worthy in your sight. Help us to bear much fruit, to your greater glory. Amen."

Suggestions for Worship

Call to Worship (Ps. 22:27-28):

LEADER: All the ends of the earth will remember and turn to the LORD,

PEOPLE: And all the families of the nations will bow down before him,

LEADER: For dominion belongs to the LORD

PEOPLE: And he rules over the nations.

Act of Praise: Psalm 22:25-31.

Suggested Hymns: "Jesus! the Name High over All"; "I Need Thee Every Hour"; "Close to Thee."

Opening Prayer: Lord of life and overcomer of death, we seek your presence at this time as we begin what we call worship. Without you, O God, our worship is empty form. But with you, it becomes life-transforming communion with the source of creation. Enter our worship now, O Lord, and make it real. Amen.

Pastoral Prayer: O God, may we witness, in both deed and word, to your reality and to your love. Save us, Lord, from blighting our witness with flares of anger or the nourishing of hatred in our hearts. Save us, too, from that worst affliction of false Christianity—self-righteousness. Help us to cheer the suffering by our sympathy, to freshen the drooping by our hopefulness, and to strengthen, in all we meet, a wholesome sense of worth in your sight and a joy in the fullness of life. If any have need, make us ready to render help ungrudgingly, rejoicing that we have been counted worthy by our God to be of assistance to a fellow human.

We continue to rejoice in Jesus' victory over death, and we look forward to the day when he shall return to fully restore this earth to the goodness with which you originally created it. In the meantime, we are yours to use in whatever ways you see fit. Use us, Lord, to your glory. Amen.

MAY 8, 1994

□

Sixth Sunday of Easter

Easter joy finds its completion in love that obeys. "These things are spoken that my joy may be in you, and that your joy may be full."

The Sunday Lessons

Acts 10:44-48: This is a part of the story of the baptism of Cornelius. It is told in the context of justifying the gentile mission. The Holy Spirit was poured out on Gentiles who heard Peter's sermon. He therefore asked, "Can anyone withhold the water for baptizing these people who have received the Holy Spirit just as we have?" (v. 47).

I John 5:1-6: Faith is the victory that conquers the world. In the context of a baptismal confession that emphasizes love for God and neighbor, this mighty claim is made: "For whatever is born of God conquers the world. And this is the victory that conquers the world, our faith" (v. 4).

John 15:9-17: Love and obedience are the themes of this lesson. First, love is shown in the relationship of the Father and the Son. "The Father has loved me . . . I have kept my Father's commandments and abide in his love" (vv. 9-10). John's doctrine of the church follows in the commandment to love one another.

Reflections

Paddy Chayevfsky in his play *Gideon* has the servant leader saying, "It is a hard thing to be loved by God." He is right about that. Love, which is free in the giving, makes a mighty claim when it is received. That claim is the call to obedience. "If you keep my commandments, you will abide in my love." The kind of love that is worthy of the name Christian is more than being loved, it is more than enjoying a satisfied feeling about yourself because you are accepted. It is much more than a warm glow in your heart. Every parent who has found joy in sacrificing for a child knows that. So do friends who are willing to lay down their lives for their friends and are even glad to do it.

We all know that love is a gift. When it wraps a body up in its warmth and joy, one is likely to say, "What did I ever do to deserve this?" Then in the first moment of loneliness when one feels unloved, there follows a whimper and cry like the newborn baby's, "Somebody love me! Somebody love me!" Unanswered, it is likely to change to the despairing complaint, "Nobody loves me!" But love will never come to the person who desperately tries to squeeze more affection out of somebody else. Love is a gift. But it is not a gift we get so much as it is something we give. So love and obedience belong together. No one ever receives the love of God without immediately being put to the test by it.

We disobey and then wonder why love is so fleeting. Neither beauty that invites attention, nor a warm feeling of gratitude is the key to abiding love. It is heeding, "This I command you: Love one another."

The obedience is not that of a slave, but of a friend. (JKB)

FAITH AS THE VICTORY
THAT OVERCOMES THE WORLD

I John 5:1-6

A SERMON BY RALPH C. WOOD

Who in his right mind would want to *overcome* the world? This is too delightful a place to be set at nought. For all its hardships, life is too full of joy, hope, and fun for us to want to defeat it. Is there anyone here who wants to overcome ACC basketball? Neither do I. And what about the things that are lasting as athletic games are not such as friendship, books, ideas, music, art, nature, science, and even politics? Are these the worldly accomplishments that faith overcomes? If so, I know why many people are not very interested in our world-overcoming faith. If this be our victory, who wants it? Peter De Vries' character named Chick Swallow certainly does not want it. When he is asked to sum up his experience in Sunday school, Swallow quotes Psalm 84 with witty ironic effect: "A day in thy courts is as a thousand." And later, having emancipated himself from the dull business of church-going, Swallow sees a stream of worshipers hurrying toward the house of the Lord, and sighs wearily: "There, but for the grace of God, go I."

It was Nietzsche who said that we Christians want to overcome the world because we are too weak and cowardly to confront life's hard realities. How right Nietzsche often is. Many of us use our religion to escape the difficulties of life, and thus to overcome the world by manipulating it according to our own selfish purposes. Conservative Christians turn God into a Good Buddy who assures us that everything will work out well, who guarantees our success, who promises us that life will be an endless joyride. Some of these folk do not believe that a Christian can fail. I know a charismatic who insists that God does not permit any of his *truly* faithful to be sick or poor, and that if we both believed and prayed sufficiently well, God would make us healthy and wealthy. This charismatic Christian does not mention whether, following Benjamin Franklin's adage about "early to bed and early to rise," prayer could also make us wise. I have no doubt, however, that if prayer were a shortcut to knowledge as well as prosperity and success, many of us would use it for such unholy purposes.

The commentators say that something not unlike our superficial religiosity was the heresy that the book of I John was written to combat. There were Christians in those days who claimed that their experience of God was immediate and perfect, that they had direct knowledge of God and did not depend on mere faith, and that they loved God so truly as to be without sin. This little tract called I John is directed, therefore, at those who have won a false victory over the world in order to show them what the true triumph of faith is all about.

It has to do chiefly with victory over the one whom Luther calls the Prince of Darkness grim. Our author calls him "the evil one." The writer of I John also says that he is writing to his readers, not in the hope that they might one day defeat the Devil, but "because you have conquered the evil one" (2:13*b*). This may sound more like the disease than the cure, as if the Christian could live in triumphant immunity from evil. Clearly, this is not what the author means, for he warns that "If we say that we have no sin, we deceive ourselves, and the truth is not in us" (I John 1:8). Sin is a very serious business, the writer all but cries aloud, and anyone who underestimates it is deceived in the worst possible way.

The point of these warnings is to make very sure that these first-century believers—and therefore we twentieth-century believers—do not misconceive the Christian life as an easy, obvious, simple-pie business. We do not have immediate, direct experience of God, he reminds us; we know God only as he is mediated to us through Jesus Christ. This seems so patent that it hardly needs stating. Yet, there are Christians in every age, our own included, who become so spiritualized that they claim to have immediate experience of God. They were called Gnostics in the first century, and they are called Fundamentalists in ours. The pamphlet writer of I John has little patience with such a naive religion because it makes a mockery of the gospel.

It mocks God by making his grace seem to be something obvious and manageable. It makes God knowable in the way we know each other and the world—knowable by argument as well as experience. I John, like Scripture in general, stands adamantly against the notion that we can reason our way to religion. Biblical faith is not a rationalist system of doctrine to which a sufficiently well-trained mind gives its assent. God is far too gracious and mysterious and unpredictable to be rationally knowable. As Jeremiah reminds us, God is sometimes inexplicably absent; God even hides. Worse still, God can seem cruel and monstrous, as when he visits insufferable evils on Job.

Such an unmanageable God—a God who does not do our bidding but who dispenses and disposes as he wills—such a God is not known directly, much less perfectly. The heart of the matter is that we believe in God; we trust in God; we live and move and have our being in God. But we *know* God in one way alone— through faith in Jesus Christ. And to have faith is to travel more like a blind man feeling his way with his cane than like an Olympic sprinter pumping confidently toward the finish line. "We walk by faith, not by sight," says Paul (II Cor. 5:7). "Faith is the assurance of things hoped for," the book of Hebrews reminds us, "the conviction of things not seen" (Heb. 11:1).

If conservative Christians achieve their bogus victory over the world by religious naïveté, we liberals triumph over it with our moralism and cynicism. I can remember preaching one of my first sermons from the passage in I John that says, "Those who say, 'I love God,' and hate their brothers or sisters, are liars; for those who do not love a brother or sister whom they have seen, cannot love God whom they have not seen" (4:20). I took this to be a plain and straightforward call to compassion, to sympathy, to what we in our time rather stupidly call caring. It was a simple summons to love that I thought I heard in the Scriptures, both here and elsewhere. And what a time I had, during the hot racial climate of the 1960s. What a time I had moralizing on this obvious Gospel. If my white fellow Baptists did not love the blacks they had seen, how could they claim to love the God they had not seen? And if you do not love your neighbor, how can God love you? Isn't that clear and cogent? Or course it is. It is perfectly clear, as Mr. Nixon used say. Yes, but it ain't Good News. It is not the logic of the Gospel; it is the logic of the world for which Jesus Christ died and that the Gospel has overcome.

I thought I had struck gold when I read that explosive little sentence in I John that declares, "God is love." If God is love, I reasoned, then so can we live lovingly. And then all the world's problems will be solved. It never occurred to me that the revolutionary thing about that sentence is that you cannot reverse it. You cannot say that "Love is God" and be speaking the truth. I John makes plain the true logic of the Gospel when it announces, with utter modesty but with staggering implication, that "we love, because God first loved us." The world tries to invert the syntax and to say that we first love because we are good people capable of good things, including the love of God and the love of our fellow humans. The Gospel insists, to the contrary, that our real hope lies not in ourselves but in the forgiving God. The love to which we are called does not flower from the bud of human goodwill and human good nature. It is an act commanded by God, enabled by God, supplied by God, and redeemed by God despite all of our terrible inadequacy.

To love as the world loves is, by contrast, to grow weary and often embittered. Our efforts to do good are not often reciprocated. Those East Texas racists did not respond to my moralizing appeal for them to stop being hypocrites and to love their black neighbors. But the fault was far from being all theirs. What I did in my self-righteous fury was only to make them feel guilty and angry. Good liberal that I was, I missed the whole point of the gospel, which is the glad news that God forgives even liars who say they love him, but do not always love their neighbors. To break the bonds of prejudice and fear, I should have told them, is not a grim obligation but a grand privilege granted by God. Christ's yoke is gentle and his load is light. As I John says, God's commandments are not burdensome. If we live with the heaviness of hatred and anger on our backs, we are guilty, not of hypocrisy, but of joylessness and hopelessness. We are guilty of being overcome by the world.

Moralism is not the only failing of liberals. We also achieve our spurious victory over the world by always lamenting how bad things are: how illiterate and Republican our students are, how much more truck drivers make than college professors, how stupid and bovine are the American masses sitting there in front of the television chewing their cud. If everyone were as moral and righteous as we are, we argue, the world would be a swell place. Our favorite pastime is to blame the likes of Mr. Falwell, Mr. Helms, and Mr. Reagan for all our religious and political troubles. We liberals need a greater sense of irony—the irony voiced by one of Peter De Vries' characters who wishes, when his spirits are cast low, that he could be a pig. For then he could grunt and mutter to himself, "Nobody knows the truffles I've seen."

I sometimes wonder what we liberals would do if we actually won a religious or political battle. I would hate for most of us to be in charge of *anything*. Walker Percy has observed that most intellectuals enjoy complaining more than winning. The true liberal's sweetest victory, says Percy, lies in losing. There is no better way to be proved right than to have fought valiantly for a defeated cause. Thus, it is that the conservatives win their cheap little victories by religious naïveté, and liberals by religious moralism and cynicism. But the real winner is neither truth nor faith nor Christ, but the world and its evil prince.

What, then, is the magnificent victory of which I John speaks—the victory that overcomes the evil one and the world he so ruthlessly dominates? It has to do with something that again appears obvious and trite, but in fact is revolutionary and explosive. It has to do, I believe, not with love as the world comprehends it, but with forgiveness that faith alone can understand and enact.

The world takes the word *love* to mean compassion and sympathy. These are words that in their root origins both mean "to feel with" or "to feel for." The world knows what love is so long as it involves such fellow-feeling, so long as it means helping someone else out of trouble. Such helpfulness undergirds nearly all of our charitable agencies—from hospitals and children's homes, to welfare and poverty programs, to drug and crime rehabilitation. Without such love life would be, as Thomas Hobbes described the state of nature, "nasty, brutish, and short." Yet, the world's love depends on reciprocity: You have to deserve what you get, to give back what you are given, and if you are unable to return the favor then be sure you are thankful. For it is being grateful that we assure the world how worthy we are of its help. This is why the Reagan administration insists on helping the *truly* needy. Only if one can grovel in either sufficient misery or sufficient thankfulness can one's neediness be established. After all, no one is supposed to get more than one is due.

Justice is always, in the world's logic, the counterside of love. The same world that demands compassion and helpfulness also demands that we live by the law and that we accept the consequences of our misdeeds. There is an awful rigor to the world's moral logic, and it runs something like this: If you smoke, you are endangering your own health and the health of others. If you get fat, you are a slob. If you turn skinny, you are a workaholic and perhaps an anorexic. If you don't publish, your perish. If you don't keep a 2.00 grade average, you can't graduate. If you cheat, you can be kicked out. If you lie, you are no longer trusted. If you get caught with drugs, your record is permanently tarnished. If you fall down on the job, you are fired. If you strike your child or spouse, you are an abuser. If you have an abortion past the first trimester, you are a murderer. If you threaten to mug a subway rider, you are liable to get pumped full of lead. In every case, both silly and serious, the world demands that we pay for our sins and crimes. Or else that we hire a lawyer to keep us from paying our penalty. This explains why there will soon be more lawyers than people.

Do not misunderstand me: I am not suggesting that we abandon the business of law and virtue and ethics. The world would smash quickly to pieces without them. And indeed the author of I John insists that we love God by keeping his commandments.

In a passage that would seem to be the moralist's dream text, he says that "all who do not do what is right are not from God" (1 John 3:10). This makes the Gospel seem like a charter for cops, who used to be called (in my childhood) the Do-Right Boys. I insist, to the contrary, that the Gospel does not mean doing right in the worldly sense of the phrase, and that I John calls God love for reasons that have little to do with what the world means by love.

Again, it is the novelist Peter De Vries who here, as in so many other places, has a witty hold on the truth. "If love is what makes the world go 'round," says one of his characters, "no wonder the world wobbles on its axis." Though calling himself a skeptic who keeps backsliding out of his unbelief, De Vries knows how shaky is the world's love, how uncertain its justice. You cannot ultimately depend on them. Valuable as they are, they are not enough. Indeed, they have to be overcome by the love of God. And God's love is neither compassion nor justice so much as it is forgiveness.

The word *mercy* literally means to give up a claim someone rightly has upon another, to remit or send back what was rightly owed by another. And this is exactly what God does in the Jews and Jesus. God takes back what he has every right to visit on us—namely, his wrath and punishment for the sorry mess we have made of ourselves and the world. God refuses to harbor resentment against us for our miserable offenses. Instead, God condemns us by pardoning us, imprisons us by setting us free, and gets his vengeance on the world by reconciling it unto himself. In short, God overcomes the world by forgiving it.

In every way, the world stands ready to defeat us. We all know the gall of disappointment and failure. We all know the sadness of betrayal and broken friendships. Most of us do not know the terror of hunger and poverty and war; but the rest of humankind knows it. We all know the fear that our world will be incinerated in a nuclear bonfire. And even if the bombs do not fall, we all know that we will die. Life would seem, therefore, to be a losing proposition, and the world would appear to be the final victor. Indeed, it *is* the victor in every way except one: The world cannot forgive. But, by the gift of faith, we can: We can believe that Jesus is the Christ, we can become the forgiven children of God, and we can live a life of forgiveness. This faith alone is what makes us more than conquerors through the Christ who loved us and gave himself for us.

Life is so dangerous a business, said Mark Twain, that he had never known anyone to survive it. Twain is almost right. No one *has* survived life on this wobbling planet except the one whom we call the Christ. He alone has emptied the grave of its victory. He alone has pulled the fangs from death. He alone has rolled back the stone of sin. He alone has overcome the world. Let us be glad and gladly forgiving. Amen.

Suggestions for Worship

Call to Worship (Ps. 98:1-3):

LEADER: Sing to the LORD a new song, for he has done marvelous things;

PEOPLE: his right hand and his holy arm have worked salvation for him.

LEADER: The LORD has made his salvation known and revealed his righteousness to the nations.

PEOPLE: He has remembered his love and his faithfulness to the house of Israel; all the ends of the earth have seen the salvation of our God.

Act of Praise: Psalm 98.

Suggested Hymns: "Come, We That Love the Lord"; "What a Friend We Have in Jesus"; "My Jesus, I Love Thee."

Opening Prayer: Lord God, save us from isolation and everything that alienates us from the presence of Christ and from your will for us. Break down the walls that separate us from others. Let suspicions give way to trust, selfishness to sharing, complaints to encouragement, fear to confidence, and resentment to love. It is you, O Christ, and your unity with the Father, that is the bond uniting us with all mankind. Save us,

O God, from isolation, through the presence of the risen Christ. Amen.

Pastoral Prayer: O Christ, we are gathered here today as part of a great multitude of Christians. Help us make a difference in our world. Help us, O Lord, so that the evidences of your faith and love, which are so visible and near in the community of faith, may be known and honored throughout the whole world.

Make us want to live by truth instead of lies. Make us value honesty and integrity more than expediency and profit. Help us to care for the good earth, for clean flowing rivers, for the clouds above us, and the oceans around us. Help us to make the welfare of all the guiding principle of our land.

Cast down, O God, those evils that have now invaded the structures of our society and the strata of our neighborhoods. Let pride be gone. Let profiteering be thwarted. Let violence be destroyed by its own destruction. Let governments that fail to serve be overthrown. Lord Jesus Christ, you died so that others might live. Crowned with thorns and enthroned on a cross, you announced the coming of our Father's kingdom. Therefore we make your faith our prayer. "Thy kingdom come! Thy will be done on earth!" Amen.

MAY 15, 1994

□

Seventh Sunday of Easter
(Ascension Sunday)

Two themes attend the Ascension of Christ. One is the enthronement of Christ and his power. The other is his command to spread the gospel throughout the world.

The Sunday Lessons

Acts 1:15-17, 21-26: The Ascension story is the prologue to the Acts of the Apostles. It recounts Jesus' promise of power "when the Holy Spirit has come upon you" and his commission to be a "witness in Jerusalem . . . and to the end of the earth" (1:8). The Ascension is not an event clearly located in a time and place. Acts reports forty days. In those days Matthias was chosen to replace Judas.

I John 5:9-13: The testimony of God concerning the Son of God is greater than any human testimony. "This is the testimony: God gave us eternal life and this life is in his Son" (v. 11). Those who do not believe have made God a liar.

John 17:6-19: Jesus' prayer for his disciples just before leaving them was that (1) they would glorify God, (2) they would continue in unity (they may be one), (3) they would be protected from evil, and (4) they would be sanctified (made holy and righteous) by the truth. They would be left in a world that hated them.

Reflections

The rational and the mysterious come together on Ascension Day. The commission to take the good news of Christ into all the world can be readily expressed in the scope of time and space. The Ascension and enthronement of Christ suggest dimensions that are beyond history. Responding to the commission of an enthroned Lord, Christians sometimes emphasize the realistic and practical mission of the church and sometimes glory in signs, wonders, and mysterious sovereignty.

The outreach of the church through our global mission reflects the tension. Few mainline missionary preachers call attention to the miraculous evidence of Christ's power. Not even on Ascension Sunday, when the Gospel lesson speaks of serpents and poison, will any one of them try to demonstrate Christ's authority by handling a rattlesnake or drinking battery acid. But many will testify to the miracle of changed lives and will preach for conversions.

From the beginning, Christian churches have engaged in relief efforts to feed the hungry and care for the homeless. Social service in missions has been a special emphasis since late in the last century. At times the motive was to make contact with potential converts, hence the charge "rice Christians." Sometimes, the service was primarily for the Christian community, such as mission schools. Often, the service was viewed as leaven in or encounter with the culture. Frequently, the motive was only a desire to serve the suffering. Missionary efforts in education, medicine, agriculture, and human rights relate very much to this world.

Science has gained increasing dominance over superstitions. Reason has displaced magic. Visible objectives associated with a time and a place receive most of the attention of the church. Yet, reason itself demands recognition of the mysterious and the unexplained. So we are left between mud and stars, between shadows of earth and light of eternity, on earth looking up into heaven. (JKB)

BLESSED IS THE CHURCH

Psalm 1

A SERMON BY RALPH C. WOOD

"I like my pastor," the man said, "because he is so completely human." Well, I guess he must have meant that his pastor is not stuffy or starchy, but easygoing and down-to-earth, a nice and friendly fellow. Yet, I can't think of a worse way to describe a pastor—or, for that matter, any other Christian—than to call him completely human. All of us sinful sons and daughters of Adam and Eve, alas, are completely human. We have fallen away from the image in which we were made. Our mere humanity will not suffice unless it is radically remade in the image of the one true man: Jesus Christ. God doesn't call us to be human, therefore, but to be holy even as he is holy. I am thus hoping and praying that our Pastor Search Committee will recommend to us a preacher who is indeed holy, and that we will not be embarrassed to call him or her a man or woman of God.

Yet it is not the minister alone who is called to holiness of life. The entire church is summoned by God to be God's holy people. We are not another civic club, not a philanthropic organization, not even a fellowship of the like-minded. We are called to be the communion of saints, the holy ones of God, the blessed church of the redeemed. Psalm 1 and the twelfth chapter of Romans tell us what this means. It means that we have our only hope of prosperity in the grace of God. It means that we are summoned to worship no commonplace God but the Lord God Almighty. And it means that we are the people whom God calls not to be caregivers, but to make ourselves a living sacrifice to his Kingdom.

Allow me, if you will, to take liberties with Psalm 1 while remaining faithful to its message: "Blessed is the church that walks not in the counsel of the wicked, nor stands in the way of sinners, nor sits in the seat of scoffers, but whose delight is in the law of the Lord. On his law this church meditates day and night. Such a church is like a tree planted by streams of water. It yields its fruit in due season, and its leaf does not wither. In all that it does, such a church prospers."

This, I submit, is a word of clear spiritual direction about what God is calling our church both to be and also what not to be. The church is blessed when we delight in the law of the Lord, when it meditates on his gospel day and night, and when it seeks nothing other than to know God and to enjoy him forever. God's law is never a heavy burden, never a boring grind. It is the highest of all honors: the way to life abundant, life reconciled to God and human, life everlasting. Jesus says that he has not come to abolish this law but to fulfill it. And we ourselves are blessed when we fulfill it.

The Ten Commandments are bulletins of liberating good news, glad guideposts to a life of blessedness before God. That we shall bow down before no other gods than the Lord God of Israel and Jesus is not a stern, but a gracious command. It is the happy offer to be freed from the silly and sinful business of worshiping our houses and cars, our families and jobs, our health and money, our politics and nation. "Give them up gladly to God, and you shall have them back again rightly!"—this is the joyful cry of the gospel. All these things are God's anyway, and God will have them sooner or later. And if we do not gladly give them sooner, then God will take them later, alas, with weeping, wailing, and gnashing of teeth. God is angry only if we will not be blessed.

Because God's law is sheer grace, worship on Sunday should be an utter delight. This is the happiest day of the week. On this day we learn first things. We remember to honor our fathers and our mothers not in grim duty, but because God in Christ has honored us with so great a salvation. We are taught not to steal, kill, covet, commit adultery, bear false witness against a neighbor. These acts are not blessed things. They are the sad way to an unblessed death of both body and soul. Such sins injure our brothers and sisters, and thus do they also harm the God who in Christ has reconciled the world unto God. Blessed is the church that meditates on these things day and night.

The psalmist also warns about what happens when the church does not live the blessed life. When we are not watered by the streams of God's mercy, we wilt in the summer heat. We put on a great burst of flowery activity, but we yield no succulent fruit. We may build great buildings and sponsor huge programs, but we lack the permanence of God's abiding grace. And so we perish like the damned, like chaff that the wind blows away.

Thus do I hear the psalmist calling us not to be panicked by a decline in our numbers, as if statistics alone were the true measure of spiritual health. Nor should we do frantic and foolish things in imitation of the so-called superchurches. Their crowds may result from the counsel of the wicked; their success may be the way of sinners; their packed pews may be the seat of scoffers. Such churches mock God with their magical plans for guaranteed growth. They sin against the Spirit when they promise prosperity in exchange for attendance. They crucify our Savior on a dollar sign.

Blessed by contrast is the church that presents itself as a living sacrifice to God, which is not conformed to this world, but that is transformed by the renewal of its mind in the holiness of God. In both the Old Testament and the New, the word *holy* means set apart, separate, radically different from anything human. The counter-notion to God's holiness is not, therefore, evildoing or unrighteousness, but rather whatever is common, ordinary, undistinguished. This is why we are enjoined not to take the Lord's name in vain, as if it were just another word that trips off our lips lightly. A prayer uttered thoughtlessly is perhaps worse than a curse, for it makes God's name common and ordinary.

Blessed is the church that refuses to make God common and cozy, a heavenly buddy, a cuddly deity of warm feelings and friendly belonging, a god of the even swap: You do God a favor and God will do you a favor in return. The God whom we confront in the Jews and Jesus is not such a wimp god who merely wishes us well. God is the Lord God Sabaoth, Maker of heaven and earth, Commander of the heavenly host, Chief of the angel army that does God's will against all the forces of evil. The book of Hebrews says God's word is sharper than any two-edged sword, piercing to the thoughts and intentions of our hearts, cutting like a butcher's knife to the division of joints and marrow. God is the one with whom we have to deal, the God before whom no creature is hidden, the God whose eyes open up all things and lay them bare (Heb. 4:12-13). Blessed is the church who worships no commonplace god, but the God of the cross, the God who has laid down his very life for us in order that we might become living sacrifices.

The call to be a suffering church is a lesson I learned, ever so sharply, while helping serve a tiny church called Paddington Chapel in London two years ago. During the terrible years of the Second War, these faithful people canceled only a single service, and that on the dreadful Sunday of September 3, 1939, when war was first declared. Yet the Paddington folks later regretted this suspension of worship. They vowed not to repeat it, even though large assemblies were discouraged because they threatened massive loss of life. Another local church at worship did in fact suffer a direct hit by a German bomb that killed more than a hundred. Yet, these Christian people at Paddington Chapel gathered every Sunday for worship throughout the Blitz. They knew that the church is never a place for safety and security, but always a house for confession of faith and sin, and thus for the praise and service of God.

These London Christians told me that their worship was charged with a life-and-death meaning they had never known before. Instead of singing sentimentally about "sweet Jesus, meek and mild," they rang out the great hymns of Gospel substance: "How firm a foundation, ye saints of the Lord, is laid for your faith in his excellent Word." In November 1940 a bomb did indeed strike the church's Mission Hall, cracking the main wall, collapsing ceilings, leaving holes in the roof. Yet the very next week, when the roads were clogged with an early winter snow, the Women's Missionary Society gathered there for regular fellowship. Though an air-raid alert had been sounded, and though a cold wind was blowing through the bomb holes, these women were undaunted. A passerby overheard them singing "Count your many blessings, name them one by one; count your many blessings, see what God hath done."

Such suffering-tested faith is what I fear we have lost in our own country, though our fellow believers in the Iron Curtain countries might help us learn it afresh. We Americans are fed a steady regimen of religious pap. We have lost our vision of God's holiness and thus of our own call to a devout and holy life. Note how embarrassed we are to declare anyone holy, even though we readily speak of people as saints. This is because we equate sainthood with extraordinary care giving. Television has taught us that those who care for the hungry and the homeless are to be regarded as saints. Mother Teresa and Millard Fuller—for whom I have great admiration—are thus hailed by the media as the saints of our time. We have now come to equate sainthood with doing good, and caring with being Christian.

My own Southern Baptist Convention contributed to this heresy when, for an evangelism campaign, our leaders adopted the theme "Jesus Cares For You." That's a little like saying that Jesus cares for broccoli rather than brussels sprouts. No, Jesus does not care for us: He died and rose for us. Far from being a mere care giver, He is Lord and Savior. And all our caring is but a deadly business unless it serves as parable and proclamation of the good news that God in Christ saves sinners.

This is why the Apostle Paul commands us not to be care givers, but to present ourselves as living sacrifices to the God whose grace alone measures what is good, acceptable, and indeed perfect. The horrible thing about sin is its deceit. It always masks itself as goodness. Caring for others—the highest of all human loves—can thus be a terrible substitute for the love of God. We can lay down our lives for the needy as a way of stuffing ourselves with our own righteousness, and thus getting rid of God. No one understood sin's subtlety better than C. S. Lewis. He said that you can always recognize those who are served by others because of their hunted look.

Blessed is the church whose peace consists not in its own vaunted good works, but solely in the grace of God. Such a church confesses its sins to God, to each other, and also to its persecutors. "If your enemy is hungry, feed him," says Paul; "if he is thirsty, give him drink; for by so doing you will heap burning coals upon his head." This is a surprisingly strange saying. The fiery briquettes from my barbecue grill, if I poured them over my enemies' heads, would set their hair on fire, and perhaps do far worse. The heaping of live coals on the pates of our foes must have some other meaning.

Perhaps there is a clue hidden in the Apostle's instruction for us not to return evil for evil, but to overcome evil with good. We Christians don't hit back, not because we are cowards, but because we know that God should hit us, even if our enemies should not. Not to retaliate, but to forgive as we are forgiven— this is the call of our Lord. Thus, we do heap burning coals on those who persecute us, thus including that burning shame that silences all hatred. To confess our sin in the presence of our enemies enables them to confess their own sin before God.

"Everyone a winner" is the motto of Texas public schools. "Show me a good loser," a Durham churchman said to me not long ago, "and I will show you a real loser." Ted Turner has called Christianity a religion for losers. What Mr. Turner and his fellow winners do not understand is that they and we are all losers in the sight of God. Christ came to seek and to save the lost.

To be lost is not to have unmet needs, but to be in the condition of sin and alienation from God. I am lost, you are lost. And all the Good Will Games in the world will not rescue us, unless God in Christ makes us truly good. We are saved not by our winning record but by Christ's victory on Good Friday and Easter Sunday. Blessed is the church that confesses itself to be a company of losers whom Christ has found. Blessed is the church that worships not a sentimental, commonplace deity, but the Lord

God Almighty. And blessed is the church whose only prosperity is God's abundant grace. Amen.

Suggestions for Worship

Call to Worship (Ps. 1:1-2):

LEADER: Blessed is the man who does not walk in the counsel of the wicked,

PEOPLE: **Or stand in the way of sinners or sit in the seat of mockers.**

LEADER: But his delight is in the law of the LORD,

PEOPLE: **And on his law he meditates day and night.**

Act of Praise: Psalm 1.

Suggested Hymns: "For the Beauty of the Earth"; "Happy the Home When God Is There"; "Children of the Heavenly Father."

Opening Prayer: Eternal God, whose name is love and whose way is faithfulness and mercy, enable us to see the great worth of all things great and small. You are the creator of everything, and you have called it good. Teach us, O God, that your care for the greatest and the least is unfailing, and that your love is mighty to save. Amen.

Pastoral Prayer: Great is thy faithfulness, O God our Father. Your mercies are new every morning. We thank you for bringing us to this new day and the beginning of this new week. We thank you for the gift of sleep and for the blessing of sabbath rest. We thank you for health and strength, and for the confidence that faith bestows. We thank you for the opportunities of work and play, and for the vision that calls us forth. We thank you for those who love us, and for those whom we love, and for your steadfast love that surrounds us all.

Now by the example of Christ and the guidance of the Holy Spirit, lead us in ways that glorify you for your many gifts to us.

Lead us in paths of righteousness, for your name's sake. Strengthen us in truth and justice. Gentle us with love and mercy. Inspire us with joy and gladness. Teach us those things that belong to peace.

When our days are heavy with burdens and long with labor, stay close beside us. Give patience for suffering, courage for trials, faith for uncertainties, and hope for despair. Let faith, hope, and love take root and grow among us, we pray in the name of Christ our Savior. Amen. (JKB)

MAY 22, 1994

☐

Pentecost Sunday

There are many themes in the Pentecost lessons. All of them refer to the Holy Spirit and promise freedom, unity, power, and joy.

The Sunday Lessons

Acts 2:1-21: A sound like the rush of a mighty wind, fire touching each of them, and the understanding of foreign tongues were manifestations of the gift of the Spirit. Some mocked, "they are filled with new wine" (v. 13). But Peter proclaimed, "This is what was spoken through the prophet Joel . . . I will pour out my Spirit upon all flesh . . . I will show portents in the heaven above and signs on the earth below" (vv. 16-19).

Romans 8:22-27: Paul teaches that the work of the Spirit in the lives of individual Christians is twofold: It directs and it empowers. In our weakness, so weak that we do not know how to pray, the Spirit intercedes "with sighs too deep for words" (v. 26). It results in prayer that is attuned to the will of God.

John 15:26-27, 16:4b-15: "When the Spirit of truth comes, he will guide you into all the truth" (v. 13). Jesus tells his disciples that he is "going to him who sent me" (v. 5). In response to their sorrow, he promises them "the Advocate" (v. 7). When he comes, "he will prove the world wrong about sin and righteousness and judgment" (v. 8).

Reflections

The sights and sounds of Pentecost are many and varied. There was the sound of wind. *Ruach* is the word in Hebrew. The same word is used for wind and spirit. Sometimes it means the breath of life. Sometimes it refers to a raging desert storm that changes everything when it has passed by. Sometimes it is the gentle murmur of a breeze like the one that caused Elijah to cover his face

161

with his mantle knowing that the Lord God was in it. When Nicodemus wondered about new birth, Jesus taught him that it was birth in the spirit and then said, "Listen to the wind."

There was the appearance of fire. The fire burned, but the bush remained when Moses stood on holy ground. Fire by night led God's children through wilderness. Fire fell on Mount Sinai when the law was given. It consumed Elijah's altar and sacrifice. And fire came again on Pentecost. Wesley spoke of "painted fire" on the altars of the churches of England. It appeared as fire but had neither warmth nor light.

There was the sound of many tongues. Confusion reigned at the tower of Babel. There was the babble of many languages, and division followed. At Pentecost there were many tongues, but a common understanding. Unity followed. When confusion threatened the church at Corinth, Paul spoke of this remarkable unity once again.

There was the word of truth. Challenges to new teachings and to those who are its witnesses always abound. The need for an authentic word and a final authority is insistent. John's Gospel proclaims that the God's truth revealed in Christ is convincingly supported by the Spirit that leads us into all truth.

There was the evidence of power. Recently, I watched a young stallion run bold and free across a broad pasture. Every step exploded with vigor and power. An old rancher remarked, "Sure wish I had some of his go." The self-generating power of the Spirit gave birth to the church. The disciples, once timid and confused, the apostles, so often doubtful and hesitant, received power on Pentecost, and the church, bold and free, was born. (JKB)

FROM AMAZEMENT TO BOREDOM AND BACK?

Acts 2:1-21

A SERMON BY GAYLE CARLTON FELTON

I was recently at Sunday dinner with a family that included two junior-high-school age children. Since we had just returned from the church service, the conversation rather naturally turned in that direction. Abruptly, the young boy exclaimed, "I hate church; it's so boring!" His parents were quite embarrassed and tried to hush him up, especially concerned that I, as a minister, might take offense. (Fortunately for my ego, I had not been the preacher for the service.) Quickly the daughter chimed in, "Oh, yes, it is boring; all they do is talk, talk, talk!" These children probably differed from their flustered parents much more in their outspoken frankness than in their honest opinions. Whenever I am able to persuade people of any age to speak bluntly about the church, I hear similar sentiments. I am reminded of Mark Twain's quip, "It's a terrible death to be talked to death." Are we in danger in the church today of talking people to death, of boring them to frustration? I fear so.

How strange that this should be true when we are given such wonderful material with which to work! The account that we just read in Acts must be one of the most exciting stories in all of history. The men and women who had followed Jesus are gathered in a room in Jerusalem waiting . . . though they are not sure for what. In the past few weeks they have experienced the miraculous events of Jesus' crucifixion, resurrection, and ascension. They have obeyed his final instructions not to return home, but to wait in Jerusalem "for the promise of the Father." Days have passed, but then on the day of the feast of Pentecost, the promise is fulfilled and astounding things happen. The room is filled with a sound like a violent windstorm, flames of fire appear and come to each of them, they are enabled to speak new languages, they are overwhelmingly aware of the presence and power of God's Spirit. They are filled with such delirious enthusiasm that those who saw and heard them thought that they must be drunk. It was not a boring occasion! Let us note carefully the words that Luke uses to describe the responses of those who heard these Spirit-filled Christians speak. They were bewildered—it was confusing and baffling to experience such things. Twice Luke says that the hearers were amazed—dumbfounded at the strange things that their senses were taking in. They were astonished—shocked by happenings unlike anything they had experienced before. They were perplexed—puzzled and troubled about what all this meant, wanting to learn more. There is no report of anyone being bored.

These events are our story—the coming of the Holy Spirit on the first disciples, our ancestors in the faith, to make them the Church of Jesus Christ. We stand in the illustrious line of this heritage; their message and their calling is ours. How is it that we have so completely calmed the wind, so thoroughly quenched the flames, so totally silenced the tongues? In our church services too often the closest resemblance to the wind of the Spirit is a stifled yawn, the flames of fire have been replaced by reflections from wristwatches being surreptitiously consulted, and the only strange tongues are the whispers of children asking when it will be time to go home.

Of course, these early disciples had the advantage of first-hand involvement. This passage from Acts resonates with the immediacy of a mighty experience before years of theorizing had worn it into dullness. Is it possible for us, at a distance of almost two-thousand years, to recapture the intensity of that experience? I believe that there is a greater gulf than that of time separating us from the Christians of the first century. Our problems with recapturing the vitality of such experiences as Pentecost is not so much a matter of passing years, but of changing attitudes. We are a modern, sophisticated, educated people. Our standards are scientific; our values, technological; our thinking, rationalistic. We are uncomfortable with what sounds to us primitive, with what appears to be simpleminded and irrational. We are likely to expend more effort on explaining away such strange-sounding stories in Scripture than we are in trying to relive them. Most contemporary Christians are suspicious of the superrational, discomfited by the supernatural. We would much prefer to rest in the realms that we can understand and explain, even control. But unfortunately for our taste, the Christian faith does not easily lend itself to such categories as logic and analysis. It is instead the incredible story of a God who brought creation into existence out of nothingness and made human beings in order to have someone with whom to share love. It is the tragic story of how humans turned against their divine creator and so separated themselves from God, from each other, from their own authentic selves, and from the natural world. It is the poignant story of God's patient, insistent love that sought through the history of the Hebrew people to bring humankind back into the covenant relationship. It is the astounding story of God who took human form and came to live among God's human children as one of us; who was rejected, suffered, and killed by them. It is the triumphant story of divine victory over evil and death when Jesus Christ rose from the dead and the joyous story of how that death and resurrection has restored our broken relationship with God. It is the dramatic story of the coming of the Holy Spirit at Pentecost to inaugurate the Church through which Christ's work of redemption of the world would be continued. It is the ultimate story of the Risen Christ who will come in final victory to establish the community of love through which the divine purpose is fulfilled. None of these stories is reasonable, understandable, or explainable. And certainly none of these stories is the least bit boring! They are, indeed, amazing beyond belief. And, praise God, they are true. This is what the Christian faith is; and our efforts to reduce it to categories with which our small minds and shrunken spirits are comfortable is to make it into another religion entirely.

We can appreciate the account of the coming of the Spirit at Pentecost only we if we are willing to suspend disbelief and open ourselves to the reality of a God who is far too immense for our comprehension, a God who works in human history in ways that mystify and bewilder us. The events of Pentecost are rooted in the prior event of Easter; indeed, the outpouring of the Holy Spirit is the fulfillment of the Easter promise. The good news of Christ's victory over sin and death, won at the bloody cross and the empty tomb, could now be proclaimed around the world. A very ordinary group of men and women were flooded with divine power, and thus transformed into the vanguard of a force that could change the world. They were imbued with a tremendous excitement and fervor, gripped by a disturbing passion. They were molded by the power of the Spirit into a courageous, energetic, and effective company of witnesses to the faith. They were amazed at what they knew had happened for and to them; surely, they were neither bored nor boring.

Is it possible for the church today to recapture that amazement, that fervor, that power? I believe that it is possible; it is, in fact, essential. The pale, anemic versions of Christianity that characterize so much of our proclamation are not only deadly dull, but fatal. It was said of these early Christians that they were turning the world upside down. What can be said of us as Christians today? Surely our world needs to be turned upside down by a new infusion of divine power, and we are called to be the instruments through which God can work. The poet Stephen Vincent Benet in commenting on the Christ event says, "Something is loosed to change the shaken world and with it we must change!" It is the wind and fire of the Holy Spirit that comes to change us and to empower us to change the world.

The Holy Spirit, as the promise of Christ and the gift of the Father, is a reality in the church today. Therefore, the account of the first Christian Pentecost brings to us a message of both judgment and hope. The effectiveness of the church in fulfilling its divine call to witness to the redeeming love of Christ is dependent on its willingness to allow the Spirit free rein. To do so will require us to give up our efforts to restrain the Spirit to activities that we can understand and control. It will demand that we recognize and accept the radically supernatural character of the faith that we profess. If we do so, we will again hear the sound like a mighty wind, see anew the flames of fire, and speak the good news in compelling languages. Those who hear us proclaim the gospel will be bewildered and perplexed at this unanticipated intrusion into the mundane round of their lives. They will be astonished by the story of God's outreaching love. We will all be amazed at the power of God in our midst, and we will no longer be boring.

Suggestions for Worship

Call to Worship (Ps. 104:33-35):

LEADER: I will sing to the LORD all my life;

PEOPLE: **I will sing praise to my God as long as I live.**

LEADER: May my meditation be pleasing to him, as I rejoice in the LORD.

PEOPLE: **Praise the LORD, O my soul. Praise the LORD.**

Act of Praise: Psalm 104:24-34, 35*b*.

Suggested Hymns: "Spirit of God, Descend upon My Heart"; "Spirit of Faith, Come Down"; "Breathe on Me, Breath of God."

Opening Prayer: O Holy Spirit, who came upon the church on the day of Pentecost, flood us anew with your presence and power. Descend into the midst of our dullness and kindle new life. Imbue us with your message and embolden us to proclaim it that the world may hear the good news of Jesus Christ.

Pastoral Prayer: Holy Lord, we praise you for the gift of Jesus Christ and for the continuation of his ministry through the church. We are grateful for the privilege of being a part of that company who are called to be your people and commissioned to call others. We confess that we have often failed to live up to the responsibilities of this great privilege. We have been suspicious of what we did not understand and uncomfortable in the presence of the supernatural. We have taken the amazing story of your reconciling love and rendered it stale and boring. Forgive us for our failures and renew us with fresh gifts of your Spirit. Set us on fire for you so that the needy world might come to see us burn and there meet you.

We pray for those with special needs, whether those be physical, emotional, material, or spiritual. Make us truly sensitive to the often unexpressed pain of those with whom we come into contact. Stimulate our compassion that we might sincerely care for our hurting sisters and brothers. Grant us wisdom that we might know how to help them. Give us humility that we might never forget that all we have comes from you.

As we celebrate this Pentecost Sunday, we remember the promise of Christ that the Holy Spirit would come to the disciples. We recognize that Spirit as the ongoing divine presence in our lives. We desire to be empowered by the Spirit for our work of spreading the gospel. May the message of Christ indeed be heard in every language that the world might respond in amazement and recognize him as Lord and Savior.

MAY 29, 1994

☐

Trinity Sunday

The one God of heaven and earth is known in Christian thought by a threeness—Father, Son, and Holy Spirit. Our baptisms, benedictions, and doxologies proclaim this Trinity.

The Sunday Lessons

Isaiah 6:1-8: The call of the prophet Isaiah portrays God as both transcendent and immanent. God is high and lifted up. God also touches and speaks. God is revealed and God's message is proclaimed through human agents. These are understandings about God that are expressed in the Trinitarian doctrine of the Father and the Son.

Romans 8:12-17: The threefold nature of God is implied. "When we cry, 'Abba! Father!' it is that very Spirit bearing witness with our spirit that we are . . . joint heirs with Christ" (vv. 15-17). The ecstatic cry, "Abba," (Aramaic for *papa*) was a familiar sound in the Corinthian church at prayer. The Spirit, not our createdness, prompts the utterance, and identity with Christ's suffering validates it.

John 3:1-17: Nicodemus wonders how one can be reborn as a child of God. "How can anyone be born after having grown old?" (v. 4). Jesus answers, "What is born of the flesh is flesh, and what is born of the Spirit is spirit" (v. 6). The Son of Man who must "be lifted up" (v. 14) is the way to eternal life with God. Notice the Trinity.

Reflections

The Apostles' Creed, in use since the second century, begins, "I believe in God the Father Almighty, maker of heaven and earth." It has been observed that the word *Father* is the only distinctly Christian word in this first article. When early Christians praised God as Almighty and Creator, they affirmed nothing new. Judaism had taught them this. But to acknowledge the Almighty Maker of all things as Father of the Lord Jesus Christ and our Father was to affirm a faith that brought heaven and earth together and spawned the controversies about the human and divine.

In the fourth century, Arius taught that Christ was neither God nor man, but a created being intermediate between divinity and humanity. To settle the disputes that prevailed, the emperor called the first general council at Nicea. Athanasius advocated the view that prevailed, and the Nicene Creed was formulated, declaring that Jesus Christ is "of one Being with the Father."

The activity of the Holy Spirit, central in the whole life of the church and confessed in the Apostles' Creed, was given fuller expression in the Nicene Creed. And "We believe in the Holy Spirit, the Lord, the giver of life, who proceeds from the Father and the Son, who with the Father and the Son is worshiped and glorified."

While most of us know the creeds, few of us know the history of Trinitarian controversy, and very few of us comprehend the subtleties of Trinitarian doctrines. But all who know the stories of heaven and earth, of starlight and stable straw, of birth in flesh and spirit, can from their experience of Father, Son, and Holy Spirit join the Christians of all ages in the praise of each. (JKB)

HERE AM I

Isaiah 6:1-8

A SERMON BY RONALD H. LOVE

After the 1860 election, and before he was to take office as President of the United States, Abraham Lincoln continued his work at the statehouse in Illinois. Late one afternoon, tired from the day's labor, Lincoln returned to his office for some rest. He lay down on the davenport to relax his weary body and quiet his mind. Looking across the room, he could see the length of his body reflected in the bureau's mirror. Suddenly, the image in the mirror changed. His body separated into two distinct images. Startled, he got up and walked over to the mirror, but the image had vanished. Once again the president-elect returned to his davenport. Supine, staring at the mirror, the image again appeared as suddenly and as mysteriously as before. However, this time the figure in the glass took on a different countenance. One face was flush with life; the other face was deathly pale. A cold chill went through Lincoln's body. Troubled, he related the vision to his wife, Mary. The meaning to her was clear—her husband would live through his first term of office as president, but die in his second. During the years to follow, Lincoln often recalled that vision. It haunted him. He said that each time it came into his mind it "gave me a little pang." Yet, Lincoln courageously kept to his appointed way. Can we do likewise? We have been elected by Christ to be the prophets of this land. Will we serve?

Do we have the courage to follow the vision before us? Do we have the fortitude to remain committed to God's calling? Do we have the stamina to endure all hardships for the name of Jesus? Do we have the confidence to know our cause is just? Do we have the steadfastness to remain uncompromising in our belief?

These are the questions that we must answer as Christians. They are not easy questions, but they are questions we all must address. How faithful will we be in preaching the name of Jesus? How determined and resolute will we be to take on the responsibility of social justice? How bold will we be in presenting the truth of the Scriptures? How willing are we to sacrifice ourselves for the benefit of others? How willing are we to suffer so others may be free?

Pondering these questions, we will be confronted with our own unworthiness. We will doubt our ability to cope with the uncertainty of following Jesus. We will underestimate our knowledge of the Scriptures, thinking we are unprepared to witness. We will consider ourselves timid and shy, unable to speak on behalf of another. We will confess our insignificance, admitting we are without authority. We will be scared, sure that our own fears will paralyze us from taking affirmative action.

We will question ourselves, doubt ourselves, as did all of the prophets before us who ventured forth in the name of the Lord. But, as those who have gone before us, we too will be empowered by the Holy Spirit. God will call us. God will touch us. God will lead us forward. We will be able to say as Isaiah did: "Here am I; send me!"

Isaiah was in the Temple when suddenly he was surrounded by the glory of the Lord. To look on the face of God would mean death, so Isaiah was protected by God's garment, which filled the sanctuary. Isaiah stood in awe as the seraphim loomed over him. He trembled in fear as the winged creatures in human form called to one another, "Holy, holy, holy is the LORD of hosts; the whole earth is full of his glory." Isaiah panicked as the ground shook beneath his feet from their thundering voices.

In the midst of such splendor and majesty, Isaiah was conscious of his own sinfulness. Standing among the company of the heavenly host, Isaiah was aware of his own inabilities. Yet, it was this quivering, guilt-ridden man that God called into service.

Isaiah cried out, "Woe is me! I am lost, for I am a man of unclean lips, and I live among a people of unclean lips; yet my eyes have seen the King, the LORD of hosts!" Before he could speak another word, before he even had time enough to think, one of the seraphim took a burning coal from the altar and touched Isaiah's mouth and pronounced this blessing: "Now that this has touched your lips, your guilt has departed and your sin is blotted out." This man of unclean lips was purified and consecrated as God's chosen prophet. The same coal has touched our lips. The same blessing has been bestowed on us. We are the Isaiahs of this age.

On January 3, 1840, a Belgian woman, Catherine de Veuster, gave birth to her sixth child. She named the boy Joseph, after the Pope. The following week, Catherine and her husband, Francois, took their child to church for his christening. Standing at the baptismal font with the child's parents were his godparents. As Joseph was anointed he raised his hand in the form of a fist. The godfather, standing in a faded soldier's uniform, a face scarred from battle, declared the boy was holding a saber and one day he would be a great general. The godmother, in her quiet way, whispered that the child made the sign of the cross and would be a priest. As the years passed, the godparents expectantly watched the child grow into manhood.

To the delight of both godparents, Joseph became a priest and a soldier. He served as a missionary to foreign lands as a soldier of the Lord. On the day of his ordination, Joseph accepted the name Damien. He journeyed to the Hawaiian islands to minister to the forsaken lepers in that land of paradise. One day Damien too became a leper, and died from that dreaded disease. Today, on the island of Molokai, there stands a tribute to Damien: a white granite cross, inscribed with the words, "Greater love hath no man than this, that a man lay down his life for his friends."

We must raise our fist and choose this day to be a soldier for the Lord. We must cast aside any thought of our unworthiness, for we have been called to the priesthood of all believers. We must disregard our state of sinfulness, for we live in grace. We must overlook our inabilities, for we have been empowered by God.

The hour is on us. It is our moment to be servants of the Word. Be an evangelist. Take upon yourself the responsibility to preach in the name of Jesus. Be a missionary. Seek out those in your own community who need the touch of compassion. Be a prophet. Declare the judgment of the Lord.

In the Temple, God called out, "Whom shall I send, and who will go for us?" Isaiah, his spirit touched by the flaming spirit of God, screamed without hesitation, "Here am I; send me!"

At the time Isaiah answered the call of God, he had little understanding of the treacherous years that stretched before him. Isaiah was not aware that he would be confronting King Ahaz and King Hezekiah, berating them for their disobedience to God. Isaiah could not foresee that he would be challenging the rich and powerful for their mistreatment of the poor. Isaiah had no realization that he would be a prophet among an exiled people in Babylonia. Isaiah never would have imagined himself walking naked and barefoot for three years; an effort to make his message heard among a despondent people. And Isaiah never could have predicted his death as a martyr, under the wicked rule of King Manasseh. Isaiah did not know these things, but he did know one thing: He was going to be a servant of the Lord.

Rosey Grier was a great football player for the New York Giants. Shortly after he retired from a noteworthy career, he got involved in politics. He became a strong supporter and campaigner for Robert Kennedy. After Kennedy's death, Grier remained with the Democratic Party until the campaign of Ronald Reagan. Adhering to Reagan's philosophy, Grier changed political parties. One day at a press conference a reporter shouted to him, "But aren't you a Kennedy man?" In a strong and firm voice Grier responded, "No, I'm God's man. I owe allegiance to no other."

We, as the prophets of this decade, owe our allegience to God and God alone. We do not know where this will take us, but when God calls—we will follow. We are unaware of the sacrifices we will have to make, but when God calls—we forsake all to serve. We are uncertain as to the hardships we will encounter, but when God calls—we will endure. We are not certain if persecutions will besiege us, but when God calls—we will willingly suffer for his glory.

John Wesley encourages us to "do all the good you can, by all the means you can, in all the ways you can, in all the places you can, at all the times you can, to all the people you can, as long as you ever can." Once we have answered God's summons, there is no limit to the sacrifices we will make, the hardships we will endure, the time we will spend, the money we will offer, the places we will travel, and the persons we will serve.

The presidential campaign of 1912 was long and bitter. Theodore Roosevelt, William Howard Taft, and Woodrow Wilson were locked in political combat. It was an election the nation took seriously. Passions ran high among the populace.

On October 14, Roosevelt came out of the front door of his Milwaukee hotel, on his way to deliver a speech for the Progressive Party. As he crossed the sidewalk to his waiting automobile, a man stepped forward and shot the former president. The bullet went through his overcoat, spectacle case, and folded manuscript; it entered his body, fractured his fourth rib and lodged a little short of his right lung. Roosevelt fell backward from the blow, coughed, then stood up and declared: "I will deliver this speech or die, one or the other." He then proceeded into his waiting car. At the convention center Roosevelt mounted the speaker's platform. He then began his address with these words: "Friends, I shall ask you to be as quiet as possible. I don't know whether you fully understand that I have just been shot; but it takes more than that to kill a Bull Moose." Fifty minutes later, the speech concluded, Roosevelt sought treatment at a local hospital.

When God summons you for service, let nothing stop you. When God calls your name, answer: "Here am I; send me!"

Suggestions for Worship

Call to Worship (Ps. 29:3-10):

LEADER: The voice of the LORD is over the deep; the God of glory thunders.

PEOPLE: **The voice of the LORD is powerful; the voice of the LORD is majestic.**

LEADER: And in his temple all cry, "Glory!"

PEOPLE: **The LORD is enthroned as king forever.**

Act of Praise: Psalm 29.

Suggested Hymns: "Holy, Holy, Holy! Lord God Almighty"; "All Creatures of Our God and King"; "Spirit Song."

Opening Prayer: Merciful God, you have decreed that those who wait on you will be saved; that in quietness and trust we will find strength. Our waiting has often been long, and days of expectation have turned out empty. Weakness has been our portion instead of strength. But still we wait, and once again we quiet ourselves before you. Give us an increase of faith, we pray, and with it new hope. Then hasten the day when Christ will come and save us. Amen.

Pastoral Prayer: Wonderful Counselor, to thee we seek wisdom. As we begin the journey through yet another week, we ask for thy divine guidance. Place each foot of ours on the path it should take. Let each word we speak bring glory to thy name. Let every thought of ours be one of purity and love.

Mighty God, let the power of thy name thunder forth among the nations. At the sound of thy voice, may every knee be bowed and every tongue confess that thou are the Lord of Creation. Let all the people bring their tribute before thy throne as an act of adoration and humble submission.

Everlasting Father, we thy children are in need of thy loving care and constant assurance. Let us be aware of thy divine presence each moment of the day, that we may be affirmed in our faith and strengthened in spirit. Comfort us. Protect us. Heal us. Embrace us with thy love.

Prince of Peace, reestablish the estranged and shattered relations between individuals and nations. May spouses once again adore one another. May parents and children speak and be heard. May neighbors reaffirm their friendships, no longer harboring jealousies and grudges. May nations declare themselves to be a global village, and share resources for the betterment of all people.

JUNE 5, 1994

□

Second Sunday After Pentecost

The oppressed constantly experience life out of control. Outside forces shape their destinies. But most of us intend to plan our own futures. Then comes the day when we, too, are overtaken by a power—sometimes good and sometimes evil—that we can neither comprehend nor control.

The Sunday Lessons

I Samuel 8:4-11 (12-15), 16-20, (11:14-15): The elders of Israel came to the prophet Samuel demanding a king. The Lord said to Samuel, "They have not rejected you, but they have rejected me from being king over them" (v. 7). The ways of a king are noted. "He will take your sons . . . he will take your daughters . . . he will take one-tenth of your grain and of your vineyards" (vv. 11-15). At Gilgal, Samuel annointed Saul as the first king of Israel.

II Corinthians 4:13–5:1: After recounting the difficulties, hardships, and persecutions he has suffered for the gospel, Paul speaks of the "spirit of faith" (v. 13) that assures him that, like Christ, he will be victorious. Therefore, he believes and speaks boldly. "We do not lose heart" (v. 16). If the earthly tent is destroyed, we have a house not made with hands, eternal in the heavens.

Mark 3:20-35: Fearing that Jesus was out of his mind, his family sought to restrain him. The scribes accredited his power over demons to Beelzebul, the ruler of demons, implying he was possessed. Jesus answered in two parables: a house divided, and plundering a strong man's house by first tying up the strong man. The sin of blasphemy against the Holy Spirit is described as "an eternal sin" (v. 29). Jesus lifts up obedience to the will of God as the primary force at work in relationships and all of life.

"Whoever does the will of God is my brother and sister and mother" (v. 35).

Reflections

Both the law and the prophets saw the intervention of God's Spirit to be a sudden, but also a continuing, influence in the life of Israel. The Gospels and the book of Acts speak of the power and guidance of the spirit as a presence that remains with the church always.

The two immediate effects of the power of the Spirit on the day of Pentecost were (1) new power for the church, and (2) the beginning of unity. Now *mission* and *community* are terms that we regularly employ to describe those sudden happenings as dimensions of the ongoing life and work of the church. The Spirit that empowers and shapes our life in Christ is sometimes experienced suddenly, but it should always be valued as a constant presence throughout all of Pentecost, and the age of Pentecost, and the age to come.

We should not be dismayed because there is such deep, recurring need for the Spirit. There are, and will be, recurring experiences of the power of the Spirit. The forces that shape and sustain life are constant. The influences that guide and direct us are also ongoing and steady. There is always a continuing need for the power and guidance of the Spirit, and for what Paul calls the "spirit of faith."

Individuals who sincerely seek to follow Christ recognize their constant need—they want a power that will enable them to live their faith every day. Churches and governments pray for it. Quite aware of lifeless structures, and confronted with multiple choices and thousands of chances for error, they seek the life-giving power and the guidance of the Spirit.

Unity is cherished wherever it is found, and it is constantly both our need and our longing. The dividing walls of hostility (Eph. 2:14) are evident in personal relationships, churches, communities, and nations; they are apparent among age groups, sexes, classes, and races. God forbid that we ever deny or blaspheme the wonderful source of our life, our togetherness, and our joy. (JKB)

DRAWN TO THE BOSOM OF GOD

Psalm 138

A SERMON BY RONALD H. LOVE

The Reverend Dr. Martin Luther King, Jr., could not sleep. He lay awake in bed, scared by the threats made against his family, fearful he would be murdered, bewildered as to his leadership role in the Montgomery bus boycott. No longer trying to sleep, he went downstairs to the kitchen and made himself a cup of coffee. Sitting at the table he felt very much alone. His parents were 175 miles away, too far to offer comfort. He did not want to share all of his anxieties with his wife, knowing it would upset her even more than she was. Then there was the awareness that nothing he learned in college or graduate school had prepared him for this. King could no longer cope with the fear, the worry, the uncertainty.

King slumped over the table and buried his face in his hands. He wept. He prayed, "O Lord, I'm down here trying to do what is right. But, Lord, I must confess that I am weak now. I'm afraid. I am at the end of my powers. I have nothing left. I can't face it alone." In the midst of that desperate prayer, he heard a voice calling his name. The words were unmistakable. "Martin Luther, stand up for righteousness. Stand up for justice. Stand up for truth. And lo, I will be with you, even unto the end of time." Suddenly, the lightning flashed, the thunder cracked, and King knew he had heard the voice of Jesus. Astonished, King sat at the table, repeating again and again, "He promised never to leave me, never to leave me alone. No, never alone. No, never alone. He promised never to leave me, never to leave me alone."

The promise we have from Jesus is that he will never leave us alone. Even in the most desperate of times, when Jesus seems farthest from us, we know he is still with us each step of the way, each moment of the day. He embraces us with his love. Delores Nick, my church organist, always petitions in our Tuesday morning prayer fellowship, "Jesus, place your hedge of protection around us." And we know he does.

We are all confronted by many problems in life. Overwhelming problems that leave us numb and without hope. Problems that seem to have no end and defy a solution. Problems that nag at us from morning till night, and, worse yet, persist through the night.

The problems that beseige us are real and unending. Estrangement from our spouse. An inability to communicate with our children. A boss who is oppressive. A co-worker who is constantly annoying. A persistent pain. An incurable disease. A difficult decision. An uncertain future. A loss of meaning to life. A feeling of aloneness. Insufficient money. The frustration of underemployment. The agony of unemployment. These problems and many others drive us to our knees seeking the comforting presence of Jesus.

In these times of great personal crisis, we are assured by the Scriptures that God is with us, that our God is personal, and that our God will deliver us from the woes of life. Let us call on the promises of the Scriptures. Let us know that each promise in the Bible is my promise, your promise. Take it. Hold fast to it. And you will find your solace.

In our lesson for the day, the psalmist recognized and worshiped a God who is protecting and steadfast. He knew our Heavenly Parent kept a constant vigilance over him. He knew that God was always present, constantly concerned.

The psalmist bows down before God in thanksgiving for "your steadfast love and your faithfulness." He is able to confess with assurance that "on the day I called, you answered me, you increased my strength of soul." It is the same confession we can make, for we, too, know that on the day we called God answered us. God strengthened us. God gave us hope. God delivered us from our tormentors. As God has done this in the past, we know God will continue to do it in the future.

Corrie ten Boom was transferred to Ravensbruck Concentration Camp. The internment of this Hollander continued because she hid people of the Jewish faith in her home. As the women entered the camp, they were taken to a shower room where they were ordered to undress. Their clothes and all their personal belongings were to be confiscated. Corrie had a Bible with her, without which she knew she could not survive. How could she hide this precious lifeline? Before undressing she asked to use the toilet, and was directed to one of the shower room drain holes. Quickly, she removed her undergarments and wrapped her Bible in them. Placing the clothes in a cockroach infested corner, she returned to disrobe and receive a prison dress. Then she went back to the corner and picked up her clothes, concealing the bundle under her prison garb.

Two guards stood at the exit from the shower room, frisking each woman as she left. Corrie knew she could not escape their searching hands; the bundle under her dress as too noticeable. Desperate, helpless, Corrie prayed, "Lord, cause Your angels to surround me; the guards must not see me." A sense of peace came over Corrie. She walked relaxed and with ease towards the door. She passed by the inspection, almost as if she were invisible.

With the assurance that comes from prayer, Corrie ten Boom knew the steadfast love and faithfulness of God. Corrie felt the strength of her soul increase. She shared in the same experience as the psalmist. The comforting presence of God will be revealed to us, if we have the faith to believe and the willingness to trust.

There are desperate, frightening, uncertain times in our lives. We need not pretend otherwise. There should be no embarrassment in admitting that we are scared. Machismo is no protection against the sufferings we so often encounter. Encircled by hardship, we have nowhere else to turn but to God.

Deliverance comes when we are drawn close to the bosom of God. A maternal God who sustains us through our times of trial and tribulation. It is the Lord joining his spirit with our spirit that strengthens our soul, that gives us the stamina to continue.

Fanny Crosby is considered one of the greatest hymn writers in the history of the church. The perseverance that allowed her to continue with her art, she testifies, came from the assurance of God's divine presence. In January, 1864, Crosby had an encounter with God that transformed her life. One night she had a dream, but really more than a dream, it was a vision—but really more than a vision—because Fanny Crosby knew it was reality. She found herself in an immense observatory; before her was the largest telescope one could ever imagine. She looked through the telescope and saw a brilliant, captivating star. Suddenly, she was moving through space towards that star, when abruptly she came to the edge of a beautiful river. The elegance of that river cannot be described. The scene was so peaceful, so inviting, that Fanny wanted to continue on. She even asked to be invited across that golden spectacle.

In response to her request she heard the voice of God. Her Heavenly Parent brought a stillness to her soul when he spoke these gentle words: "Not now, Fanny. You must return to the earth and do your work there, before you enter those sacred bounds; but ere you go, I will leave the gates opened a little way, so you can hear one burst of the celestial music."

Whenever she became discouraged or uninspired, or whenever her handicap of being blind since she was an infant became too much of a hindrance for her, she recalled that vision and listened for a chord of celestial music to regain the inspiration she needed to continue her work.

God has given us a vision. God has spoken to us. We know God's faithfulness. We have felt the presence of God within our soul. We have felt our bodies strengthened, our minds enlightened, our spirits lifted, because God breathed into us new life.

The psalmist continued to testify to the awesome power of God when he made this confession: "Though I walk in the midst of trouble, you preserve me against the wrath of my enemies; you stretch out your hand, and your right hand delivers me. The LORD will fulfil his purpose for me; your steadfast love, O Lord, endures forever."

The psalmist continues to express the trust he places in the Creator. The psalmist finds himself in trouble daily. He is walking in the midst of it. He cannot avoid it. There is no escaping it. Yet, God stretches out a hand and guides the forsaken soul through the valley of despair. You and I are in the same predicament as the psalmist. Our problems are as real and as painful as his. Desperate, we grasp the same hand that reaches down from the heavens, and receive comfort and assurance, hope and peace.

As a child, Norman Vincent Peale enjoyed visiting his grandmother in Lynchburg, Ohio. Norman recalled that whenever she served him a meal, she would seat him at the dining room table opposite a painting that hung on the wall. Norman contends that his grandmother acted deliberately so he could study and one day internalize the artist's message. The painting was of a terrible stormy sea, with a dark, overcast, foreboding sky. The scene was one of desolation, except for a rock rising in the middle of the tossing sea. Planted on the rock was a large cross, anchored from the ravages of the storm. Sitting at the bottom of the cross was a lady. Her arms were wrapped around the cross, clinging to it for security. She wore a long white robe that floated out over the water. Her beautiful hair was shimmering in the wind. Beneath the picture were the words: SIMPLY TO THY CROSS I CLING. Grandma, looking at the picture, would often say to young Norman, "Everything else may be swept away, but as long as you hold on to the cross, you will have security in life."

Clinging to the cross we are secure this day, and all days. The psalmist expresses his confidence in God's constant vigilance when he writes the steadfast love of the Lord "endures for ever." We have no fear of tomorrow, because of the deliverance we have experienced this day.

Sunday, July 5, 1863. General Daniel Edgar Sickles was hospitalized in Washington, D.C., for a wound he received at Gettysburg. When the President came to visit, the general had only one question—was the President anxious about the outcome of the battle. The President replied that his Cabinet was, along with the members of Congress, but he was not concerned. Then Abraham Lincoln went on to say: "I went to my room one day, and I locked the door, and got down on my knees before the Almighty God, and prayed to him for victory at Gettysburg. I told him that this was his war, and our cause his cause, but we could not stand another Fredericksburg or Chancellorsville. And I then and there made a solemn vow to Almighty God, that if he would stand by our boys at Gettysburg, I would stand by him. And he did stand by our boys, and I will stand by him. And after that, soon a sweet comfort crept into my soul that God Almighty had taken the whole business into his hands that things would go all right at Gettysburg. And that is why I had no fears about you."

Today, tomorrow, every day of your life, you can rest on the bosom of our Lord. Do not fear the day that is unfolding or the one that is to follow, for the Lord will be with you. Believe in the word of the psalmist. Let his promise be your promise.

Suggestions for Worship

Call to Worship (Ps. 138:6-8):

LEADER: Though the LORD is on high, he looks upon the lowly, but the proud he knows from afar.

PEOPLE: **Though I walk in the midst of trouble, you preserve my life;**

LEADER: With your right hand you save me.

PEOPLE: **Your love, O LORD, endures forever.**

Act of Praise: Psalm 138.

Suggested Hymns: "How Firm a Foundation"; "O God in Heaven"; "Be Thou My Vision."

Opening Prayer: O Immortal, Invisible God, you have created us to seek you, and have put deep within us the hope of finding you. Therefore, we grope through the darkness of our ignorance, and the shadows of your mystery, with our great need to know you. We are nearsighted creatures and cannot look upon your face, but grant that we, in fresh new ways, may behold your only son, our Lord Jesus Christ, so that in seeing him we may see you. In his name, we pray. Amen. (JKB)

Pastoral Prayer: Blessed are the poor in spirit, for theirs is the kingdom of heaven. Dear God, may we be pilgrims.
   Blessed are those who mourn, for they shall be comforted. Dear Lord, may we be consoled.
   Blessed are those who are meek, for they shall inherit the earth. Dear Lord, may we be humble.
   Blessed are those who hunger and thirst for righteousness, for they shall be satisfied. Dear Lord, may we be just.
   Blessed are the merciful, for they shall obtain mercy. Dear Lord, may we be compassionate.
   Blessed are the pure in heart, for they shall see God. Dear Lord, may we be sincere.
   Blessed are the peacemakers, for they shall be called sons of God. Dear Lord, may we be forgiving.
   Blessed are those who are persecuted for righteousness' sake, for theirs is the kingdom of heaven. Dear Lord, may we be steadfast.

JUNE 12, 1994

□

Third Sunday After Pentecost

Spectacular, star-studded casts are in some circles deemed essential for success. A recurring theme in Scripture is that God uses the small and lowly.

The Sunday Lessons

I Samuel 15:34–16:13: When Saul was rejected as king, the prophet Samuel was sent to anoint one of the sons of Jesse as the new king. Seven of his sons passed before Samuel, but none was chosen. The youngest son was keeping the sheep. He was ruddy, had beautiful eyes, and was handsome. David was anointed, "and the spirit of the Lord came mightily upon David from that day forward" (v. 13).

II Corinthians 5:1-10, (11-13), 14-17: Paul knew firsthand the weakness, suffering, and rejection of apostles of Christ. As he reflects on dying, he speaks of faith, "If the earthly tent we live in is destroyed, we have a building from God, a house not made with hands" (v. 1). "We are always confident . . . for we walk by faith, not by sight" (vv. 6-7).

Mark 4:26-34: The mustard seed, smallest of all seeds, becomes the greatest of all shrubs. The lesson contains two parables of the Kingdom—the seed growing and the mustard seed. Christ's kingdom grows although no one (not even one who cares for it) notices. The small will become great.

Reflections

We live in an age of impatience. Journeys that once took months are completed in minutes. Ready-made garments can be worn out of the store. Instant cereals and quick-rising flour were absolutely foreign to the culture of the first century, but not to ours. Yet, one thing remains the same in cultures paced either slow or fast. There are always persons among us who want to

184

hurry the coming of a new age. Many of them promote violent revolutions, social convulsions, and economic and personal catastrophes. Even in times constantly changing, for them change comes too slowly.

Yet, there is no ready-made kingdom stored up on the shelves of glory, ready to be brought forth as soon as one pays the price for revolution. We may long for the Kingdom. Work for it. Pray for it. Yet, we must wait for it. While we work and while we sleep, the gospel runs its course—a small green shoot, a new-formed ear, and finally the full-formed harvest.

And the new age is not ushered in by the powerful or the elite. That part is hard to believe. Important missions demand recognized leaders. Do not send a child to do an adult's job. Can you imagine a national television presence without famous and influential personalities? The power to overkill is what guarantees success in everything from athletics to war. But "God chose what is low and despised in the world, things that are not, to reduce to nothing things that are" (I Cor. 1:28). (JKB)

SEED THOUGHTS

Mark 4:26-34

A SERMON BY JUDITH A. OLIN

Jubilee Gardens feeds urban dwellers on the east side of the city. Volunteers cleared the vacant lot of broken bricks, shattered glass, and paper trash. They plowed under the hardcrusted earth, enriched the soil, and divided it into sections. Today, interested families may claim a small garden plot and produce fresh vegetables all summer long.

Elderly gardeners remember long-ago successes down home in Alabama and Georgia. They share their expertise with younger, less experienced tillers of the soil. Scattered seeds sprout and grow while the gardeners fight the battle of the weeds. Neighbors become better acquainted.

Best of all, Jubilee Gardens represents a hopeful harvest. Not only do people eat nourishing food, but the sight of a waving cornfield next to a concrete sidewalk sparks a promise of better days. Jubilee Gardens offers health, happiness, and hope—a vision of God's reign on earth.

When Jesus told parables to his disciples he used common, everyday places and situations to convey deeper truths about God. There was no Jubilee Garden in his panoramic view, but the Valley of Jezreel stretched out before him. Jezreel, that geological fault basin, receives an abundance of water that makes it one of the most fertile areas in that part of the world.

Could it be that Jesus had in mind such fat land as Jezreel—ripe with grain, vineyards, and olive trees—when he wanted to make clear God's promise of harvest? Jezreel means "God sows, or may God make fruitful." Because Jesus wanted to introduce the kingdom of God in familiar images, he chose colorful word pictures.

Listen to the rhythm of the growing grain, "Scatter seed . . . sleep and rise . . . night and day . . . sprout and grow."

In this parable of the seed growing secretly, the kingdom of God may be compared to the bumper crop that needs immediate attention. Never before has there been a day like today. God has been sowing seeds for many centuries, through seasons of flood and seasons of drought. Now to the surprise of all, there stands Jesus knee-deep in golden grain, sickle in hand, calling for field hands.

"Carpe diem!" he shouts. "Seize the day!"

By God's grace, prior to all human activity, the seeds were sown. And now the harvest is ripe, requiring faithful laborers to bring it in. Arise, reapers. Come, in-gatherers. Follow, disciples. Follow the bent-grain path. Join the sun-brown one with the sickle in the air. Plunge headlong into the midst of the ripened fields, because the harvest has come and you are needed.

God's kingdom harvest is plenteous. There is enough food to feed the world, if ways for providing can be developed.

The Ecumenical Sharing Kitchen takes poverty seriously. Hungry people become dinner guests at least two evenings every week in one local church. Faithful disciples spend the afternoon chopping vegetables for salad and mixing bread stuffing, enough for an army. That in itself is a major job. But nothing can compare with the experience of meeting the church's dinner guests face-to-face. A golden harvest aura radiates from their eyes. Recipients of God's generous bounty as they follow the free

bread line, these guests become as glowing grain themselves—
God's harvest—yearning for the in-gathering.

There is ample land for all God's people, if by intentional
effort, persons are helped to belong.

A small group stands at the Jordan River boundary, looking
over to the other side. Those who were landless are about to
become landed. The people of Israel have been on a journey and
now are coming home. What grace to finally have place!

Contrast their relief with the deep disappointment of thousands
of Brazilian peasants. In response to the state government promise
of "Land for the Landless," these persons emigrate from thousands
of miles away in the hope of finding arable land. Disappointed and
frustrated when nothing is available, the peasant families are
forced to work for absentee landlords or they move into burned-
out rain forest areas to scratch an existence for themselves.

As our eyes are turned toward the burning of acres of Amazon
rain forests, we see there in the charred remains the faces of people. They appear everywhere, as green shoots from the scorched
earth. It would appear that trees can be protected, but unless it is
done as part of the care of people, the poor who are landless will
never find home.

Our generation has cried out, "Give me space," when in truth
we long for place. We sing our faith in God's promise to gather
us in:

> For the Lord our God shall come, and shall take the harvest home;
> From the field shall in that day all offenses purge away,
> Giving angels charge at last in the fires the tares to cast;
> But the fruitful ears to store in the garner evermore.

"With what can we compare the kingdom of God?" Jesus told
the parable of the sheltering shrub that grows from the mustard
seed, "the smallest of all the seeds on earth." It is not difficult to
gaze across the flaxen fields and imagine a lone mustard seed
shrub rising above the heads of grain. It becomes a place of
refuge for the birds of the air, symbolic of God's sanctuary for all
people.

Through God's reign, all manner of life receive protection and
shelter: the strong and the weak, the wealthy and the poor, educated and illiterate, African-American, Korean, Hispanic, Anglo.
They are all there, Sunday after Sunday—and midweek, too.

They sing in the choir, share in the disciple Bible study, lead meetings, teach Sunday school.

The time has come when the harvest blessings of God are available to all people. Imagine a long banquet table spread beneath the sheltering shrub. A great feast is prepared for the multitudes. The table stretches around the world, including those with all manner of eating habits.

The miracle of the mustard seed is that out of that poor, tiny, unremarkable band of followers, few wise and mighty, most surprisingly insignificant, comes the great purpose of God. The kingdom of God is destined to span the earth giving life wherever the seed is planted.

The fruit or the harvest is in the seed. Trust the insignificance of the beginning for the sake of the triumph at the end. Go ahead, place your faith in those dry, brown, dead seeds. You will wake up to discover waving cornfields. You may find yourself waving back with pure delight. Do not be surprised to discover the waving hand of the one who calls us to harvest. Do not delay; the time is right; the time is now.

Suggestions for Worship

Call to Worship (Ps. 20:6-8):

LEADER: Now I know that the LORD saves his anointed;

PEOPLE: **He answers him from his holy heaven with the saving power of his right hand.**

LEADER: Some trust in chariots and some in horses. Some trust in tanks and some in missiles;

PEOPLE: **But we trust in the name of the LORD our God. We rise up and stand firm.**

Act of Praise: Psalm 20 or Psalm 72.

Suggested Hymns: "Sing Praise to God Who Reigns Above"; "Nobody Knows the Trouble I See"; "Precious Name."

Opening Prayer: Almighty God, Maker of heaven and earth: Yours is a creation of beauty and order. Night yields to day; seed-time leads to harvest. In your divine providence, grant growth from that which you plant. Bring to harvest and fruition the seeds of your kingdom. Teach us your lessons of faithful stewardship and we will always give you thanks through Jesus Christ, Lord of the harvest. Amen.

Pastoral Prayer: Eternal and gracious God, we come into your presence with thankful hearts for the blessings of life, which come from your hand. We humbly confess that we misuse and abuse your gifts. Our sense of the sacred has become dulled and mystery reduced to commonplace. Forgive us for our failure to tend your garden earth with responsibility and a will to peace. Plant within us a desire and determination to treat all creation as holy: air and water, trees, fruits, and flowers, birds and fish and cattle, all children, youth, women, and men. Be especially near those this day for whom life is more burden than gift. May your word of hope flow through us as an encouragement to others. Bring your kingdom to fulfillment as your servant church seeks to be a faithful witness to Jesus Christ, in whose name we pray. Amen.

JUNE 19, 1994

☐

Fourth Sunday After Pentecost

The sovereignty and power of God are shown through the victories of God's servants. Christ's authority is manifest in the stilling of the storm.

The Sunday Lessons

I Samuel 17:32-49: King Saul worried that David was no match for the giant, Goliath. But David, putting aside the armor of the king, went out to face the giant with a slingshot and five smooth stones. The boy challenged the warrior saying, "You come to me with sword and spear and javelin; but I come to you in the name of the Lord" (v. 45). David threw one stone, which struck the giant's forehead. "And he fell face down on the ground" (v. 49).

II Corinthians 6:1-13: Paul reviews the sufferings and endurance of his ministry: "great endurance, in afflictions, hardships, calamities, beatings, imprisonments, riots, labors, sleepless nights, hunger" (vv. 4-5). Endurance is expressed as "punished, and yet not killed; as sorrowful, yet always rejoicing; as poor, yet making many rich; as having nothing, and yet possessing everything" (vv. 9-10). His concluding counsel is also to open wide your hearts.

Mark 4:35–5:20: When a great storm arose on Lake Galilee, the disciples awakened Jesus, who was asleep in the boat. "Teacher, do you not care that we are perishing?" (v. 38). Jesus stilled the storm with the words, "Peace! Be still!" (v. 39). Two questions follow. One is asked of the disciples, "Have you still no faith?" (v. 40). One is asked about Jesus, "Who then is this, that even the wind and the sea obey him?" (v. 41).

Reflections

A tornado had destroyed most of the downtown businesses and every residence in its path. Wondering why God had allowed this to happen, more than one person questioned, "If God is almighty, he certainly is not good. If God is good, he must not be almighty."

Such questions attended the suffering of Job. The disciple's question, "Teacher, do you not care that we are perishing?" is a persistent question, especially when we are faced with life-threatening disasters.

If miraculous deliverance is the only basis for one's faith, that one is poor indeed. The power of God and the love of God may be seen in both the ordinary and extraordinary. Almost any man or woman will note the exceptional, and then reflect on the power and mystery of God. It requires a mature faith to see God in every commonplace detail.

Edward Schweizer observes that "it is no longer possible for us to separate on principle the miraculous events from the nonmiraculous." Science continually accepts the fact of strange occurrences with the simple acknowledgment that it is not yet explained or understood. Schweizer suggests, "An event is a miracle only if God speaks to us in it; therefore, whether God speaks in the form of the miraculous or the nonmiraculous is immaterial."

It is easier to be impressed by the unusual than it is to be a faithful soul. True faith also shows more humility.

In an amazingly accepting way, such faith stands in awe before every evidence of the sovereignty of God and the saving authority of Christ. "Have you no faith?" (JKB)

WHO'S IN CHARGE HERE?

Mark 4:35-41

A SERMON BY JUDITH A. OLIN

Every Christmas card we received that year from friends on the Isle of Man referred to it. The winter storm lashed against the shores of this tiny island. Weather patterns went wild. The Irish Sea raged furiously. The normal four-hour passage from Liverpool to the Douglas Harbour stretched to eleven. Only Peel Harbour on the west side of the island was open, and what a relief to land safely on its shores.

People who live by oceans and great lakes attest to the powerful combination of wind and water. Hurricanes, typhoons, and heavy thunderstorms are common and wreak havoc on property and human life. It is amazing that persons will endure a Hurricane Camille, losing many possessions, hopes and dreams, only to rebuild on the very same spot.

Van Bogard Dunn, former Academic Dean of the Methodist Theological Seminary in Delaware, Ohio, once observed, "The sea is not friendly." He referred to the Sea of Galilee as described in this scripture. How quickly the storms whip up these relatively shallow waters when mariners least suspect them. Fishing boats—snapped as so many matchsticks—have sunk to the bottom over the centuries, never to sail again.

"The sea is not friendly," could also be said with some realism when earth creatures invade the sea unprepared. A twenty-one-year-old Marine lost his life to the sea when his helicopter crashed upside down off the coast of California. Trapped inside, he succumbed to the salt water that gushed in through broken windows. Out of his earth-element, he was an alien intruder in the water-element and died.

Dunn's statement could also be stated as a metaphor for life. Human existence on planet Earth frequently takes on the character of riding an unfriendly, turbulent ocean. Persons struggle and are nearly overwhelmed by both external and internal waters and windstorms. Indeed, many take on much more water than they can handle. Try to bail out as they might, bucket by bucket, they may even abandon the effort as they fear being swamped.

Turbulence takes its toll in the individual arena. Broken covenants may lead to estrangement and divorce. Unexpected losses of job or position may contribute to a further loss of self-esteem. A decline in health or a reversal of financial circumstances cause significant anxiety and dread for the future. Tossed and turned by doubts, many persons think they have no way out of their dilemma. Life can be experienced as a negative in a hostile environment at the individual level. Considerable effort must be made to stay afloat in the midst of all those factors that would pull a person under.

On a much larger scale and in a broader arena, considerable suffering occurs when whole populations of people are affected by catastrophe. An earthquake in Turkey, a volcanic eruption in the Philippines, a flood in Bangladesh, a nuclear accident in Chernobyl, and forest fires in California all dislocate whole communities of people. Sifting through the rubble, cleaning up the mud, and burying the dead can become overwhelming to those involved. Lee Tzu Pheng of the National University of Singapore writes, "Can you see how we are racked upon the axis of this world—drawn between a sky and ocean, heavenly air or heaving water?"

Frustration and anguish move in to live with disaster victims, often plunging them into bitterness and cynicism. "Who's in charge here?" they demand. "What are we supposed to do now? Who will get us out of this mess? Where in the world is God?"

In the national and political arena, people are often in over their heads. Every nation has to deal with its own economics, foreign policy, a defense budget, human welfare issues, trade agreements. The psalmist in Psalm 9 joins the chorus of concerned citizens who struggle with the raging storms of politics.

> The nations have sunk in the pit that they made;
> in the net that they hid has their own foot been caught. . . .
> The wicked shall depart to Sheol,
> all the nations that forget God. . . .
> Rise up, O LORD! Do not let mortals prevail;
> let the nations be judged before you.
> Put them in fear, O LORD;
> let the nations know that they are only human.

Once again the underlying question remains, "Who's in charge here?"

Mark 4:37-38 records, "A great windstorm arose, and the waves beat into the boat, so that the boat was already being swamped. But he [Jesus] was in the stern, asleep on the cushion; and they woke him up and said to him, 'Teacher, do you not care that we are perishing?' " What a frightening situation! To be caught in a sudden squall was one thing, but to feel abandoned by their leader in the midst of the windstorm was another matter indeed. The impression the disciples had of Jesus was that he was unaware, oblivious, perhaps even uncaring about their dangerous circumstances.

This episode brings to mind the account of the prophet, Jonah, who took a ship to Tarshish. He intended to get away from the presence of the Lord. His ship got caught in a storm, too. And all the while, Jonah, who had gone down into the hold of the ship, had lain down and was fast asleep. To be sure, Jonah's response to his predicament was pure escapism, not unlike our too common response to the realities of some people's everyday pain, captured in this segment of a poem I wrote more than a decade ago:

ASLEEP ON THE DEEP

I curl up on a comfortable couch
Unaware of those who crouch
In the dark, alone in the park,
With nowhere to go. . . .

Inside my bed I cover my head
And shut out cries of the dying and dead
The wail of the midnight specials:
Grass for sale,
Bodies for sale,
Souls for sale,
Going, going, gone. . . .

Jonah sleeps upon the deep,
Do not wake the baby . . . (JAO)

No, Jesus was not another Jonah. Quite the contrary, Jesus responded immediately to his disciples' needs. With a word, he rebuked the wind and said to the sea, "Peace! Be still!" Mark would have us know that with those few words, the wind ceased, and there was a dead calm. His critical question to the disciple follows: "Why are you afraid? Have you still no faith?"

The stark contrast is here drawn between Jesus and the disciples. The disciples are not models for faith. If they have any courage at all, it fails them in their hour of crisis. They express great anxiety about their own lives. Such a response is a complete and utter different one from that of Jesus. The stakes are high in this particular episode. Van Bogard Dunn's assertion that "the sea is not friendly" has a very special meaning. The sea is the enemy of human life. It is metaphor for death—that ultimate and irreversible calamity that comes to all.

Mark presents Jesus through the eyes of resurrection faith. Jesus serene, asleep in the stern on a cushion, rests as the crucified, risen Lord who has conquered the final foe and has nothing to fear. Sweet sleep in this case is not an act of human courage, but a sign of God's victory over sin and death forever and ever.

All is well, there is nothing to fear. Make no mistake about it, God is in charge. The sea may not be friendly, but the Lord who made the seas is. Who is this, that even the wind and sea obey him? Jesus the Christ, Son of the living God, is that one. Alleluia!

Suggestions for Worship

Call to Worship (Ps. 9:9-11):

LEADER: The LORD is a refuge for the oppressed,

PEOPLE: A stronghold in times of trouble.

LEADER: Those who know your name will trust in you.

PEOPLE: For you, LORD, have never forsaken those who seek you.

LEADER: Sing praises to the LORD.

PEOPLE: Proclaim among the nations what he has done.

Act of Praise: Psalm 9:9-20.

Suggested Hymns: "How Great Thou Art"; "To God Be the Glory"; "Many Gifts, One Spirit."

Opening Prayer: O God, you are Lord of all. At your word, storms are stilled, diseases are healed, the dead are raised. Grant by your mercy such faith among your people that possibilities become fact. During this hour of worship, lead us into the eye of those storms that rage within our hearts. Grant us the gift of quietness of spirit, so that in the midst of fury we may hear your voice of calm direction. In the name of the risen Christ. Amen.

Pastoral Prayer: Eternal God of compassion and strength, we gather together at your invitation. You have designed us for fellowship and community. Forgive us for those times we turn our backs on you and one another. May this be a day for reconnection as we learn the lesson of faith and dependence on others. Especially grant that we place our trust in you. You are mindful of your children's needs, more ready to respond than we are to make them known. Give us a quiet confidence that carries us in personal conflict and struggle. Increase our faith as we carry that same spirit into arenas of community life: education, commerce, government, and nations. Hasten the day when making peace will be a way of daily life. May patience, kindness, truthful speech and genuine love on our part contribute to the shalom you desire for your world. We seek your blessing as we live each day by faith in your grace and power. Through Christ our Lord, we pray. Amen.

JUNE 26, 1994

□

Fifth Sunday After Pentecost

The touch of Jesus brings healing and life. God is the author of life, and rejoices in the lives of his servants, not in their destruction, poverty, sickness, and death.

The Sunday Lessons

II Samuel 1:1, 17-27: David, grieving over the death of King Saul and his friend, Jonathan, wrote a song and ordered that it be taught to the people. "Saul and Jonathan, beloved and lovely! In life and in death they were not divided . . . How the mighty have fallen . . . my brother Jonathan; greatly beloved were you to me" (vv. 23-26).

II Corinthians 8:7-15: Encouraging the Corinthians to raise funds to help the church in Jerusalem, Paul notes the example of the Macedonians who, out of their own poverty, "gave according to their means, and even beyond their means" (v. 3). He points to the example of Jesus, who "though he was rich, yet for your sakes he became poor" (v. 9).

Mark 5:21-43: Two miracle stories are told. One demonstrates Jesus' power over disease. A woman touched his garment and was healed of her disease. The other demonstrates his authority over death. A Jewish official's (Jairus) daughter was already dead, and mourners were wailing when Jesus arrived. He spoke the words, " 'Talitha cum,' which means, 'Little girl, get up'!" (v. 41). Immediately, the girl got up.

Reflections

Sometimes, one seeks a miracle. At other times, the miracle is unexpected. One might pray to have a withered hand made strong, but would not expect a hand long ago severed and lost to be miraculously formed. Prayers to forestall death are commonplace, but those prayers all cease after the patient has been pronounced dead.

197

The raising of Jairus' daughter, just as the raising of Lazarus, finds Jesus arriving when it is seemingly too late to do anything. But Christ has a power and authority that never runs out of time. As the Old Testament so frequently states, "God's mercies never come to an end."

It is nearsighted to read these miracle stories from a historical point of view asking, "What really happened?" Mark's purposes are clearly theological. His question is, "What happens?" He points to the Resurrection with its new life and new creations that are much more than a mere return to an earthly existence.

Jesus Christ triumphs over disease before it ushers in death. He triumphs over death even after it has made its claim. Christ triumphs in the hour of his own death.

In spite of that, there remain in the church timid souls, forever earthbound, who are left saying, "You must of course realize that there are some very practical limitations that make it impossible for us to do anything now. We can't give a dime." (JKB)

EVEN THE MIGHTY FALL AND DIE

II Samuel 1:19-25

A SERMON BY MILFORD OXENDINE

The story of David, Saul, and Jonathan reveals their very mighty characters. It tells us about their personal relations in both life and death. Further, the story reveals to us that great value was attached to their inspiring influence on others. No one can fully understand and evaluate the benefits that arise from it. God had given them power. It affected others with harm and good. Likewise, their influence inspired others. But life ended for a king and his son. David laments over his deceased friends with his fellow Israelites. David wails the defeat of the Israelites on the battlefield at Gilboa. Israel's glory has fallen with the death of their mighty leaders. David curses the place of battle where the heroes were slain (v. 21).

In today's scripture, we find the elegy delivered by David. The words—"How the mighty have fallen" (v. 19)—cut deep into the ears of those experiencing mournful harmony as David spoke. The memory of a king and his son is celebrated as Saul chose to follow the devices of Satan. Saul's heart was not right with God. Even his desires were not centered in God. Saul forgot that "it is from within, from the human heart, that evil intentions come . . . deceit" (Mark 7:21-22). His heart had received him as he refused to yield it to God. The thought of his relations with others was not a motive to deter him from sin. Thus, Saul, the foe of David, involves Jonathan, David's friend, in his own fall.

For many of us, the term *mighty* is bestowed on others because of their birth, position, abilities, or noble exploits. Further, the title is usually placed on kings, princes, and other nobles of the earth. However, the term is more peculiarly adapted for a military general experienced in war (e.g., Generals Colin Powell and H. Norman Schwarzkopf during Operation Desert Shield/Storm). In I Chronicles 26, the princes of Israel were mighty because of their valor and skill. The word *mighty* fittingly agreed with the character of the deceased whom David mourns. The mighty had fallen, but they had fallen down dead. Those in attendance were filled with sorrow on hearing the words—"And the weapons of war perished!"

In our world today, the noblest of princes, world leaders, or the most valiant and honorable of the earth are liable to fall. A member of Congress is overtaken in a career of business unworthy of the meanest criminal in jail. The clergyperson who ought to set forth and live under God's word does not practice the truth he or she preaches. One furnishes a warning rather than an example. A married business person attending a convention is entertained by an escort service. A young woman is attacked and raped. The flower that promised such glory to a bright future is now an outcast. Yes, the mighty fall. Indeed, the greater the eminence, the deeper and deadlier the fall.

When the mighty fall, depending on their power and influence, the glory of a people is departed. By their fall, the strength of a people is impaired. This is one reason for mourning when strength has been removed. The mighty—who once held rank and high honor for the welfare of others—was once the defense for their followers. The known mighty—who once destroyed the enemy and caused others to rejoice—who availed themselves of the loss a people sustain when the young warriors die is another reason for mourning their fall. This explains why David joined Israel in mourning the deaths of Saul and Jonathan. Individuals have a just cause and reason for mourning the fall of great people because grief spreads throughout the nation. Even under such awful pains created by the fallen, every one in the land who seeks its prosperity is sensibly afflicted.

Since the mighty do fall and die, and the most valiant are liable to perish, let us take heed that we do not place an absolute dependence on them. As we live and abide under God's rules, there is an expectation and confidence we are asked to give to all leaders and rulers. They are to be honored and trusted. Yet, since they will die, our hope, trust, and faith must not totally be placed in them. Also, this shows how foolish and vain it is for great and mighty people to exalt themselves as though they were gods. In one word, when the mighty fall on their own sword, honor and beauty decease. The advantages gained by the exploits of the mighty are only temporary. However, one thing is needful. There should be an interest in the triumph of the cross and the redemption obtained by the precious blood of Jesus Christ, the Son of God.

Remember that though fallen sinners are expelled from the world's society, Christ will receive them if they do not fall into a deeper pride of heart. It is still true that Christ "eat(s) with sinners" (Mark 2:16). Isn't it good to know that God takes the world's outcasts and gives their weary and broken hearts an eternal inheritance? Yes, the publican and harlot enter the kingdom of God before the self-righteous. Notice the concluding words, "How the mighty have fallen in the midst of the battle!" (v. 25). Such language teaches us about the conflict of evil with good and darkness with light, which is raging around us at all times. The danger is not past. Remember, "If you think you are standing, watch out that you do not fall" (I Cor. 10:12). Let us find our strength, our safety, and our all in Jesus as we rest in his bosom. Let us recall Proverbs 16:8—"Better is a little with righteousness than large income with injustice."

Suggestions for Worship

Call to Worship (Ps. 133):

LEADER: How good and pleasant it is when the faithful gather together in unity!

PEOPLE: **It is like precious oil poured over us.**

LEADER: It is as if the dew of Hermon were falling on Mount Zion.

PEOPLE: **For there the LORD bestows his blessing, even life forevermore.**

Act of Praise: Psalm 133.

Suggested Hymns: "All Hail the Power of Jesus' Name"; "Jesus, Savior, Pilot Me"; "Lonely the Boat."

Opening Prayer: Lord, our true source of righteousness, remind us that you can mark our lives with happiness. Give us strength to overcome the conflicts in life, and when our life is ended, allow us to sit in triumph forever with the King of kings and Lord of lords. Amen.

Pastoral Prayer: O God, the mighty have fallen under the supreme power of death! O Death, the king of terrors, the conqueror of conquerors—whom riches cannot bribe or power resist, whom goodness cannot soften or dignity and loyalty deter, or even awe to a reverential distance.

Dear God, remind us how death intrudes into palaces as well as homes, and attacks both the rich and the poor. How astonishing and lamentable is the stupidity of humankind! Can the natural or the moral world exhibit another phenomenon so shocking and unaccountable? Death destroys thousands of our loved ones every year. Our neighbors, like leaves in autumn, drop into the grave. Our attendance on funerals and memorials are almost as frequent and formal as our visits of friendships. Yet, how few of us realize the thought that we, too, will die. We imagine we will be everlasting residents here on earth. We view eternity as a family land and see heaven and hell as majestic chimeras.

Almighty God, since the mighty is fallen, how vain are all things under the sun. Vanity of vanities; all is vanity. Lord forgive us. Amen.

JULY 3, 1994

□

Sixth Sunday After Pentecost

Rejection is painful. Even hard-nosed prophets are intimidated by it. That is likely the reason that so many of us are quick to compromise with ordinary expectations, and thus become ordinary ourselves.

The Sunday Lessons

II Samuel 5:1-5, 9-10: When David was thirty years old, he began his reign and ruled for forty years. He ruled over Judah (at Hebron) for seven years, and over all of Israel, both northern and southern kingdoms (at Jerusalem), for thirty-three years. "David became greater and greater, for the Lord" (v. 10).

II Corinthians 12:2-10: Paul speaks of visions and revelations other than the Damascus road experience. Then he speaks of his thorn in the flesh. "To keep me from being too elated, a thorn was given me in the flesh" (v. 7). He learned to be content with weakness, insult, and persecutions, "for whenever I am weak, then I am strong" (v. 10).

Mark 6:1-13: The account of Jesus' rejection by the people of his hometown concludes Mark's account of his ministry in parables and signs. They ask, "Is not this the carpenter, the son of Mary and brother of James" (v. 3). The Greek work *skandallzein*, translated "took offense," literally means "stumbled." Rejection is the reality. "A prophet is not without honor, except in his own country."

Reflections

The teaching is not questioned, but rather the teacher. There is no reference to the content taught, but only to the authority and wisdom of the teacher. This is what the home folks of Nazareth rejected—the Christ himself.

Their first response was amazement, but it was soon replaced with familiar names and categories. "Is not this the carpenter,

Mary's son? We know his brothers and sisters." Then they set him aside.

To name someone or something is to bring that strange other within our power to define and control. The practice is more common in the scientism of the twentieth century than it was in the first. We have developed more explanations, and psychological insights provide more categories.

Yet, the result remains the same. When we name a thing, the wonder goes out of it. A child's eyes, wide with amazement, are soon dimmed with commonplace explanations. A sophisticated five-year-old will thus announce, "That's just an old bug!"

When God comes among us, hidden in homeliness and concealed in the commonplace, we may for a moment be astonished. Then wanting to gain control or keep control, we, too, are quick to say, "This is the carpenter, Mary's son."

Independence Day provides fine examples of those who, discontent with the way things are, strive in the face of ridicule and repression to make new claims for truth. (JKB)

PROSPERITY

II Samuel 5:10

A SERMON BY MILFORD OXENDINE

Tomorrow our nation will celebrate its 216th year of independence and freedom from England. During this time the United States has indeed become a great and prosperous nation. Perhaps it is the most powerful nation allowed by God to have ever survived such prestige, honor, and valor. But let us never forget the many conflicts, battles, and turmoil we have undergone and endured. Many men and women indeed sacrificed and gave their lives for the country they loved so much. Saul, too, had given much to Israel from the time he was appointed its ruler. However, he fell on his own sword after he had pleaded with the young man carrying his weapons to kill him. With his death, Saul lost his greatness.

There are people who grow great among and above their peers, while the Lord is not on their side. Such growth and greatness are neither to be desired, nor to be admired. Also, there are people with whom the Lord is on their side, who do not go on, as they might go. Further, there are yet more of them who do not grow great by what they do or by the Lord's doing. Having the Lord with us on our side is a great thing. Going on while the Lord is with us is more important than growing great. However, if one is to grow great, let that person see to it that he or she does not grow away from the Lord. Also, one must have the Lord with one in all one's going and in all one's growing.

The scripture tells us that David became the sole ruler over Israel. However, the tide of prosperity was about to begin. Just as every tide has a turning point, David's misfortunes began to flow. Judah had for seven-and-a-half years been subject to David's sway. Now Israel was anxious to array itself under his banner and leadership. The account given in II Samuel 5:1-5, 9-10 is very skimpy. First Chronicles 12:23-40 gives a fuller account of the pomp and proceedings of David's coronation. Adding up the total number of military escorts for the event was 340,800. The festival lasted for three days. The former shepherd was officially honored and at last recognized as sovereign over all of God's chosen people.

As the sovereign ruler, David was a great military conqueror. Soon after his installation as king over all Israel, David turned his wistful eyes toward Jerusalem. It was considered the Gilbraltar of Canaan. The Israelites had attempted to capture it on many efforts. Only on one occasion were they partially successful. Therefore, David made plans to take it with his mighty army. He did conquer it and make it his capital. From Jerusalem he established a religious center from which he ruled his people.

Being the king over Israel, David's prosperity at home was quickly recognized by the sovereigns of other nations. Among them was Hiram, king of ancient Tyre. Soon distant rulers sought alliance with David as they courted his favor. This allowed David to advance even more, and he became great among all nations. The tide of prosperity swept far as David enjoyed the times of happiness and plenty.

David knew the cause of prosperity was not linked to his own sake. He knew God had prospered him for Israel's sake. If David had stopped to think for a moment, he would have soon realized that he had no more talents than Saul did. Saul had begun well as he took over the throne. In some respects, Saul indeed had the advantage over David. At this time in David's life, perhaps he recognized all this as he ascribed the glory to God, to whom it belonged. If only he had borne this earlier in his mind, he would have made fewer mistakes and committed fewer sins than he did. So long as his thought ran God-ward he was safe. However, as soon as David's mind began to say "by mine own might and power," he lost power and fell. Yes, the first few years of his reign were among the happiest times of his whole life. His hardships as an exile had ended. He no longer laid down and rose up in fear of his enemies killing him. David was with his families and friends. No longer was he driven from post to pillar like a wild beast. David's heart was not tried by the apparent contradiction between God's promise and God's performance. The promise from God to provide David a good kingdom was upheld, and David felt that all's well that ends well. Further, the Israelites had not yet been alienated, and thus standing off at a distance from David. Their enthusiasm created a united and prosperous nation as they were led by wise and talented military chieftains. This great and overwhelming temptation of royalty had not yet destroyed the moral character of their king. An enlarged life, filled with many unusual opportunities for usefulness, soon spread like wild fire before him. This filled David with enthusiasm that caused him to reach full manhood. Yes, this was David's golden age. He stood at the beginning of a career that might be almost perfect in all of its achievements.

The same thing is true for many of our young men and women today. Life stretches out before them as it is full of grand possibilities and rewards. The restraints incident to childhood and the years of tutelage are over. Powers of body and mind are in full vigor and strength. Hope stands with its face erect and confidence on its brow and awaits them eagerly. Friends applaud for them with the words, "It is there for you to take. Go for it." Friends and loved ones predict great success in their future. But it is only well for those who remember that God is the source of all their talents and of the conditions of their future success.

Here lies the secret of prosperity. Remember—"The Lord God of Hosts was with David." The secret of all real greatness is in having the Lord on our side. How can we secure God's presence and help? How did David secure these? He trusted God. He acknowledged and consulted God. He obeyed God. The same method of ensuring the divine help is open to all. If we would go on and grow great and if we would prosper in all right ways, we must begin to walk in God's ways.

Progress and improvement are everyone's duty. It is not right to remain as we were or as we are. We ought to be all the time gaining and growing in experience, attainment, and love. It may be to our shame that we are just where God put us and that we have just what God gave us. Remaining just as God made us may be the cause of our condemnation.

If the United States is to remain a powerful and mighty nation, let us not take our prosperity lightly. To do so may cause destruction, on our part, as we turn away from God. Let us be thankful and serve God faithfully. Maybe this country can reach another 216 years of independence. May our nation continue to be blessed as "the land of the free and the home of the brave."

Suggestions for Worship

Call to Worship (Ps. 48):

> LEADER: Great is the LORD, and worthy of praise.
>
> **PEOPLE: Within your temple, O God, we meditate on your unfailing love.**
>
> LEADER: Like your name, O God, your praise reaches to the ends of the earth;
>
> **PEOPLE: Your right hand is filled with righteousness. Mount Zion rejoices, and our land is glad because of your judgments.**
>
> LEADER: For this God is our God for ever and ever;
>
> **PEOPLE: God will be our guide even to the end.**

Act of Praise: Psalm 48.

Suggested Hymns: "Now Thank We All Our God"; "O How I Love Jesus"; "Precious Lord, Take My Hand."

Opening Prayer: Lord God Almighty, in whose name the founders of this country won liberty for themselves and for us, and lofted the torch of freedom for nations then unborn, grant that we and all the peoples of this land may have grace to maintain our liberties in righteousness and peace. Amen.

Pastoral Prayer: Dear Lord, as a nation we were convinced that we could not endure half slave and half free. No one can celebrate liberty as long as one's brothers and sisters are in chains or shackled by poverty or ignorance or a denial of basic rights that enables them to the good of society.

Our most elusive dream has been the pursuit of happiness, for no person can give happiness to another. It is a state that each must find for oneself. Help us to discover the secret that comes not from selfish pursuit of ingrown indulgence, but from sharing not just what we have, but who we are.

Re-create in each of us the dreams of our founding fathers, who by your grace knew that where there was no dream there could be no destiny. Amen.

JULY 10, 1994

□

Seventh Sunday After Pentecost

David danced before the Lord in recognition of a spiritual power and blessing that attended the ark. Herodias danced before Herod the King and forever stained her hands with the blood of the beheaded John the Baptist.

The Sunday Lessons

II Samuel 6:1-5, 12b-19: The ark was a portable shrine that symbolized the presence of Yahweh. David and his men went to get it and brought it up to Jerusalem. The procession to Jerusalem was a loud and joyous affair. "David and all the house of Israel were dancing before the Lord with all their might" (v. 5). Special blessings from God attended that person who was in possession of the ark: "blessed the household of Obededom . . . because of the ark" (v. 12b).

Ephesians 1:3-14: Ephesians begins with this ancient hymn of thanksgiving. God has "blessed us in Christ with every spiritual blessing . . . made known to us the mystery of his will . . . to gather up all things in him" (vv. 3-10). Christ is the ultimate truth by which all human values are tested.

Mark 6:14-29: At a birthday party for Herod, the daughter of Herodias pleased Herod and his guests with her dance. "Ask me for whatever you wish, and I will give it" (v. 22), Herod promised. At her mother's prompting, she asked for the head of John the Baptist on a platter. John was immediately beheaded in prison. King Herod believed that Jesus was John the Baptist, raised from the dead (v. 16).

Reflections

"Who are the most competent pastors in this city?" he asked. The answer named some for their training in Ivy League schools, some for their ability as administrators, some because of their public appeal, and some because they were appointed to a wealthy and influential church. Competence in ministry is often judged by the quality of one's education, the size of the crowd, and the significance of the budget.

When a group of pastors were naming the five best appointments in their conference, it was not merely coincidental that the churches paying the largest salaries were listed. Churches often employ the size of a congregation and its financial wherewithal as primary criteria for evaluation. The Bible teaches that loyalty to Christ, dependency kept independent, and faithfulness to the message are primary considerations.

To be sure, any pastor serving a local church must expect to pay the rent. That means raising the budget. Moreover, church growth is mandated by Christ himself. God's power and revelation reflected in the Old Testament and the epistle places a limited value on money and members. Even though the need is genuine, Christians must disengage themselves from the control of such loyalties.

We are always beholden, but we must never be compromised. Civil religion, which is always more intent on serving a nation than in honoring Christ, is challenged by the Old Testament text, which portrays an awesome God. A church more concerned for its life than its mission is rebuked by the martyrdom of John the Baptist. (JKB)

LOSING YOUR HEAD

Mark 6:14-29

A SERMON BY MICHAEL T. MCEWEN

Think about it for a moment . . . how many times have you said, or heard someone else say, "I lost my head," or "He lost his head"? This is not just intended to be a superficial or crudely humorous comment on the story of John the Baptist heard in our lesson from the Gospel According to St. Mark today. As a matter of fact, though it may be a bit of a pun, there is a deep, poignant, and theological point behind the story of John losing his head to the evil machinations of Herodias and her daughter, Salome.

Try to remember times when you "lost your head." For me, a couple of times come to mind very quickly.

One Sunday night in the summer of 1988, my wife and I were awakened about nine o'clock by a call from the Emergency Department of a hospital fifteen hundred miles away. We were told that our ten-year-old son had been in an auto accident with his grandfather, that he had internal injuries, and that permission was needed for immediate surgery. Believe me, in some very real ways, I lost my head. Fear, concern over our separation by those many miles, worry about my dad, agony that I knew how my wife was suffering—all these things came pounding into my consciousness, and I literally could not function in a rational manner. I will tell you that everything came out fine for my son and my dad, but that is not my main point. The real issue here for me was how fear and powerlessness can cause you to lose your head.

On the other hand, it is not always the negative that causes this result. When I think about my ordination service, I remember so very vividly that I had really lost touch with reality. After the years of study, prayer, and self-examination, I found myself at the point where the bishop was laying his hands on my head saying those words that would change my life forever. I was in a daze. I knew what was going on, but I was so overpowered by the sense of God's presence and the love of his people, that I truly was not in any kind of normal state of mind.

So, I think we can lose our heads, and we can do it in positive or negative ways, or as a result of positive or negative situations. A good question is: Where is God in all this?

Maybe we begin to get some insight by looking at the example of John the Baptist. He certainly might have found himself in the figurative sense of losing his head over a number of negative factors.

For one thing, there was the terrible injustice of his situation. He had been imprisoned because he had been faithful in preaching the sinfulness of the marriage between King Herod and his wife, Herodias. (You may recall that Herodias was originally the wife of Herod's brother, Philip, and that Herod took Herodias in clear violation of Jewish law.) John insisted on confronting the royal couple with their illegal relationship. When Herodias decided to use Herod's weakness and lust for Salome as a tool to bring about the death of John, a perfect example of injustice and immorality came into play. Surely, John must have felt the agonizing pain of this unrighteous and despicable situation. Another negative factor for John would have been his own human fear and trepidation. Even though he as a powerful prophet who was undoubtedly filled with the spirit of God, he was also human and must have known the despair and agony of imprisonment, uncertainty, and the fear of an approaching death.

What might have sustained John through these negative feelings and times? We do not know for certain, of course, but there are some possibilities that are very consistent with the witness of faith that we have seen in the lives of so many martyrs.

First, there must have been some comfort from knowing that he was on the side of God and was doing what was right according to God's law and according to his own call as a prophet. Right does not make might, but it does make the righteous one more confident. Wouldn't you rather know that you were following God's law instead of violating it? This is not a call to the kind of hypocritical self-righteousness that seems to affect some of us. Instead, it is a call to remember that God has given us some standards, and we can use them to judge whether or not we are doing what God wants us to do.

For me, it is vitally important to remember that the English word *rule* and the Latin *regula* both refer to a similar idea that we have tended to lose in our modern usage. The original meanings carried the same connotation that survive in our words ruler, yardstick, or tape measure. The rules or laws were intended as a means to *measure* where we are. If all modern Christians—as John the Baptist—-use God's rule or law as a means to measure, then when we find ourselves in a good place with respect to those rules—as John would have—we should draw strength and courage from knowing that we are doing what God wants us to do.

Even more important than this idea of rightness according to the law must have been John's knowledge that he was close to Christ and that he had fulfilled his role. The words in the Gospel according to St. John make it clear as the Baptist said, "He must increase, but I must decrease" (John 3:30). In fact, the testimony of John the Baptist rings out clearly in all the

Gospel accounts. He knew he had met the Christ and that his life had been fulfilled.

Can you imagine the peace that comes from feeling that you have fulfilled your call by God and that you have really come to know his son? Even in his depths of fear and despair, John knew that he had found the Messiah. The power of that belief is what sustained John—and all the martyrs over the ages.

For us, the issues may not seem as concrete. After all, John the Baptist met Jesus in person. We deal with the resurrected Christ whose presence is a different matter altogether.

What should we do? What can we do?

This may seem like a long stretch of the points, but I think we can do just as John the Baptist did. We can follow his lead with respect to both the negative and the positive issues. If we feel injustice and unfairness in pain or suffering we face, let us try to take heart in being right with God according to his laws. Of course, I am not talking about the rule-bound absurdity of the Pharisees. I am referring to the confidence in God's law and justice that John would have felt in the midst of the human injustice that had been thrust on him. It is comforting to know in your heart that you are right—especially if you can truly know you are right according to God's way.

In another of the negative modes, we can remember that there is nothing unchristian or unfaithful in confessing our fear and frailty. Even Jesus did as much in the Garden of Gethsemane. Admitting our fear and pain is the first step in asking God to help us through it.

On the positive side, when we face fear, uncertainty, or the negative side of life, we can take courage from the knowledge that we are part of the "communion of saints." That is a rather theological phrase that has very profound and personal meaning. The church, as the body of Christ, is composed of all those who have been its members—now, in the past, and in the future. The saints—the people who have found that God's grace sustains them when they are faced with the worst the world can offer—are part of God's kingdom and are with us in a mysterious way that we cannot fully understand even though we can know that they respond to the same strength and power that is available to us when we stay open to God in times of trial and crisis. All of those saints were people like us. Women and men, old and young, all races and nations.

What made them saints is as much a part of our life in Christ as it was in theirs. God's love never changes. God never deserts us.

Finally and most importantly, we can remember the example of our Lord and Savior. Though he suffered in agony and felt the pain and despair that are part of our human existence, his time on the cross and his resurrection were proof that God is with us. Easter, Pentecost, the birth and growth of the church, the witness of the saints, the lives of people today like Mother Teresa and Desmond Tutu are all proof of God's eternal and enduring presence. Dear ones, choose to live in that love and in the power of his presence. Amen.

Suggestions for Worship

Call to Worship (Ps. 24:3-5):

> LEADER: Who may ascend the hill of the LORD? Who may stand in his holy place?
>
> **PEOPLE:** **He who has clean hands and a pure heart, who does not lift up his soul to an idol or swear by what is false.**
>
> LEADER: He will receive blessing from the LORD and vindication from God his Savior.

Act of Praise: Psalm 24.

Suggested Hymns: "He Leadeth Me: O Blessed Thought": "Morning Has Broken"; "Dear Lord and Father of Mankind."

Opening Prayer: Dear Father in Heaven, you are the source of the ultimate peace and power that can sustain us when the very worst happens. Give us a sense of your presence and grace. Let us remember the faith of those saints who have come before us. Help us follow the example of your blessed Son. We pray in his holy name. Amen.

Pastoral Prayer: Lord, sustain us when we hurt and doubt. Remind us of the examples of John the Baptist and all those who faced the worst injustice the world had to offer and triumphed because they lived in the reality of your love. Direct us according to your will and make your will for us present as a clear and certain faith, even when we do not understand the inequities and cruelties that may beset us.

Always, Father, give us an undimmed and glowing vision of the perfect faith of your son whom you sent as the proof of your love. We offer ourselves and our prayers in his name and ask for the empowerment of your Holy Spirit. Amen.

JULY 17, 1994

□

Eighth Sunday After Pentecost

Apart from Christ, it is impossible for the church to satisfy the
hunger of humanity. Our human resources are too meager. The
world's hunger is too great.

The Sunday Lessons

II Samuel 7:1-14a: David was settled and at peace with his enemies. In a vision, the prophet Nathan received God's covenant
with David. "I have not lived in a house . . . but I have been moving about in a tent and a tabernacle. . . . I took you from the pasture, from following the sheep to be prince . . . I will make for
you a great name . . . the Lord will make you a house. . . . I will
not take my steadfast love from him, as I took it from Saul
. . . your throne shall be established forever" (vv. 6-16).
Ephesians 2:11-22: Both Jew, "those who were near" (v. 17),
and Gentile, "you who were far off " (v. 17), have access to the
Father through Christ, who is our peace. "So then you are no
longer strangers and aliens, but you are citizens with the saints
and also members of the household of God" (v. 19).
Mark 6:30-34, 53-56: Jesus and his disciples had withdrawn to
the wilderness. Crowds followed, and soon they needed to be
fed. "Send them away" (v. 36), said the disciples. But Jesus
answered, "You give them something to eat" (v. 37). With five
loaves and two fish the whole multitude—five thousand men—
were fed. "And all ate and were filled" (v. 42). Jesus likened the
multitude to "sheep without a shepherd" (v. 34).

Reflections

"I'm always hungry," he said, but he was not thinking of bread.
At least not the kind of bread used for peanut-butter sandwiches,
not the bread carried to work in brown paper bags, not the kind
of bread—white, whole wheat, or rye—that can be ordered in

any deli. He spoke about the hunger that attends one's constant need for one more experience. It is a constant sense of emptiness—that vanity of vanities described in the book of Ecclesiastes. It is a deep yearning that never goes away. The eye is not satisfied with what it sees. The ear is not satisfied with what it hears. The tongue is not satisfied with what it tastes.

Often our whole existence is merely this: hunger, emptiness, need. The story of the wilderness crowd is our story. A flock wandering in barren wasteland, unfed, scattered, and lost. People who had come too far and stayed too long. Sheep without a shepherd.

We are people who indulge our appetites, worship our possessions, and complain when we do not always have all we want. We fill ourselves with bread that perishes (John 6:27). We are better fed than any people in history, yet we are restless and greedy. Whatever our eyes have desired, we have not kept from them. Whatever our appetites have longed for, we have sought to provide. And it is all emptiness of emptiness, a striving after the wind (Eccles. 2:11).

The central theme of this text, however, is not the hunger of the crowd. Rather, it is the power of Christ to satisfy. He is the shepherd who cares for the sheep. The bread was divided among them all, and they all were satisfied. And there was no shortage. Twelve baskets full of broken pieces were left over.

These baskets full of broken pieces are symbols that should remain important to us. (See Mark 8:19-21.) They imply the abundance and extravagance of God. Have you wondered what was done with the leftovers? Oswald Chambers, the evangelical mystic, often spoke of discipleship as broken bread saying, "If God would only use his own fingers, and make me broken bread and poured-out wine in a special way." (JKB)

A MIRACLE OR HIDDEN SANDWICHES?

Mark 6:30-34, 53-56

A SERMON BY MICHAEL T. McEWEN

It has been nearly ten years now, but I remember the experience quite clearly. Eight of us were gathered together in a small teaching chapel at our seminary. We were in our practical course on preaching in which we took turns preparing and delivering sermons. We had to preach once each week to each other, the professor, and lay volunteer listeners from local churches. Each trial sermon was followed by very frank comments from our little congregation. We were also videotaped and had to later undergo the agony of self-criticism.

It was an extremely effective way of learning to preach better. Among other things, it was a time when each divinity student learned how to be carefully attentive to the scripture texts that were assigned. We always hated it when we got a tricky lesson, and today's story of Jesus and the feeding of the five thousand was considered by all of us to be one of them.

This particular miracle account is one that we studied extensively in our New Testament courses. There are many fascinating aspects to it. For one thing, it is included in all four of the Gospels. Most scholars do feel that the accounts in Matthew and Luke have their source in Mark's version that we heard today. As you may know, the Gospel According to Mark is considered to have been the first Gospel written, and Matthew and Luke often seem to use it as a source. However, they did not simply copy Mark's work, and when a story appears in all three of these Gospels, it is usually considered to be a sign that it was very important to the early church's understanding of who and what Jesus was.

To make the story even more significant, it is one that John includes in his Gospel. Although there is a high degree of similarity in Mark, Matthew, and Luke, John usually covered material that they did not. The fact that he also includes the feeding of the five thousand makes the story even more significant.

So, we have an account of an event that was apparently considered highly important to all the Gospel writers, and presumably, to the entire early church. Obviously, a preacher, either seminary student or pastor, needs to take such a story very seriously. Another complicating factor for this lesson is its very status as a miracle story. Many modern folks, Christian or not, simply do not like to seriously entertain the idea of a supernatural miracle such as the multiplying of loaves and fishes.

This has led to a number of ways of explaining what happened in more scientifically acceptable terms. Perhaps the most popular is called the "hidden sandwich theory." According to this explanation, when the people in the crowd saw that Jesus and the disciples were willing to share what little they had, this inspired everyone to share their own food for the road, which people of that day commonly took with them on an outing or journey. Now this is a nice, comfortable explanation for the scientifically-sceptical mind, and it even rings true with our current experience. Think how often you have been amazed at the overflowing tables of food you encounter at a pot-luck dinner! So, whether we want to call it the hidden sandwich theory or the pot-luck phenomenon, this is certainly one way to look at the feeding of the five thousand.

We might call this a modernist view of the scriptures. The other end of the spectrum would be a conservative or literalist interpretation. It has power and appeal, too. In this understanding of the story, we are invited to enter whole-heartedly into the faith that Jesus is the son of God who fully and completely exercises his father's power. God created all that is, including the laws of nature, and it is certainly within his power and authority to suspend those laws if he wants to make a point. Even the most scientifically-oriented person, if open-minded, will usually admit that things sometimes happen that either cannot be explained or seem to directly violate some natural law.

Maybe the feeding was exactly what it purports to be: A demonstration of the miraculous power of God working through his son.

Another approach to understanding the story has favor with technical scripture scholars. For instance, some have pointed out that a basic story about a feeding miracle was around in both Jewish and Gentile religious tradition long before Jesus lived. In fact, the account of Elisha in II Kings 4:42-44 bears remarkable similarity to Mark's story about Jesus. This sort of historical and comparative view of the story looks for eternal and universal religious truths in the scriptures much more than it is concerned with the factual events of a given event in the life of Jesus. From this type of perspective, the assumption is made that something dramatic happened in an actual event involving Jesus, and the well-known feeding miracle story was used as a means to communicate that to the people of his time for whom such an account would have had a familiar ring.

Can you see why the feeding of five thousand can look so inhibiting to a preacher? There are so many factors to consider, and so many different possibilities for interpretation and understanding. What is a preacher or any reader of the Bible to do when faced with so much diversity and so many persuasive arguments and explanations?

My response is to accept them all on some levels and reject them all on others. When I do this, I see truths begin to emerge that go beyond human attempts to analyze and explain the scriptures. Since I believe the Bible to be God's word and not man's, this approach gives me some hope that I may be seeing his truth as it is dimly reflected in all our various human attempts to explain and understand him.

Here is how the feeding of the five thousand makes sense to me: First, Jesus did *something* involving an unexplained feeding of a large number of people. The details of the event may be lost in the mystery of the past, but something incredible happened. God is like that. He does wonderful and unexplainable things for us.

Second, the event was so powerful and dramatic that it became part of the story of Christ as remembered by his followers and told by all four of the Gospel writers. When God showed his grace and glory through the work of his son, people paid attention. They may not have remembered all the details the same way, but the basic truth stuck with them. When we pay attention to God's power working through his son, then we are on the same track.

Third, the story is about Jesus *and* his disciples. They had a part in it, too. The feeding begins with the work of Christ and incorporates the work of his followers. That is true today. Whether it is the literal feeding of the poor and hungry of the world or the spiritual feeding of those desperate souls who are looking for God's love, it still begins with Christ and incorporates us as his disciples.

Finally, when we read scripture, we are going to encounter passages like this one that can strain credibility and create real confusion. This need not lead directly to doubt. There are always going to be aspects of God's work in the world that we cannot understand. That is true of our reading of the Bible, *Time* magazine, or the local newspaper. In all of it and behind all of it is the mystery of God. God will always be beyond human understanding, but never beyond our reaching out to him in our need. What we must sometimes do is try to love him and not try to understand him, to trust him and not try to explain him.

I know to the depths of my soul that in some special way, Jesus fed the five thousand. He has fed his untold millions of followers since. He stands ready right now to feed you and me. Thanks be to God! Amen.

Suggestions for Worship

Call to Worship (Eph. 2:13-18):

LEADER: Now in Christ Jesus you who once were far away have been brought near through the blood of Christ.

PEOPLE: **For he is our peace, who has destroyed the barrier, the dividing wall of hostility,**

LEADER: He came and preached peace to you who were far away and peace to those who were near.

PEOPLE: **For through him we all have access to the Father by one Spirit.**

Act of Praise: Psalm 89:20-37.

Suggested Hymns: "Come, Ye Disconsolate"; "O Happy Day, That Fixed My Choice"; "Let Us Break Bread Together."

Opening Prayer: Dear Lord, you are the God of mystery and power for whom the feeding of five thousand is like the batting of an eyelash. Help us to believe in your power and in your love. Feed us with the spiritual food that will make our souls grow in faith. We ask this in the name of your Son, our Savior, Jesus Christ. Amen.

Pastoral Prayer: God of miracles beyond human understanding, guide us into acceptance of your eternal truth. Direct our minds to understanding your will for us. Touch our hearts so that they may reflect your immeasurable love. Empower us to be witnesses to your son's glory so that all the world may come within his loving embrace. Day by day, make all of us in this world more sure of your presence and more convinced of your care for us. Make us true members of the body of Christ. We ask these things in his name. Amen.

JULY 24, 1994

□

Ninth Sunday After Pentecost

Sometimes it seems there is just not enough to go around. Faith and love express themselves through sharing. Anxiety and selfishness are reflected in our careful and calculating ways.

The Sunday Lessons

II Samuel 11:1-15: David's adultery with the beautiful Bathsheba led to an unwanted pregnancy, and then intrigue, deception, and the arranged death of her husband, Uriah. The king was unable to get the disciplined soldier, Uriah, to spend time with his wife, and thus assume paternity. Therefore, he sent a letter in the faithful officer's own hand that would ensure his death.

Ephesians 3:14-21: There are four petitions regarding the mystery revealed in Christ. Paul prays "that you may be strengthened in your inner being" (v. 16), that "Christ may dwell in your hearts through faith" (v. 17), that "you may have the power to comprehend . . . the breadth and length and height and depth" (v. 18) the dimensions of God's love, and that "you may be filled with all the fullness of God" (v. 19).

John 6:1-21: Five barley loaves and two fish; what are they among so many? The Gospel lessons for the next three Sundays will speak of the bread of life. The multiplication of the loaves and fishes, as John records it, provides more detail than Mark. It is the Passover. Barley loaves are used. The meal is on a mountain. The crowd followed because of his miracles. The eucharistic pattern is evident—took bread, gave thanks, distributed it.

Reflections

Today's generation of young persons will not have as much as their parents have had. Heretofore, each succeeding generation has anticipated more of everything—more educational opportunities more chances for jobs, more things to buy, and more money to spend.

Now educational costs are more than many can afford. Student aid programs are drastically reduced. Housing costs make the American dream of owning one's own home an unreality. A father recently spoke of his grown son's employment and economic problems. "We have tried again and again to launch him, but he keeps getting stuck in the tube."

In the first century, need resulted from scarcity. There simply was not enough bread. In the Third World, it is still the case. However, in America the problem is surplus, surfeit, economic waste, and a wretched disunity brought about by personal greed.

When there are only a few barley loaves and we consider, "What are they among so many?" we are not prompted to "humility and gentleness, with patience, bearing with one another in love" (Eph. 4:2). Rather, our style becomes increasingly anxious, aggressive, and assertive. If there's only one loaf of bread to be had, we intend to have it. It there's only one barrel of oil to buy, we reason that we should get it.

The texts begin with apparent scarcity, but conclude with abundance. The child of God and the Christ are not distressed by the lack of bread. The words are so simple, yet so profound. "Make the people sit down," "give thanks," "distribute." "Gather up the fragments left over, that nothing may be lost." (JKB)

A STORY OF SIN AND DEATH

II Samuel 11:1-15

A SERMON BY JOHN K. BERGLAND

In the Australian bush country grows an attractive little plant with a lovely name. It is called the sundew. It's blossoms are red and pink. Its stalk is slender and its leaves are small and almost round. Each leaf glistens in the sunlight. The leaves are fringed with tiny hairs and each hair is tipped with a drop of fluid as delicate as dew. Colorful and bright in the sunshine, the plant is worthy of its name—an inviting name—sundew. The blossoms are sweet and safe enough, but any insect that seeks their nectar risks its life. Those glistening hairs on every leaf are sticky tentacles, that will catch and hold and finally devour any insect that saunters in their sweetness. The sundew is carnivorous. Not even the quick and the strong escape its cluthces.

Sin is like that; attractive but deadly. Deceit is like that; inviting, but ultimately destructive. Adultery is like that; no one expects to hurt or to be hurt, then trust dies and family is degraded. The story of David's sin with Bathsheba, the Old Testament lesson for today, is a story of the ways of sin. Sin's consequences are not intended; they are seldom foreseen, but they are real and tenacious and ruthlessly destructive.

When David was attracted to the beautiful Bathsheba, sent for her, and lay with her, he never intended to get her pregnant. Then he hoped to escape that unwanted consequence by arranging for her husband Uriah to come home from war. "Send him home, Joab," was the king's message to his general. "I'll make sure that he goes to be with his wife and when that baby is born he will think it is his."

But Uriah, a disciplined and loyal soldier, after reporting to his king would not go down to his own hosuse. "I won't sleep in my own bed. Not when my comrades, not when the ark of Israel, are all out in open field in combat," he said.

David thought, "Well, that didn't work. I'll get him drunk." But even this drunk soldier would not return to his own bed to sleep with his beautiful wife. David never intended to betray the loyalty of a faithful soldier, but he needed to get out of a messy situation. And so David wrote a letter. He put it in the hand of his faithful soldier; a treacherous letter that was Uriah's own death sentence. "Put Uriah in the midst of the fighting," it said. "Let him face the most valiant warriors of the enemy." David wanted him dead. The final solution was to arrange a husband's death so that he could marry the woman who carried his child.

Like David, we never intend the suffering of sin. We always expect to escape the consequences. But still, the sticky tentacles of sin entangle and demand their dues. Today, as we reflect on the story of David and Bathsheba—a story of adultery, deceit, and treacherous murder—we know there's no escape from wrong choices. Not in God's world. Not in David's and not in ours.

Now, with the word of God before us, consider how it really is. *Sin will take you further than you want to go. It will keep you*

*longer than you want to stay. It will cost you more than you ever
intended to pay.*

Do you think that you can somehow escape the consequences
of sin? You cannot! True, we live in a society that believes that if
caught we can still get free. A good attorney can get us off. Somehow, in some way, we will escape the consequences we never
intended. But in the final analysis, one cannot count on it. *Sin
will take you further than you want to go.*

Can any of us really hear this story in 1994—in this day and
age. We respond to unwanted pregnancies with abortions.
There's horror in the story when David decides his faithful soldier must die. There is tragedy in the story, when the prophet
says, "You won't die, David, but the child must die!" In the abortion clinics of our world, countless thousands of unwanted babies
have died, and more will die. Some defend it as right. Others
condemn it as wrong. This preacher wants to say, "It's tragic! It's
all tragic! It's always tragic!" Surely, all of us must know and
believe, whether pro-life or pro-choice, that promiscuous intimacy will sometimes, too many times, *take you further than you
want to go.*

The fact that most persons in our society do not consider it
always wrong to engage in sex before marriage, and that many do
not find sex beyond marriage always wrong either, does not
change this reality. We may defend pornography as an expression
of free speech. Adultery may be described as a brief affair. The
deep knowing of premarital sex may be casually called living
together and illegitimate children may be described as love
babies. Celibacy in singleness and fidelity in marriage may be
more rhetoric than reality, but not one of us, not any of us can, in
any way, change this fact about sexuality without covenant. *It will
take you further than you want to go.*

Observe that you cannot play with the animal in you without
becoming wholly animal, play with falsehood without forfeiting
your right to truth, play with cruelty without losing your sensitiv-
ity of soul. Dag Hammarskjold writes, "He who wants to keep his
garden tidy, doesn't reserve a plot for weeds."

David's affair with Bathsheba was sin. There was no doubt
about that, not in the Hebrew law. Bathsheba was not just a
woman, she was the daughter of Eliam. She was the wife of
Uriah the Hittite, the faithful soldier. Bathsheba was not a

woman of the street, a slave, or a concubine. She was not an object to entertain David's lust, or a convenience to satisfy it. She was somebody's daughter, somebody's wife. And in the law of Moses, sex with Bathsheba was a capital crime.

But David did not expect to be caught, and he surely did not expect to be held accountable. If there were unwanted consequences he expected them to be temporary, not lasting. *But sin will keep you longer than you want to stay.*

Have you considered lately how unforgiving, how absolute and final some choices are? A little girl was out walking with her daddy one day when she saw a flower in the midst of many flowers.. Pointing towards it she said, "Daddy will you pick that flower for me?" He stooped down, picked the flower, and reached out to hand it to her. "No, no, not that one Daddy," she said. "I want the other one. Put that one back." And the father, in his wisdom knew that could never be done. "All the king's horses and all the king's men can't put it together again."

The lines of George MacDonald's poem are as compelling as the title, "Sweet Peril":

> Alas, how easily things go wrong.
> A sigh too much, or a kiss too long,
> And there follows a mist and a weeping rain,
> And life is never the same again.

Life in David's house was never the same again.

Bob Greene is a columnist who writes for the *Chicago Tribune*. One of his columns discussed, "The Death of the Permanent Record." Do you remember days in school when teachers would remind you, indeed warn you, concerning the permanent record? You could do some things bad and think to yourself, "Well, they will probably forget that by the end of next week." But if the teacher said, "This is going to go on your permanent record," you knew it was serious. You might not get into college. You might not get a job. Permanent record meant that it would follow you all the days of your life. Bob Greene wrote "Aren't you glad that that's gone?" I think I am. They can't write it down now and tell it forever, they can't. We have the Right to Privacy Act and the Right for Information Act. But is the old poet still right? "The moving finger writes . . . tears won't wash out a word of it." *Sin keeps you longer than you want to stay.*

I wonder why they told it. Why did the chronicler write it down in the permanent history of Israel? Why is David's adultery, deceit, and murderous treachery recorded in Holy Scripture? David was a favored king. For forty-two years he ruled Israel. It was a golden age. He wrote many of the psalms. He was the spiritual leader who made Jerusalem the Holy City. Even now it is a holy place for over half of the world's population. Why would anyone write down, as permanent record, the account of King David's lust, adultery, lying manipulation, and his ruthless plotting of a good friend's death. Why?

The scripture is written for our edification. For your help and for mine. This historian in David's kingdom was so close to his beloved king that he knew every intimate detail of his life. He also knew, as everyone knew, the tragedy, the grief, the awful violence, and death that attended the royal family. Why he wondered, "Why has God's annointed king suffered so?" And he answered, "It is the consequence of sin." He wanted history to know. He wanted you to know, and the whole world to know that *sin will cost you more than you ever intended to pay.*

When I was growing up, the kids who smoked wanted others to smoke. The kids who were drinking beer seemed almost zealous to convert the uninitiated. Then it was marijuana, cocaine, and crack. The missionaries and salespersons for these drugs promised a special feeling, a thrill, and new experiences of human potential. They promised that it wouldn't hurt you. A promised thrill has always been a temptation for the young, especially those who want to grab all the gusto. Promised safety and no consequences—you will not die—is as old as the temptation of Eve. It scored then and it still does.

Now warnings of dangers to health appear on cigarette packages. It is criminal to sell beer to minors. We all know how easily one becomes hooked and that once addicted the drug is very expensive, a cruel master, a deceitful thief—that it steals, enslaves, wastes, and destroys. *It costs more than you ever intended to pay.* The sexual revolution with its promiscuity and "if it feels good, do it counsel, now fears the HIV virus and AIDS. Warnings are everywhere. The warning from David's story of sin and death is not new, but it is always needed. *Sin will take you further than you want to go. It will keep you longer than you want to stay. It will cost you more than you ever intended to pay.*

Now, the rest of the story. David prayed for a new and a right relationship with God. He wanted to be reconciled. He sought mercy and forgiveness. This was his prayer: "Have mercy on me, O God, according to your steadfast love; according to your abundant mercy blot out my transgressions. Wash me thoroughly from my iniquity, and cleanse me from my sin. For I know my transgressions, and my sin is ever before me. Against you, you alone, have I sinned, and done what is evil in your sight. . . . You desire truth in the inward being; therefore teach me wisdom in my secret heart. Purge me with hyssop, and I shall be clean; wash me, and I shall be whiter than snow. . . . Create in me a clean heart, O God, and put a new and right spirit within me" (Ps. 51:1-10).

There is no way to get us innocent, but we can go from this place with a new beginning today. We can leave here with new resolve, with a new reach for righteousness, purity, and goodness. We can leave here with sins forgiven, and with a new and right spirit within. Let it be, O God, let it be.

Suggestions for Worship

Call to Worship (Eph. 3:15-19):

> LEADER: We kneel before the Father, from whom his whole family in heaven and on earth derives its name.

> **PEOPLE:** **We pray that out of his glorious riches he may strengthen us with power through his Spirit.**

> LEADER: So that Christ may dwell in our hearts through faith.

> **PEOPLE:** **That we may have power, together with all the saints, to grasp how wide and long and high and deep is the love of Christ.**

Act of Praise: Psalm 14.

Suggested Hymns: "I Need Thee Every Hour"; "I Want a Principle Within"; "Make Me a Captive, Lord."

Opening Prayer: Holy God, you have set before us the ways of righteousness and virtue. We confess that many times we have chosen to satisfy our desires and have failed to obey your will for our lives. Help us to learn from our foolishness and sin, the truths that will call us to lives of purity, faithfulness, and joy. Strengthen us so we can follow your will for us, we pray in the name Jesus Christ our Lord. Amen.

Pastoral Prayer: Gracious and merciful God, give us the grace and wisdom to truly repent of our sins. Inspire in the hearts of your servants, those affections and desires that will set aside and destroy the base imaginings and sinful thoughts that conflict with the truth and goodness of our Lord Jesus Christ. Help us to think on those things that are pure and true and lovely.

Free us from our fascination with sin. Keep us from the allurements of this world. Lead us not into temptation and deliver us from evil. O Holy God, cause us to see the hurt and shame that accompanies sin. Cause us to see the ugliness of lust and the ruthlessness of vice. Make us hate what is evil and love what is good.

Prompt within us, O God, a true reverence for righteousness. We do not pray only that we may do the right thing. We pray that we might be in such a right relationship with you, that we will honor what you honor, love what you love, and will hasten to obey our commandments and do your will.

Merciful God, you have promised forgiveness to all those who with true repentance turn to you. You remove sins as far as the east is from the west. You remember them no more. Help us to put all of our failure and sin behind us today. Through the grace of Christ, enable us to let it go. Let his redeeming grace make us clean and untarnished vessels, ready to be filled with the goodness of his love. Have mercy on us, O Christ. Have mercy on us. Amen.

JULY 31, 1994

□

Tenth Sunday After Pentecost

One need not encourage a desire for daily bread. Every good provider keeps at least one loaf in the house. Such bread gets old and moldy. We need the bread of always.

The Sunday Lessons

II Samuel 11:16–12:13a: King David was rebuked by the prophet Nathan for his adultery with Bathsheba. He told the famous parable of the ewe lamb. "He took the poor man's lamb, and prepared that" (v. 4). The king's anger was kindled against such a man, and he decreed that he deserved to die; and that he "restore the lamb fourfold" (v. 6). Nathan said to David, "You are the man!" (v. 7). The king repented.

Ephesians 4:1-16: For three chapters, Ephesians argues that we are justified by faith. The fourth chapter is the beginning of the ethical teaching of the letter. It is therefore goodness—not an imperative, and not a condition to be met—that is called forth by grace. Therefore, lead a life worthy of the calling to which you have been called. All Christians are to share in the spiritual gifts and virtues that will build up the body of Christ.

John 6:24-35: After recording the miraculous feeding of five thousand, John begins the Bread of Life discourse. Rebuking those concerned only with bread for their bellies ("Why do you labor for bread that perishes?") and encouraging the work of God ("This is the work of God, that you believe Jesus said, 'I am the bread of life; he who comes to me shall not hunger'").

Reflections

The priority for a hungry man is bread. The thing most needed by a thirsty woman is water. The bread lines filled with hungry people in times of economic need, and the employment agencies besieged by the unemployed underscore that reality—bread is

229

what we need. Not ethereal, nebulous, spiritual values, not something to believe, not even freedom to be. Staying alive today is what really matters.

Bread is solid stuff. It tastes. It is real. Therefore, we reason, "You can help a hungry child more with a peanut butter sandwich than with a prayer." But do not preach that. The church must be more concerned for the unconverted than it is for the unemployed.

Now we are faced with major shifts in the economies that support our standard of living. In America, every child has expected that his or her life would be better in material ways than that of the parents. Better houses, better comforts, better food, better clothing, and better employment opportunities have been taken for granted. But today a home and food as good or better than that of our childhood is, for many young persons, a lost dream and for others an uncertainty.

If our children move into such a wilderness without faith and values, they will be at fearful risk. Why do we labor for bread that perishes? (JKB)

A CALL TO CONFESSION

II Samuel 11:16–12:13a

A SERMON BY JOHN K. BERGLAND

High in the hills above Carmel Valley in California lives a man who watches over his sheep and writes about life and the world around him. In his book, *Thoughts While Tending Sheep* (New York: Crown Publishers, Inc., 1988), Willard "Tex" Ilefeldt records his response to visitors who are horrified at the thought of innocent lambs being butchered. Charmed by a flock of lambs that leap and gambol, like a bunch of kids at recess, they ask, "You don't slaughter them, do you?"

He wants to respond, "Man does not live by bread alone." Roasted lamb has been the main course in the Middle East for centuries. But, knowing this is not what Jesus meant to imply with the words, he resists and lets them "go on thinking lamb chops are stamped out by machines in the back rooms of supermarkets. I let them go on denying reality because I often deny it myself; which, I suppose, is also one of nature's ways of helping us endure those things which we wish were otherwise."

This is the truth! One of our favorite ways of dealing with things we wish were otherwise is to pretend they never happened. Denial is the human weakness addressed by true confession. As a minister of Jesus Christ, I often let folks go on denying reality, because I often deny it myself. We all act as though sin never happened.

The prophet Nathan demonstrates a different approach to sin in his confrontation with King David. Displeased by David's adultery with Bathsheba, his deceit and murderous treachery in the killing of her husband Uriah, God sent Nathan to tell David that he had sinned, and that his innocent child would die. "Death (the sword of violence) will not depart your house," was the harsh warning God wanted David to hear. When Nathan delivered the message, he wrapped it in a story.

His familiar parable of the stolen, slaughtered lamb begins, "The rich man had very many flocks and herds; but the poor man had nothing but one little ewe lamb." It grew up with him and with his children.

Tex Ilefeldt describes a lamb like that. "Nearly every year there is at least one little lamb that becomes quite friendly . . . he will butt me in an affectionate way, usually only a gentle nudge of its head, inviting me to touch it back." Then came the day when he "had to face the reality of having a close friend put down. It's bad enough to witness the death of any creature in the springtime of life, but it is worse when it is one that has come to trust you." His wife, Louise, gave up naming them. The poor man's lamb of Nathan's parable, would "drink from his cup, and lie in his bosom, and it was like a daughter to him" (II Sam. 12:3).

When a traveler came to visit the rich man, the host did not want to slaughter one of his own flock (we do not want our own to die), so he prepared the poor man's lamb for their dinner. When King David heard the story he was outraged. "The man who has done this deserves to die," he said. That is when God's prophet looked him square in the eye and said, "You are the man! It's you David. You have done this selfish, ruthless thing."

God had made David king. He had saved his life and given him the throne of Saul. David had the love of wives and the loyalty of both Israel and Judah, the whole territory of Palestine. "And if that had been too little, I would have added as much more," said the Lord God. "Why have you dispised my word? You have struck down Uriah and taken his wife." David was confronted with the reality of his adultery, deceit, and murderous treachery. David had to face his sin.

And now before God, to whom no secrets are hid, I, as servant of God's Word, must proclaim this truth to you. It is not kindness, it is not goodness; it is not mercy to deny what has really happened, and is still happening. It is not the least bit gracious to pretend that we are innocent.

There is no way to get this crowd innocent today. We do not need to review the catalogue of sins to know that "we have all sinned and come short of the glory of God." "All we, like sheep, have gone astray." "There is none righteous. No not one." There is no way to get this preacher innocent. And there is no way to get you innocent, my dear sister, my dear brother. You are the man! You are the woman! And there is a better way than denial for dealing with the things we wish were otherwise.

If we cannot be innocent, we can be this: We can be responsibly guilty. David's response to the prophet's reproof was to confess his sin. "I have sinned against the Lord," he said. He did not blame anyone else, did not try to get the woman to share his guilt by suggesting that she had enticed him. (That was Adam's ploy: The woman gave me the fruit.) He did not make any empty speeches wishing it had not happened, wishing he could bring Uriah back to life. He could not be right before God, but he could be forthright—and he was. He simply said, "I've sinned. I've sinned against God."

A man, found guilty of murder in the first degree, spoke to the court before he was sentenced. His speech was filled with a lot of unreal wishing. "A lot of things happened that shouldn't have happened. I wish they hadn't happened," he said. Then speaking of the man he had killed, he pined, "Many, many times I've wished that I could bring him back, but I can't." David didn't try to undo what was done. There were no empty wishes in his meeting with the Lord God. God knew and he knew that the whole messy affair was a done deal. He made a full confession.

Father Philip Leach writes, "I want us to focus on one fear that so often controls our lives as Christians . . . We are afraid to go to confession." Noting that it was a little easier for Roman Catholics to confess to a priest hidden behind a screen, he says that some find reason to be afraid "now that the church asks us to celebrate the sacrament of penance 'face to face.'" He goes on to tell of his first full confession. "I told him *everything* . . . all those things that I had never wanted to admit to myself, much less to any other living person." And he writes that he was "set free from all those fears and anxieties that had controlled me."

I remember my first full confession, made before God and with the guiding counsel of a good minister of Jesus Christ. I had sought—or perhaps it was arranged—a series of counseling sessions with my mentor in a course on pastoral care. After several sessions he did something that I found completely disarming. He told me about a tragic failure in his own life. I remember thinking, "Wow! If *they* knew about that they would never let him be a teacher in theological school." But his conversations with me had become so candid and honest, that denying the reality of any failure, deceit, or sin was unthinkable. And so it was, at a later session scheduled for 7:00 in the morning, I was to "make my first full confession." I began haltingly, speaking in broad generalities. But the more guilt I confessed, the more I wanted to be rid of all of it. The more that I shared the fragile things of my life with this minister and friend, the more he seemed to care for me, and for my soul. There was no curiosity, no probing, no surprise, no excuses, no denial. I can't remember if it was a long time or a short time, but when it was over, he turned from the window— how gracious it was for him not to look hard at me—and said, "God loves you. Always has. Always will. Now just let it go." I found the power of penance that day, and the sweet land of beginning again.

Have you ever made a first confession? Have you ever heard in a deeply personal way John Wesley's probing question, "What sins have you committed since last we met?" Have you found the courage and discovered the reality of being responsibly guilty? I think many of you have and some more of you will. I have been your preacher. Now let me be your priest and declare for all who truly and earnestly repent of your sin, "God loves you. God loves you very much."

The prophet Nathan's last words to David were, "Now the Lord has put away your sin." It causes me to remember another of John Wesley's compelling questions. "Have you found the grace of God for it?" Psalm 51, David's psalm after being confronted by Nathan, begins: "Have mercy on me, O God, according to your steadfast love; according to your abundant mercy blot out my transgressions. Wash me thoroughly from my iniquity, and cleanse me from my sin." The psalm, always the consolation of sinners, concludes: "The sacrifice acceptable to God is a broken spirit; a broken and contrite heart, O God, you will not despise." David's sin did not determine his destiny. His experience of God's mercy, his passionate love for God, his freedom found through forgiveness are a benediction to us all.

There was a fraternity hazing on the campus of a large university that turned tragic. Pledges were being taught humility and obedience and were told to always respect the decisions of their seniors. To make the point more memorable the pledges were lined up across a country road just beneath the crest of a hill. They were told that a car, driven by a fraternity brother, would soon come speeding over that hill. But they were ordered not to move until they heard the command, "Jump!" They were to trust themselves to their fraternity brothers.

The car crested the hill and sped toward them. At seemingly the last safe second, they heard the order, "Jump!" and they all ran to safety—all except one. He stood there frozen in fear. The last thing he saw was the anguish in the face of the young man driving the car.

After the death there were investigations, court hearings, and legal decisions. Hazing was forbidden and the fraternity was censored. The young man who was driving the car left school for a while, intending to take some incompletes and not fail any courses. He started fresh the next semester, but soon dropped out completely. Later he enrolled in a local college, and again he failed. He was not able to keep a job. His life story was a history of unfulfilled dreams, broken relationships, disappointments, divorce, alcohol, drugs, loneliness, and self-hate.

One evening, when he sat alone in the squalor of the slum apartment where he stayed, there was a knock at the door. He opened it to see an elderly woman standing there looking deep into his eyes. Her eyes were filled with tears. "Will you forgive me?" she asked. "I am the mother of the boy killed in the hazing. All these years I have followed you with my hatred. I've hoped you would fail at everything, and I've been glad when you did. But recently, through therapy and God's mercy, I've been set free from that hatred. Please forgive me."

Long months later, on the other side of addiction and in a place of wholeness and promise, a man, now made new said, "And in her eyes I saw freedom—freedom to be the kind of man I might have been, if it never would have happened."

The most compelling words of the story of Nathan's confrontation with David are these: "Now the Lord has put away your sin." If this story is your story, as it is my story, let these words be for you. "The Lord has put away your sin!" Amen.

Suggestions for Worship

Call to Worship (Eph. 4:3-6):

LEADER:	Make every effort to keep the unity of the Spirit through the bond of peace.
PEOPLE:	**There is one body and one Spirit—we were called to one hope.**
LEADER:	One Lord, one faith, one baptism;
PEOPLE:	**One God and Father of all, who is over all and through all and in all.**

Act of Praise: Psalm 51:1-12.

Suggested Hymns: "I Love to Tell the Story"; "Pass It On"; "A Charge to Keep I Have."

Opening Prayer: Merciful God, we have disobeyed your will, and disregarded your love. Confront us today with our failure and sin, and make us know the harm and hurt of it all. But do not forsake us, we pray. Lead us to a true confession of sin, and then help us to realize the full meaning of sins nailed to the cross of Christ. Have mercy on us, O Christ. Amen.

Pastoral Prayer: Gracious Father, you supply all our needs through our Lord and Savior, Jesus Christ. Therefore, teach us the prayer:

> that is relief to a burdened spirit,
> that can set a prisoner free,
> that restores a sinner,
> that heals a broken heart.

Teach us the prayer:

> that makes right the things that are wrong,
> that gives hope to the lost,
> that is wisdom for kings,
> that gathers the wayward,
> that reveals salvation.

O Risen Christ, teach us the prayer:

> that brings your blessing,
> that makes us truly fulfilled,
> that adds no sorrow,
> that makes us one with you now and forever. Amen. (JKB)

AUGUST 7, 1994

□

Eleventh Sunday After Pentecost

True life, that was before the beginning and lives beyond the end, is nourished by the bread of heaven. It is this strength of holy bread we need.

The Sunday Lessons

II Samuel 18:5-9, 15, 31-33: When Joab led King David's warriors out to fight against the rebellion of his son, Absalom, it was with the words, "Deal gently for my sake with the young man Absalom" (v. 5). There was a son who wanted his father dead. There was a father who wanted his son to live. Absalom was killed. When the news of his son's death reached David he wept openly saying, "O my son Absalom, my son . . . Would I had died instead of you" (v. 33).

Ephesians 4:25–5:2: Conduct that befits our calling as children of God is set forth in immediate and practical ways such as: "speak the truth" (v. 25), "do not let the sun go down on your anger" (v. 26). Christ is the great example. "Be imitators of God . . . and live in love, as Christ loved us and gave himself up for us, a fragrant offering and sacrifice to God" (v. 1).

John 6:35, 41-51: This reading is central to John's discourse on the Bread of Life. It is the Father who sent Christ as bread from heaven. Faith is also the gift of God. "No one can come to me unless drawn by the Father who sent me" (v. 44). "Whoever eats of this bread will live forever" (v. 51). The relationship of faith and Eucharist is set forth. "The bread that I will give for the life of the world is my flesh" (v. 51).

Reflections

A young woman, reflecting on this bread of heaven that satisfies all hunger mused, "It feels good—this idea of being always full. It's probably pretty peaceful. But it bothers me, too. I like to order for myself; to pick out my own groceries. This bread of heaven arrangement sounds like I really have to leave myself open—take what I get. Is there any guarantee that I'm going to like the taste?"

To be sure, bread of heaven is said to be better than all other breads. It is from God. So is the appetite for it. Taught to like it by God, the creature craves it and comes to it like a cat comes to a dead herring.

We cannot devise other nourishment to desire, so rare, so perfect, as the gifts that God so freely gives—from the single living cell, to a field of wheat, a sunrise, a newborn baby, love one for another, and the bread of Christ. And this bread is not temporary. It is always. Whoever eats this bread will live forever.

Often persons come to faith out of great personal loss or pain. They are left with an emptiness and hunger so demanding that they just are not picky. When you are truly hungry you will eat almost anything that is set before you. Then, growing stronger and becoming satisfied, we are inclined to want it our way.

One thing is needful. A singular hunger for the presence of the risen Christ. How blest are those who hunger so. (JKB)

YOU ARE WHAT YOU EAT

John 6:35, 41-51

A SERMON BY EDITH L. GLEAVES

Have you had your loaf of bread this week? According to the American Institute of Baking, the average American consumed fifty-and-a-half pounds of bread last year, and this year is projected to eat over half a pound more! This does not even include wonderful items like cakes, pies, cookies, and doughnuts! We eat more bread in this country than any other single item, and we eat more bread than any other country in this world.

You have probably heard the popular saying, "you are what you eat." You know, that really is a principle of life. It says our bodies are nourished and built up by what we put in them. With all the breads we consume, it is amazing that more of us do not resemble the Pillsbury doughboy or doughgirl! It is almost an inherent thing to consume plenty of bread. Bread is known as the staff of life. It is the stuff of our physical lives. It is basic to life. Whole grain bread provides essential vitamins and minerals our bodies need to survive. In these modern times, bread still is the most widely eaten food, and it provides a larger share of people's energy and protein than any other food.

This was true for people in Jesus' day, too. At the time of our text, Jesus had just performed the miracle of feeding the five thousand men, plus women and children. He had blessed and multiplied two fishes and five barley loaves of bread that a young boy had brought for lunch. Immediately after the miracle, Jesus went into the mountain alone because he knew the crowd would attempt to take him by force to make him their king. They realized that here was one who could give them all the bread they would need, even until they were full and satisfied. With Jesus as king, they need no longer worry about having this essential of life. Because he could offer them bread, he could in a sense offer them life. So the crowd went searching for him in Capernaum.

It has been said that humanity is divided into two classes— those who are looking for food and those who are looking for an appetite. Jesus knew that they wanted food, but he responded by making them aware of a more important appetite. He offered them the bread that would satisfy that hunger. He spoke to them of himself using a metaphor as basic to their day-to-day existence as the bread they sought. Jesus said "I am the bread of life. Whoever comes to me will never be hungry, and whoever believes in me will never be thirsty."

A tragedy occurred at one of our beautiful local beaches not too long ago. A woman and some friends went down to the beach for a religious ritual. She was buried in the sand—completely covered—with a plastic bag over her head and a tubular device in her mouth through which was she to breathe. The purpose of this process was to purify her, make her whole and new, enable her to better live in harmony with nature, people, and God. When she came up out of the sand, it was to be like a resurrection from the old life. She was to arise cleansed from impurities to a new life. When her friends went back to dig her out several hours later, they noticed immediately that something was not right. They dug her out as quickly as possible, but they were too late. She had regurgitated into the plastic bag, choked, and suffocated. Her hunger, acted out in this search for new life, ended in death. Her thirst for cleansing from impurities found no quenching on the shores of the vast ocean waters.

There is a hunger more fundamental to each of us than that for food. There is a thirst we experience that demands quenching that drink cannot satisfy. It is a hunger for love, joy, and peace. It is a thirst for purpose, meaning, and direction. It is a yearning for cleansing, wholeness, and health. Augustine speaks of it as the restless searching of the soul, whose quest for rest is in vain until it finds its rest in God.

The principle that we are what we eat, also applies to spiritual food. What we take into our spirits determines who we are spiritually. "I am that living bread that comes down from heaven," Jesus tells us. We need Christ as much as we need food. At life's most basic, fundamental essence, our hunger and thirst is satisfied only in Jesus Christ. As bread gives the essentials to the body to sustain life, Christ gives the essentials of life to the spirit. Christ **is** life, and he gives us himself.

What does it mean to feed on Jesus Christ? How can we eat of his flesh and drink of his blood? Eating flesh and drinking blood were repulsive thoughts to the Jew. It was associated with the prevalent pagan practices of sacrificing animals to the gods. The gods were believed to inhabit the offerings. The worshipers would consume the flesh and blood, thereby taking in the very essence of the god. Living under the influence of that god, they believed they had found salvation and safety. Even in Jewish thought, blood stood for life. Life was understood to ebb away with the loss of blood. It may sound repulsive, primitive, and ridiculous to the sophisticated and sensitive modern-day ear. Yet, this metaphor is nothing less than the meaning of true discipleship, the secret of Christian faith and Christian living.

Not everyone who heard Jesus accepted his metaphor or message then. So it is today. When offered the bread of life, some prefer to starve. A pastor told me of a young man he had been visiting in the hospital. This young man had lived a dissolute life and his life-style resulted in a terminal illness. As he lay dying, he said to his pastor "There was a time I considered giving my life to Jesus Christ, but I put it off. I wanted to live life like I wanted to. Now, as I lie here I discover I can't give my life to him. I find I simply don't care." Sometimes, when we are ill we lose our physical appetites and turn away from food. Those who are ill spiritually, indeed who are dead spiritually, have lost their appetite for God. They turn away from the very food that will give them life. They are like the ones described by the prophet Isaiah in chapter 53 who when they looked upon the Messiah, saw no beauty that they should desire him. Yet, he was wounded for our transgressions, bruised for our iniquities, and on him was the chastisement that made us whole. We have healing and salvation for our souls because of what he did for us on the cross.

In her book, *A Gift for God*, Mother Teresa gives good expression to what it means to eat of this heavenly bread. "Put yourself completely under the influence of Jesus, so that he may think his thoughts in your mind, do his work through your hands, for you will be all powerful with him to strengthen you." Our Gospel texts offers the way to eat of this bread in manageable portions. First, in order to eat—realize that God calls us! It is the grace of God that gives us the hunger, the appetite for God. We respond to the divine initiative that is always at work. Not only does God call us, God draws us. God is always seeking that we might come closer. We do well to remember during the good times, and when we go through difficult times, that God allows these experiences in the hope they will draw us closer to God. Second, we eat of this bread when we acknowledge God saves us. There is a story of a yacht that was sinking somewhere off the east coast. The captain of the yacht radioed the Coast Guard. This captain also was a very famous financier, but he was in dire straits. The Coast Guard spoke reassuringly—we'll come and get you. What's your position? The man said "I'm president of the board of First National Trust." No matter what position we do or do not hold in this world, if we are without Christ then we are in a desperate position. We are lost and in need of rescue. How wonderful it is that God opens our eyes to the example of Christ that we can see. How marvelous it is that God opens our ears to hear the Word and believe! Because of God's love for us, we can receive Jesus Christ and abundant life, now and for eternity. Finally, we eat of this bread when we understand that God alone truly satisfies. Our life with God is not one of a long face and protracted sighs. It is one of joy and victory! Do we not know that it gives God great joy to give us fullness of life! We can rest in the assurance that when we face a mountain too high to climb God will make a way. When it is too wide to go around, God will make a way. When there is no way to go through, God will make a way. The Lord renews our exhausted inner strength, gives us resources we never dreamed were there, and fills our lives with vitality. We are given the power to be more than we are. We are given power to be all that Christ calls us to be. When we eat bread and are full, we want no more—we literally cannot stomach it. But the more we eat our fill of God in Jesus Christ, the more we want to be filled. The greater our hunger for God, the greater is our capacity to receive God. The more God draws us into God, the deeper we will be drawn into God.

It is possible for the body to exist on bread and water alone, for they provide the essentials of life. But Jesus warns us that humanity cannot live by bread alone. Life without Christ is merely existence without the essence of life. God has brought Christ graciously near, and made him more available to us than the bread we eat. We are what we eat—let us feast on the Bread of Life!

Suggestions for Worship

Call to Worship (Ps. 130:1-5):

LEADER: Out of the depths I cry to you, O LORD;

PEOPLE: **O LORD, hear my voice. Let your ears be attentive to my cry for mercy.**

LEADER: If you, O LORD, kept a record of sins, O Lord, who could stand? But with you there is forgiveness; therefore you are feared.

PEOPLE: **I wait for the LORD, my soul waits, and in his word I put my hope.**

Act of Praise: Psalm 130.

Suggested Hymns: "Guide Me, O Thou Great Jehovah"; "Savior, Like a Shepherd Lead Us"; "Amazing Grace."

Opening Prayer: Dear heavenly Father, we confess that we have not always been ready to hear your word. We have not always been open to receive the bread and water of life that is in Christ Jesus our Lord. Give us ears to hear today, and grace to accept those spiritual blessings that nourish and sustain our souls now and forever. In the name of Christ, we pray. Amen. (JKB)

Pastoral Prayer: Gracious God, Give us of the living bread that we may never hunger. Let us drink that we may never thirst again. Let us be filled by your life, so that your life can be full in us. God, be in our head and in our understanding. Be in our eyes, and in our looking. Be in our mouth, and in all our speaking. Be in our heart, and in our thinking. And God be at our end, at our departing, receiving us unto yourself, and raise us on the last day. In the name of the Living Bread, we pray. Amen.

AUGUST 14, 1984

□

Twelfth Sunday After Pentecost

God is among us. Full of grace. Full of truth. One of the visible expressions of that Presence is the partaking of bread that becomes our very life. It is nearer than breathing.

The Sunday Lessons

I Kings 2:10-12, 3:3-14: When King David died, his son, Solomon, "sat on the throne of his father" (v. 12). As the new king of Israel, he prayed for wisdom. He loved the Lord and followed his commandments. The Lord appeared to Solomon in a dream and said, "Ask what I should give you" (v. 5). He asked for an understanding mind and was given, along with wisdom, both riches and honor.

Ephesians 5:15-20: Continuing the exhortation to be imitators of Christ, the Ephesians letter counsels wisdom. "Mak[e] the most of the time, because the days are evil. So do not be foolish, but understand what the will of the Lord is" (vv. 16-17).

John 6:51-58: "My flesh is true food and my blood is true drink. Those who eat my flesh and drink my blood abide in me" (vv. 55-56). The Word made flesh announced in John's prologue is now offered in immediate and very present terms. It is to become a part of our bodies as we partake of Christ's flesh and blood in Holy Communion. For some, such intimacy is shocking and abhorrent. "How can this man give us his flesh to eat?" (v. 52).

Reflections

"Just don't get serious" is the counsel given teenagers in their first fragile attempt at personal relationships. Intimacy is volatile stuff and deep involvement leaves permanent scars.

Some folks never want to get serious. Afraid of intimacy, they fantasize and tease and then devalue the idea of flesh being one. Sexual activity is the dominant motif of intimacy in our culture.

There is nothing more immediately present and intimate than this—"eat my flesh and drink my blood and so abide in me." That is getting close. Very close!

For some, it is too close. They look for space and find a bit by spiritualizing the reality. Others achieve the distance they want by analyzing, labeling, and categorizing the elemental stuff and so only think about it. Most of us just do not get serious.

Some impetuous young person, about to plunge headlong into faith and service, is likely to be cautioned, "Don't get too involved. It's O.K. to go to church and youth fellowship and even a retreat. You might even want to give some money and mow the church lawn. Just don't get too serious about it."

God was serious about the world. He sent his only Son. Christ is serious about you—about being very present in your very body and your very life. "The bread that I will give for the life of the world is my flesh." (JKB)

LIVING BREAD

John 6:51-58

A SERMON BY ROBERT ERIC BERGLAND

From July 25th through August 22nd, next Sunday, the Gospel lessons have come from the sixth chapter of John. There is enough bread in this chapter to supply an entire bakery! Today is the fourth bread Sunday, so what more appropriate way for us to celebrate it than to make bread.

This is a rather unusual sermon to hear and see on a Sunday morning: the dough for a loaf actually being prepared, but all that is done symbolizes God's real presence and action in our lives.

In his book, *Sunday Dinner*, Will Willimon remembers when he began teaching worship at Duke Divinity School. He asked a Roman Catholic liturgical scholar at another seminary to give him some advice on how to excite Protestant seminarians about the rich possibilities for the sacrament of the Lord's Supper. "You should begin by teaching cooking classes," he was advised. Willimon confesses his astonishment. "What would that have to do with the Lord's Supper?" The scholar explained, "Because, they will never lead the Eucharist with conviction until they first learn the joy of giving food to hungry people."

He is right. We are hungry people: We hunger to have our empty lives filled with living bread. We are thirsty for living water that will quench our brokenness. So today, we prepare the dough for a loaf of bread to be broken and shared at the Lord's Supper.

We come to a table where the vessels to prepare are set to provide this bread of life. (*Enter one who will prepare recipe.*) All is ready. The recipe has been handed down—like the traditions and teachings of the church—so we will remember who we are, so we will be nurtured and given guidance in our journey as Christians. There is a bowl for the ingredients to be prepared, much like our Sunday school. And a board for the dough to be kneaded, much like we often struggle and work through our own doubts and questions, so that faith will be strong. All is ready. (*Choir sings first stanza of hymn, "Become to Us the Living Bread."*)

In preparing dough for bread there must be leaven—that ingredient that will make the dough be alive and rise. We know the leaven as yeast. (*Prepare the yeast and add to bowl.*) The apostle Paul reminds us in I Corinthians 5:6-7, "Do you not know that a little yeast leavens the whole batch of dough? Clean out the old yeast so that you may be a new batch, as you really are unleavened." The yeast symbolizes the presence of the Holy Spirit that brings us life and renews us as the body of Christ.

There is a basic ingredient in preparing bread dough that we all know: It is the flour. (*Bring flour forward and give to preparer.*) In it we are reminded of God's wonderful creation, how he created the heavens and the earth and placed man and woman in the midst of it and gave them dominion over it. Through sin we were cast from the garden and told that "By the sweat of your face you shall eat bread," (Gen. 3:19a). Yet, we can approach the table through the gracious gift of God's Son, Jesus, who said, "I am the bread of life . . . so that one may eat of it and not die."

Another ingredient for our loaf is salt. (*Bring salt forward and give to preparer.*) Salt checks the action of yeast and gives flavor and wholeness to the loaf. In our lives as Christians we are reminded of the words of Jesus. "You are the salt of the earth; but if salt has lost its taste, how shall its saltness be restored? It is no longer good for anything except to be thrown out and trodden under foot by men." Remember, you are the salt that gives flavor and wholeness to the body.

Sugar is an ingredient in our loaf that also acts with the yeast to bring life to dough. (*Child brings sugar and gives to preparer.*) The body of Christ, the church is made up of people of all ages. Yet, so often we neglect the care and nurture of our children. We put them in a place where they will not be heard or seen. Remember these words of Jesus, "Let the children come to me, do not hinder them, for to such belongs the Kingdom of Heaven." Our children offer a life giving aspect to the body we cannot forget.

There is a special ingredient that we will add to our loaf—cinnamon. (*Bring cinnamon to preparer.*) Our life as the body of Christ is diverse. Each of us brings something that is very special to the community of faith that adds to the richness of it, yet we are one through our baptism. Paul reminds us of that in Galatians 3:27-28—"As many of you as were baptized into Christ have clothed yourselves with Christ. There is no longer Jew or Greek, there is no longer slave or free, there is no longer male or female; for all of you are one in Christ Jesus."

Shortening provides texture and a keeping quality to our loaf. (*Bring shortening to preparer.*) It is a quality that can be likened to the love that Christ calls us to. "Love one another as I have loved you." We are reminded as the shortening is mixed with the other ingredients, "In this is love, not that we loved God but that he loved us and sent his Son to be the atoning sacrifice for our sins. Beloved, since God loved us so much, we also ought to love one another" (I John 4:10-11).

The final ingredient is water. (*Bring water to preparer.*) We are knit together through our baptism. Water symbolizes that washing away of sin. We are reminded in the baptismal liturgy how water has been a significant symbol throughout the movement of our faith. In the beginning, when there was nothing but chaos, God swept across the dark waters and brought forth light. In the days of Noah, God saved those on the ark through water. The children of Israel were led from captivity to freedom through the sea and were brought through the Jordan to the promised land. In the fullness of time, God sent Jesus, nurtured in the water of a womb. He was baptized by John, and called his disciples to share in the baptism of his death and resurrection. So we bring the water and are reminded once more of our baptism.

What do we do now with this lump of dough? It will be kneaded and will be allowed to rise and then it will be baked so it may be shared at this table once more. It will take time. But isn't that also a quality of our lives as Christians? It takes time—to build community, to discern discipleship, to grow in faithfulness.

Jesus said, "This is the bread that came down from heaven . . . the one who eats this bread, will live forever." Amen.

Suggestions for Worship

Call to Worship (Ps. 111):

LEADER: Great are the works of the LORD; they are pondered by all who delight in them.

PEOPLE: Glorious and majestic are his deeds, and his righteousness endures forever.

LEADER: The fear of the LORD is the beginning of wisdom; all who follow his precepts have good understanding.

PEOPLE: To him belongs eternal praise.

Act of Praise: Psalm 111.

Suggested Hymns: "I'll Praise My Maker While I've Breath"; "God of the Sparrow, God of the Whale"; "What Wondrous Love Is This."

Opening Prayer: Eternal and almighty God, you do not need our worship, yet you desire it. You do not need our service, yet you enlist it. You do not need our companionship, yet you invite us into your holy presence. Therefore, it is with thanksgiving and gratitude that we bow before you in prayer; that we stand before you in praise; that we wait to learn your will for our lives. Bless our meeting today with the power and presence of your spirit. In Christ's name we pray. Amen. (JKB)

Pastoral Prayer: O God, you are from eternity to eternity and not set in one place at one time. O God, you are before and beyond every day and your immensity cannot be contained in the heaven of heavens, much less in the small arenas of our lives.

We now seek to know our destinies as your children. We are poor, we are weak, we are mortal. Yet, you have made us in your image. In our frail flesh, you have placed a longing for eternal life.

Please God, in this small room and in this short hour, give living bread. Turn us away from all that is transient. Save us from trusting in things that cannot save. Drive from among us all earthbound gods and be for us, today, the bread of life. Amen.

AUGUST 21, 1994

□

Thirteenth Sunday After Pentecost

Confronted by hard choices, we often choose what is comfortable and deny that which holds the promise of life.

The Sunday Lessons

I Kings 8:22-30, 41-43: Solomon's prayer at the dedication of the temple acknowledges that "even heaven and the highest heaven cannot contain you, much less this house that I have built" (v. 27). He pleads that all who pray in this holy temple, even the foreigner, will be heard and find mercy.

Ephesians 6:10-20: "Put on the whole armor of God, so that you may be able to stand against the wiles of the devil" (v. 11). The battle is not against flesh and blood, but against principalities and powers and spiritual hosts of wickedness. Pray at all times, Paul counsels.

John 6:56-69: Offended by the hard saying, "my flesh is true food" (v. 55), and his claim to be from God, many disciples drew back and did not follow Christ. When Jesus asked the twelve, "Do you also wish to go away?" (v. 67). Simon Peter answered, "Lord, to whom can we go? You have the words of eternal life . . . You are the Holy One of God" (vv. 68-69).

Reflections

Bertrand Russell noticed "a strange strained sadness" in the eyes of apes at the zoo when they were not occupied with cracking nuts or trapeze gymnastics. He imagined that "they feel they ought to become men, but cannot discover the secret of how to do it . . . They have lost their way." Then he speaks of that same strain and anguish in the soul of civilized man. "He knows there is something better than himself almost within his grasp. Yet he does not know where to seek it or how to find it."

250

The gospel offers Christ as that best way. He is the revelation of God and the source of abundant life. Many have come close enough to hear and see but have turned away.

It is sad to see one who has been given freedom return to prison, to see one taken from ignorance disregard the hard won insights of civilized enlightenment and embrace superstition and fear once more. It is hard to see a people achieve opportunity for some of their poor and despised races, only to see oppression gain power again. We despair when war shatters a hard won peace.

Yet, this is always the possibility. Faced with choices we may go forward or turn away. We may choose to be merely of this world when we could choose life in Christ. Russell is right. There is something better than ourselves within our reach. Will you choose so little and lose so much?

But it is also true that there is no regression for truth. Its dawning is always a point of no return. (JKB)

GOD'S PROTECTION PLAN

Ephesians 6:10-20

A SERMON BY SCOTT J. JONES

Miss Hannigan is a wicked woman. In the movie *Annie* she is the evil administrator of the orphanage where the little girls live. With her brother, Rooster, and his girlfriend, Lil, she plans a fradulent scheme to get a lot of money fast. Using Miss Hannigan's information about Annie, Rooster and Lil plan to pose as Annie's parents and claim the reward from Daddy Warbucks. They will get rich quickly, they think, and so they sing "Easy Street." The song tells how wonderful it will be when they are rich, how luxuriously they will live, and how easy it is to get there by cutting a few moral corners. Life is great on easy street, and they will get there easily. The only problem? Their scheme fails, and easy street becomes hard labor as they are arrested for fraud.

The illusion of easy street is far too common among us today. It underlies all kinds of get-rich-quick schemes, from selling drugs to bank fraud. Gambling has become more widely acceptable, and is even sponsored by state governments. When our states sponsor lotteries, we are simply sending the message that people should quit working hard, quit getting educated, and start playing the odds to get rich quick.

The image of easy street even abounds among some Christians who proclaim that belonging to Christ will mean the end of their troubles. They say it is the quick way to put everything right. Some go so far to say that in exchange for a contribution, prosperity and health will quickly follow. In Dallas, Texas, one television evangelist promises, in the name of God, that sufficient faith will always lead to healing and wealth. The prosperity gospel brought the unusual step of a government investigation into the evangelist's preaching because of the possibility of fraud.

The God of the Bible promises something entirely different from easy street. The God of Abraham, Moses, Deborah—the one who sent Jesus as our Lord and Savior—that God promises to walk with you through the valley of the shadow of death in such a way that you will fear no evil, and that you will be comforted. God does not promise that you will have no enemies, but God does promise to set a banqueting table for you in the midst of your enemies. With all the difficulties that life inevitably brings, believers in God will be able to say, "Surely goodness and mercy shall follow me all the days of my life, and I shall dwell in the house of the LORD my whole life long" (Ps. 23:6).

The letter to the Ephesians makes our Christian situation abundantly clear. Being a Christian is not easy street. We are not invited to follow a Lord who made it as a big success and achieved fame, riches, or honor. Instead, Jesus "did not regard equality with God as something to be exploited, but emptied himself, taking the form of a slave, being born in human likeness. And being found in human form, he humbled himself and became obedient to the point of death—even death on a cross" (Phil. 2:6-8). We are invited not to a life of material prosperity and ease, but to "take up [our] crosses and follow" Christ (Matt. 16:24). We are told that we are enlisting in a fight that is not against normal, everyday people, but against the spiritual hosts of wickedness that plague us and all of humankind.

Sin has an infectious character that can never be quite contained and prevented from spreading. Racism plagues our country, and rears its ugly head in both personal and institutional forms. Greed infects both our business practices and our political lives. Atheism and materialism affect our views of the world so that we think that God no longer matters and prayer no longer works. Young people are convinced that the pleasures of today are more important than the consequences of tomorrow. Disease, tragedy, and death take away our health, our well-being, and even life itself.

Against such foes we are given spiritual help as a gift from God. Ephesians tells us that in this spirtual warfare, we do not count only on our own strength and abilities. Most importantly, we are given God's armor for protection in this spiritual warfare. Ephesians gives us a list of several gifts from God that protect us.

Your loins are girded with truth. Ephesians has in mind a leather apron worn by Roman soldiers that protect the midsection of their bodies. The truth is seen as covering your vital organs, because the most powerful form of spiritual evil is the lie. There are lies about happiness, lies about God and religion, and lies about particular circumstances. We tell ourselves the big lies about what life is all about, what constitutes happiness, and what we ourselves are really like in God's eyes. People rarely choose evil things for the sake of evil, but because they have been duped by the false presentations that evil makes. As a protection, Jesus tells us "you will know the truth, and the truth will make you free" (John 8:32).

Righteousness is a breastplate, and salvation is your helmet. Through faith, God's righteousness becomes our righteousness. We are covered by the atoning blood of Jesus and saved from guilt, fear, and anxiety. When temptations come, our trust in God and commitment to God's kingdom protect us from caving in to their pressure. The helmet of salvation means that we are protected from doubts about who we are and whose we are.

Far too often the world sends negative messages. The boss comes in and chews you out. Not only did you do a bad job last week, but you are a bad employee and, by implication, a bad person who is not worth very much. Maybe it is not your boss, but a customer or a teacher or a student. When those negative messages come, salvation is a helmet that can ward off the blows. The poster of the poor child is right: "I know I'm somebody, because God don't make no junk." Because of the righteousness of Christ and the gift of salvation, we know the love of God in our lives.

In a world filled with conflict, the gospel of peace is on your feet. Peace is the message of the reign of God. Peace means wholeness, restoration of relationships, and the love that should exist between God and humanity, and between people. We carry the message of peace into situations where everyone else sees only conflict.

In 1973, a group of demonstrators from the American Indian movement took over the village of Wounded Knee to dramatize the cause of Native Americans. They were heavily armed and were soon surrounded by heavily armed law enforcement officers determined to end the protest. John Adams, a United Methodist minister, came there to mediate the dispute. Among widespread predictions of violence and bloodshed, Adams patiently served as a conduit for negotiations between the two sides. He literally rode a horse from one group to another because no other form of communication between them was possible. The seige lasted seventy days, but only the violence was much less than many people predicted. Picture, if you will, a lonely man riding a windswept prairie between implacable enemies bent on killing. His mission was the gospel of peace. If it had not been for him, great bloodshed would have taken place.

So many times, ordinary Christians are like John Adams. They work with a troubled family, or in the office, or at a school, and are agents for reconciliation between people who appear to hate each other. These peacemakers are called to carry the same message so that peace can replace conflict, love can replace hatred, and anger can turn to contentment.

Faith is a shield that turns back the flaming darts of evil. When you are up to your neck in alligators, it is hard to remember that your orignial objective was to drain the swamp. Because of our faith in Christ, we know that the swamp will be drained someday. We have read the book and we know the end of the battle. Our job is to get rid of the alligators and drain our portion of it as God enables us to do it. We seek the little victories, knowing that the total victory has already been won.

For offensive capability you have the sword of the Spirit, the word of God. The Spirit gives you words to say when you do not know what to say. Life in the spirit of God is a life of prayer, a life of study of God's written word in the Bible. It becomes a spiritual weapon to push back evil and to defeat it.

At Sea World of San Antonio, Texas, the trainers are also performers. It looks like a fun job, getting to swim around in the pools with whales and dolphins, interacting with them in one-to-one relationships. A trainer was asked how someone could get a job like his, and the answer started with getting the right college education. But then one comes for the interview. Before the interview starts, the applicant must swim underwater the length of the pool, swim back on the surface, dive twenty feet to the bottom, retrieve an object there, get out of the water, and immediately read a script into a microphone. If you have the abilities and the strength to do all of that, you are qualified to begin the interview. The message is that being a trainer requires a lot of preparation.

People face evil sitations every day, and the amount of spiritual preparation is an important factor in how well they are able to cope. The Christian who has accepted the whole armor of God is fully prepared for the difficult testing that occurs in life. When the evil day comes, make sure you have put on God's armor, and having done all, you will be able to stand.

Suggestions for Worship

Call to Worship (Ps. 84:1-7):

LEADER: How lovely is your dwelling place, O LORD Almighty!

PEOPLE: **My soul yearns, even faints, for the courts of the LORD; My heart and my flesh cry out for the living God.**

LEADER: Blessed are those whose strength is in you, who have set their hearts on pilgrimage.

PEOPLE: **They go from strength to strength, till each appears before God.**

Act of Praise: Psalm 84.

Suggested Hymns: "Stand Up, Stand Up for Jesus"; "Tis So Sweet to Trust in Jesus"; "God of Grace and God of Glory."

Opening Prayer: Almighty God, our rock and our salvation, our ever-present help in time of trouble, give us the gifts we need to conquer the evils that we face. Strengthen our faith, confirm our hope, and perfect us in love, that we might overcome the obstacles that have been set in our way. In Christ's name we pray. Amen.

Pastoral Prayer: Eternal and ever-present God, we pray today for all those who are beset by the problems of life and death, disease and disaster, evil and oppression. We pray for those who have recently lost loved ones, that you might comfort them. We pray for those who are facing death themselves, that their faith might be strong and that they might be kept free from pain. We pray for those who are ill, that they might be healed, and for those who suffer from natural disasters that they might rebuild. We pray for those who suffer from racism and oppression, from poverty and political tyranny. Help all such persons to claim your aid in the struggle for justice and genuine peace. We pray for those who do not yet know you as their savior, that they might come to commit their lives to you and pledge allegiance to your reign on Earth. In our fight against evil give us your armor, that we might be protected from harm, both spiritual and physical, and that we might have the gifts we need to win victories in your name. Through Jesus Christ, we pray. Amen.

AUGUST 28, 1994

□

Fourteenth Sunday After Pentecost

The tension between traditional values and practices and new revelations of God's truth is the theme of this lesson.

The Sunday Lessons

Song of Songs 2:8-13: This is a springtime rhapsody. "The winter is past, the rain is over and gone. The flowers appear on the earth" (vv. 11-12). It is a time for singing. It is also a time to "catch us the foxes, the little foxes, that ruin the vineyards" (v. 15). It is a time for love.

James 1:17-27: "Every perfect gift, is from above, coming down from the Father" (v. 17) writes James, "Therefore rid yourselves of all sordidness" (v. 21). Hearing the gospel prompts obedient response. "Be doers of the word, and not merely hearers who deceive themselves" (v. 22).

Mark 7:1-8, 14-15, 21-23: A controversy between Jesus and the Pharisees centered in the conflict between traditional practices and the truth of God. "You abandon the commandment of God and hold to human tradition" (v. 8). Ceremonial cleansing before eating was the specific issue. Some Pharisees were more interested in the pots and pans than with the bread of life.

Reflections

Religious practice, ritual, and doctrine that at first were intended to support truth, may finally displace it so that the cultus becomes more important than the thing itself.

Morris West's novel, *The Shoes of the Fisherman,* describes the life and work of a French priest whose teaching was considered to be dangerous for the tradition. Some see the character named Telemand as the fictional counterpart of the French Jesuit, Teilhard De Chardin.

A special commission, assigned to study and report the work of the scholar priest, wrote, "It is our considered opinion that the Reverend Father Jean Telemand be required to reexamine this work, and these later ones which depend on it, to bring them into conformity with the traditional doctrine of the Church. In the meantime he should be prohibited from preaching, teaching, publishing."

When new truth interrupts old habits, it does not begin in the masses. Neither the way everybody does it, nor the accepted standards agreed on by noted authorities is the criteria for testing truth. It breaks in on our thought through the intuitive insight and special obedience of a Moses or a Paul.

Old traditions do not stand a chance against new revelations of God. Twelve ordinary men with a bit of zeal for the Christ they had seen and heard turned the world upside down. (JKB)

THE INSIDE OUT GOSPEL

Mark 7:1-8, 14-15, 21-23

A SERMON BY SCOTT J. JONES

I first met Susan when she was thirty-one years old. She had been raised in a church, but her eyes were opened to the good news of the gospel for the first time as an adult. The church she attended as a child had drilled it into her—you must say prayers before bedtime, before meals, you must go to Sunday school, you must attend church, you must be at all the meetings of the youth group. The routine of religious ceremony had been part of her life all through those first eighteen years.

Being out on her own provided an opportunity to escape from the routines of church life. She never attended church, and neither did her friends. Every now and then she thought about God and about religion, but those thoughts made her feel uncomfortable, because she was not doing all of the rituals that she was supposed to do.

She married Jeff, and they had two children. About age thirty she felt a strange and new desire to get back to church. Maybe it was for herself, but definitely it was for her children. The rituals were familiar, the people friendly in a distant sort of way, and the whole exercise of getting there on Sunday morning was a herculean effort. But they made it, week in and week out.

Susan's eyes were opened in a disciple Bible study. Her sister-in-law had decided to join the thirty-four-week study group, and she signed on, too. The very first week of the study, Dr. Albert Outler spoke on the videotape saying, "It is a story about covenant-making and covenant-keeping on [God's] part, and covenant-making and covenant-breaking from our side." During the discussion about covenant as a relationship with God, she suddenly realized that she should look at religion not from the outside, but from the inside.

That basic insight is at the heart of Jesus' message to the Pharisees. One of the basic warnings he made to them over and over was to avoid an overly scrupulous observance of the law that detracted from the main purpose God had intended for the law to serve.

We should not be quick to condemn the Pharisees. Many of them were honorable and holy men seeking to serve God the best they could in difficult times. We should empathize with them, for the same process that led them astray often leads us astray as well.

Take the case of hand washing. Leviticus 22:1-16 emphasizes the holiness of the offerings made to God at the temple, and insists that the priests who eat the food dedicated to God must themselves be pure and clean. One way of removing ceremonial uncleanness is to wash the body. So the priests were commanded to wash every time before they ate. The Pharisees reasoned that if priests were to be holy and to be clean while eating holy things, then lay persons should do the same. Thus, if Israel is to be a holy people, all persons should wash their hands before eating. The logic is impeccable.

How often do we have the same logic? It was drilled into me, during my rebellious years, that proper clothing was necessary to the worship of God. Saturday night was the time to polish shoes. One always wore a coat and tie to church. Never mind that they were uncomfortable. Never mind your rebellious ideas about casual clothing. Looking nice was a way to honor God.

Or consider the kind of music that is played during our worship services. I know a local church where the musicians play

Bach preludes and sing Handel chorales during worship. Viewed from a classical, professional point of view, this church has one of the best music programs anywhere. But the congregation is dying. Its members' average age is over fifty, and few young people are joining. Most of the members have not made the connection that playing dead German music during worship does not reach people of the baby-boomer generation. The leaders who see the problem refuse to give up their cherished musical program for the uncertainties of new evangelistic opportunities.

Please understand me. I love classical music. My favorite piece of music in all the world is Beethoven's "Ninth Symphony," followed closely by Handel's "Messiah." I play them frequently for my personal enjoyment. That is not the issue here.

The real issue is what kind of music enables persons to have a closer relationship with God. There is nothing intrinsically wrong with Pharisees' practice of ceremonial hand washing. But to turn that into a religious requirement was wrong. It was not commanded in Scripture, but was added on to Scripture by humans. Further, it was burdensome to the common people. They had little access to water, and for them to wash ceremonially three times a day would have been very difficult, with little or no religious benefit.

So Jesus teaches them the basic lesson: "There is nothing outside a man that by going into him can defile him; but the things that come out of a man are what defile him."

At its most basic level, true religion is not a matter of externals. Someone who thinks that Christianity consists of observable behaviors such as attending church, going to Bible studies, giving money, and attending committee meetings has missed the point. Christianity is a relationship between the individual and God where the individual hears the gracious offering of a relationship. That relationship includes an offering of forgiveness for past sins and the promise that God's grace will continue to help the individual grow toward Christian maturity. Christianity is salvation by grace through faith, to the end that each person might become the kind of man or woman God intended them to be.

The Pharisees, whom Jesus criticized, were worried about getting all the external behaviors right. They were concerned about tithing the little things—mint and dill and cummin (Matt. 23:23). They were concerned about the precise words used in formulating oaths (Matt. 23:16). Over and over Jesus emphasized not the observable behaviors governed by the law, but the interior virtues of faith and a holy heart. He says in verses 20 and 21 of our text, "It is what comes out of a person that defiles. For it is from within, from the human heart that evil intentions come: fornication, theft, murder, adultery, avarice, wickedness, deceit, licentiousness, envy, slander, pride, folly" (vv. 21-23).

This is an inside-out gospel. What is most important is the condition of your heart, your relationship to God. What will save you from the guilt of your past sins and the power of sin over the rest of your life is not any set of behaviors, however noble and religiously right they are in themselves. What saves you is a heart that is right with God, a commitment you make to follow Jesus and pledge allegiance to his reign.

All of the outward observances, like attending church and Bible studies and tithing and moral behaviors are of secondary importance, because they tend to help your heart worship in spirit and in truth, and to help you live the life you truly believe in.

Three conclusions can be drawn for our own practice from this important truth. First, pay attention to the condition of your relationship with Christ. If you have not made a commitment to Christ, if you are uncertain about your salvation, if you are lukewarm in your faith, then focus on your relationship with God and seek to grow to a stronger relationship as one of God's daughters or sons. Make the commitment today!

Second, use the outward forms of religion only as means to a spiritual end. Religious rituals are important. Rules of behavior are important. My friend Susan received a great blessing from her parents when they taught her the value of religious discipline. I always advise people that attending worship every week is a means of grace where God has a greater opportunity to touch your heart and help improve the relationship that is so important. However, those outward behaviors are only means. They are avenues or channels whereby we can get to what is really important, a heart that is right with God.

Third, where the outward forms of observance obstruct the importance of the inward gospel, then change or modify them. If the style of music at our church is not helpful for truly spiritual worship, let us change it. If relaxing our dress code would enable people to come and worship with us, let us do it. Whatever stands in the way of helping people build that relationship with God, let us get rid of it so that, as much as possible, we can live in spiritual obedience to the Lord.

In 1786 John Wesley wrote in his *Thoughts Upon Methodism,* "I am not afraid that the people called Methodists should ever cease to exist either in Europe or America. But I am afraid lest they should only exist as a dead sect, having the form of religion without the power." The possibility of being spiritually dead, having only the form of religion without its spiritual power is a real temptation for all Christians. Let us pray that we are delivered from that danger, both individually and as a church.

Suggestions for Worship

Call to Worship (Ps. 72:18-19):

LEADER: Praise be to the LORD God, the God of Israel,

PEOPLE: Who alone does marvelous deeds.

LEADER: Praise be to his glorious name forever;

PEOPLE: May the whole earth be filled with his glory.

Act of Praise: Psalm 45:1-2, 6-9 or Psalm 72.

Suggested Hymns: "Let All the World in Every Corner Sing"; "Leave It There"; "More Love to Thee, O Christ."

Opening Prayer: Dear God, we confess to you our preoccupation with the outward forms of religion rather than the power of faith. Help us to use rituals, ceremonies and traditions not as the final acts of obedience, but simply as means of grace. Help us focus on truly spiritual worship of you, with praise and thanksgiving for your mighty acts of salvation. In Christ's name we pray. Amen.

Pastoral Prayer: Almighty God, help us to beware of the leaven of the Pharisees in ourselves. Help us to avoid a religion that has only the form of godliness without its power. Help us to focus on our relationship with you. We pray for ourselves that we might worship you in spirit and in truth. Help us to use our rituals and ceremonies as means of truly giving you praise and glory. We pray for those who have not yet come to know you as Lord and Savior. Help them to make commitments of their lives to serve you in everything. We pray for our church, that it might see the movement of the Spirit in our times and answer the call to be used by you for the salvation of the world. In Christ's name we pray. Amen.

SEPTEMBER 4, 1994

☐

Fifteenth Sunday After Pentecost

To become rich in faith we must become poor in spirit. Our deaf ears need the miraculous touch of our Lord.

The Sunday Lessons

Proverbs 22:1-2, 8-9, 22-23: These wise sayings of Solomon counsel generosity. A good name is better than riches. "Those who are generous are blessed" (v. 9). The Lord cares for the poor and oppressed (pleads their cause), therefore do not "rob the poor . . . or crush the afflicted" (v. 22).

James 2:1-10, 14-17: "Faith by itself, if it has no works, is dead" (v. 17). This central emphasis of the book of James is preceded by a practical discussion of partiality and privilege. "Has not God chosen the poor in the world to be rich in faith and to be heirs of the kingdom?" (v. 5).

Mark 7:24-37: A gentile woman begs for the healing of her daughter, arguing that even dogs get the crumbs beneath the table. In recording the healing of the man who could neither hear nor speak, Mark alludes to Isaiah 35:5-6. "He even makes the deaf to hear and the mute to speak" (v. 37). The miracles take place in a gentile region. Tyre and Sidon are on the Mediterranean coast. Decapolis refers to ten Greek cities east of the Jordan river. Jesus' command to the deaf mute was, "Ephphatha" (v. 34), which means, "open up!" The good news of God is for all, both Jews and Gentiles, who have ears to hear.

Reflections

We take the miracle of hearing for granted. We are surrounded by sound. Whether we are awake or asleep, we hear all the time. The wonder of it soon becomes familiar and grows ordinary.

Listen for a moment. Now list ten sounds you hear and recognize. The subtle tones—like those that make a mother know her baby's special cry among all the world's cries—are beyond description. Hearing is indeed extraordinary, but seldom appreciated.

The hearing of the gospel, that language of the boundary, is also taken for granted. One just assumes the sounds are always there—the reading of the lessons, the singing of the hymns, the telling of the story, the preaching of the Word, the absolutions, the blessings. We simply assume we can hear it all and understand most of it anytime we want to pay attention. Having ears to hear, we do not hear.

Christ's command, "Ephphatha," which means "open up," is the word to be heard today—not just by the hearers, but also by the preacher. Christ is the chief actor and controlling power in that hearing—both in the miracle story and also in the hearing of the gospel.

After reading this account of a deaf mute healed, I read again the scientific analysis of the human ear. The mystery of sound vibrations translated into recognized messages is described in three parts: outer ear, middle ear, and inner ear. Each has special parts—tympanic membrane, malleus, incus, cochlea, acoustic nerve—to list only a few. Thus described, the miracle of hearing is traced but not defined. Finally, at the point where mechanical vibrations become awareness and awareness becomes understanding, the discussion concludes, "The exact nature of this conversion is still unknown."

Both hearing, and hearing the gospel, are miracles indeed. Tracing it through traditions and theologies we are finally left saying, "The exact nature of this conversion is still unknown." (JKB)

THE CONVERSION OF JESUS

Mark 7:24-37

A SERMON BY R. BENJAMIN GARRISON

The very idea that Jesus might have needed to be converted would strike many people as strange, if not blasphemous.

It seems odd, I think, because we have failed or refused to take seriously the utter humanity of the man. We have forgotten that, when he was cut, he bled; that when he was sad, he wept; that anger and error were as real to him as they are to us.

Thus it seems not only odd but blasphemous to suggest that he needed conversion. Does the Savior need saving?

Consider the Gospel lesson, the (in many ways) distressing story of the Syrophoenician woman.

Jesus had withdrawn from his native province to the town of Tyre. We do not know why he went into retreat. To celebrate the Passover in some comparative calm and quiet? To secure the leisure to think about the goals of his ministry?

As a result of the earlier wilderness temptation, he had become clear about what his ministry was not to be: namely, a worldly maneuver resulting in temporal success. But that told him nothing about what, positively, it was to be.

He was about to discover.

One who had heard about him was a mother whose "daughter had an unclean spirit" (v. 25). Or, as we might put it, the little girl was emotionally disturbed. The mother, a Gentile, "came and bowed down at his feet" (v. 25). Do not underestimate the difficulty and drama of that act.

From her point of view, Jesus was a member of an alien people and, as she was soon to rediscover, even a hostile one. It was as if the Irish Protestant, Ian Paisley, were to drop to his knees before the Pope, or as if the National Organization for Women were to beg Pat Buchanan to be its president.

Under circumstances like that, this Syrian woman begged the famed rabbi Jesus, whose reputation as a physician had preceded him, to heal her ailing child.

In Matthew's version Jesus says, "I was sent only to the lost sheep of the house of Israel" (15:24). In addition, both Matthew and Mark remember Jesus saying, bluntly:

> Let the children [that is, the children of Israel] be fed first, for it is not fair to take the children's food and throw it to the dogs. But she answered him, "Sir, even the dogs under the table eat the children's crumbs." Then he said to her, "For saying that, you may go—the demon has left your daughter." So she went home, found the child lying on the bed, and the demon gone (vv. 27-30).

It offends our sensitivities and defaces our image of the gentle Jesus to hear him call her "a dog." It is amusing to read the numerous efforts of biblical scholars to escape the plain and painful intent of his words. What Jesus' words plainly said was that the woman was a dog because of her nationality. That was racial arrogance. That was political provincialism. And that means that Jesus of Nazareth had yet to experience the liberating, ennobling, enlarging religious conversion that made him at last the Lord of all life and the king of all persons.

This provincialism of Jesus was not, however, absolute—even in those early days of his ministry. It is only fair to note that he did not say the dogs should not be fed, but only that the children should be fed first. Even so, clearly something else was needed.

This crucial, converting encounter with the foreign woman proves, too, that his provincialism was not invincible. The woman, out of love for her ailing offspring, was not about to be put off by nationalism, by parochialism, by preoccupation—by anything.

So to his ill-conceived remark about dogs, she shot back, "Sir, yet even the dogs under the table eat the children's crumbs" (v. 28).

Matthew says that Jesus was silent for a moment before he called her people dogs. I wonder if the silence did not occur after she gave him as good as she got. Silence: big, pervasive, shocked; apprehensive, thoughtful. Silence before the pained realization that he had been guilty of foreshortening his vision, limiting his mission, and degrading another human being.

Not on purpose, of course (few of our worst sins are on purpose). He had been accidentally arrogant, unintentionally small-minded, unconsciously callous.

Silence, while he pondered the big faith of this brave woman, a faith bigger and braver than any he had thus far witnessed among his own children of Israel, a faith (could it be?) larger than his own.

And then he broke the silence, and with it the chains of his past. "You're right," he replied quietly but, I am sure, fervently. "You may go—the demon has left your daughter" (v. 29).

Jesus had been converted.

The yearning "To brother all the souls on earth" (Masefield's boxer) has marked Christian discipleship at its best from the beginning. But it is in us only because before us, it was in him.

This incident was far from incidental in his life. It enlarged his vision, broadened his horizons, tempered his judgment, deepened his compassion, converted and transformed a minor prophet into a major force to brother all the souls on earth.

What a tribute it is to the rigorous honesty of the New Testament writers that this story was preserved at all! It must have been hard on the man's messianic image. But there was no Madison Avenue in Jerusalem to change or distort his image.

The fact that the story now jars and even shocks us is evidence of how thorough our Lord's conversion was. Much of the rest of the New Testament is paced with a note of eager and inclusive universalism: standing in the temple in the very week of his death, he declared, quoting Isaiah and Jeremiah: "My house shall be called a house of prayer for all the nations" (Mark 11:17). Note that: *all* the nations.

Later: "Go therefore and make disciples of all nations" (Matt. 28:19a).

And Paul: "There is no longer Jew or Greek, there is no longer slave or free, there is no longer male or female; for all of you are one in Christ Jesus" (Gal. 3:28).

But it had not always been so.

In our day, too, Christian conversion is incomplete unless we leap over some walls, like Masefield's converted boxer, or like the New Testament's Lord. Christian conversion is fundamentally a turning toward Jesus Christ, a grateful and faithful acknowledging of him as Lord.

But, he warned us, even this is not enough: "Not everyone who says to me, 'Lord, Lord,' will enter the kingdom of heaven" (Matt. 7:21a). Not everyone who calls himself a Christian has enlarged his heart enough to let Christ in.

Some of the people and groups who have bleated most about conversion have not been conspicuously gymnastic about leaping over walls. Consider, for instance, the following examples.

Studies by Glock & Stark at the University of California at Berkeley discovered that the incidence of anti-Semitism among church people is higher than among so-called nonbelievers!

Research by Milton Rokeach at the same university concludes that "Christians who valued *salvation* were not necessarily the same ones who valued forgiving."

A man anonymously phoned my home and called me a murderer because of a sermon on abortion. Apparently, that brave fellow Christian has mistaken conformity for Christianity and dissent for disloyalty. He is still walled in.

Not only he, but also we: The libelous and widespread substitution of labels for understanding is sufficient evidence that the forthright and expansive reversal that Jesus was honest enough to undertake is still beyond too many of us.

Examples of such epithetical substitutes for thought? WASP, reactionary, rabble-rouser, phony. Each betokens a benumbed brain, a hardened heart, and a will unwilling to love and let live.

While I was on sabbatical leave at Cambridge, my wife and I were boarding an English double-decker bus. We happened to overhear the following: a woman was trying to identify her wanted bus and said to the female fare agent, "Are you number fifty-eight?" "No, dearie, I'm Margaret. The bus is number fifty-eight." No one enjoys being reduced to a number, or to a thing.

One of the results of conversion is an impatient unease with anything that makes persons less than persons. The police officer directing traffic is a person. The man with an earring in his ear is a person. For the Christian, even an enemy invites reconciliation more than he incites retaliation. Barriers exist to be brought down.

What counts with God and with the people of God is not the color of one's face, not the shape of one's smile, not the cause of one's snarl. What counts with God and with God's people is simply and solely the person.

Until we can see that, something is lacking in our religion. Until we can say that, something is missing from our conversion.

Conversion, in any tested and total sense, involves the pit of the stomach and the whole of the brain. It invokes heart and hand and checkbook; it includes beliefs and hesitations. It leaps over any wall, responds to any need, bears any rebuke, and goes to any length to meet and greet and gain the brother and sister, even if, at the moment, they are not acting like brothers and sisters.

The conversion of Jesus occurred when he ventured beyond his borders.

That is a hint and a hope for you—and for me.

Suggestions for Worship

Call to Worship (Ps. 125:1-2):

> LEADER: Our help is in the name of the LORD, the Maker of heaven and earth.

> **PEOPLE: Those who trust in the LORD are like Mount Zion, which cannot be shaken, but endures forever.**

> LEADER: As the mountains surround Jerusalem,

> **PEOPLE: So the LORD surrounds his people both now and forevermore.**

Act of Praise: Psalm 125 or Psalm 124.

Suggested Hymns: "From All That Dwell Below the Skies"; "Sweet Hour of Prayer"; "Soldiers of Christ, Arise."

Opening Prayer: O God of all order and harmony, who brought yourself close to us in your Son, Jesus Christ, that we might draw near to you with faith, come into this hour of worship, that we, hearing you speak in clear accents, may tune our lives to yours. In the name and through the power of our saviour Christ, we pray. Amen.

Pastoral Prayer: O God, in your wonderful and awesome creation you have provided the model of all creativity. We bow before you on this Labor Sunday. We are here as individual workers who seek respite from our labors and from the tedium of our toils. We are here as citizens of a nation that has set apart this day to honor our workers.

We pray for those who own the tools with which our workers labor and the resources that are processed into items of usefulness. Grant that their aim may be the provision of the means by which all persons may have the benefits of a fuller life and a more secure living.

We pray for our workers. We thank you that you have given

both substance and spirit to preserve freedom, in which the well-being of all can flourish. May we resolve to give a full day's work for a full day's wage, and a full day's wage for a full day's work. May we so use these rich resources hovering in our forests and streams and beneath the surface of the earth—lumber and energy, nutrients, coal and oil—that all persons everywhere may benefit from our just stewardship. In your divine providence empower us to develop and encourage leaders whose devotion is to the entire citizenry. Forgive us for our blindnesses. Lift us to a new spirit of service, and let that spirit be humble trust. Through Jesus Christ our Lord, we pray. Amen.

SEPTEMBER 11, 1994

□

Sixteenth Sunday After Pentecost

Jesus' life and mission were shaped by the cross that awaited him. Anyone who wants to share one's life must be willing to lose one's own.

The Sunday Lessons

Proverbs 1:20-33: The call of wisdom often goes unheeded. "I . . . have stretched out my hand and no one heeded" (v. 24). The complacency of fools will finally destroy them. "Those who listen to me will be secure" (v. 33).

James 3:1-12: In his discussion of the taming of the tongue, James notes how small things have great power to control and guide. Examples are the bits that control horses, and rudders that guide ships. The tongue, a small member, has power to "stain the whole body" (v. 6), yet it cannot be tamed. It is a restless evil, sometimes blessing, sometimes cursing.

Mark 8:27-38: When asked, "But who do you say that I am" (v. 27), Peter confesses every true disciple's faith, "You are the Messiah" (v. 29). This one from God, the only one who has it right, tells of his suffering, rejection, and death. Those who follow must come to terms with their crosses, and other crosses shaped by the world's sin. "Those who lose their life for my sake, and for the sake of the gospel, will save it" (v. 35).

Reflections

Confronted with a crucified God who just will not be defined in power establishment terms, those who truly hear are faced with a costly response. Three things are required—deny self, take up your cross, follow me.

We know what it means to deny oneself. That is about our selfishness. We know what Christ means with his invitation to follow. We need to get his style. What we cannot quite grasp is "take up your cross." What does this mean?

One thing it means is this: The Christ, and also his disciples, will bear the world's sin. You accept the fact of it, contend with the grief of it, and carry the cost of it. Christ bears the sins of the whole world. Anyone who honors his or her Christian name will also bear some portion of the sin of the world.

"I have to accept my share of the blame," said the father of a young man who had robbed and then killed. But accepting blame is not bearing the cross. Victims of crime bear the consequences of crime, even as the convicted criminal. Grace is not interested in assigning blame, but it does carry the sin and guilt of the world.

One may choose to be isolated and separated from any kind of failure. When a child, a church, a community, or a nation messes up, the one who wants only "to save self" will be quick to say, "I had nothing to do with that." "I'll have everything to do with that," says the true disciple. Then, like Isaiah's suffering servant, "You give your back to the smiter." Like Jeremiah, you speak judgment through tears. Like Paul you pray, "Let me be damned if they may be saved." (JKB)

THE LOCALE OF THE CHURCH

Mark 8:27-38

A SERMON BY R. BENJAMIN GARRISON

I have learned not to volunteer to my seatmate on the airplane that I am a clergyman. Sometimes, though, this information slips out. So your seatmate's question pops out, Where is your church, Reverend?

The cause of the pause that then follows is two-fold: (1) the reverend is trying to suppress some very unreverend remarks. (2) I do not really know how to answer. If I say, "My church is on the university campus" or "at the corner of Green and Goodwin in Centerville," I have already made a couple of mistakes: (a) It is not my church. (b) Giving a street address may be justifiable geography, but it is deplorable theology.

In order to identify the locale of the church, one does not need a new map, but a New Testament.

I contend for a concept of the church that is not geographical or locatable, not architectural or buildable.

As a preliminary to that contention, however, we had better be very clear that such attributes of the church are not unimportant. What the church is is not unrelated to where the church is.

My seatmate's question on the plane was not pointless, after all. Where the church is: the environment it occupies or ignores, the shapes it takes, the life it lives out—gives out, or holds back—all these are important clues to what the church is. Those purists who would have the church exist in somebody's mind and heart, but not in somebody's town or street—or in some nebulous perfect structure, but not in some needy, fragile one—are not talking about the church at all. They are talking about a ghost—and not the Holy One.

Where is the church? In order to answer this question, let us look at the crisp gospel exchange between Peter and Jesus (Mark 8:27-38, Matt. 16:13-20).

Jesus and the twelve have arrived at the site of the ancient city of Paneas, named for the god Pan, renamed Caesarea Phillipi in honor of the emperor and his local functionary. Jesus has just come from an encounter with the Pharisees, some of whom had an almost perverse capacity to misunderstand him automatically. Perhaps, sensing his hour was near, he knew it was time to begin to take his friends more completely into his confidence. Anyway, he indulged himself in that peculiarly human question: What do people think of me? Or, as our text phrases it, "Who do people say that I am?" (v. 27).

Like most friends, they do not immediately declare themselves. Rather they are content to repeat what they have heard by the grapevine: "John the Baptist" (v. 28). (The authorities were superstitiously petrified that the wilderness prophet whom they had slain might come back to life to haunt them.) Others, with greater insight, thought that Jesus resembled the prophet Jeremiah. Then came the clincher question: But what do you think? That one they could not dodge or postpone. Nor could they merely and safely quote what others were saying.

Now, I would imagine: silence—except in the big, pounding heart of Peter. He had always been the impulsive one, ready to blurt out whatever was bugging him. As a result he has left us with some of the wisest—and some of the most stupid—statements in the New Testament.

Well, why shouldn't Peter say it? He had been thinking it for quite a time. It had begun as an intuition, as gentle, tentative, and elusive as a passing breeze. It had become a conviction, as new, growing, and tender as the roots of a young olive tree. It burst forth as affirmation rising from his heart and hurrying out into the Palestinian air like a breathless runner with a crucial message. I do not care what others think, Peter reflected, or refuse to admit they are thinking. "You are the Messiah" (v. 29).

The drama closes quickly. One would be hard put to say whether the climax is what has just happened or what is about to happen. Jesus blesses Peter for a knowledge beyond knowing, for his soul's invincible surmise. Now it is the master's turn to give voice and verity to what has been burning him up inside. In Matthew's account, Jesus says, "You are Peter"—petros, which means the rock—and (Jesus must have shouted this) "on this rock I will build my church" (16:18).

We have now the answer to our question, Where is the church? The church is wherever persons stand with Simon Peter and side with Jesus Christ and name him Lord. Peter by himself is nothing. Peter with his affirmation is no longer by himself. He is saying, "That's the way it is in my life because that's the way it is in all of life. "As life latches on to that life, the church is born.

We may blurt it out. Peter did. We may think it out. Paul did. We may pour it out. The martyrs have.

Across the ages, it is an affirmation with which Christians have buried their loved ones, sung their liturgies, and given away their treasure. The institutional forms of it vary. The theological explanations of it change. The social implications of it shift. Our wars are its judgment on us. Our peace is its gift to us. But that affirmation, and nothing else, is the locale of the church. That church and no other is the church of Jesus Christ.

The church lives in the tension between its confession of faith and its confession of failure. If it is very difficult to affirm the one, it is more difficult still to admit the other. The church is where Christ is Lord, whether in judgment because we fail and hinder him, or in triumph because we follow and serve him.

This litmus test of lordship helps us make sense, or nonsense, of a lot of things being said about the church. To hear some people talk, one would think poor old God could not possibly make it without the church, like trying to box with hands tied behind your back. While I am not about to suggest that God will work with humanity without human instruments, I do not think God is tied to us, not ever and surely not forever.

On the other hand, to hear other people talk, you would think the Lord God Almighty will never be able to make it while encumbered with the church. That would be like trying to box with handcuffs on. And while I am not about to deny that the church is at times a drag on deity, I rather think God has enough imagination and initiative to exercise divine power even through us. We are imperfect instruments, but we are God's instruments.

The litmus test of lordship will not approve our use of the words *institution* or *structure* as if they were cuss words. Nor will it permit us to idolize our institutions.

What it will ask is: Is the church here because Christ is Lord? Or is the church absent because Christ is merely a name we name instead of a Savior we serve?

The point for Peter and for us is that there is enough in Christ's disclosure of God to warrant our venture, but not enough ever to spare us that venture. The church is the fellowship of those who are willing to take the risk of being wrong. Faith is that for which there are very good reasons—and against which there are also good reasons. So the essence is the risk. I am obliged therefore to bear testimony to what the church means in my life. Oh, I get as irritated with it as anybody does. Nevertheless, it is to the church of Jesus Christ that I owe what I know of the living God. Therefore, I am determined not only to hear its confession, but also to heed its proclamation. Because I love the church, I want the best for it, which means that I also want the best from it. That requires a message that is clear even when it is uncomfortable. That means a life that is warm, contagious, and joyful even when it requires sacrifice, correction, and pain.

That means me, and that means you: thoughtful, serious, ready, committed and on the move in the name of Jesus Christ.

Suggestions for Worship

Call to Worship (Ps. 19:1-4):

LEADER: The heavens delare the glory of God;

PEOPLE: **The skies proclaim the work of God's hands.**

LEADER: Day after day they pour forth speech;

PEOPLE: **Night after night they display knowledge.**

LEADER: There is no speech or language where their voice is not heard.

PEOPLE: **Their vocie goes out into all the earth, their words to the ends of the world.**

Act of Praise: Psalm 19.

Suggested Hymns: "O For a Thousand Tongues to Sing"; "Open My Eyes, That I May See"; "Where He Leads Me."

Opening Prayer: O God, who has made us messengers of peace in a world of strife, and messengers of strife in a world of false peace, make strong our hands, make clear our voices. Give us humility with firmness and insight with passion, that we may fight not to conquer, but to redeem, through Jesus Christ, our Lord. Amen.

Pastoral Prayer: Almighty God, who in Jesus Christ has graciously granted us new life, who has created us by your power, re-created us by your love, and sustained us by your Spirit, hear and heed us as we pray.

O Holy Spirit, who enables us to know you, like your holy apostles long ago, let our tongues speak in a language that all people can understand. Let our lives flower with the fruit of your presence, our churches pulse with the lifeblood of your power.

Measure our hearts, O God, with the rule of love. Grant us the humility to know that, when measured by your love, our hearts are too centered in self, too weak in faith, too small in deed. In your great mercy cleanse our pride by him who is meek, harness our deeds to him who is strong, fasten our faith to him who is Lord.

Hear our petitions for those who need you in the secret chambers of their souls. Give strength to the weak and humility to the strong; give generosity to the gifted and patience to the afflicted. Show hope to the despairing and comfort to the bereaved.

Keep us ever in your favor. Hold us always in your care. Bless our lips with holy fervor. Drive us to our knees in prayer, for we pray in the name of Jesus Christ our Lord. Amen.

SEPTEMBER 18, 1994

☐

Seventeenth Sunday After Pentecost

The most significant station in the Christian life is not the place of privilege and high favor. Compassion produces a harvest of good deeds, says James, while desire for privilege results in conflict and strife.

The Sunday Lessons

Proverbs 31:10-31: This ode to a good and capable wife emphasizes humility and service. She reaches out to the needy. "Charm is deceitful, and beauty is vain, but a woman who fears the Lord is to be praised" (v. 30). Such a woman is honored by her children and praised by her husband.

James 3:13–4:3, 7-8a: Draw near to God, and God will draw near to you. Friendship with the world must be subordinated to one's devotion to God. Selfish ambition is not found in a true follower. "Wisdom from above is first pure, then peaceable, gentle, willing to yield, full of mercy and good fruits, without a trace of partiality or hypocrisy" (v. 17). Faithful disciples are peacemakers, not dividers.

Mark 9:30-37: Jesus foretells his death and resurrection again and speaks of true discipleship. The twelve argued about who would be greatest and Christ taught them, "Whoever wants to be first must be last of all and servant of all" (v. 35). Care for the child and the powerless is the way of important service.

Reflections

A minister, visiting a multi-generation farm family in his parish, found himself left in the house with the women and young children. Later he complained about being left out of the activities and conversations of the men and youth. "This parish must believe a minister's place is with women and babies," was the lament of the cleric. He did not recognize the chauvinism implied. He just wanted to be in the center of things.

Most of us want to be where the action is. We would like to be, or at least be with, the shapers and movers of the world. The ways of greatness are not perceived in such ordinary stuff as quieting a crying child, managing children's play or cleaning a cluttered kitchen. That is considered too common to be noteworthy.

Most of us need to be recognized and like to be honored. We would like a bit of glory. But it is vain glory that is mainly sought and treasured for the glitter. True greatness has deeper luster and lasting shine.

The pathetic and humble Cinder of the Cinderella story abounds in varieties of characters in folk tales having the last becomes first motif. More than 345 versions, belonging to cultures of the last three centuries have been collected. The Scottish variant is "Rashin Coatie"—Coat of Rushes. The English version is "Cap o' Rushes."

A Native American version exists among the Algonquin Indians. The barefoot and ragged, Oochigeaskow, the Rough-Faced Girl, is the homely, humble slave of all the fair ones. Finally, she is shown to be the fairest of them all. (JKB)

HIDDEN SECRETS

Mark 9:30-37

A SERMON BY RICHARD ANDERSEN

The Gospel texts for Pentecost seventeen and eighteen have a common setting. From Mark 9:33-50, it is evident the themes raised come from the same conversation in the same Capernaum house. It is possible that it is Peter's home, and that the child Jesus singles out (v. 36) is a progeny of the big fisherman. While some of this is justifiable speculation, it lends itself to a two-part series that might be entitled overall, *Family Discussions*.

There is a certain charm to the scene surrounding our text. Jesus and his companions are walking home to Capernaum. They are coming from northeastern Galilee that juts into Syria. They are going in a southerly direction toward the Sea of Galilee. In that locale there is a particularly placid enchantment to the countryside. There are lush fields, thriving with grain, that span outward from the grey-green waters of the upper Jordan River. Olive trees line some of the country lanes and vineyards climb the rounded hills. Jesus and the twelve are returning home from an extensive visit to Caesarea Philippi. The Transfiguration took place only days beforehand. Some believe that happened on snow-crowned Mount Hermon thirty to thirty-five miles from the fishing fleet at Capernaum. Now they are stretching their legs over the familiar highways close to home. There is probably a delightful jocularity among the twelve. With prospects of going home and their long journey away from the Sea of Galilee nearing conclusion, one can imagine a restive light-heartedness. Possibly, among some, there is a weariness from the tiring trek and an impatience with entering the gates of their own hometown. One can well imagine some sporty jesting, as well as some testiness from the tired members of Jesus' entourage. Yet, Jesus is not as blithe as his disciples might have been, nor as weary. Something seems to be gnawing within his soul, something tremendously important. It is the vision for which he came into the world. It is the fulfillment of the divine plan that he must accomplish.

"The Son of Man is to be betrayed into human hands," says the pensive Lord, "and they will kill him, and three days after being killed, he will rise again" (v. 31). In a few words, out in the middle of nowhere, Jesus once more revealed the greatest secret of the universe. It is the hidden secret of heaven itself. It is the gospel sewn up in a few chosen words. It seemed lost on the twelve. They were probably too caught up in the prospects of dining at their own table and sleeping in their own beds to comprehend the seemingly dark words of their master about betrayal and death. They even missed the words focused on the Resurrection.

When they arrive in Capernaum, Jesus' demeanor changes again. No longer caught in introspection, he is wondering about the conversations along the way. He is curious about what he missed. The twelve, never overly calm and frequently arguing about this and that, were embroiled in a conversation that probably began with jokes and quips and wound up with insults and boasts. As Jesus walks over to some of them in the house in which they were staying, he asks about their noisy conversation. Their boastfulness fell to silence. They became as quiet as fish in a giant sea. One has the distinct impression from Mark's words that they were embarrassed, and not just embarrassed, but deeply mortified. "Why did Jesus have to ask that?" a disciple might have wondered.

"Well, it was nothing really," one might haltingly admit.

"No, nothing," a more caustic disciple could add, "because they were arguing over who is the greatest, and *none* of *them* won." A final sting added to the stabs already thrust at one another just might awkwardly float to the surface.

Eventually, someone spills the whole sordid truth.

It is enough for Jesus to seize the opportunity to share still another secret. If the first hidden secret was about the evangel, the gospel, the bad news of his impending death and the good news of his imminent resurrection, the second secret concerned the evangelists themselves, those who are to live and share the good news afterward. Divine truth is revealed on the homeward journey as they trudge the final miles, but its human application is divulged around the family circle in the intimacy of a familiar home.

In the midst of their interplay, it is evident that Jesus expects heavenly truth to be humanly lived. That is the challenge of the Christian home. It is not merely to tell Bible stories at bedtime and sing Bible camp songs on awakening, but to take the most sublime ideas ever to brighten this world and employ them eagerly to life.

Here are the two elements of an essential family discussion. On the one hand, we have the lofty theme of love and sacrifice that ultimately turns into victory. On the other hand, we have the mundane matter of human conceit, arrogance, and indifference to others . . . not to mention out-and-out disregard. How can we take the towering themes of the gospel and apply them to day-to-day struggles?

How would Jesus handle them?

Let us go back to the first secret he unveiled as they wandered along the rocky roadway to Capernaum. Out of the blue, Jesus makes a startling observation. Or is it so startling? It seems to me it is a calculated effort on the part of the Redeemer to deal lovingly and thoughtfully with a family matter, and just to shock his compatriots. Mark is careful to point out that Jesus did not want anyone to know he was passing through that region. He wants to concentrate on his disciples and their need to know the divine plan. The author makes it clear that Jesus is teaching the twelve. He also makes a distinction between the words Jesus uses in revealing this hidden secret now and the time before . . . just days before when he and the inner circle climbed the Mount of Transfiguration (8:32-38).

Jesus said something very different, very revealing: "The Son of Man is *to be betrayed into human hands*" (v. 31). He had not shared with them previously that his death begins with *betrayal* and also *into human hands.*

This is a unique family, and yet it is Jesus' extended family. He is aware that dark thoughts have crept into the deep recesses of the soul of one of those he loves. He knows Judas is stewing with thoughts of betrayal, perhaps eager to push the Great Rabbi into a role he does not want: the role of an earthly king or revolutionary commander or Roman antagonist—a role Jesus does not seek at all. Still, it may have been Judas' desire to push Jesus in that direction for he was a political zealot bent on the restoration of independence and the ridding of Israel's Roman scourge.

Jesus had shared the secret before, but never with this specific awareness: human hands would be involved! It is almost as if Jesus is reaching out, straining to restrain a maniacal friend from becoming his own worst enemy. Jesus shares the gospel in that conversation, but he does more. He lives it in all its implications. There is grace offered, and the opportunity for forgiveness extended. There is love and the encouragement to abandon the despicable plan put forward in a gentle, oblique way.

Back at the house, once they are settled in and the evening meal is concluded, we imagine the time for relaxing engulfs the whole household. The women clean the dishes and put the food away. There is the smell of cooked fish and red wine and olive oil lamps hanging in the room. The sounds of light conversations between the twelve and their hostesses, among themselves or with Jesus punctuate the lively scene. This is probably Peter's house. His wife and mother-in-law probably did the cooking. His children are probably spilling underfoot, happy to see their father, and joyous over Jesus and his attentiveness. As he inquires about the argument along the way, he settles down on the floor, cross-legged. The twelve stand about, some leaning against the walls. The women eavesdrop. The children continue to roll around on the floor and play with their primitive toys until Jesus lifts up one of the children and places it in the middle of the circle.

"Whoever wants to be first must be last of all and servant of all" (v. 35), he says. Here is a lively visual aid, an ideal argument against their non-productive discussion of who is the greatest. The humble little one; always dependent, always vulnerable is his example.

Then he lifts the little one into the crook of his carpenter strong arm and explains, "Whoever welcomes one such child in my name welcomes me, and whoever welcomes me welcomes not me but the one who sent me" (v. 37).

The evangelists could not begin to preach the *evangel,* the good news, until they master this important concept—nor can we, really. It is fundamental. Love must be lived, not just preached. Love must be extended to the lowliest, the smallest, the least of all before it becomes a love that can reach into other dimensions. Yet even here, Jesus is focused on Judas. If the other eleven need to learn this lesson, the man of Iscariot needs to learn it more. If James and John fight over who sits at the Lord's left and right hand, while Judas is bent on demanding a lesser throne in a decadent kingdom instead of a place in heaven's realm, Jesus must teach them all. Jesus is reaching out to the very least of the twelve, as he wants us to attend to the needs of those within our families and neighborhoods that others overlook. Jesus, ever the consummate teacher, is also an image of his Father and deals with the squabbles of his children as a patient, but righteous, parent should.

Hidden secrets are exposed. They are the gems of faith. One is the gospel. The other is how it is lived out in the world of human beings patiently, lovingly taught.

In the fall of 1991, as the former Soviet Union invited Christians to bring a renewed faith to their depleted spirituality, nineteen evangelicals went to Moscow at the invitation of President Gorbachev and the Supreme Soviet. Philip Yancey tells the story in his remarkable article in the pages of *Christianity Today.* They were staying in a posh hotel and were royally received by Soviet authorities, scholars, the press, and other leaders. One day, however, a surprise guest show up. His name was Basil, a huge hulk of a man with a voice that had the blast of a launched rocket. He was an ex-convict. He sought five minutes to address the American Christians. Then he blasted away like ignited kegs of dynamite.

The KGB had arrested him for publishing Christian tracts and distributing them in his homeland of Moldavia in 1962. He spent ten years in prison for that crime. Disillusioned, he wondered why God abandoned him. Then he came to the conclusion he was not abandoned. God had a ministry for him right there. As the prisoners at the labor camp assembled in an open space for roll call at sunup, he discovered the camp guards were not as punctual as the prisoners. He used those minutes to preach. That is why his voice had grown to freight train decibels. He had no microphone. It took him two weeks to deliver a single sermon, since he only had two minutes a day to preach. There were all kinds of prisoners. Some were actual convicts. Others were imprisoned, as Basil was, for Christian preaching, or criticizing the government. But his captive audience proved to be a receptive crowd to hear the gospel. Among them, as a convicted felon, he sought to live out its message under the scrutiny of guards and prisoners alike.

Basil had heard that the American Christians were in Moscow. He once listened to the clandestine radio broadcasts of several of the evangelicals in the group. Picking apples and grapes from Moldavia, he rode a train fourteen hours to give them a welcome with fruit from his homeland and a prayerful wish. "Be bold!" he asserted. "Where I come from the believers are praying for you at this minute. We believe your visit will help reach our country for God."

Basil could not leave the secrets of the gospel hidden from his fellow prisoners, nor could he fail to live it out in the *gulag*. He found his family to embrace everyone inside the barbed wire confines of that prison camp. Our family is just as broad and wide and deep, if not much more free. In imitation of Jesus, we are to share divine truth by applying it to the humanity around us. That is the way to ensure these hidden secrets will be hidden no longer.

Suggestions for Worship

Call to Worship (James 3:17–4:8):

LEADER: The wisdom that comes from heaven is first of all pure;

285

PEOPLE: **Then peace-loving, considerate, submissive, full of mercy and good fruit, impartial, and sincere.**

LEADER: The Scripture says, "God opposes the proud, but gives grace to the humble."

PEOPLE: **Submit yourselves, then, to God. Come near to God and he will come near to you.**

Act of Praise: Psalm 1.

Suggested Hymns: "Of All the Spirit's Gifts to Me"; "There's a Wideness in God's Mercy"; "Ask Ye What Great Thing I Know."

Opening Prayer: Wondrous Father, we adore you for sending your Son to travel the roads of human life and experience the tensions between friends and enemies, relatives and strangers, laborers and managers. Equip us with the determination to live in love of everyone, so that as Jesus' disciples today we follow him in applying the gospel to life. Amen.

Pastoral Prayer: Creator-Father, it is the splendor of this planet that you have created the seasons, so that we are able to rejoice in the progress of the sun and the adventure of the changing landscape. We praise you for the beauty of each season, but particularly for now we rejoice in the colors of beginning autumn and the beauty of a promising harvest.

Let us not be so distracted by the grandeur of the countryside that we forget to walk with Christ at the lead and your Spirit behind all that we do and everywhere that we go. Guide us away from the torturous tensions of this age and past the intriguing temptations that we might arrive at our destinations healthy and whole.

Mold fathers into men of strength and tenderness.

Shape mothers into women of thoughtfulness and boldness.

Let the children be formed with the caution of the law and the encouragement of the gospel.

Draw us together, Lord, as families who widen the circle to include all who seek the family of God. In this hour, this day, this week, nurture us, we pray through Jesus Christ, our Lord. Amen.

SEPTEMBER 25, 1994

□

Eighteenth Sunday After Pentecost

Pride, place of privilege, and self before others are subtle sins—yet deadly. Discipleship requires discipline.

The Sunday Lessons

Esther 7:1-6, 9-10; 9:20-22: When Queen Esther was asked by the king, "What is your request? Even to the half of my kingdom" (v. 2), she asked nothing for herself, but asked for the freedom of her people, the Jews. Haman, who had undertaken to destroy the Jews, was hanged on the very gallows he had prepared for Mordecai. A holiday was established.

James 5:13-20: When you are suffering, pray. When you are cheerful, sing. James encourages both prayer and praise, and then prescribes prayer and anointing for the sick. "The prayer of faith will save the sick" (v. 15). The prayers of the righteous are lifted up as "powerful and effective" (v. 16). Elijah's prayer for rain (I Kings 18:41-46) is an example of the prayer of faith.

Mark 9:38-50: Mark continues his discussion of discipleship with a collection of sayings. Working with others in Christ's name, causing the little ones to stumble, and warning aginst self-interest and self-service are some of the themes. Private domain, pride, and indulging one's person are the central issues. "Whoever is not against us is for us" (v. 40). "If your eye causes you to stumble, tear it out" (v. 47).

Reflections

Sometimes we battle against the wicked and evil forces of the world. There is a harder battle to fight. It is against the sin within us, among us, and against our very selves. Selfish pride and foolish deception are the marks of it.

Pride and deceit are subtle warriors, and just when you think you have conquered them, they begin a skirmish on another front.

Consider for example the young man who, reckless as the prodigal, wastes his property, risks his health, and disregards his honor to satisfy the desires of his own heart—to grab all the gusto. He quite literally kills himself living only for self. Then older, wiser, and reformed, that man hordes his property, pampers his health, preens his reputation. He once was unscrupulous. Now he has become uncharitable. Once he was self-indulgent. Now he is self-righteous. Phillips Brooks called it, "The killing of sin by sin, of selfishness by selfishness, of death by death."

If you would win the battle within, you must surrender every personal consideration. You cannot save yourself. The lesson suggests the way of it. Hate selfishness, pride, and deceit in every form it takes. Count it a disease and be rid of it. Get all the help you can. Offer yourself for correction.

Suppose that a bride found a stain on the spotless white of her bridal gown. Would she console herself by saying, "Every dress is soiled sooner or later." Would she reason, "It's only a speck and hardly noticeable." Without reservation she wants it gone, and all the evidence of it.

Count every sin within you as being against God. Employ every power of God and every ally of judgment and every means of grace to have it gone. (JKB)

RECOGNIZING FAMILY

Mark 9:38-50

A SERMON BY RICHARD ANDERSEN

Invariably it happens. People recognize those they have not met, not because of pictures or signs they carry, but because of the family traits. I see it at weddings and funerals. People who have not seen one another for a long while recognize offspring they have never met because of family mannerisms. It may be a father's peculiarities or a mother's characteristics bred into the kids that readily identifies them.

Once when I visited my parents' homeland, eleven relatives converged on us at a charming little hotel in Randers, Denmark. I knew they belonged to me, although I had never seen any of them before, because my father's brother—though years older than he—could have been his twin. The family features were unmistakably there. His children likewise favored those family traits. They were *Andersens*.

The opposite can be equally true. When someone is totally opposite, completely foreign to you, it is readily apparent that they cannot claim the same family ties. Race and ethnicity have nothing to do with it. The color of eyes, the curl of hair, the facial profile may be very much alike and still there will be a great family difference. It is discovered in the internal things. Not the mannerisms, but the morals. Not the doctrines, but the rejection of Christian faith. Not the language barrier, but the inability to communicate at all. They cannot be recognized as being part of the family.

Jesus is at home in Capernaum. Our text is probably part of the same conversation he had with his disciples in that house near the Galilean lakeside that we discussed last week. We heard the first part of the dialogue then. Today we hear the rest. As a child figured in last week's lesson, so a child becomes illustrative of the Lord's concern for the innocent in today's text. There is, seemingly, a concern for the family of the faithful being voiced in Jesus' comments both last week and this week. Not just the nuclear family, but the total Christian family is the subject of Jesus' comments. He sees the family traits that lead to unity. He recognizes the dissimilarities that erode into pain. It is a family discussion and it concerns us.

The apostle John shares an incident with his Lord in that evening visit. As they traveled throughout northern Galilee, he observed someone casting out demons in the name of Jesus. "We tried to stop him, because he was not following us," explained the youngest disciple.

"You missed something," Jesus might have said. "You didn't note the family trait, did you?" Instead, our Lord cautioned John rather than scolding him, and the rest of us also. "Do not stop him," said Jesus of the one exorcising demons in Jesus' name, "for no one who does a deed of power in my name will be able soon afterward to speak evil of me." Here was more than clever psychology, but patient understanding that left the door open to a relative still discovering his identity.

Jesus coined a phrase that we hear often, "Whoever is not against us is for us." That is the family trait. Jesus saw it. John failed to look. It is the similarity that hints at a broader, deeper relationship. It is the clue that a greater connection links us. We are closely related by that desire to serve the one who is almighty. There is a unifying relationship in all who support the name of Jesus.

But if we find a comrade with similarities, we also will find the opposite characteristic is a stumbling block to the innocent. Without the unifying factor of the Savior, we cease to be the close family we yearn to have.

Jesus fondly eyes the children in the household where he is staying. They are probably Peter's kids, and they are undoubtedly filled with life. The Lord sees them as defenseless against the mean and the corrupt who would lead them away from him to stumble into tragedy. Those who cause little ones like this to stumble are not members of his family, but aliens of the worst kind. Jesus describes a punishment fitting such stumbling blocks: He suggests that they be adorned with millstones and cast into the sea.

He cautions us to remember in whose family we have relationship. We belong to him. For that reason, he uses some extreme examples so that we will remember the importance of keeping the family traits. They are what we call *hyperbole*: exaggerations and overstatements intended to register in our mind, but not intended to be carried out precisely.

Once my father playfully suggested at the breakfast table to my oldest daughter, then only five or six years of age, that by putting so much pepper on her eggs she would grow hair on her chest. My daughter is now the mother of teenagers, and she still does not use pepper. The effect of her grandfather's hyperbole was more than he anticipated. Jesus did not intend to be taken literally either, but he wanted to make it clear that any kind of wrongful act that destroys faith or leads one to fall away from God is worthy only of drastic action. "It is better for you to enter life maimed than to have two hands and to go to hell" (v. 43), observed Jesus.

But there is a better way to stifle a wayward hand, stumbling foot, or willful eye than by literally discarding it. It is to retrain it. It is to teach it something better, as Jesus did in that Capernaum house. Get the hand, the foot, the eye back into the spirit of the family again, get it to respect the relationship to God. It is to salt life with fire, but the fire of faith and hope and love.

Alcoholics' Anonymous does that. So do organizations that help gamblers and drug abusers break their bad habits and adopt the family traits anew. Churches do it all the time when the gospel is proclaimed and people come to Jesus. It is the nature of God's family to be compassionate and to offer others a cup of water in the heat of suffering, and to do so in the name of Christ. Here is the secret to recognizing the long lost members of the family. It is in recognizing their desire to rejoin the family they may have rejected in the past.

Gerry Phelps was an economist and a lecturer at a leading university. Her social concerns got her involved in zealous actions. She was not subversive, and yet her involvement led to what the government said were illegal acts during the Viet Nam conflict. Gerry Phelps wound up in a Texas prison. She was a very socially-conscious individual. She had a social gospel of concern for freedom, human rights, and peace. She was an agnostic on the fringes of the real gospel, but not yet a part of it. In some ways, Gerry Phelps was like the man who cast out demons in Jesus' name, but did not follow him. She had some of the truth, but not all of it—and it led to wrong conclusions and drastic actions.

In prison, however, she looked back at the family of faith that she had ignored. Something, someone beckoned her home. There in that hostile environment, she found a cup of refreshing water handed to her. She read the Bible and heard God speak to her. There she discovered the open door to God's family circle. As Jesus called Paul from being a persecutor to being a preacher, so he called her. She is a Methodist pastor today.

Gerry Phelps is still socially conscious. She has retrained her wayward hand, stumbling foot, and willful eye to work effectively for the kingdom. From scratch she started a shelter for the homeless in Bakersfield, California. A few years later, she began a shelter for homeless families in San Jose that serves the whole Silicon Valley. In five years, the organization went from a zero to a $750 million budget. Nearly 150 residents are housed, fed, and retrained for new jobs in programs available right at the shelter site. There, small children have daytime care, while after-school programs aid the older ones. The concept is to take homeless families and assist them in breaking the cycle of homelessness by getting them retrained for the labor force, and then into dependable jobs and permanent housing. It has become a model program for the nation. The Reverend Gerry Phelps recognized in others the family traits of God's family and called them from the bitter streets into a caring environment. She is very good at recognizing family—those yearning to join God's family circle. Through Gerry Phelps, the door has been opened to many.

She is salted with fire. It is a salt that preserves and gives flavor. It is a salt that adds value and remains constant. It keeps the families whole and draws them into the greater family of God. If I understand the Lord's expression correctly, it has reference to the sacrifices made in Jerusalem's temple. The roasted meat on the altar of burned offerings had to be salted ceremoniously according to the Levitical law. Salt's symbolic nature was to emphasize soundness, sweetness, wholesomeness, and acceptability. Yet, we are aware that sacrifice means pain, even if salt means sweetness. In Pastor Phelps' own life, as well as the shelters she has founded, sacrifice that has been salted with love has preserved the best and purified the worst by building on the pain.

What Gerry Phelps has done is inspire others to recognize the homeless as long lost family members. Others are being seasoned with her salt. Rita Olsen is the leading volunteer. She masterminds ways of getting people to help the families after they have completed the program at the shelter and are in permanent housing. There is fire in the salt with which she sprinkles the clients, too. It is the loving fire of compassion and concern. Rita enlists other volunteers, and the family keeps widening. Many volunteers come from the churches, but some come from outside the churches for she heard Jesus tell John not to stop those who cast out demons in Jesus' name, but who do not follow him as yet.

Here are living members of the family of God who take literally the rhyme that goes:

> He drew a circle that shut me out—
> Rebel, heretic, thing to flout.
> But love and I had the wit to win—
> We drew a circle that took him in.

In my college years, I attended a small school founded by Danish Lutherans. Though I had few relatives in this country, I felt immediately at home the day I arrived on the campus of Dana College, Blair, Nebraska. I looked like no one there, but there was something in the atmosphere that permeated the environment and I felt as though my family had somehow materialized out of Danish blue onto the lush green hillside campus overlooking the Missouri Valley.

The faculty did not know that I was a first generation American. Somehow, the idea got around that I was the son of a popular pastor who had died some years before. My dad was a house builder. I had the same last name as that sainted pastor, but Andersen among Danes is like Jones or Smith in this country. Frequently, when being introduced to parents of other students, they would ask if I was Pastor Andersen's son. My answer was usually, "No. I'm the child of a *carpenter*."

"Aren't we all?" they would answer in pious, but sincere tones. "Aren't we all!"

They recognized a greater family than I saw then, but a family I never want to leave. Friend, recognize the similarities that lead to unity in Christ, and avoid those traits that evidence such a dissimilarity that nothing but the pain of a plucked eye or discarded hand or lopped off foot will do to get away from it, for they lead away from joy. They snatch us from our rightful family to an alien life in which we do not belong.

Pinocchio did not realize that until almost too late.

We have someone better that Jiminy Cricket to encourage us. We have Jesus Christ. Recognize him, and you will be in the right family always. You will ensure that others come into that family as well.

Suggestions for Worship

Call to Worship (James 5:13):

LEADER: Is any one of you in trouble?

PEOPLE: He should pray.

LEADER: Is anyone happy?

PEOPLE: Let him sing songs of praise.

Act of Praise: Psalm 124.

Suggested Hymns: "Come Christians, Join to Sing"; "Take Time to Be Holy"; "I Am Thine, O Lord."

Pastoral Prayer: Make us compassionate and faithful, gracious Holy Spirit, so that we are neither stumbling blocks to others, nor a detriment to ourselves. Season us with the salt of sacrifice so that we flavor our world with the zest of a true conviction and earnest service that glorifies Jesus Christ, our Lord. Amen.

Pastoral Prayer: Teacher-Savior, clear our clogged hearing and distracted minds so that we may accurately heed your guidance and cause no one to stumble.

Fill us with such love for you that we neither ignore those outside our comfortable realms of faith and action, nor reject those who cast out demons in your name who differ from us. Yet, Lord Christ, teach us to sift the wheat from the chaff in issues of faith so that we do not blindly accept every teaching that purports it comes from you, but instead to separate mindless concepts from biblical truths, and apply the latter. Let us not become so tolerant of every idea that we lose the essentials of the gospel's ideal, nor so intolerant of others that we fail to see them as the children of God. Strengthen the church of Jesus Christ to look beyond denominational boundaries to discover brothers and sisters of faith beyond human limitations. Stir us to celebrate your love and share it eagerly together with a world weary of our squabbles and anxious to find the body of Christ undivided and whole.

Now grant peace to those disturbed within their souls, and healing to those who ache within their bodies. Draw all nations together in concern for each other, as we beg your Spirit's presence to end our prejudices and inspire our proclamation that Christ is Lord. Amen.

OCTOBER 2, 1994

□

Nineteenth Sunday After Pentecost

Thank God for the table. The time-honored rituals of the Eucharist, and especially the prayer of thanksgiving, have helped to shape and conserve community. Families that gather to share a meal are blessed. Christ honored the children.

Sunday Lessons

Job 1:1, 2:1-10: Job, who was blameless and upright, feared God and shunned evil. But this man, greatest in all the east, was tested. Job's second test (vv. 1-10) was one of personal suffering. "Skin for skin!" Satan said, "All that people have they will give to save their lives" (v. 4). Job was covered with sores, but he still honored God. "Shall we receive the good at the hand of God, and not receive the bad?" (v. 10).

Hebrews 1:1-4; 2:5-12: In former days, God spoke through his prophets, but now he speaks through his son. Jesus, who was made a little lower than the angels, is now crowned with glory. All things are subject to him who was made perfect through suffering.

Mark 10:2-16: The Pharisee's controversial question, "Is it lawful for a man to divorce his wife?" (v. 2), is answered by Jesus' commandment that goes beyond the law of Moses. Divorce is forbidden. A teaching regarding children follows. "Let the little children come to me . . . whoever does not receive the kingdom of God as a little child will never enter it" (v. 15).

Reflections

A young mother who honored her Baptism and came often to the Holy Table went through a painful and humiliating divorce. During those difficult times, she felt isolated from the church and especially from the sacrament. Jesus' statements forbidding divorce and the church's longstanding opposition to it combined to make her feel separated from the family of God, too. Later, the ministry of the church, which faces clearly the reality of guilt, brought her, as one of all the scattered, to this feast of mercy.

Divorce for her became a symbol of repentance—a facing up to failure. It was for her a confession that she had not lived in marriage according to the highest in God's plan of creation. Let it be noted that some marriages, stubbornly maintained though long ago dead, can blind one to his or her failures and the pervading emptiness.

The commandment of our Lord (the Pharisees sought their rights, the Lord's answer sought obedience) must not be compromised lest the gift of the Creator (that the two shall be one) be devalued. The church is plain in its opposition to divorce. It has, however, made concessions regarding remarriage.

The institutions of marriage in first-century Jerusalem and in twentieth-century America are very different. Even though granted a divorce, a Jewish wife was still the possession of her husband and unable to remarry without his permission. Roman law was changing all of that, hence the Pharisee's question. We see the fault in first-century values. Is the modern institution of marriage, and our all too common marriage failures, nearer to God's will for his creation of man and woman? Surely not. (JKB)

EQUALITY THROUGH CHRIST

Mark 10:2-16

A SERMON BY JERRY L. MERCER

As Jesus approached the time he was to die, he made the implications of his teachings increasingly clear. And, as the Bible shows again and again, many religious authorities did not for one minute like what he was saying!

At every opportunity, Jesus hammered away that those who follow him are one in spirit with each other and one in standing before God. This means that no one gets special treatment. There are no perks, no doles of privilege—not even for apostles. No one rides at the head of the parade.

Because of our Lord's strong teaching on unity and equality, on power-sharing instead of power-hoarding, the Romans saw him as a threat to the empire, and Jewish leaders saw him as a threat to religious tradition.

And threat he was—and still is, for that matter. Because wherever Jesus makes his presence known, things change. This is as true for us as for those who heard him in the first century. You see, Jesus turns dominance into servanthood, the spirit of getting into the spirit of giving, and selfishness into love of neighbor. Only in Christ can all peoples have true dignity and true equality!

Nowhere in the gospels is this point made with greater force than in the lesson for today. Jesus and his disciples had come from Galilee to the rugged south country of Judea and the Transjordan. Tension choked the air. The disciples were restless. Jesus had been talking about what lay ahead of him in Jerusalem; deep suffering—terrible death. They were only days from Jerusalem. Yet, Jesus did not appear apprehensive, rather he spoke freely to the many people that crowded around him. He spoke of prayer and humility—and he warned them against hypocrisy.

In one of these gatherings, some Pharisees approached Jesus with a puzzling question about their laws: "Is it lawful for a man to divorce his wife?" (v. 2). On the surface, this sounds like a simple, straightforward question. But when we read the way Matthew reports it, we see at once that it was a clever attempt to trap Jesus. "Is it lawful for a man to divorce his wife *for any cause?*" (Matt. 19:3).

This matter of divorce was a hot topic in Jesus' time. There were two schools of thought, and they were so opposite that they were stirring up a lot of controversy. Some rabbis were saying that sexual infidelity was the only legitimate ground for divorce. Other rabbis were teaching that a man has the right to divorce his wife for any reason that seemed good to him. Burning the evening meal was to them a just cause for either a beating or a divorce. And there was nothing a woman could do. She was literally at the mercy of her husband.

The Pharisees favored the conservative position, that adultery was the only proper reason for divorce. But suspecting Jesus to be a radical wanting to tear down their Law, the Pharisees hoped to pin him down and show him up for what he seemed to be, a person who had no regard for the sacred traditions. To the surprise of the Pharisees, not only did Jesus hold the line with them on divorce, he was even more demanding! The law of Moses was itself a compromise, he said. Divorce is a tragedy touching the deepest human relationship we can know. But the issue for Jesus was not so much divorce as it was fidelity—and responsibility—and caring.

The question then—and now—is not what the Law allows, but what God intends. Here Jesus did not beat around the bush. "From the beginning of creation," Jesus said, "God made them male and female. For this reason a man shall leave his father and mother and be joined to his wife, and the two shall become one flesh . . . they are no longer two, but one" (vv. 7-8).

No man has the right to dehumanize his wife, to divorce her at the snap of a finger. In God's sight, a woman and a man are equals, with equal rights and equal responsibilities. No one dominates the other! At this the crowd must have gasped for breath.

As if to aggravate the situation even more, Jesus opened his arms to the little children people were bringing to him for his blessing. Even for Jesus' disciples this was too much. If women had few rights in the eyes of society, children had no rights at all! Children were routinely regarded as property, and it was not unusual for a child to be sold to the highest bidder. There were no child labor laws, no child advocate groups, no courts to protect against abuse. Besides, a public figure the stature of Jesus could not be bothered by children. That was an insult! But Jesus scolded his disciples for scolding the children and their mothers. Not only did the Lord receive the children, he said the kingdom of God could not be entered unless one became as a child!

Do you see what was happening in all of this? Jesus attacked a long-standing assumption of his society: That some people are better than others, that the stronger rules the weaker, that the powerful are privileged. This is still a raging battle; every minority group in the United States knows this only too well. With all the advances we have made in our country during this century, we still have an uneasy feeling that the many are at the mercy of the few, that color begets privilege, that money buys power, that oppressors have more rights than victims. It was just these assumptions that Jesus met head-on! So he took those who were weak and socially neglected in his arms and blessed them.

These teachings and actions of the Lord certainly were not oil on troubled waters. Quite the opposite! They were inflammatory. They were profoundly disturbing because they hit at the heart of a society where prejudice reigned: prejudice against Gentiles, prejudice against women, prejudice against children. And Jesus would have nothing to do with such attitudes—and he did not allow his followers to have anything to do with them either. Paul the apostle understood this quite well. Speaking of the power of faith and baptism, Paul wrote to the Galatians: "As many of you as were baptized into Christ have clothed yourselves with Christ. There is no longer Jew or Greek, there is no longer slave or free, there is no longer male and female for all of you are one in Christ Jesus" (Gal. 3:27-28).

We must always remember that on that road to Jerusalem— moving relentlessly toward death *and resurrection*—Jesus was living out the song Mary sang just before his birth: "My soul magnifies the Lord . . . he has shown strength . . . he has scattered the proud in the thoughts of their hearts. He has brought down the powerful . . . [he has] lifted up the lowly; he has filled the hungry with good things" (Luke 1:46-53).

Do you see how deep Jesus' response is to this question? He took the issue to another level! This episode comes right in the middle of a section of Jesus' teachings on true discipleship. Along with his sayings on humility, obedience, renunciation, and how to deal with money, are these statements on equality and unity. Do you feel their force? Do you understand?

If we are to be serious about following Jesus, we must be serious about equal rights for all people, equal status for all people, and also equal opportunity. What Jesus says becomes our standard for fairness, for protection, for self-worth. It is a shame for some to lord it over others, for women to fear sexual harassment on the job, for children to be in danger in their homes.

As modern disciples of Jesus, it is impossible for us to sit back quietly and allow prejudice and abusive power to go unchallenged. We must speak out! Let our voices and votes be heard! As the church, we set the example: in our agencies, on our boards, in our ministries, with the little children. And in this congregation, too! We are called to minister Christ to the scapegoats of society, to the helpless, to the minority.

The mission Jesus sends us on is not an easy one. You can see that! It will certainly not always be popular. It is difficult to redirect power from grasping to caring. It is hard to consider others to be better than oneself. It is natural to hold on tightly to stereotypes, especially ones that put us high on the pecking order. Yet, into our shattered lives, controlled as they are by family pressures and social expectations, comes Christ with what each of us needs most: recognition, acceptance, love, and forgiveness.

So what are we to do? Some of us can study our community to see exactly where the needs are. Others of us can bear our witness in groups and agencies that serve battered spouses and abused children. Still others can join forces with our own church work areas that make matters pertaining to unity and equality a high priority. All of us can pray for the spirit of the season after Pentecost to strengthen us for Christ's great work. "And he took them up in his arms, laid his hands on them, and blessed them" (v. 16).

Suggestions for Worship

Call to Worship (Ps. 25:4-5):

> LEADER: Show me your ways, O LORD, teach me your paths;

> **PEOPLE: Guide me in your truth and teach me,**

> LEADER: For you are God my Savior,

> **PEOPLE: And my hope is in you all day long.**

Act of Praise: Psalm 26 or Psalm 25.

Suggested Hymns: "Joyful, Joyful, We Adore Thee"; "Spirit of God, Descend upon My Heart"; "Spirit of the Living God."

Opening Prayer: Almighty God, you alone can lift us above our brokenness and enable us to live together in unity and fairness. Grant your people grace to practice tolerance, work for equal rights, and protect those who cannot protect themselves. Help us open our hearts to the fullness of your presence through Jesus Christ, who lives and reigns with you and the Holy Spirit, one God, now and forever. Amen.

Pastoral Prayer: Great and living God, who has created every person in your image, please hear our prayer. We are happy today to recognize your majesty. We delight to sing your praise. We rejoice in every expression of your grace, so freely given to those who seek you. Receive our thanksgiving.

Our petitions are many, Father [or Lord], because our needs are many. There is so much hurt in the world. We are constantly reminded how fragile life and fortune are—and how necessary it is to know what is really important. We ask you to reinforce their faith, strengthening them during these days of trial and anguish.

You know, O God, that we have a special concern today. Your Son, Jesus, taught that every person is special in your sight. He also said that Christians are known by their selfless service. In the light of these emphases of the Lord Jesus, we ask you to enlighten and empower us as the people of God to live free from cultural prejudices, to model in our family and church life human relationships of equality and unity, and to proclaim the ethics of Jesus as the norm for the human community.

Receive our praises and petitions through this same Jesus Christ, who reigns with you and the Holy Spirit, one God, now and forever. Amen.

OCTOBER 9, 1994

□

Twentieth Sunday After Pentecost

Poverty is no virtue. Neither is wealth a sin. Yet possessions, whether many or few, may create the illusion that riches are life's best goal.

The Sunday Lessons

Job 23:1-9, 16-17: Job dares to seek a day in court with God. "Oh, that I knew where I might find him . . . I would lay my case before him" (vv. 3-4). He acknowledges that God knows the way he takes, and that the Almighty has terrified him.

Hebrews 4:12-16: The word of God is alive and active. It judges even our thoughts, none of which are hidden from God. Christ is our great high priest. He sympathizes with our weakness, and has been tempted in every way, just as we are, but without sin.

Mark 10:17-31: A rich man knelt before Jesus saying, "Good Teacher, what must I do to inherit eternal life?" (v. 17). His obedience to the laws of Moses lacked one thing. "Sell what you own, and give the money to the poor . . . come, follow me" (v. 21). The man went away sadly, Jesus then said to disciples who had left everything to follow, "It is easier for a camel to go through the eye of a needle than for someone who is rich to enter the kingdom of God" (v. 25).

Reflections

The decision to follow Christ is not the beginning place of discipleship. Commitment of talent and possession is not the bedrock of Christian life. The fundamental factor for faith is poverty. The beatitude says it best, "How blest are they who know they are poor."

Possessions blind one to his or her poverty. They encourage what Thomas Carlyle called "the chirpy optimism" of Emerson. One lives with the illusions that whatever is needed can be had and whatever should be done can be achieved. That arrogance is evident in the self-righteous conceit of a man who was both rich and good. If this good teacher would offer the ultimate discipline for a righteous life or even one more commandment, he intended to obey. "What must I do?" is a works-righteousness question. It takes a long time to learn that we are poor. We try to avoid the futility of absolute poverty. So we learn slowly, and sometimes not at all, that we are wholly dependent on Christ. We turn away, not because discipleship is too demanding. We turn away not because wealth and comfort are too alluring. We turn away because the right and might of Christ seem only an illusion, while possessions appeal as reality. If you will follow, you must desire him more than a dying person wants one more breath. More than you desire possessions, honor, or any other relationship. (JKB)

IT'S NOT THAT SIMPLE ANYMORE

Mark 10:17-31

A SERMON BY JAIME POTTER-MILLER

When I fell in love with my husband, I mused over an idyllic sense of romance and togetherness; it never occurred to me that one day I would look back over twenty-two years of marriage and wonder how we ever made it so far. When I dreamed of having children, I thought of *infants*: portable, huggable, lovable. I never considered that I would eventually be the mother of teenagers. When Jesus Christ first claimed my life, I rejoiced in redemption. I did not count the cost of discipleship that loomed on the horizon. In this account of the rich man whom Matthew calls young and Luke calls a ruler, Jesus insists that those who are potential followers must move beyond the initial path of faith toward an uncharted journey into eternal life.

When our son and daughter were aged three and five, respectively, our family took a vacation and went to the zoo where they each were permitted to select one souvenir. I do not remember what Janna took home with her; Jordan chose a stuffed chipmunk, which he christened "Little Nephew Squirrel." Little Nephew

Squirrel became Jordan's constant companion. When we moved to a new community shortly after the vacation, old friends assumed even greater importance. Little Nephew Squirrel traveled on the tricycle with Jordan, rode on the swing set with Jordan, waited under the permitted climbing trees for Jordan, and even sat beside the swimming pool. Jordan was quite possessive of Little Nephew Squirrel. Three-year-old children are not known for their generosity anyway, but Jordan was adamant: Little Nephew Squirrel was *his* and was not to be shared.

Jordan had another fixation at age three. He was fascinated about the devil. He asked more questions about the satan than any other topic. It was an obsession. So, my husband and I tried to compensate on the other end of his spectrum. Much more suitable, we believed, for a child whose parents are both clergy of the Wesleyan tradition to know of prevenient grace and saving love than always to be pondering damnation.

One day as I was washing dishes, I looked out at my youngsters playing in the yard with some new friends. I heard that song that always signals a prelude to pending disaster. That antiphonal chorus that rings out, "Uh huh!" "Nuh uh!" "Uh huh!" "Nuh uh!" There was a crescendo, and then the chant: "Jordan's goin' to the devil! Jordan's goin' to the devil!" followed by the universal refrain, "Nya nya nya nya nya!" Jordan's cries were frantic. "No, I'm not! No I'm not!" Neighbor Chad taunted, "Yes you are! If you don't share Little Nephew Squirrel, you'll go to the devil!"

I started toward the door. Then I heard my three-year-old son's quavering voice. I had been watching from the window his little red face, tears welling up in those big, shining eyes. "No I won't!" He stood as tall as he could with his hands clenched in fists at his side, "I have Jesus in my heart. I won't go to the devil 'cause I have Jesus in my heart. And if you don't believe me, ask my mom. She's a preacher and she knows *everything*!"

In July of 1987, Jordan and I spent five days primitive camping on Assateague Island while Jeff and Janna were on a Youth Work Mission in Alaska. We talked about everything, solved all the problems of the world and told stories about the good old days. We were then nine years removed from the altercation over Little Nephew Squirrel. Nephew Squirrel occupied an honored space on the shelf reserved for old, loyal friends. Jordan was as tall as I, his face still glowed red when he was upset, and his eyes were just as clear. He displayed generosity nearly to a fault. He did not worry too much about the devil. When this saga from his childhood was rehearsed, Jordan smiled and nodded, "That's true. I have Jesus in my heart, so I won't go to the devil. But it's not that simple anymore, is it?"

Central to Jesus' message is a difficult paradox. Come to him as guileless as a little child; make profoundly difficult mature choices. How simple life would be if all we had to read in the tenth chapter of Mark were verses 13-16. But we have more. As Jesus raises up from the children's innocent embraces, he begins to make his way to the next place. A man hastily appears and kneels in front of him, asking the question begged by what Jesus had been teaching: What must I do to inherit eternal life? Jesus speaks words the pious and devout Jews of his world would understand: keep the Law. The man indicates he already has done that. We have no reason to think that he was being arrogant; some rabbis believed that it was perfectly possible for someone to perfectly keep the Law. Jesus perceived his earnest spirit and said, in effect, the Law is still true, but it is not that simple anymore. Potential followers must move beyond the initial path of faith toward an uncharted journey into eternal life.

Do you remember the quickening of faith in Jesus Christ in our life? I think back and marvel at the sense of abandon I experienced. Rushing into the embrace of Love Incarnate, tumbling headlong over the edge of reason, fully trusting that the net of faith would check my descent into whatever might await me. And through the changing experiences of life, I have reflected back to moments of rekindling when the realization of Immanuel left me breathless once again. The faith that I knew as a newborn believer is still true—but it's not that simple anymore. Just like the man of Mark 10, I understand that elemental components of religion are commitments of ethical and moral candor. Jesus intentionally chose only the second table of the Law, those commandments that speak of a universal commitment to human dignity and responsibility, omitting those exclusively and ritualistically Jewish. Those directives are still true; inheriting eternal life is not that simple.

Simplicity represents a virtue that claims much energy from those who examine the inner life. We are encouraged to simplify our schedules, our accumulations, our evaluative measures of other's behaviors. The simple truths of the gospel are clutched to our hearts as we sort out, categorize, and file the experiences of our journeys for the gospel's sake. What freedom is experienced when the compelling reason for simplification reflects Jesus' intention in this story from Mark. What dangers lurk when we seek to rid our lives of those suggestions we do not like and those responsibilities we had just as soon discard. Intolerance is not simplicity; keeping the law is no substitute for surrender to the whole gospel. Childlike does not mean childish; having Jesus in your heart represents the genesis, not the finality, of Christian life.

Jesus asserts many, many things about abundant life, both eternal and temporal. The foundation of law is to be fulfilled, our awakening experience leads us on to perfection. While initiation can be expressed by commonly understood phrases such as "having Jesus in my heart," the flowering of faith is individualized. "Go, sell what you own, and give the money to the poor, and you will have treasure in heaven" (v. 21). The Gospels reveal that Jesus gave that instruction to only *one man,* just as he told only *one man* to be born again, only *one woman* that she could exchange an introduction to her husband for a drink of living water. The subjectivity with which Jesus addresses those who have him in their hearts is expressed clearly in this account. God knows which idol will separate each person from abundant life. One person's devotion is another person's temptation. To encapsulate eternal life in the Decalogue robs living of grace. To reduce the teaching of Jesus to one act—having him in our hearts—blinds us to the prospects of abundance. The saying is sure and worthy of full acceptance that the Christian life is fraught with heartwarmings and replete with personal salvation. But it is not that simple.

In his book *Quantum Spirituality,* Leonard Sweet writes about going beyond the specific, measurable and attainable into a place that is not so simple anymore.

> All truth ends in mystery. The Enlightenment, which emphasized more the mastery than the mystery of nature, never realized that God leaves more fingerprints than blueprints . . . As one rabbi has observed, "If there is not more than one explanation to an event, then it is not of God" (p. 228).

Sweet then recalls an incident in the life of Albert Einstein. One day Einstein received a letter requesting a rephrasing of the theory of relativity in simple terms explainable to the letterwriter's grandchildren. Einstein wrote back his conviction that reason, no matter how simplified, simply will not do. Only something straight from the heart as music would suffice.

> Dear sir, I am sorry that I cannot comply with your request. The theory of relativity cannot be reduced to simple terms. We find it to be true, the further we look. I hate to disappoint you, but, if you would be willing to come by Princeton some afternoon, I will try to play it for you on my violin (pp. 231-232).

It is essential to have the assurance of belief's basic foundation. However, the fullness of eternal life is a gift entrusted to those who understand that it is not that simple. Sometimes it is not even expressible. John Wesley's Aldersgate Street experience, as profound as it was for Wesley, never became the focus of his ministry. His heart was strangely warmed, but his ministry was never that simple. Through words and music, he and brother Charles lived and sang of the soul "lost in wonder, love, and praise" moving to perfection from the beginnings of personal salvation.

A dream that recurs in my life forms in a misty billow of shapes and images. I stand at the foot of the cross, retching at the sight of torn flesh and smell of oozing blood. I am afraid to look up, yet I feel the magnetic gaze of the one above me. I cower and cover my face in the folds of my robe when I hear the strains of a melody whispered. I cannot hear the words, but I know that Jesus is singing. Singing? In a language I cannot comprehend, Jesus is singing as he dies. I finally raise my eyes to see that it is from my own face that Jesus' voice echoes.

I do not know how I feel about this dream. Although I experience a wash of emotions upon awakening, I sometimes wish that it would not recur. Other nights, I settle onto my pillow praying to feel Jesus that close to me once more. Although the nausea and stench overcome me, I want to be there in the stark presence of his love. It is not a simple matter. It is not Jesus in my heart at issue here; it is me lost in Jesus, allowing his voice to sing through my mouth, his compassion to touch through my hands, his wisdom to be expressed through my mind, his love to reach others through my offering of all that I have. Maybe the dream is given to remind me that the center of my life is grounded in those experiences that speak more of whose I am and what I have to offer than of who I am and what I possess, or strive to inherit.

The man of Mark 10 sadly left Jesus' side and returned to his search for a simple answer. He coveted eternal life to add to his possessions and missed the point of Jesus' answer. So did the disciples, for that matter. So will we if we dwell on the tangibles of riches, the camel and the needle's eye. Instead, hear the intent. Begin with the obvious—keep the Law; let Jesus come into your heart. But do not stop there. Jesus' presence is not yours to be possessed; it is yours to give away. The truths that were foundational are still truth. It is just not that simple anymore.

This passage illuminates a difficult paradox. Receive Jesus in your heart as though you were as guileless as a little child; make the profoundly difficult mature choice to give yourself away by allowing yourself to be lost in him. Those who are potential followers must move beyond the initial path of faith toward an uncharted journey into eternal life. What you believed when you came to faith may still be true, but it is not that simple anymore.

Suggestions for Worship

Call to Worship: (Ps. 22:2-5):

LEADER: O my God, I cry out by day, but you do not answer, by night, and I am not silent.

PEOPLE: **Yet, you are enthroned as the Holy One; you are the praise of Israel.**

LEADER: In you our fathers put their trust; they trusted and you delivered them.

PEOPLE: **They cried to you and were saved; in you they trusted and were not disappointed.**

Act of Praise: Psalm 22:1-15.

Suggested Hymns: "Maker, in Whom We Live"; "O Master, Let Me Walk with Thee"; "Take My Life, and Let It Be."

Opening Prayer: Called by grace and gathered by choice, we your people wait. Listening for the winds of the Spirit, attentive to your brooding presence, alert to Christly surprise, we are content to know that as we open in worship, you are here. Amen.

Pastoral Prayer: Holy, holy, holy! No phrase more sacred escapes our lips as we perceive anew the truth of Jesus' words: only God is Good. And so, we bow in grateful praise before the sunshine of your face. As your radiance streams toward where we stand, we can only allow the rhythm of our heartbeats to speak our joy! Holy, holy, holy! Illuminate this room, this gathering of your children, and be enthroned on the praise of your people.

Yet, the closer we stand to your light, the more we see our shadows and the sharp, defining line of where we stop and you begin. Our condition is clear; your call beckons.

We are creatures of the safe past. But you, Spirit of surprises, invite us to risk our lives for the new thing you will do. We are content to be sheltered in our dens of darkness. But you, Christ who reveals, lift us into the light of exposure. We are burdened by our limited interpretations of reality. But you, expansive Creator, call us to dream dreams and see visions. We are determined to mold the Word of salvation into a narrow familiarity. But you, God of many faces, voices, and pigments, show us a global diversity.

In worship, you open your eyes to obstinate obstructions and over-simplifications. We, who are Christ's followers, will move beyond the initial path of faith into uncharted journeys toward eternal life. For the sake of those who seek life, we will be channels of grace. For the sake of those who search for answers, we will become your divine *yes*. For the sake of those who turn away sorrowfully, we will be your reaching arms.

Give us energy and wisdom to know you, to trust you, and continually to receive you. Grow us into the full measure of witness, love, and grace that Jesus embodied. Sing through our mouths, touch through our hands, convey wisdom through our minds, and love through our lives.

Let it be known that it is not we who live, but Christ who lives in us, with strength, integrity, and courage, and always in God's grace.

Holy, holy, holy! In Jesus' name! Amen.

OCTOBER 16, 1994

☐

Twenty-first Sunday After Pentecost

There is a suffering that saves and a surrender that frees. In God's order, the one who serves is first and greatest.

The Sunday Lessons

Job 38:1-7 (34-41): The Lord God answered Job out of the storm. God began to ask the questions. "Where were you when I laid the foundation of the earth?" (v. 4). "Or who shut in the sea with doors?" (v. 8). "Have you commanded the morning since your days began?" (v. 12). Job's questions became narrow and small.

Hebrews 5:1-10: Every high priest is selected from among humankind to represent them before God. A high priest, who is subject to weakness, will deal gently with the failings of others. Christ did not "glorify himself in becoming a high priest" (v. 5). God called him saying, "You are my Son" (v. 5). Though a son, he was submissive and obedient.

Mark 10:35-45: James and John asked for chief places in Christ's kingdom and were asked in return, "Are you able to drink the cup that I drink?" (v. 38). The disciples, indignant with the Zebedees, were told, "Whoever wishes to become great among you must be your servant" (v. 43). Privilege and triumphalism are not the way of the Son of Man.

Reflections

"Who gets what?" is a pervasive question in every society. Coleman and Rainwater in their study, "Social Standing in America," frame the question as "the relative desirability of life situations." Is it better to be landlord or tenant, management or labor, the servant or the served?

We may readily affirm the importance of a servant style and point to the rewards that attend disciplined work. We may say that status should be based on moral goodness and faithfulness, but in this culture and the modern church, the power of position and the privilege of wealth are the standards by which we usually measure personal worth.

Servant obedience that takes the shape of surrender is simply not honored. A woman, making shallow speeches about liberation, was counseling assertiveness. She said, "I was a slave because I surrendered."

There is truth in it. But it is also true that a child allowed to have his or her own way will become the slave of selfishness. A man willing to satisfy his lust will soon be owned by his passions. A woman asserting her pride may become the slave of her narcissism.

Many are possessed by what they own, bound by their own power. Such sin cannot be corrected. It needs to be redeemed, atoned by the perfect obedience of one who "gave his life as a ransom for many." He invites a surrender to service and offers a bondage that frees.

Persons are shaped more by what they believe to be of greatest value, than by their present station or wealth. (JKB)

TO SERVE THE PRESENT AGE—
OUR CALLING!

Mark 10:35-45

A SERMON BY REGINALD W. PONDER

One of the first Charles Wesley hymns I remember learning is "A Charge to Keep." It was the first hymn I learned to play on the piano in my brief and undistinguished career in music. Written in the key of C (no sharps and flats), it was very easy to play and easy to sing. It is still one of my favorite Charles Wesley hymns, not because of its unsophisticated musical setting, but because of its simple and sound theology. In the second stanza of this familiar hymn, we find these poignant words:

> To serve the present age
> My calling to fulfill,

OCTOBER 16

O may it all my powers engage
To do my Master's will.

There is no doubt in my mind, as there was no doubt in the minds of the Wesleys, that God is calling us to serve our present age—"To Serve the Present Age—Our Calling!" John and Charles Wesley and the early Methodists made a tremendous difference in eighteenth-century England. Will you and I, as servants of the risen Christ, make a dramatic difference in the world where we live? Are we committed to the extent that we are willing to engage all of our powers (strength and energy) in that servanthood to which Jesus calls us?

Being a Christian disciple is more than a privilege, a place of honor and distinction. It is primarily an opportunity to serve. This is what Jesus attempted to share with James and John when they came to him on the road to Jerusalem and asked for the places of honor in Jesus' eternal kingdom (Mark 10:35-45). One wanted to sit at his right hand, and the other at his left. We can share the feeling of resistance (anger) that the other disciples had toward the two brothers because of their presumption.

Jesus, however, was quite patient with them and used their presumption as an opportunity to teach them and the others about the true nature of right relationship in the kingdom. He reminded them of how things were in the world. "You know that among the Gentiles [literally, the people of the nations] those whom they recognize as their rulers lord it over them" (v. 42). It is still that way, isn't it? Almost everywhere I go, even in the church, there is such a preoccupation with position, with rank. I grew up on army bases and was taught to be very rank-conscious. In that environment, everything revolves around rank. When you are the colonel's son, it is hard to be one of the boys.

Jesus gives us another way. He says, "But it is not so among you; but whoever wishes to become great among you must be your servant, and whoever wishes to be first among you must be slave of all" (vv. 43-44). The nature of the Christlike life is *diakonia*—servanthood, ministry. Nowhere is that note needed to be sounded more than among the clergy of our generation. Often we have become so concerned about our status, our professionalism, our salaries, and our pensions that we forget that we are first of all servants of the body of Christ. Jesus even uses the word *doulos*, which means a bond slave.

But lest we think that this message is for the ordained clergy in our midst, let us be reminded that Jesus' words refer to all Christian disciples. Laity, too, are called to be servants. There are some very powerful words in *The Book of Discipline* of The United Methodist Church about the servant role of all baptized Christians. I would like to share them with you because they say so much better than I can articulate what the nature of this servant ministry is.

> The heart of Christian ministry is Christ's ministry of outreaching love. Christian Ministry is the expression of the mind and mission of Christ by a community of Christians that demonstrates a common life of gratitude and devotion, witness and service, celebration and discipleship. All Christians are called to this ministry of servanthood in the world to the glory of God and for human fulfillment. The forms of this ministry are diverse in locale, in interest, and in denominational accent, yet always catholic in spirit and outreach.

> The Church as the community of the new covenant has participated in Christ's ministry of grace across the years and around the world. It stretches out to human needs wherever love and service may convey God's love and ours. The outreach of such ministries knows no limits. Beyond the diverse forms of ministry is this ultimate concern: that men and women may be renewed after the image of their creator (Col. 3:10). This means that all Christians are called to minister wherever Christ would have them serve and witness in deeds and words that heal and free.

> This general ministry of all Christians in Christ's name and spirit is both a gift and a task. The gift is God's unmerited grace; the task is unstinting service.

It is worthy of note that business and industry realize how important service is to their success. The modern management gurus all are focusing on how we are each other's servants. The church must rediscover its servanthood role in the world if we are to make a significant difference in our local communities and the world.

Christian servanthood begins with commitment to Jesus Christ, is extended in a commitment to the church, and is completed in our commitment to the world. We can fulfill our calling to serve this age only as we renew these commitments.

OCTOBER 16

The writer of the Epistle to the Hebrews teaches us that Jesus is "the source of eternal salvation for all who obey him." We know that the word we usually translate *salvation* is the Greek word *soter*, which also means wholeness, health, and well-being. Jesus fulfilled his servant role as an obedient son. You and I are called to that same commitment of obedience.

My father was a very stern man. Though he loved his children deeply, he demanded obedience above all else. He believed that obedience was the key to maturity. We were taught to obey our parents without question or hesitation. Some would call that blind obedience. I came to know it as a way of seeing, a way that utilized the eyes of those who are wiser and more mature. So it is.

Obedience to Jesus enables us to see life through the eyes and mind of Christ. It focuses us to look beyond ourselves and our needs. It transforms our mirrors into windows. We take on a new nature, the nature of a servant, the nature of one who cares for others. Indeed, obedience is the pathway to at-one-ment. Jesus said, "The Father and I are one." That oneness was a result of Jesus' obedience. Jesus also implied that he and his disciples were to be one through their obedience of his way of life. You and I share in the holy privilege through our commitment to obey Jesus' teachings as our way of life. The United Methodist *Book of Discipline* correctly states: "Christian ministry is the expression of the mind and mission of Christ." As we obey Jesus, we express to the world his mind and mission.

Our second commitment of obedience is a commitment to the church. When we are received into the membership of Christ's church, we make commitments of loyalty and faithfulness—to pray, to give, to serve, to attend. We become a part of the body. The apostle Paul teaches us that no part of the body is unneeded; therefore, our part in the body of Christ is essential, and it is important for us to do it. Again, I remind you of a powerful sentence in that statement on the ministry/servanthood of all Christians: "There can be no evasion or delegation of this responsibility."

I am not speaking merely of the "churchy" things we are asked to do. I am also calling to our remembrance the teachings of Jesus that send us out to feed the hungry, to give drink to the thirsty, to give clothing to the naked, to visit the sick and those in prison. When the Church dares to express the mind and mission of Jesus, the people around us take notice. When we fail to be obedient to him, "we lose our vitality and impact on an unbelieving world."

Commitment to Christ.

Commitment to the Church.

Commitment to the world.

"God so loved the world that he gave his only Son" (John 3:16). That Son calls us to love the world, too. In fact, we cannot love God, whom we know in Jesus, unless we love the world. It is my belief that our love for the world has at least two dimensions. The first is a love for people, all people. The second is a love for the earth, the planet, the universe.

"Jesus loves the little children, all the children of the world. Red and yellow, black and white, they are precious in his sight. Jesus loves the children of the world." It sounds so easy when we sing about loving the children. They are innocent. Loving the adults in the world is another matter. There is a force at work in our culture that tends to make enemies out of those who are not like us, who do not live where we live, who do not believe the way we believe, who become our industrial and political competitors. Competition and hate seem to be easier emotions than cooperation and love. Jesus, however, calls us to love and cooperation, to transform our enemies into friends. This may be the miracle our world needs to see coming from the spiritual forces of the church more than any other. I believe that Jesus is calling on the church to be his instrument in the healing of the nations in our generation. We have seen unparalleled political changes in recent years. Can we love enough to make the political changes become changes of the hearts?

Jesus is calling us to love the world through our care of the environment. Perhaps there is no arena in which our selfish desires and wanton wastefulness is more evident than in the way we treat the earth and its resources. Acid rain, the depletion of the ozone, solid waste disposal, nuclear waste disposal, the erosion of farmlands, and the depletion of the forests are some of the ecological issues facing our world. As persons who are called to love the world and to be committed to its betterment, you and I must become better stewards of creation and help others to share this sense of stewardship. On this twenty-first Sunday in Pentecost in the year 1994, you and I, along with all the people in the world, are being summoned to a new sense of caring for the gift of creation. Perhaps there is no test of our sense of Christ-like love that is greater than this.

Yes, you and I are challenged by our master to be servants—servants of Christ, servants of the church, and servants of the world. Will we who wish the place of prominence be willing to take the role of servants in the name of Jesus, the Servant-Savior? "To serve the present age" is our calling! Amen.

Suggestions for Worship

Call to Worship (Ps. 104:1-5):

> LEADER: Praise the LORD, O my soul.
>
> **PEOPLE: O LORD my God, you are very great;**
>
> LEADER: You are clothed with splendor and majesty.
>
> **PEOPLE: He makes winds his messengers, flames of fire his servants.**
>
> LEADER: He set the earth on its foundations;
>
> **PEOPLE: It can never be moved.**

Act of Praise: Psalm 104:1-9, 24, 35c.

Suggested Hymns: "Praise to the Lord, the Almighty"; "Jesus Is All the World to Me"; "Close to Thee."

Opening Prayer: Almighty God, through your Son, Jesus, you showed us that the secret to greatness is in serving. Help us to commit our lives to service, not so that we might become great, but that we might become like him. Help us to commit whatever we perceive to be greatness in us to serving, so that the likeness of Jesus may be seen in us and that others may want to serve in his name, too. Amen.

Pastoral Prayer: Dear God, how much like James and John we are. We struggle to be successful, and often ignore others as we achieve success. We compete with colleagues and hurt the feelings of friends. It seems so silly when we reflect on it in our prayers; yet, we keep on doing it. Please forgive us for our selfish desires and competitive drives that do damage to our discipleship. Help us to seek to serve others in all of our relationships—at work, in our homes, in the church, in our recreation. Enable us to experience the glory of following Jesus through the taking of the mantle of servanthood. We pray in the spirit and name of the one who came to serve and calls us to be servants, too, even Jesus Christ, our Savior. Amen.

OCTOBER 23, 1994

□

Twenty-second Sunday After Pentecost

Blindness, ignorance, and wandering are the prevailing needs in each of the lessons. It is the predicament of each one who would be a follower on the way.

The Sunday Lessons

Job 42:1-6, 10-17: In Job's last reply to the Lord, he acknowledges that he spoke of things "too wonderful for me, which I did not know" (v. 3). He had only heard about God. But now he had actually heard and seen God. He repented, prayed for his friends, and the Lord made him prosperous again.

Hebrews 7:23-28: Our great high priest, Jesus, is "holy, blameless, undefiled, separated from sinners, and exalted above the heavens" (v. 26). Other priests cannot continue in their office because they die. Jesus "holds his priesthood permanently, because he continues forever" (v. 24). It is forever perfect.

Mark 10:46-52: Mark's discussion of discipleship ends as it began—with the healing of a blind man. Bartimaeus was at first rebuked, but then told, "Get up, he is calling you" (v. 49). His request was, "My teacher, let me see again" (v. 51). "He regained his sight and followed him on the way" (v. 52).

Reflections

Some folks are content in their blindness. They believe that a stumbling, wayward style is the way of life. These are the persons who do not want any major disturbance or radical change. They expect the blind man to remain silent in his darkness, and the beggar to be satisfied with his crumbs. But this is not the way of the gospel.

Mark tells the story of blind Bartimaeus as an illustration of faith and following. He sat by a thoroughfare. Hearing that Jesus was passing by, he began to plead. Rebuked and shushed, he only shouted louder. At the first invitation, he threw off his cloak, got to his feet, and with joy came to meet the Christ. He welcomed the questions and was outspoken about his need.

Persons who always remain casual and only follow on their own terms are those who will likely never know the life-changing power of Jesus Christ. They will always wear commonplace shoes in commonplace ways. They may see what Jesus does, but never learn who he is.

If we would meet him, we must have our eyes opened. We must be willing to forsake convictions that stifle, creeds that control, and experiences that blind, until there is nothing between ourselves and God. (JKB)

BLIND SPOTS

Mark 10:46-52

A SERMON BY REGINALD W. PONDER

It was a beautiful fall afternoon. The sky was as clear as it could be. There was not a cloud anywhere. I was driving on Interstate 20 between Atlanta and Birmingham. I had my cruise control set on sixty-five miles-per-hour, and all was going well. As I started up a hill, I pulled out to pass a tractor-trailer rig. I got about half of the way around the truck, and the truck pulled out to pass another truck that was in front of it. There was no place for me to go. I blew my horn, but to no avail. The truck just kept coming out. I pulled all of the way onto the median still blowing the horn. Finally, the truck driver saw me and pulled back into the right lane, allowing me to pull back on the highway. Later as I was telling this story to a friend, he said that I had gotten in the truck driver's blind spot. I know that I have blind spots, too, when I am driving. Also, I have them in my relationship with my wife, in my relationships with members of my staff, in my relationships with other Christians, and especially in my relationships with persons I do not know.

Last Sunday, our focus was on the relationship between discipleship and servanthood. Today, our lessons point us to the relationship between believing and seeing. I plan to look primarily at the Old Testament lesson from Job 42 and the Gospel lesson from Mark 10:46-52. Surely there is no physical sense more essential to life than seeing. Blindness is a serious curtailment to life. But the distinction between those who see and those who do not see is not always as clear as we might imagine. Many of us who have the ability to see adequately do not see things that are in front of our eyes. We have blind spots.

Many of our blind spots have to do with our faith, our believing. We love God. We believe in God. We trust God. But when things do not go our way, we question why God let this happen to us. This was Job's situation, wasn't it? Job knew God, and certainly considered himself to be a righteous man. When things began to go bad for him and his friends began to question Job's relationship with God, Job argued with God, too. In the end, however, Job acknowledges his blind spots and utters one of the great statements of repentance in the Bible: "I had heard you by the hearing of the ear, but now my eye sees you; therefore I . . . repent" (vv. 5-6).

How easy it is, when we are focused on ourselves, to fail to see God or others clearly. We hear the words. We see what is happening all around us, but we do not see God in our midst. The drug problem—illegal drugs, addiction to drugs, drug-related crime—is probably the most hideous influence in our American culture in this last decade of the twentieth century. Yet, many of us in the church pay no attention to it. It has not affected our lives, or so we believe; therefore we do not see it.

Bishop Felton E. May has led The United Methodist Church in addressing this issue. He tells us how the drug culture is tied to persons in poverty who see the trafficking of drugs as a way out and up. He also points to the high involvement of black men in drugs and drug abuse. He makes the startling statement that the drug problem is genocidal for black males. Because many of us are not black, and because many of us do not live in metropolitan centers in which drugs are the number one commodity, we are blind to the crisis that confronts us.

Lest we think that this problem is restricted to the poor and the black, we need to know that the drug epidemic is rampant among affluent white youth and young adults, as well. For them, the escape is from a materialistic world that has no meaning and holds before them no adventure in life. These are youth from the neighborhoods in which the mainline churches have the greatest representation and influence; yet, we say little about the issue. It is our blind spot.

What is more, we are blind to the relationship between alcohol and other drugs. Alcohol is the most widely abused drug in our society, and there are few families in our churches that have not been affected by the pain and loss that accompanies alcoholism. Nevertheless, beverage alcohol has become such an accepted part of our social structure that the church has little or nothing to say about the potential danger of this drug. We have become blind to it.

In a recent volume, *Quantum Spirituality,* Leonard I. Sweet sums up the magnitude of this issue:

> An estimated 75 percent of all convicted felons have drugs in their bloodstream when a crime is committed. Drug consumption outpaces growth in every other human enterprise, except the arms trade. With 5 percent of the world's people, the United States consumes 50 percent of the dangerous drugs. The world's most prescribed drugs? Benzodiazepine tranquilizers with the brand name Valium and Librium. The world's most popular drug? Alcohol. The Sickness treated by the three best-selling drugs in America? Stress.

Bartimaeus, the blind son of Timaeus, who lived in Jericho in the days of Jesus of Nazareth, was not just another person with a blind spot. He was blind. He could not work and had to beg for his sustenance. He was truly blind, or was he? When he heard that Jesus was in Jericho, he cried out, "Jesus, Son of David, have mercy on me!" (v. 47). His friends did not want him to create a scene, and encouraged him to keep quiet. But Bartimaeus knew that his great opportunity was at hand, and kept on crying out to Jesus. Suddenly Jesus stopped and said, "Call him here" (v. 49). His friends told him that Jesus was calling for him, and he threw off his cloak, jumped up, and came to Jesus. Jesus asked him, "What do you want me to do for you?" (v. 51). Bartimaeus replied, "Let me see again" (v. 51). Jesus said to him, "Go; your faith has made you well" (v. 52). Immediately, he regained his sight.

Bartimaeus had a special category of blindness. He had lost his sight. At one time in his life, he could see. Then something happened that caused his blindness. The miracle of this healing was that Bartimaeus' faith in Jesus enabled him to be well, to be whole, to see. The statement, "Your faith has made you well" has a form of the Greek verb, *sodzo,* which is the same verb that is translated "to be healed," "to be made whole," "to be saved." The relationship with faith is clear—faith makes us whole, well, healed. Wholeness or salvation is the result of one's faith is Jesus Christ.

That same faith heals our blind spots, too. Faith in Jesus enables us to see persons with drug and alcohol dependencies, to see persons who are enslaved by poverty and hunger, to see persons who are lonely and depressed, to see persons who are abusive and angry. One of the things we note in this pericope about Bartimaeus is that Jesus noticed the blind man and told the crowd to beckon him. The first step in healing is awareness. The person who has a need must be aware of that need. We find this so true in ministry with alcoholics. There must be awareness on the part of the healer, too. That is where you and I come into the picture. Our faith in Jesus has given us a special sight that enables us to see the brokenness in others. We cannot offer them the healing of the gospel until we are aware of their hurt.

Several months ago, I was walking with a friend in one of the major metropolitan centers of our nation. We passed a man huddled against a building in the dark. When we were about a block away, I asked my friend if he had seen the man against the building. He said that he had not seen him, although he was closer to the man than I was. Isn't that the way it is so often with us? The closer you and I are to the brokenness and hurt of another person, the less likely we are to see it. This is certainly true as it relates to the pains and needs of our spouses and children. Closeness and intimacy often create blind spots. In contrast, Jesus utilized intimacy as a means of seeing clearly, of being aware. Through faith in him and becoming like him, you and I are enabled to see with eyes of awareness.

In addition to being aware, Jesus responded with healing power. We are the body of Christ in the world. Jesus has given to the church the power of healing. We need to believe that in the name of Jesus we can offer healing power, the power of Jesus, to the broken and hurting people of the world. I know that this sounds a bit hokey to many persons in our congregations today. The reason is that we have not been taught about, and we have not seen, this healing power. We read of Peter and John offering this healing power to the crippled man in Jerusalem, but we are not sure that such power has anything to do with us. Let me assure you that it does, for it is the same power that enables Bartimaeus to see. And it is the same power that will offer hope and healing to the people around us who are calling out to the church for help.

We have been given this power, spiritual power, so that others can be made whole. Contrary to what so many think, the power is to help, to heal, others. It is not so that we can brag about what we have. It is a power to share, to give away. Peter said, "what I have I give you." That is all that Jesus asks of you and me. Will we dare to give away the spiritual power of healing that Jesus has given to the church, to us? Is the reason that we do not offer spiritual power because we believe too much in the power of silver and gold? Must the church be impoverished in order to see with healing eyes?

May God grant us the grace to believe Jesus enough to have our blind spots healed, and to offer healing and hope to our broken brothers and sisters who live next to us. Amen.

Suggestions for Worship

Call to Worship (Ps. 34:1-8):

LEADER:	I will extol the LORD at all times;
PEOPLE:	**His praise will always be on my lips.**
LEADER:	Glorify the LORD with me;
PEOPLE:	**Let us exalt his name together.**
LEADER:	Those who look to him are radiant; their faces are never covered with shame.
PEOPLE:	**Taste and see that the LORD is good; blessed is the one who takes refuge in him.**

Act of Praise: Psalm 34:1-8, 19-22.

Suggested Hymns: "All Creatures of Our God and King"; "Heal Me, Hands of Jesus"; "Open My Eyes, That I May See."

Opening Prayer: Eternal God, we know that our blind spots are symptoms of our selfishness, and prevent us from seeing our mission at home and throughout the world as clearly as you desire. Strengthen our faith that our eyes might be opened to see the needs of the world and those needy persons around us, and to offer to them the healing touch of Jesus Christ. Amen.

Pastoral Prayer: O God of infinite love, discipleship is so difficult for us because of the blindness of our way. Show us the way of Jesus so that we might follow his way and discover the joys of true ministry in the world. Help us to see the road of discipline that leads us to others and their need for the healing of the master. Forgive us for being so comfortable in our own circumstances that we have neither heard the cries of broken and hurting persons around us, nor have we seen their sores when they stand before us. Give us sensitive and caring spirits, O God, that we may be more like Jesus in the way we see and in the way we care. Fill us with your Holy Spirit that we might have the healing power to offer to those who cry out to us for health and salvation. We make our prayer in the name of the Great Physician, even Jesus Christ our Savior. Amen.

OCTOBER 30, 1994

□

Twenty-third Sunday After Pentecost

The first and greatest commandment is to love God. Its claim takes precedence over every other loyalty. These are laws with absolute authority—love God and love your neighbor.

The Sunday Lessons

Ruth 1:1-18: A famine in Judah causes Elimelech of Bethlehem to move his wife, Naomi, and their two sons to the country of Moab. He died, as did the two sons. Naomi was left a widow with two foreign daughters-in-law who were Moabites. When she decided to return to her homeland, Judah, she encouraged the two girls to remain with their own people. But Ruth said, "Where you go, I will go. Where you lodge, I will lodge; your people shall be my people, and your God my God" (v. 16).

Hebrews 9:11-14: Jesus is the guarantee of a better covenant (v. 8:22). The temple had been destroyed, but there was now no need for a temple or for temple laws and sacrifices. Jesus has entered the holy place—a tent not made with hands. With his own blood he has obtained eternal redemption.

Mark 12:28-34: Jesus and one of the scribes agreed that the two great commandments are these: (1) Love the Lord your God with all your heart, soul, mind, and strength; and (2) Love your neighbor as yourself. When the scribe added, "This is much more important than all whole burnt offerings and sacrifices" (v. 33), Jesus commended him. "You are not far from the kingdom of God" (v. 34).

Reflections

There were 613 laws in Judaism. Three hundred and sixty-five of them were prohibitions. "You shall not!" The remaining 248 laws were positive. "You shall!" One could perhaps refrain from doing the things prohibited, but how could anyone possibly do all that was required. It was necessary to establish some priorities. What should one do first? Which of the laws is the most important? What is the greatest commandment?

In response to the scribe's question, Jesus aligns himself with those who emphasize obedience to the Mosaic law (not ritual observances) as the lasting foundation of Israel's faith. He cites the shema and its two primary requirements—love the Lord your God above all else, love him with all your heart and soul and mind; and love your neighbor as you love yourself.

Love is not a duty to be done. In Christ, we are not commanded to get it all right. We are told to be in such a right relationship with God that no foolishness can upset our trust in him, and no guiltiness can destroy our belonging to him. Nothing can separate us from the love of God.

Law expressed as love suggests a way of living in the world. It does not prescribe specific duties and observances. Yet, there are two observances that both the Old Testament and the New Testament honor. They are the sabbath and the tithe. Both are very helpful in our love for God and neighbor. Moreover, they are safeguards against love for self.

The recovery of sabbath rest will help us to celebrate our love for God. You cannot be in love with any one without having time for them. The tithe will strengthen our worship of God and our service to neighbor. If you can give a significant part of your money away, it is not likely that that which you possess will end up possessing you. The tithe helps keep us from loving too much the things of this world. (JKB)

VICTIM, SURVIVOR, REDEEMED

Ruth 1:1-18

A SERMON BY LOUISE STOWE JOHNS

[Note to the preacher: This sermon states that the congregation is one that can help heal the pain and scars of victimization. That should not be said without knowledge that in addition to yourself, others in the church are committed to such a ministry. The sermon gives you the opportunity specifically to offer yourself, and special caring ministries within your congregation. Providing a listing of social service agencies and resources for victims in state and government offices reinforces your desire to be of assistance. If done verbally, a list should also be made available. That will take research, but is well worth the effort. The sermon offers good possibilities to "Response to the Word."]

All have been victims at some time in their lives. You have been a victim. If you are nodding yes—at least mentally—stay with me while I touch base with the more skeptical. Being a victim is more than the result of criminal activity (although that is a highly significant cause of victimization). A victim is someone who has been injured, hurt, killed, or is suffering due to the actions of another—intentional or unintentional. Without being so wide in definition as to lose meaning, one can be a victim in a car accident, a fall due to slippery or treacherous surfaces, child abuse or neglect, spouse abuse, in addition to being a victim of a crime such as robbery.

Some do not think of themselves as victims, because when tough and unfair things happen to them, they pick themselves up, brush themselves off, and go on! That seemingly casual description of how one can respond makes it sound like it is all up to the victim. In fact, life experiences make a great difference in how easily one is able to mend after being victimized. Just as the body has built-in self-healing properties, so we can have emotionally, but that comes to a large degree from one's sense of self-worth, self-respect and faith in God, who cares for us individually. These all are related to interactions and messages we have had throughout our lives.

If you do not consider yourself to be a victim, I ask you to dig down and understand how you overcame seeing yourself as one. Our growing concern for the rights of victims is still young, but throughout history bad events have fallen on good people. If you are one who knows well that you have been victimized, suffering that is perhaps too deep and secret even to speak of, I want you to know that within the love of God that is in this community of faith and within yourself there is comfort and cure.

Let us turn to our reading today from Ruth to help us explore one example of a woman who suffered through no fault of her own.

Naomi, the mother-in-law of Ruth, can easily qualify as a victim through untimely deaths. Escaping famine in their own country, Elimelech, Naomi, and their two sons moved to Moab. It was a reasonable thing to do to protect the family; it was also risky—not the least being the enmity between Judah and Moab that was intense. In Moab, the first strike of death fell on Elimelech. Suddenly husbandless in a strange, hostile land with two sons, Naomi had to take charge. When the sons got to the age of marriage they did not return to Bethlehem to find wives. They married two Moabite women. After ten years, the book of Ruth tells us of a mother and wife completely bereft. The sons, "Mahlon and Chilion also died, so that the woman was left without her two sons and her husband" (1:5).

Providentially, Naomi heard then of better times in her home country and longed for her own kin. She and her two daughters-in-law started out and the familiar scene was enacted: tears, blessing, pleading, parting, and determination to remain. The text ends today with Naomi's yielding to Ruth. Naomi was bankrupt, but seeing Ruth's determination, she debated with her no more (1:18). Perhaps, Naomi worried about Ruth's being a burden on Naomi. How would her people feel when they learned that both sons had married Moabite women? Moabites were not to be admitted to the assembly of the Lord—nor were their descendants (Deut. 23:3-6). Marriage to a Moabite would have raised more than a few eyebrows. The book of Ruth does not let the reader forget for long just which side of the tracks Ruth came from! Moab is referred to seven times and Ruth is described as a Moabite or Moabitess, also seven times! In a book only four chapters long, the point is well made.

The return to Bethlehem is less than joyful for Naomi. As a testimony to her emptiness and sense of abandonment, she tells her old friends,

> "Call me no longer Naomi [that is, Pleasant],
>   call me Mara [that is, Bitter],
>   for the Almighty has dealt bitterly with me.
> I went away full,
>   but the LORD has brought me back empty;
> why call me Naomi
>   when the LORD has dealt harshly with me,
>   and the Almighty has brought calamity upon me?"
>   (Ruth 1:20-21)

Naomi's blame and anger at the Almighty seem uncomfortably close to profaning. One should not talk out loud about God in such a harsh manner. It is the rare person, however, who has not had at least a twinge of anger at God: God is, we know, all powerful. Why do senseless, unfair tragedies wreck the lives of innocents with God standing idly by? The Psalm for today is 146. It is a song of hope for all, but especially for the weak and disenfranchised. It is intentionally set in the context of praising the Lord and putting one's trust in God. In many ways, it matches Naomi's plight even as it speaks to us today.

Verses three and five of Psalm 146 warn people not to trust in mortals of any stature, but those whose help and hope are in the God of Jacob will be happy. Naomi decided to return to Judah when she heard that "the LORD had considered his people and given them food" (1:6). Although Naomi never fully understood the consequences of her decision, it was the will of God that she return. She did not comprehend the truth the psalmist wrote that God "lifts up those who are bowed down . . . loves the righteous," and "watches over . . . the widow" (146:8-9). She focused on her grief. At the birth of Obed, Naomi's grandson through Ruth and Boaz, and the heir of Elimelech and Naomi, it is the neighbors who point out Naomi's blessing from God: "Blessed be the LORD, who has not left you this day without next-of-kin . . . [Obed] shall be to you a restorer of life and a nourisher of your old age; for your daughter-in-law who loves you, who is more to you than seven sons, has borne him" (4:14-15). Calling Ruth of more worth than seven sons has a double meaning: Naomi had lost her own sons and the number seven has the symbolic meaning of something that is perfect or most complete.

One need not forever remain a victim. I suggest five ways that hope can be found. The first is to engage yourself in scripture. It will help you know what God has already done, and what God is willing to do in your life. As we read the Bible, we can see how God as acted in the lives of others. They had their ups and downs, and in the midst of that they did not shrink back from calling out to God in anger or despair. God listened and understood, and God hears us today and empathizes with us. The study of scripture can foster a developing sense of peace and hopefulness. As you study, you can be aware of a second way to move from victim to survivor. With God's power and direction, you can begin to overcome a perception of yourself as victim. That will take being honest with your own feelings, and being honest with God. The psalms are a great source for hearing earlier voices that sound very much like our own. The third way is to look to this community as a place to assist you in sustaining your faith; the encouraging word may not always be spoken and any one of us may blunder in expression of concern, but the spirit of God is present here for us as we worship, work, and live communally.

Fourth, you need to determine and face any responsibility you had in your victimization. This could be as harmless as saying to yourself, "the soles on those shoes are too slippery to wear on slick floors," to "I've been enabling her addiction for years." I hasten to add that many are victims in circumstances in which any preventive measure would have been impossible. Therefore, in those times you bear no responsibility. An objective, trained listener is probably essential in sorting out the fine points of this part of your exploration. This part of the process includes the aspect of forgiveness. You may need to accept God's forgiveness for whatever role you played. But if there is no guilt, there is no need for forgiveness—except for the one who victimized you. Realizing the loving compassion and forgiveness God has for each of us, no matter what our sin is, should enable us to begin to extend forgiveness to those who have hurt us. Do not be dismayed if others cannot fathom your desire to forgive. Perhaps they are relying on an external, legal purification—not the internal cleansing that comes through Christ's death.

The fifth way is to utilize your experiences to help others. All you may truly comprehend about the suffering of another is that the person is deeply wounded. Get in touch with that and be willing to be present in the other's suffering.

If those five are placed in a different order, we can spell HOPES to aid in remembering these ways:

H: Help others through your experiences.

O: Open yourself to God's direction, will, and power.

P: Put your life back in your own hands by taking reasonable responsibility—if there is any, receiving and extending forgiveness.

E: Engage yourself in study of scripture.

S: Sustain your faith by being a part of the Christian community.

It is God's parental pleasure to free us, to lift us up, to watch over us. When we praise God, and put our trust and hope in God alone, God will take us beyond being victims, move us through being survivors, to becoming people whose lives have been redeemed.

Suggestions for Worship

Call to Worship (Ps. 146):

LEADER: Praise the LORD. Praise the LORD, O my soul.

PEOPLE: I will praise the LORD all my life; I will sing praise to my God as long as I live.

LEADER: Blessed is he whose help is the God of Jacob, whose hope is in the LORD his God,

PEOPLE: Praise the LORD. Praise the LORD, O my soul.

Act of Praise: Psalm 146.

Suggested Hymns: "Holy God, We Praise Thy Name"; "Jesus, Thine All-Victorious Love"; "Where He Leads Me."

Opening Prayer: We gather to praise you, God of Naomi and Ruth. Gather us together as a worshiping community that loves you and loves one another. Move us to be of one accord devoted to the redeeming work made visible in the sacrificial death of your son. Amen.

Pastoral Prayer: You command us to hear, O Lord, and we do not always want to listen. You tell us that you are the only God, but we run after other gods. You call us to love you completely: with our heart, our soul, our mind, our strength. We find excuses that distract us. Then you command us to love our neighbor.

Surely you do not mean that literally, or surely you want us to love the neighbor who does not require anything and who loves us with baked bread and clean fence lines. We had rather give to mission work for the heathen than to deal with our own personal mission field—within ourselves and near us.

You say you will set people free, but do not take away my crutches and tell me I can be free. You lift up the bowed down, but don't they deserve to be bowed down? Eternal Ruler, even as we honestly question and speak with you, we believe enough to recognize the absurdity of our situation. You bind us up time and time again. Your patience seems to have no end. Help us to commit our heart, mind, soul, and strength to you and risk loving others as we know you love us and as we should love ourselves. Amen. (Based on Mark 12:28-34 and Psalm 146.)

NOVEMBER 6, 1994

□

Twenty-fourth Sunday After Pentecost

Jesus, a poor, homeless carpenter from Nazareth, entered the very gates of heaven. He withheld nothing for our salvation, and so was the perfect gift and sacrifice for the sins of the whole world.

The Sunday Lessons

Ruth 3:1-5, 4:13-17: Ruth's mother-in-law, Naomi, wanting to provide security and well-being for the young woman, sent her to the threshing floor to meet her kinsman, Boaz. "So Boaz took Ruth and she became his wife" (v. 13). She bore a son, Obed, the father of Jesse who was the father of David. They said of the child, "He shall be to you a restorer of life" (v. 15).

Hebrews 9:24-28: Christ did not enter a temple made by human hands. He entered heaven itself. Nor did he offer himself again and again, as a sacrifice for sin. "He has appeared once for all . . . to remove sin by the sacrifice of himself " (v. 26). He will appear again for those eagerly awaiting him.

Mark 12:38-44: Jesus denounced the scribes who parade in long robes, take the best seats, and devour widow's estates. Then he referred to a poor widow's offering, two small copper coins, as the largest gift given. "This poor widow has put in more than all" (v. 43). The gift was measured, not by how much was given, but by how much was left. Some gave large gifts and were still wealthy. After she gave her two copper coins, she was left with nothing.

Alternate Readings for All Saints: Isaiah 25:6-9; Psalm 2; Revelation 21:1-6a; John 11:32-44.

Reflections

"For All the Saints" is a great hymn, and one that is likely to be sung in many churches on this Sunday that is nearest All Saints'

Day (Nov. 1). Who are the saints that are being remembered? Are we singing of all the baptized or only about those who honor their baptism? The Gospel lesson honors a widow who was faithful and generous in spite of the cost.

One thing is certain about those worthy of being remembered as Christian saints: There is no calculating self-interest in their devotion to Christ and in their service to others. Never would such a one expect a place in Christ's Hall of Fame so others could marvel— "See what God has done for her." Never would a true saint stake a future claim on God—"I will get blessings and honor later."

Yet without seeking to be noticed, they are noticed. Without expecting praise, they are praiseworthy. Intending only to be ordinary, just a faithful worshiper, they become examples of devotion for all of us. In *Camelot,* King Arthur remarks, "He was just one more drop in the deep blue sea, but you know, some of those drops sparkle."

It is never easy to recognize a saint, is it? In Jesus' time, the scribes and Pharisees were considered most holy. Today, we think of good Christians as missionaries, ministers, faithful church members, and pious souls. I look for examples of right living among persons who are well adjusted, morally upright, and socially dependable. I hope that that poor widow did not look like a bag woman from the streets of New York; like the one I saw sitting on the steps of St. John's. But I cannot be sure. I am most times confused, and always surprised concerning the identity of the saints. (JKB)

CRYING SAINTS

Revelation 21:1-6a

A SERMON BY LOUISE STOWE JOHNS

As tears well up within someone, often those same tears are quelled by a resolve *not* to cry. Though tears borne of pain are therapeutic, generally we do not want others to see our distress. If you are a person who thinks there is no such thing as a good cry, you will be glad to hear that apparently in the New Jerusalem, God wants to eradicate the root of crying. In Revelation, John describes that new heaven and new earth, as he recalls Isaiah 25. In creation renewed by God, "[God] will wipe every tear from their eyes. Death will be no more; mourning and crying and pain will be no more" (Rev. 21:4).

It is important to us that Jesus experienced emotions, including crying. It helps us, especially on dark days, to call on Jesus and feel confident that he understands. The narrative of Jesus, Mary, Martha, Lazarus, and other Jews in John 11 is a moving description of grief over the death of one who was greatly loved. A message was sent urgently to Jesus by Lazarus' sisters that he was sick. "Lord, he whom you love is ill" (11:3). But Jesus remained where he was. When Jesus and the disciples arrived in Bethany days later, Lazarus' family and friends were devastated. Lazarus was no longer ill. Lazarus was dead.

Artists who desire to depict Jesus have quite a challenge. The results have shocked people whose ideas of Jesus differ from that of the artist. I have never seen a work of art of Jesus with tears flowing down his cheeks as he became completely immersed in the turmoil of mourning Lazarus' death. Would that cause us to think that Jesus was weak? Would we be shocked? When Jesus saw Mary, weeping over her brother's death—and what could have been if Jesus had come sooner—he was "disturbed in spirit and deeply moved" (11:33). After Jesus asked where Lazarus had been laid, he was told to follow them. Jesus felt the sorrow of earthly death. He wept; his grief was not hidden. Some who saw were moved by Jesus' great love for Lazarus. Others, who obviously had belief in Jesus' powers, wondered if those powers could not have saved Lazarus (11:36-37).

I think people were surprised at Jesus' crying. I doubt the disciples were prepared. After word was brought of Lazarus' near-death condition, Jesus calmly explained to the disciples that this was an opportunity to increase their belief. He told them, "This illness does not lead to death; rather it is for God's glory, so that the Son of God may be glorified through it" (11:4). Without hurry and with the precise intention of teaching the disciples and others, it was at least four days after news of Lazarus that Jesus appeared in Bethany. One certainly cannot fault the disciples for not anticipating Jesus' expression of deep emotion, but this story raises a question: How attentive are we to what pleases or gives pain to those whom we love?

The college class was made up of professional women, with years of experience in rearing children, and more recently experience in paying jobs. The subject at hand in the class on "Women and Religion" was sacrifice and servanthood. One woman spoke, confirming the mutual love she and her husband had for each other. "I have no doubt my husband would lay down his life for me. But, he wouldn't vacuum the stairs." The class's laughter of recognition showed they identified with her feelings. They also heard her unspoken plea, "Understand my simple, daily needs. I don't live in a world that demands life-saving efforts on an ongoing basis. I live in a world of dirty dishes, spills on the floor, unfolded laundry, and dust on the stairs."

A woman in her mid-eighties had been trapped for years in an almost useless body; her mind was alert, but communication was virtually impossible. Her family anticipated her death, some days even wishing for an end to her suffering. The news of death did come early one morning, and her son accepted it without a break in his voice. There was no question of the love between son and mother. This was to be faced and embraced as God's gracious freeing of a soul, long-bound toward heaven. But the son's wife understood that there was pain and sadness. She tried reaching out to him, wrapping him in her arms, but he seemed to pull away. She tried talking about his mother's death, but the responses were routine and matter-of-fact. As she felt more and more on the fringes, unable to cry with her husband, she searched within herself and prayed to know what more she could do. Several days passed, and then she recalled what he had told her when his father had died when he was a teenager. "I went to the woods to be alone, to think. My brother found me and told me to come home. That made me very angry. I needed to be by myself." The wife determined to be ready when her husband began his return from the woods. She also determined not to urge him out prematurely.

A story is told in Madeleine L'Engle's book, *Walking on Water,* about a Hasidic rabbi known for his piety. One day the feelings of a devoted, young disciple spilled over in exuberance, "My master, I love you!" Looking up from his books the rabbi asked the man, "My son, do you know what hurts me?" The disciple was taken completely aback and wanted to be sure the rabbi had understood the depth of his adoration. "I'm trying to let you know how much I love you and you have confused me with your trivial question." The rabbi responded, "Oh, my question is nei ther confusing nor trivial. For if you don't know what hurts me, how can you truly love me?" (Madeleine L'Engle, *Walking on Water; Reflections on Faith and Art* [Wheaton, Illinois: Harold Shaw Publishers, 1980], pp. 70-71.)

November 1 is recognized in the Christian world as All Saints' Day. I have been describing one attribute of a saint: One who tends to the wounds of others. Sainthood is not something lived on a blissful plane of existence. The saint lives in the present, and open to the Holy Spirit's in-breaking. Saints are wiling to give up their lives for others by vacuuming the stairs, or waiting at the edge of the wood. George Bernard Shaw said, "I want to be thoroughly used up when I die." Maybe that is another way of saying what Jesus told the people about being a good shepherd, "The good shepherd lays down his life for the sheep . . . No one takes it from me, but I lay it down of my own accord. I have power to lay it down, and I have power to take it up again. I have received this command from my Father" (John 10:11-18).

A fourteen-year-old daughter, as she struggled with the impending death of a close friend, reached out in love to her mother. The mother was on a trip a year after the death of her father and sister. The child sent a letter to be opened on the anniversary. Later the mother wrote of the importance of the child's mourning with her, "Her sweetness and thoughtfulness were touching. The walk of grief can't always include the presence and comfort of others. But all three of my family have been solicitous—and available; that has made it more bearable."

The words to the hymn, "I Sing a Song of the Saints of God" were written by Lesbia Lesley Scott for her children. Later, she said she disliked it because it made becoming a saint sound pretty easy. I respectfully disagree. At the end of each verse, Ms. Scott reacts to the possibility of being a saint—each time quite on target and hardly easy. The first verse ends with a resolve to be a saint—with God's help. The third verse describes how saints light up the world and concludes with a statement of Ms. Scott's resolve: "The world is bright with the joyous saints who love to do Jesus' will. . . . and I mean to be one too." Sainthood is not an honorary title. It *is* earned, but never sought for itself, or selfbestowed.

We look forward to the time of God's lovingly drying the tears from our eyes. But in this life, we must have saints to weep with us. You and I can be saints, and as a sign of our love, cry with those who stare into the dark tomb.

As Jesus cried with empathy and personal sorrow, I wonder if the disciples cried with their Master and friend.

Suggestions for Worship

Call to Worship (Ps. 127:1-2):

LEADER: Unless the LORD builds the house, its builders labor in vain.

PEOPLE: **Unless the LORD watches over the city, the watchmen stand guard in vain.**

LEADER: In vain you rise early and stay up late, toiling for food to eat,

PEOPLE: **For he cares for those he loves.**

Act of Praise: Psalm 42 or Psalm 127.

Suggested Hymns: "Great Is Thy Faithfulness"; "O Zion, Haste."

Opening Prayer: We come today as your people, holy and pure God, seeking your face and longing to be in your glorious presence. Ruler of all heavenly and earthly beings, fling wide the gates to your temple that we may enter in and worship you. Amen.

Pastoral Prayer: Our Alpha and Omega, it is with joyful and thankful hearts that we recall and honor your saints who have lived and died and who are now part of the heavenly host. They have been shining stars of our faith—shining not because of sinlessness, but because of obedience, faith, and great compassion. We recall Sarah and Abraham, Ruth, Micah, Elizabeth and Zechariah, Andrew and Peter, Paul and John. May their witness that is so rich in our biblical tradition become our story.

We lift up leaders in the church over the centuries: Monica whose piety and devoted praying were instrumental in the conversion of her son, Augustine; St. Francis of Assisi and St. Clare of Assisi; Martin Luther; John, Charles, and Susanna Wesley; Antoinette Brown; Gandhi and Kasturba his wife. These noble witnesses have lighted the way giving us a glimpse of your kingdom on earth. We praise you for continuing to raise up saints in our time: theologian Karl Barth, Pope John XXIII, Martin Luther King, Jr., Billy Graham, Marjorie Mathews, and Rosa Parks.

We give you thanks for the saints unknown to us, but whose witness has changed lives and inspired others to live in your way. We are indebted to saints in this church whom we name in silence now. [Pause] May we look to these great women and men as models of faith and be inspired by their lives of devotion. With your help we desire to be saints, too, loving to do your will.

We look toward the new heaven and new earth in which you will wipe away all tears from our eyes, and in joy and gladness we will sing with all the saints in one glorious chorus. Amen.

NOVEMBER 13, 1994

□

Twenty-fourth Sunday After Pentecost

The Epistle articulates our need. "You need endurance" (Heb. 10:36). "Do not, therefore, abandon that confidence of yours" (Heb. 10:35).

The Sunday Lessons

I Samuel 1:4-20: Hannah grieved because she was childless and barren. One day she prayed, "If only you will . . . give to your servant a male child, then I will set him before you as a nazirite until the day of his death" (v. 11). *Nazirite* means one separated or one consecrated. She conceived and bore a son and named him Samuel. "I have asked him of the LORD" (v. 20).

Hebrews 10:11-14 (15-18), 19-25: The final authority of Christ, who made a single sacrifice and "sat down at the right hand of God" (v. 12), will outlast every enemy. Abuse, suffering, and loss are joyfully accepted by his followers "since you knew that you yourselves had a better possession and an abiding one."

Mark 13:1-8: Jesus' disciples were amazed when they saw the majestic temple that Herod had built in Jerusalem. "Look, Teacher, what large stones!" (v. 1). Jesus replied, "All will be thrown down" (v. 2) and foretold its destruction. On the Mount of Olives, they wanted to know, "When will this be?" (v. 4). Signs of the end (wars, imperialism, earthquakes, famine, persecution, cosmic signs) are noted by Mark, but no immediate date is forecast. Steadfast faith is encouraged. Though the sun dims and stars fall, the faithful shall be gathered "from the ends of the earth to the ends of heaven" (v. 27).

Reflections

At a memorial service for the late Jameson Janes, his friend and colleague Bishop Dwight Loder helped all who gathered to remain confident in faith. He spoke plainly about the realities of grief and loss, and profoundly about our victory in Christ.

The profound was made simple, even humorous, through the sharing of some of Jameson's favorite stories. One told of a man who advertised for his wife's lost cat and offered a five-thousand-dollar reward for its return. The man taking the advertisement said to him, "That's a rather risky thing to do. Somebody may find that cat." He said, "No, they won't." And the man said, "But how do you know; five-thousand dollars is a lot of money for a cat." The man said, "When you know what you know, you can afford to be extravagant. I personally drowned the cat and buried it myself." Then Jamie went on, "The moral of that story is when you know what you know, then what appears to be taking a risk to others is no risk to you."

There is no fear when you know what you know about the love of God. There is no uncertainty when you know what you know about the power of God. There is no despair when you know what you know about the eternal Christ.

Henri Nouwen writes about a spiritual pilgrimage that he calls the movement from illusion to prayer. There are ten-thousand things that appear to be more permanent in power and more final in conquest than the victory of Christ. Such things threaten all our tomorrows and are plainly seen. War can be seen on the six o'clock newscast. Sooner or later, disease visits every home. When the earth trembles and mountains fall, it is seen, felt, and heard. The careful sightings of astronomers suggest that the sun grows dim.

The faithful seer looks beyond the last day to "see the Son of Man coming in the clouds with great power and glory." (JKB)

SHE GAVE HIM TO GOD

I Samuel 1:4-20

A SERMON BY JOHN K. BERGLAND

She was loved. She was cared for. She was adored by her husband. He provided more than she needed—a double portion of everything. But she was unhappy, envious, and bitter. Her name was Hannah, and she was barren.

To be childless in ancient Israel was to be bereft of all worth and significance. There was no burden heavier than that of failing to provide an heir for the husband who loved and favored his wife above everyone else. Elkanah had an impressive pedigree in the tribe of Ephraim. His fathers had provided him a glorious past. But his favorite wife, Hannah, could provide no future. Hannah's pain was made greater when a second wife, Peninnah, gloated over the children she had borne for Elkanah and ridiculed the fruitlessness of Hannah.

But it was not the criticism of a rival wife that finally made Hannah desperate. Her's was a sadness rooted and grounded in her reality. God had closed her womb. It was not the cattiness of another woman that hurt her. Neither could the gentleness of her man console her. Elkanah tried to help. He tried to comfort is wife saying, "Why are you so sad? Am I not more to you than ten sons?" Neither ridicule nor consolation changed the hard truth about Hannah. There was no child, no prospect of birth, no anticipated heir, no future generations, no hope for the promise. Her life was desolate because God had closed her womb. Only God could answer her need.

Israel's story begins like this again and again. Faith and future are threatened by a present circumstance of hopelessness. Sarah was the old and barren wife of Abraham. She laughed at the prospect of bearing a child. Abraham's faith and God's promise seemed to have failed after all.

This story is for persons for whom hope seems hopeless. If you are here today with failed dreams and a broken spirit, listen! Like the poet Auden writes, "In the deserts of our hearts, let the healing fountain start. In the prison of our days . . ."

One Sunday, following a week when there had been three funerals in our parish and more failure, brokenness, and grief than we could bear, our parish visitor commented, "There was at least one sad and broken heart in every pew." So at the outset let those persons who find life barren, hopeless, and seemingly desperate hear this story and this good word, "In the midst of hopelessness there is answer to your prayers."

There is reward for waiting—even bitter waiting. There is new life to be had, and its gifts are beyond anything for which you have hoped or dreamed. For Hannah, sadness gave way to song. Her grieving spirit was healed with a flood of joy. But first there was prayer—heart felt, soul searching, deep down, true desire prayer.

It happened like this. Elkanah and Hannah had gone to Shiloh, the center of worship for Israel in those days. In this holy place, a barren woman found her wailing wall. Her heart was centered on her deepest need. Her vow was pointed towards her dearest dream. "Give me a son," she prayed, "And I will give him to you."

Her prayer came only from the deepest recesses of her being. Her heart prayed, no words could be heard. The old priest watching her thought she was in a drunken stupor. "Give up the wine!" he scolded. Then Hannah answered. "I'm not drunk. I've been speaking out of my deepest anxiety and the heavy vexation of my spirit." Eli, the priest assured her that such prayer does not go unanswered. Hannah left that praying place with new hope and a new shining face.

In a short time, she conceived and gave birth to a son. She named the boy child Samuel, "I have asked him of the Lord." Now comes the part of the story that I cannot comprehend. This little boy, this only son, this one more precious to her than her own life, was surely the dearest thing she had in all this world. And she gave him away. She gave him to God.

Theodore L. Cuyler was for thirty years the respected and loved pastor of the Lafayette Avenue Presbyterian Church in Brooklyn. Near the end of his ministry, he gave a window as a memorial to his mother. The artist was instructed to portray Hannah with her infant son, Samuel. Beneath it were the words, "As long as he lives I have lent him to the Lord."

A young mother, wholly devoted to her three young children asked, "Do you think I'm doing a good job?" Almost every parent wants to, but isn't it true that as the years pass and we look back over the difficult decisions and impossible circumstances—when we see the conflict and failure in our children's lives—we wonder if there were not some things we could have and should have done better.

Do you think Hannah was a good parent? I know that her prayers, her thanksgiving, and her commitment have been held up as a worthy example for parents. She has been used as the model for a good mother in more than one Mother's Day sermon. But do you think she had it right?

I tested this story with two of our grandsons, aged six and eight. I told about a sad and brokenhearted woman who thought that her life was barren and wasted because she was childless. She prayed with such heaviness and grief that her praying and groaning were like a drunken stupor. But God heard those anguished prayers and God answered her. She conceived and gave birth to a baby boy. She named him Samuel because she got him from God.

For three years he was her whole life. In fact, she probably nursed him for three years. This was often the custom in the arid regions of the Middle East. Child care was made easier this way. Moreover, rabbis taught that children were to have no duties or responsibilities in the first three years of their lives. Like a tree that is not expected to yield fruit until the fourth year after its planting, so children were expected to be wholly dependent on their mothers for the first three years of their lives.

But then came the day when Samuel was weaned. Hannah took him to the temple and gave him away. She gave him to the old priest Eli to be his helper and servant. "She lent him to the Lord!"

My grandsons, who love Bible stories, listened intently without asking a single question. So I asked one. "Would you like to have a mother like the baby Samuel's mother?" I asked. "No!" they exclaimed. "Why not?" I asked. Together they answered with the same sentiment I have felt toward this story through all the years that I have known it. "Because she gave him away. We wouldn't want a mother who takes you to a temple and leaves you there."

They had been taken to church from the time they were babies and often they had been left for mother's morning out, super Wednesday children's programs, vacation church school, and varieties of programs for Christian education, but this was different. It was like the poor, bereft father who, unable to care for his two young daughters, took them to a convent and left them there. From that time on it would be their home and family. He left them there.

In his autobiography, Bishop Edwin Holt Hughes tells of the ordination of his oldest son as a Methodist minister. When this young man was ordained a deacon his father, Bishop Hughes, was the family representative. But when he was ordained an elder in the church, his mother gave the charge. As a part of her charge to him she said, "We gave you to God. We have never taken our gift away from him. . . . We have not felt that in giving you to God we have taken you away from ourselves. Rather, have we felt that since the day when you concluded to preach the gospel of his grace and love, you have been ours more that ever—because our parenthood is itself from God, with whom we reverently and gladly share his own gift" (Edwin Holt Hughes, *I Was Made a Minister* [Nashville: Abingdon-Cokesbury, 1943], pp. 256 ff.]). Surely, she must have had the story of Hannah's dedication of Samuel in mind. "She lent him to the Lord."

The boy Samuel was the dearest thing she had. She gave him to God. The desire for a child completely obsessed Hannah, but when Samuel was born, she was able to give him up. Gerald G. May is a psychiatrist who serves as a spiritual guide at Shalem Institute in Washington, D.C. He writes about attachment and detachment in his book, *Addiction and Grace* (Harper and Row, 1988). We can become addicted to beliefs, to relationships, to possessions, and to almost every dimension of human behavior and experience. Obsessions like tobacco, alcohol, and drugs are not the only addictions that claim our freedom. We can become addicted to our children.

May defines addiction as "a state of compulsion, obsession, or preoccupation that enslaves a person's will or desire." He calls the way by which desire becomes addiction *attachment*. "We succumb because the energy of our desire becomes attached, nailed, to specific behaviors, objects, or people. Attachment, then, is the process that enslaves desire and creates the state of addiction. . . . Detachment is the word used in spiritual traditions to describe freedom of desire. Not freedom from desire, but freedom of desire" (p. 14).

Obsessions use up our time and energy. The highest goal for human personality, says Jesus, is to love God with one's whole being. The scriptures make plain to us that the Lord God intends for us to desire him above all things. When we become obsessed with and wholly committed to anything or anyone, that desire becomes idolatry. It makes such a compelling claim, such a costly demand, that we fail to cherish the creatures greatest need—the love of our Creator.

Hannah's desire for a child was an obsession. But the child she desired so much, and indeed loved so much, brought her her greatest joy when she lent him to God.

Abraham's willingness to sacrifice his only son Isaac; Hannah's willingness to "lend to God" her only son Samuel, at first seem radical and excessive. But consider how basic it is for a right relationship with God, and therefore with others. The first commandment of both Judaism and Christianity is, "You shall have no other gods before me." God has been saying throughout the long years of salvation history, "Nothing and no one, no one and nothing, shall be more important to you than I am." God is the source of love that enables all love. He is the ultimate treasure by which every other treasure is given worth.

Bishop Hughes' wife concluded her charge to her young clergyman son with these powerful words. "It does not seem long since that morning when God placed you in my arms. I had no feeling then that you left his arms when you came to mine. Again tonight, as I have so often done, I place you in the arms of God. I have no feeling now that you leave my arms when I place you in his. You are my son the more because you are his son the more. I gladly give you to Christ—utterly and forever. You are to be the Saviour's minister. He will keep you, guide you, comfort you, strengthen you" (p. 258).

When Hannah gave her first-born son, Samuel, as a minister to the Lord, her heart filled with joy. Once, when burdened with bitterness and grief, she had come to the temple with groaning and tears. But this was no sad woman anymore. Her whole life was a song. Her words were like these: "My heart exults in the Lord. My strength is exalted in the Lord. There is none holy like the Lord, there is none besides thee; there is no rock like our God."

This happy mother sang more wisely than she knew, for the Lord God was raising up his prophet and getting ready to deliver his people. Don't you wish that every child was so well placed?

Suggestions for Worship

Call to Worship (I Sam. 2:1-8):

LEADER: My heart rejoices in the LORD; There is no one holy like the LORD;

PEOPLE: **There is no one besides you; there is no**

Rock like our God.

LEADER: The LORD brings death and makes alive; he brings down to the grave and raises up.

PEOPLE: **The LORD sends poverty and wealth; he humbles and he exalts.**

LEADER: For the foundations of the earth are the Lord's;

PEOPLE: **Upon them he has set the world.**

Act of Praise: I Samuel 2:1-10 or Psalm 113.

Suggested Hymns: "All Praise to Thee, for Thou, O King Divine"; "My Hope Is Built"; "Leaning on the Everlasting Arms."

Opening Prayer: O God our Father, it is you who gives to all people life and breath, a place to be, persons to love, work to do, and strength to do it. You have freely given us all things. Grant this one gift more: More love for you. Free us from the attraction and addiction of things made, and help us to desire their maker. O God, forbid that we should take any gift from your hand, and neglect to take your hand. Draw near to us as we seek to draw near to you through Jesus Christ, our Lord. Amen.

Pastoral Prayer: Lord God, You know the things we want and you know how willfully and proudly we seek them. You know the hunger and thirst, the longing and desire, the passion and involvements of our hearts. We are a people who have sought safety in power, security in possessions, and satisfaction in self. We write our own plan of salvation, and expect deliverance through our own discoveries. But we are a people who have failed to satisfy our spiritual longings with any novelty of our making, or with any created object or attraction.

Even when we know that our hunger is for you alone, O God, we try to keep our attachments to things and people. We have sought you in ways that require no sacrifice, and in covenants that protect our power. We want deep peace, ultimate satisfaction, and eternal salvation, but we want it through relationships that we can shape and define.

Your word teaches us that you are a jealous God. Your law requires that there be no gods besides you. Your blessing is for the pure in heart who will only one thing. Your Son, our Lord, invites his disciples to leave lesser things and follow him. It is in yielding that we are satisfied. It is in surrender that we are saved.

Create a new and right spirit within us, O God. By thy grace let true affection, love, and longing remain in us, but transfer, purify, transform, and set on fire the desires of our hearts. Purge and sanctify our longings, so that we may be set free from all that enslaves us. Give us clean hearts that we may love you, even as you have loved us. Amen.

NOVEMBER 20, 1994

□

Twenty-sixth Sunday After Pentecost
(Christ the King)

On this final Sunday of the church year, Christ is praised as
King of kings. "Through days of preparation thy grace has
made us strong. And now, O King Eternal, we lift our battle
song."

The Sunday Lessons

II Samuel 23:1-7: In his last words, King David said, "the spirit
of the Lord speaks through me" (v. 2). He likens ruling in the
fear of God to the sun and the rain—"like sun rising on a cloud-
less morning . . . rain on the grassy land" (v. 4). The godless are
like thistles and thorns—"they cannot be picked up with the
hand" (v. 6), and are burned on the spot.
Revelation 1:4b-8: The beginning of the messages to the seven
churches bears greetings, "Grace to you and peace" (v. 4) from
Jesus Christ who is "the ruler of the kings of earth" (v. 5). He
made us a kingdom. "To him be glory and dominion forever and
ever" (v. 6). An announcement of the parousia follows the doxol-
ogy.
John 18:33-37: Jesus was led to the praetorium, a magnificent
palace that Herod the Great built for himself, and that Roman
procurators (agents of the emperor) used when they came to
Jerusalem from Caesarea. It was the judgment hall. Christ was
standing in this palace when Pilate entered and asked, "Are you
the King?" (v. 33). The humble Galilean, on his way to a cross,
answered that he was born a king. "My kingdom is not from this
world" (v. 36).

Reflections

Isaac Watts has given us the words for praising Christ the king.
"Jesus shall reign where'er the sun does its successive journeys

run; his kingdom spread from shore to shore, till moons shall wax and wane no more." One cannot sing them without realizing this is a cosmic Christ with eternal dominion.

The historic role of kings and queens was one of absolute power and sovereignty. Not only did they own everything; they also established the laws and decrees that determined the way of life for their subjects. Everyone was subordinate to the king, but that rule only reached to the far edge of the kingdom. He ruled in his castle and courts, in his fields and forests—but not everywhere.

The kingdom of our Lord spreads from shore to shore. It outreaches the sun. It outlasts the moon and stars. We can never get far enough away to get away from the power of God. Surely such cosmic rule should humble us, intimidate us, and leave us trembling in fear. It is a terrifying thing to be surrounded by a power, so great, that one can neither define nor modify it.

Christ the King contradicted the usual ways of sovereigns. He is more powerful than any. His riches exceed all others. His kingship outlasts all others. But he did not and does not use any of his sovereign power and glory to lord it over his subjects. Instead, he became their servant and, indeed, their sacrifice.

The nearness of Christ the King is not terrifying. His presence is neither aloof, nor are his ways unknown to us. His shed blood does not need to be avenged, but is instead redemptive. Our king is gracious and merciful, yet he rules from the throne of God.

An ancient drama, both comedy and tragedy, centers on the practice of killing the king as a sacrifice before he became old. His blood was offered as fertility for his kingdom. The practice arose of making a condemned prisoner "Shadow King" for one day, so that a pretend king might die instead of any of the true royalty. Dressed in purple and crowned in mockery, he would be led away to die.

Some, indeed many, thought they were crucifying a pretender when they nailed Jesus of Nazareth to the cross. Not so! His dominion and power reach to the ends of the earth. (JKB)

CRAIG M. WATTS

THE ODD KING AND
HIS NONCONFORMIST PEOPLE

John 18:33-37

A SERMON BY CRAIG M. WATTS

We are impatient with complexity, aren't we? Whether it comes in the instructions that accompany those some-assembly-may-be-required toys we regretfully buy for our children, or in the policies proposed by politicians, we want simplicity. Amazing grace, how sweet the sound of an answer untainted by convolution, uncluttered by jargon, unmuddled by obscurity. We long for a straightforward yes or no.

But we have to be careful that our desire for simplicity does not short-circuit our search for truth. As playwright Oscar Wilde once noted, "The truth is seldom plain and never simple." Sometimes it is necessary to walk through a labyrinth of flawed assumptions before we find our way to the truth.

Pontius Pilate wanted a simple answer from Jesus. "Are you the king of the Jews?" Spit it out. Yes or no. Answer plainly. Answer quickly. Above all, answer briefly. "Are you the king of the Jews?" (v. 33). The question is clear enough, isn't it? Surely you can respond with equal clarity, Jesus. No more than a single breath of air should be necessary to bear the message. Let's hear it. "Are you the king of the Jews?"

I cannot help but think that Pilate asked the question with some amusement. There stood Jesus, wearied by a night of interrogation and abuse. He had been ushered before Pilate with accusations, not fanfare. He was unaccompanied by an entourage. He was unsupported by an army. His position was certainly not fit for a king.

The very idea that the bruised and beleaguered man that stood before him could be taken for a king must have seemed ridiculous to Pilate. He allowed his soldiers to humiliate Jesus. They heartlessly mocked him, shoving a crown of thorns on his head, and bowing before him. King Jesus, indeed! There was nothing royal about him. At least nothing that could be seen by Pilate's eye.

Pilate's eye had been trained by what he had previously seen or heard of kings. His past experience had not prepared him for

Jesus. He knew only of kings whose reign was sustained by blood and steel. A king who was not a power-broker was without meaning to Pilate. No doubt he was familiar with the murder and treachery that characterized the Jewish King Herod the Great, and his successors. He would have been ever better acquainted with Tiberius Caesar who did not hesitate to put to death his rivals on trumped-up charges. The stories of the Caesars that preceded Tiberius would have been known by Pilate. With all of this as a backdrop, he asked Jesus if he was a king.

There could be no simple answer that would not produce more misunderstanding than truth. Too much clutter of preconceptions had to be swept away first. Jesus tried to probe Pilate about the question he asked concerning Jesus' kingship. Pilate rebuffed him and then insisted, "What have you done?" (v. 35). Why have you been dragged before me? Jesus' reply seemed to ignore Pilate's question. Instead, he spoke of the distinctive nature of his own reign. "My kingdom is not from this world. If my kingdom were from this world, my followers would be fighting to keep me from being handed over to the Jews. But as it is, my kingdom is not from here" (v. 36).

"Not of this world." No turf to protect. No borders to defend. No soldiers to train and arm. No enforced subjugation of the populace. A kingdom without coercion. That is Jesus' kingdom. Chances are Pilate believed that a king without an earthly domain is destined to have a rule of irrelevance. After all, what is a king if not an embodiment of power? And what is power if not the ability to control people and institutions on earth?

There have always been those who believe that power comes out of the end of a gun, or by the edge of the sword. But Jesus knew that the only power that matters is the power that comes from submitting to God. He demonstrated that dominating and manipulative methods are not the true signs of power. The grasp of control and the capacity to coerce are not its genuine identifying marks. True power is seen in that vulnerability that does not lash out in self-assertion or fear, but hangs from a cross in a demonstration of love.

From first to last, the royal might of Jesus was manifested in vulnerability. Not only the way he ended the days of his flesh, but the way he was introduced into the world made a statement about the quality of his kingship. Only as we allow the quality of his kingdom to capture our imaginations and shape our lives will we discover what really matters.

In Michel Tournier's novel *The Four Wise Men,* a young deposed prince encounters the infant Jesus in Bethlehem. Prince Taor had been reduced to rags. Daily he dreamed of retaking the throne that was rightfully his and exercising the power that was his birthright. He resented the poverty into which he had fallen. But after seeing the Christ Child his perspective changed.

Another asked Prince Taor, "What did Bethlehem teach you about power?" The prince answered, "The example of the crib . . . taught me the strength of weakness, the irresistible gentleness of the non-violent, the law of forgiveness. . . . In view of all this, I laid the gold coin struck with the effigy of my father King Theodenos at the child's feet. It was my only treasure, my only proof that I was the legal heir to the throne of Palmyra. In relinquishing it, I renounced the kingdom to search for the other kingdom promised me by the Savior."

This is a lesson that many—even among those who pledge allegiance to King Jesus—need to learn today. A considerable number of church members continue to bewail the abolition of organized prayer in public schools. They long for the bygone days of Blue Laws that would restrict business and entertainment on Sundays. They look for a righteous rule that is enforced by the very worldly power of governmental authorities. Instead of seeing Jesus as a nonconformist king who calls us to be a dissident minority, they would grasp the political might to make the majority step in line.

We uphold the reign of Jesus, not by seeking to impose his will on those who do not honor his name. Rather than trying to enlist the structures of society to reinforce our way, we need to recognize ourselves as outsiders who follow the one "who was in the world . . . yet the world did not know him" (John 1:10). Faith in the odd not-of-this-world king put us out of step with the wayward march of the world.

The nostalgia for an America where Christ is King is misguided. The traditional values of the past were rarely, if ever, full-bodied Christian values. Certainly some facets of traditional values resemble values rooted in the reign of Christ. But others were products of the frontier experience and other less-than-Christian influences. I recall a cartoon I came across some time ago that pictured an elderly man and woman conversing with one another. The woman says, "I'm so glad traditional values are comin' back, values like prayin'. " "And killin'," adds the man with a grin.

To be people of the odd King Jesus, we need to be willing to keep a critical distance from every status quo. We need a distinctiveness of vision and an independence of judgment derived from utter submission to the crucified and risen king. We need to learn to live from an account of the world that has at its center the saving acts and intentions of God, rather than the dubious endeavors of the powerful, successful, and wise of our time. For nothing else will do for a divinely dissident people.

Of course, not all forms of nonconformity are created equal. There is no virtue in being different for its own sake. We are called to be different for Christ's sake. The character of his reign determines the character of our response. It is what Christ has done that shapes what we are to do. Hence, if we are in step with the God who "loved the world" (John 3:16), we are bound to be out of step with those who insist on a narrower kind of love, one limited by loyalty to nation, race, or class. If we accept the way of the God who gave God's own Son for us, we will reject the way of consumerism and materialism that leads us to seek continually for what we can get for ourselves. If we turn to the one who came in vulnerability and "emptied himself, taking the form of a slave" (Phil. 2:7), we will turn away from the quest for security based on military might and the mastering of others.

Perhaps, the majority may scoff at us and consider us cranks. But if so, we would do well to have the courage and clearsightedness to say with economist E.F. Schumacher, "I would like to be known as a crank because a crank is a part of a small hand-operated machine which causes a revolution." If we are faithful to Christ the King, our lives will manifest a nonconformity that very well may cause a revolution of truth and love.

Suggestions for Worship

Call to Worship (Ps. 132:7-9):

> LEADER: Let us gather in the place where God's presence is honored.

PEOPLE: **Let us go to his dwelling place; let us worship at his footstool;**

LEADER: O LORD, come to your resting place, you and your power and might.

PEOPLE: **May your ministers be clothed with righteousness; may your saints sing for joy.**

Call to Worship (for Christ the King):

LEADER: Lift up your heads, O you gates; be lifted up, you ancient doors, that the King of glory may come in.

PEOPLE: **Who is this King of Glory? The LORD strong and mighty; he is the King of glory.**

Act of Praise: Psalm 132:1-12.

Suggested Hymns: "Come, Thou Almighty King"; "We Gather Together"; "Lead On, O King Eternal."

Opening Prayer: Our God and Maker, we gather here to magnify your name. You have given us life and have put hope in our hearts. You have poured your mercy upon us and have forgiven us of our sins. We lift our hearts to you in joy.

On this day, we especially thank you for Jesus Christ, who is our king. Empower us that we might give ourselves to him as willing subjects, without reservation and with singleness of mind. Enable us to live lives that will bring honor to his name. Guide the church, O Lord, that it might live in faith and truth always.

To you we give honor and praise, O God Almighty. All creation proclaims your glory. May we live so that all of our movements praise your name. Through Christ Jesus we pray. Amen.

Pastoral Prayer: Our Lord, we give you thanks and praise that you have called us to be subjects of your son. May his reign over us fill us with joy and peace.

Open our eyes to the meaning of his sovereignty in our time. Clear away those obstacles that block our vision and hinder our submission to his rule. Strengthen us that our knees never bend before any other Lord.

Put your word within our hearts. May it take hold of our limbs. May it move us to praise you and serve the world in your name. Through Christ the King, we pray. Amen.

NOVEMBER 27, 1994

□

First Sunday of Advent

The second advent is the theme of these lessons. They are addressed to persons who are growing weary of waiting.

The Sunday Lessons

Jeremiah 33:14-16: Having prophesied that the conquered and wasted Jerusalem would be restored, Jeremiah goes on to promise a new king who will bring justice to the land. "A righteous Branch" (v. 15) will spring forth for David. Judah will be saved and Jerusalem will dwell securely.

I Thessalonians 3:9-13: Paul prayed for his converts, "may he so strengthen your hearts in holiness that you may be blameless before our God and Father at the coming of our Lord Jesus" (v. 13). Then he exhorted them to live in ways pleasing to God, following the teachings he had given them.

Luke 21:25-36: "Stand up and raise your heads, because your redemption is drawing near" (v. 28). The apocalyptic discourse in Luke notes the "distress among nations" (v. 25) and "people will faint from fear" (v. 26) and then addresses the hopeless hearts that bend beneath the weight of "the worries of this life" (v. 34). He counsels the church (Luke expects it to last) to watch and pray, always ready "to stand before the Son of Man" (v. 36).

Reflections

We found a vantage point along the parade route at Disney World and sat down to wait for Mickey Mouse and the others to march. Forty minutes is not too long for those who want to be up front; but it was too long for our four-year-old grandson. "I'm tired of waiting!" he said. "Let's go!"

In the book of Isaiah, where the sins of Israel have been named, and their rebellion declared, God asks, "Have you grown weary of me, O Israel?" This is one of the first signs that a people has become morally weak and spiritually unhealthy. They get a sense of weariness in their worship and service of God.

Possessed by this deep weariness, we lose both our longing for God and our relish for the things of God. Joyful obedience becomes drudgery, prayer becomes a yearning, and watching becomes an empty bore. Then follows our conclusion that Christ will never come, prayers will never be answered, there is no God.

Speaking of a family no longer active in the life of the church, a friend said, "I don't know what happened. They just stopped coming. Maybe it was burnout." Recently a good man, who loved Christ and the church, was lamenting his loss of spiritual eagerness. I remember his last words in our conversation. "I'm just a little weary, I guess." (JKB)

ACTIVE WAITING

Luke 21:25-36

A SERMON BY CAMILLE YORKEY-EDWARDS

This is the time of year when we in North Carolina begin our love/obsession with basketball, all in preparation for the Final Four and the NCAA Tournament. I remember a couple of years ago, when Duke was playing Michigan in the last game to see who would be national champions. Duke had won the title the season before, but now was only one or two points ahead of Michigan. Duke had gotten into foul trouble and several players had been injured. In the last seconds of the game, the coach, Mike Krachewski had to put Marty Clark on the court, a player that had been on the bench the whole game and most of the season. There was anxiety on the court, tension on the bench, and tension in the crowd. What would happen?

With Duke still a point or two ahead, Michigan had to foul to save time on the clock and get possession of the ball. Of course, you know who they fouled. Yes, time after time they fouled the weakest link, the easiest mark. A true time of anxiety and turbulence. Life had gotten tough.

In a similar incident about three weeks later, I had an irate phone call after 10:00 one night from one of the softball players on our church team. We were a brand new team in the league; at the time we had lost five games and won zero. Tempers were short, morale was low, self-esteem not much higher. We had a band new coach with fifteen new players who not only had not jelled into a team, but who did not even know each other's names. So after the fifth game of the season, this player called me not only threatening to quit the team, but never to come to church again because he had not played in the last two games. He yelled that things were confusing and tense and if I did not make the coach change things next week, he was not ever going to participate again. Things had definitely gotten turbulent. Life had gotten tough!

Today, we encounter Luke's scripture as Jesus is describing times that are anxious, turbulent, and tough. Perhaps the listeners understood this as a prediction of the destruction of the temple. After all, the Jews to whom Jesus is speaking are proud of their temple. It took almost six hundred years to build, and was built with huge white stone pillars forty feet long, twelve feet high, twenty feet wide. Jesus tells them that the temple will be shattered just like a child playing with building blocks. Now that caused anxiety!

Or perhaps the listeners understood this as a prediction of end times. Either way they ask, "How will we know when the kingdom is at hand?" Jesus did not specify by using a date, but he said things will be turbulent—you know, devastating floods, earthquakes, senseless wars, turmoil, famine, disaster, political upheaval—the end of an era. My goodness, that even sounds worse than the NCAA Tournament. Seriously, Jesus says that even though this foreshadowing is rough and causes anxiety, it is conquered by hope and is a sign that deliverance is near and rescue is at hand.

Look at the trees when the buds begin to sprout, and you can tell that winter is over and the advent of summer is near. Just like that, you will know when the kingdom of God is near. Jesus is so emphatic about this understanding of the advent of the kingdom of God that he makes an oath similar to my grandmother saying "Mark my word, Child, mark my word, this is the gospel." He makes a similar vow. "Heaven and earth will pass away, but [what I have just told you] my words will not pass away [That's the TRUTH!]" (v. 33).

But he follows that with the words, "This generation will not pass away until all things have taken place" (v. 32). For Mark, as well as for Luke, the generation of Jesus has already passed away, if this is predicting the end of the world and the final coming of the Kingdom. The kingdom of God, future and forever fully realized and yet to come, has not come by the time of Luke's writing. In fact, it has not even come by the time of the writing of this sermon. So what relevance could Luke's passage have for us at Christmastime?

I believe we must question the generation about whom Jesus was speaking when he said, "THIS GENERATION WILL NOT PASS AWAY." Is it (A) the generation in which the temple was destroyed? (B) the generation in which the Jews were destroyed by the Nazis? (C) the generation when the Native Americans were ravaged and their homeland destroyed? (D) the generation when there were sit-ins in Greensboro and marches in Washington, D.C. and senseless riots and bloodshed in the name of racial equality? (E) the generation when AIDS was rampant and education was not? (F) all of the above?

No, we must not stop there. Perhaps there should be a (G)— the generation that covers several lifetimes or several hundred lifetimes, the generation with hopeless hearts, constant worry, crippling anxiety and foreboding fear; the generation facing unemployment, destructive fire, hazardous waste, damaging pesticides, unsafe drugs, and debilitating depression. This generation, when all about us appears to be falling in and we see with our own eyes nation against nation, family dysfunction, cancer, hypertension, hurricanes, wars, floods, tornadoes, and Christmas crazies . . . amid all of this, we come to this Advent passage of hope.

This is not a message of gloom and doom, or damnation and destruction, but of wholeness and grace, mercy and glory, of hope and peace, when and only when we recognize the signs and are actively awaiting the arrival of Jesus the Christ into this maddening world. Only then can you and I conceivably experience the truth of this text in the Kingdom present, in Advent 1994.

Hear the words of Jesus the Christ as they come to us on this first Sunday of Advent. Do not be too occupied with the worries of this life, or you might not be ready when the Kingdom comes. That message strikes home hard to me. Worries, anxieties, concerns. More than any other time in the year, I seem to be over-burdened with turmoil of getting ready for Christmas—decorating, cards, shopping, cooking, company, social activities, caroling, preparation for the cantata, the "remember those less fortunate than you." In addition to all of that, we must be on guard, alert, and prepared. Not like the words from the song, "Don't Worry, Be Happy," but do not be *too* occupied with the burdens of this life or that day when the Word becomes flesh, that day when our Savior is born, that day when the Incarnation will come will catch you unprepared like a trap.

Advent is a time of active waiting and preparation for the Christ Child. And in this season, we celebrate the revealed Christ, past, present, and forever. Advent is about the God who comes in mercy to comfort and renew that which has decayed and to heal that which is unhealthy, and to mend that which is broken. God comes in the form of a babe to offer a new life for that which is dead, and to awaken that which is asleep. This is a time for active waiting as we make preparations for the birth of our Lord.

These verses of apocalyptic literature were to encourage Christians under persecution to offer them a word of hope, and a confidence to survive, to stand upright. To us they resound in the certainty of hope, that the God who came in the birth of a babe born in Bethlehem two thousand years ago is coming today and will continue to come to you and to me as long as we are prepared to accept him. This Bethlehem babe inaugurates the kingdom of God, making whole the devastation of our turbulent lives. This birth strengthens our faith. So hold your head up high in the face of nuclear winter, ecological disaster, thinning ozone layer, exploding populations. Hold your head up high, for the world survives.

This Advent waiting is more than just a wish. It is an assurance, an expectation. Hope, not like hoping to get a surfboard for Christmas, not like a store putting up the Christmas decorations right after Halloween in hopes of getting more business. No, this is an assurance of things to come—an active waiting for the future. A hope that is almost a certainty—as when the future is already in process in a pregnant woman. The signs occur, changes begin to take place. The body changes shape, hips increase in size, breasts change shape and increase in size, the abdomen area begins to swell. No one can ignore these signs. They are both signs of the end of the pregnancy, as well as signs of the beginning of a new life. That is what I hear from Jesus in this Advent scripture, being prepared in the midst of change and turbulence for that which is to come—the birth of the Christ Child.

Before that record crowd in Minneapolis at the NCAA tournament, Marty Clark—the bench sitter—was fouled time and time again. Time and time again he walked slowly to the line, time and time again he took aim, released the ball and time and time again the ball hit its mark, went perfectly through the hoop scoring priceless points. Duke won the National Championship for the second year in a row, because of a young man prepared, actively waiting for his opportunity.

Today's question for us is, do we recognize the signs and how in the next four weeks do *we* actively wait for the birth of the Christ Child? Amen.

Suggestions for Worship

Call to Worship (Ps. 25:1-5):

LEADER: No one whose hope is in God will ever be put to shame,

PEOPLE: Show me your ways, O LORD, teach me your paths;

LEADER: Guide me in your truth and teach me,

PEOPLE: For you are God my Savior, and my hope is in you all day long.

Act of Praise: Psalm 25:1-10.

Suggested Hymns: "O Come, O Come, Emmanuel"; "Come, Thou Long-Expected Jesus"; "Jesus Shall Reign."

Opening Prayer: Loving God, we hear today in your word that when world and personal conditions are at their worst, you come to us, for Christ promises to return when the time is ripe. O God, the time IS ripe. Just as we know summer is coming when a tree begins to bud, so we will know by our present circumstances that Christ's Advent is near. We who are followers of your son, Jesus the Christ, pledge to wait, prepare, watch, and pray for his coming during this Advent season. For it is in the name of Jesus Christ that we pray. Amen.

Pastoral Prayer: O God, we come together on this first day of Advent thankful that as we turn our eyes toward Bethlehem, we do so hoping and praying for a new onset of serenity and love among us. But we know that means you must take us where we are, and remold us into new creatures capable of experiencing and expressing the wholeness of your kingdom. O loving God, do not let us be too busy with carols, cookies, and calendars to hear the message. We often fly through this season at a frantic pace, so rushed to maintain the momentum, that we never hear the whisper of the angels, "Glory be to God on High."

Be with all those this day that have broken bodies, broken hearts, and broken spirits so that your presence will minister to their every need. Encourage and enable us to be your instruments of peace as we journey toward the manger. In Jesus' name, we pray. Amen.

DECEMBER 4, 1994

□

Second Sunday of Advent

Always reaching for something, but with a reach that has come up short, we are reminded of a God who comes to us.

The Sunday Lessons

Malachi 3:1-4: The prophet tells of a messenger who will prepare the way for the sudden appearance of the Lord. He will be like "refiner's fire" and "fullers' soap" (v. 2) in the community of faith. Priests (the sons of Levi) will be purified and their service and sacrifices, which have wearied the Lord, will become pleasing to him.

Philippians 1:3-11: Remembering his Philippian converts, Paul thanked God for their partnership in the gospel "from the first day until now" (v. 5). He expects them to grow in love, knowledge, and discernment as they wait for another salvation event yet to come: "the day of Jesus Christ" (v. 6).

Luke 3:1-6: Noting the times and places associated with earthbound rulers and established priests, Luke introduces John the Baptist. Like Isaiah, John's message was spoken in the wilderness to people who needed hope. With Isaiah's words he declared, "prepare the way of the Lord . . . all flesh shall see the salvation of God" (vv. 4-6).

Reflections

Dietrich Bonhoeffer wrote that "God is with us in the evening as the morning, And most certainly on each new day."

There is strength and boldness in those words written from his prison cell. They are of the same mood and style as the baptist's wilderness promise that all flesh shall see the salvation of God.

Sometimes I wish I could be that sure. It is not that I do not wait. Everyone does some waiting. We wait for a child to be born. We wait for a birthday, for school to start, for vacation days, for a paycheck, for a broken bone to mend. We wait to retire, we wait for death. We wait for Christmas.

Waiting comes with the territory, with the very nature of life. But waiting with confidence and boldness is not that ordinary. Much of the time anxiety, doubt, and fear mock the way we wait. We are not certain about the salvation for which we long, and we are very sure that we never get all the crooked places straight and the valleys made level. We never quite get everything ready.

The first line of Bonhoeffer's poem is the message we need—"With good powers wonderfully surrounding." The lessons all speak of it. As surely as we wait for God, he is coming to us. "All flesh shall see the salvation of God." (JKB)

DO YOU RECOGNIZE THE WILDERNESS?

Luke 3:1-6

A SERMON BY CAMILLE YORKEY-EDWARDS

It has started already, hasn't it? The hustle, the bustle, the parties, the planning, the writing, the wrapping, and never-ending list making. You look directly at me and say this morning, "Why do I have to listen to you talk about preparing the way? Can't you see that I don't have time for one more thing; I'm up to my eyeballs in preparation."

Sure you are. And no one understands that better than a minister during the season of Advent. This month seems to get here earlier each year. But John's message to us today is for a different kind of preparation. God called John while he was in the wilderness and John gives it to us, "You prepare for the Lord. Fill in those valleys, cut down those hills. Take your crooked, rough life and make it straight and smooth so that you'll be ready to see God." Well, there you have it. A simple straight-forward message. So where's the problem?

John was rather radical, even for an Essene, a brash young man—often appearing impetuous, brazen, insolent, and even tactless and rude. John comes into our sanctuary this morning, and in his cocky audacious manner makes the assumption that each and every one of us need to clean up our act (certainly before December 25). What a pompous assumption. He must not know that just last week I took a name from under the tree to buy a gift for the needy. He must not know that I am making cookies for the choir when they return from singing at the nursing home. He must have no idea that I plan to drive my mother-in-law to the next town to see the luminaries on Christmas Eve. How dare he say there is some other way I must prepare for the Christ Child.

I am always guilty of saying this text has to be for someone else. But you know none of us can hear John's message until we first recognize our need for redemption. We cannot hear the message to make straight that which is crooked until we acknowledge that which is crooked in our own lives. First, we recognize our separation from God, self, and others. Then, we cast off our sin in order to be able to live a life of wholeness and wellness, and completeness and joyfulness. For there is no possibility for repentance if recognition has not occurred first. John has no message for you or for me if we do not even know that we are in the wilderness. Recognition and acceptance of this wilderness time, this separation, is a must. In order to heed the words of John, to level the valleys and mountains and to smooth out the rough spots, awareness of those valleys and rough spots is the beginning. There is no message in this scripture for any of us if acknowledgment has not come first. And for many of us admitting our separation, our sinfulness is not only a difficult process—it is almost impossible.

Let me tell you about a girl I had known in college twenty-five years before. I ran into her at her office. She began to relate the sad story of her life to me. Her older child had been satisfied with taking a low-paying menial factory job right out of high school. Of course, it would not support him so he continued to live marginally and at home. Her youngest child, a daughter, dropped out of high school and worked at a fast food restaurant, only partially paying for a new car while she also lived at home. My friend's well-educated husband had lost his job. With a husband out of work and four mouths to feed, the bills piled up and money was almost nonexistent. Eventually, their home was foreclosed and all four of them moved in with the grandparents. It did not take long for the husband to begin to feel unproductive and worthless. He started running around at night and became totally irresponsible, while my friend worked nine to five and took classes at night at the college.

She said to me, "Who would ever have thought when we were in college that all of this would happen to me? And what a terrible time it is, right here at Christmas too!" I suggested to her a twelve-step group for dysfunctional families, for support and self-help. She complained about the cost, I told her there is no charge. The groups are open to all. I certainly thought it would help the family situation. Then she said, "But why should I go? There's something wrong with all of those other people, but nothing is wrong with me." She did not even know she was in the wilderness!

But the message in our scripture today is you repent. You who think your life is so together, you in your wilderness, you repent so that you can participate in the joy of the Kingdom. This message is most appropriate for each of us, since we are the ones to whom it is written.

Several years ago, my twenty-year-old son was applying for a job at one of our United Methodist summer camps. He told me, "On the application there was a space that said 'list your personal strengths,'" He told me he wrote: "Sometimes I am trustworthy, loyal, helpful, friendly, courteous, kind, obedient, cheerful, thrifty, brave, clean, and reverent." I am sure I was shaking my head and looking skeptically at him and he said, "Don't worry Mom, the next one said, "List your weaknesses.'" I said "Good, what did you write?" He said he wrote: "Sometimes I'm not!" I think he set me up for that, but the point is ever so clear. Sometimes we are on paths that are straight and narrow, and sometimes our valleys are low and our paths are crooked. Like my son said, sometimes we are and sometimes we are not.

We cannot hear the message of John the Baptist until we recognize that we are in the wilderness. There is no hope for repentance, no hope for change in the course of direction, no hope for taking a different path until we recognize our need for John's message of repentance. We cannot even hear and definitely cannot respond to the message that John has of "prepare the way of the Lord," change your life, and make way for the Savior until we know that the message is directed at us.

Let me tell you of another woman. She had moaned for several months about her marriage. One day she came in distraught and in tears, relating to us the scene from the preceding night. Evidently, her husband had grabbed the bedpost of their colonial four poster bed and threatened, as she cowered in the corner of the room, to beat her until she was unrecognizable. The members of the group were appalled and immediately went into action. Fearing for her health, her safety, and her life, the members called appropriate agencies, set up interview sessions for her, offered shelter, offered company at her house until we were sure she would be unharmed. We did everything we could do legally to help her. We even called an emergency meeting for the following day to assure her she was out of danger. But, after all of that, her expression changed. Now in a state of composure, she said, "No thanks, I think I'll give him another chance." She calmly got into her car and drove home. She did not even know she was in the wilderness!

Until we hear the message of God that came to John in the wilderness, until we hear the message to us that in order for the Christ of Christmas to come into our lives we must first repent, take a different path, change our ways, then there is no message from John for us. That thought disturbs us.

But the mundane preparations, the buying of gifts, putting up our tree, making wreaths, baking treats, the shiny paper and crinkly bows, the twinkling lights—these are not enough. We can only truly be prepared for December 25 when we hear our personal call to repentance. For only when we both hear it and act on it, will we have a share in the coming kingdom of God. Do you even know you are in the wilderness? Can you hear the voice? Do you hear the voice? Will you have prepared your way before the birth of the Christ Child? Hear the voice of John crying in the wilderness. Amen.

Suggestions for Worship

Call to Worship (Luke 1:68-79):

LEADER: Praise be to the LORD, the God of Israel, because he has come and has redeemed his people.

PEOPLE: **He has raised up a horn of salvation for us in the house of his servant David**

LEADER: To give his people the knowledge of salvation through the forgiveness of their sins,

PEOPLE: To guide our feet into the path of peace.

Act of Praise: Luke 1:68-79.

Suggested Hymns: "Angels from the Realms of Glory"; "Hail to the Lord's Anointed"; "Lift Up Your Heads, Ye Mighty Gates."

Opening Prayer: Loving God, how could John's message be for me? After all, I am here, I participated in the Advent Candle Reading, and I sing the hymns. I give my money, not as much as I could, or as much as God would want me to, but I give. God, how could the John of two-thousand years ago know that I am a sinner? How could he know that I separate myself from you, my God, from my neighbors, and even from myself? I want my life to shine with the radiance and joy of you. So I cry out for you to lead me in your ways, help me to look deeply inside so that with your help, my paths will be made straight, my valleys will be filled, and my mountains leveled. In the name of the Babe of Bethlehem, I pray. Amen.

Pastoral Prayer: O God, you are the giver of every good and perfect gift and for this Christian community, this body of believers, I give you thanks. For the excitements and expectations of the seasons, I give you thanks. For the noises of choirs, bells, carols, for the smells of pine, holiday foods, smoke from the Christmas tree lot, for the sights of lights, colors, bows, and berries—for all of this, I give you thanks. Be with the others, God, those who do not have dinner tables or communion tables, those whose wants are as great as our abundance, those whose bodies, hearts, and souls do not laugh during this season.

But let my joy and radiance of this season be infectious within my community, in my place of work, and help me to perpetuate your peace to all. For it is in the name of the Bethlehem Babe that I pray. Amen.

DECEMBER 11, 1994

□

Third Sunday of Advent

Say it again: All joy be yours.

The Sunday Lessons

Zephaniah 3:14-20: Joy and hope conclude the prophet's message as he looks for the restoration of Israel. Confident that God is love and power, he counsels, "Sing . . . shout . . . rejoice" (v. 14). God has taken away the judgments against you. God is in your midst.

Philippians 4:4-7: "Rejoice in the Lord always" (v. 4) is Paul's counsel as he ends his letter. Urging his converts to be patient and unworried, he reminds them that the Lord is near. His wish for them is peace, as he commends things honorable, just, pure, lovely, and worthy of praise.

Luke 3:7-18: Luke begins his message of salvation with John the Baptist's sermons of judgment. In the groves, he spoke of an ax laid to fruitless trees. In the fields, he spoke of separating wheat from chaff. Beside the water he baptized them to symbolize their repentance. Responding to people "filled with expectation" (v. 15) he promised that one mightier, one whose sandals he was not worthy to untie, was coming.

Reflections

They never heard her laughing loudly, never heard her singing or shouting, never saw her skipping or dancing—so some called her a sad, quiet person. But those who knew this saintly woman spoke of her deep quiet joy.

I think it was her sense of acknowledgment that told of it most. She seemed always ready and receptive for life's opportunities. She never hid from its harsh realities. How often we have seen lives of quiet desperation; how good it is to see a life marked by quiet joy.

One of the great misconceptions of joy is that it is raucous and

370

loud. Commenting on the false view of prayer that is always talking to God, whereas the best part of prayer is listening to God, Fosdick writes, "We hammer so busily that the architect cannot discuss the plans with us. We are so preoccupied with the activities of sailing, that we do not take our bearings from the sky. When the Spirit stands at the door and knocks, the bustle of the household drowns the sound of his knocking."

The vision and strength of the faithful comes from quiet receptive hours. Paul counsels, "The Lord is near, in everything make your requests known to God in prayer and thanksgiving." (JKB)

ON REJOICING . . . ALWAYS!

Philippians 4:4-7

A SERMON BY VICTOR A. SHEPHERD

It is easy to be happy some of the time—when things are going our way, when the ball is bouncing for us, when our ship is coming in day after day. Yet, it is the command of God that we rejoice all the time. If our circumstances are what give us joy, then what happens when our circumstances change, as they always do?

I have used the words *happiness* and *joy* as though they were synonyms. But in fact, they are not. Happiness depends on circumstances and, therefore, is relatively superficial; joy depends on something else and is ever so much deeper.

The difference is illustrated in the correspondence between Martin Niemöeller, a pastor in the Confessing Church in Nazi Germany, and his wife, Else. Niemöller had been a submarine captain in World War I. When Hitler came to power and molested the church, Niemöller opposed him vigorously, with the result that Niemöller was imprisoned for eight years. In one of his letters to Else, he allays his wife's anxiety about him by telling her that he is faring better than she fears. His life now resembles the fierce storms he encountered during his submarine days: terrible turbulence on the surface, but unfathomable peace in the depths. A threatened man can rejoice always only if there is something so deep in his life that it is beyond anything that circumstances can alter.

We should be realistic and sensible about the distinction between happiness and joy. There are circumstances where no sane person is happy. When people are bereaved we expect them to be sad; when people are in pain, we expect them to groan; when people are betrayed, we expect them to be shocked. These are normal responses. When responses are not normal (that is, when someone's emotional response does not square with what is happening in life), that person is mentally ill.

Not only should we be realistic and sensible, we should also be compassionate. Paul instructs us to weep with those who weep, and rejoice with those who rejoice. Our hearts are to be attuned to theirs. We are neither to disregard their sorrow out of insensitivity, nor diminish their joy out of envy.

And of course there is one situation where we are never to rejoice. Love does not rejoice at wrong, the apostle says in I Corinthians 13, love rejoices in the right.

Let us look again at the command of God "Rejoice in the Lord always" (v. 4). To rejoice in the Lord *always* means that we have settled something in the deepest depths of our lives. Think for a minute of John Newton, Anglican clergyman, hymn writer, counselor, and former slaveship captain. John met Mary Catlett when he was fourteen and she was twelve. They loved each other ardently. Newton spent years at sea on merchant ships, warships, and slaveships. He saw Mary infrequently. Yet, their love for each other was undying. By age thirty-nine Newton had become a beneficiary of the amazing grace for which he would be known ever after. He was now finished with the sea and would spend the rest of his long life as a preacher and pastor. He had always assumed that he would predecease his wife, unable as he was to imagine living without her. She, however, died first. Newton was seventy-five. Mary was buried on a Wednesday. Four days later, on Sunday, Newton stood up in the pulpit of his church in London. Everyone wondered what text the brokenhearted man would preach on that day. It was from the book of Habakkuk. "Though the fig tree does not blossom, and no fruit is on the vines . . . the flock is cut off from the fold and there is no herd in the stalls, *yet I will rejoice in the LORD; I will exult in the God of my salvation*" (Hab. 3:17-18). I will rejoice—not in my circumstances [for the time being at least they were dreadful], but in the God of my salvation.

Far from being exceptional, in the early days of the church, Newton's experience was considered normal. Paul exults in the fruit that the apostles' preaching brought forth in the people of Thessalonica. "For our gospel came to you not only in word, but also in the Holy Spirit and with full conviction . . . you received the word in much affliction, with joy inspired by the Holy Spirit." The cumulative force of Paul's vocabulary is unmistakable: gospel, power, full conviction. The climax is Spirit-inspired joy that comes to birth and thrives even in the midst of hardship. The gospel is the bedrock of it all.

Bedrock suggests foundation. As we probe scripture, we learn that the Christmas announcement of the incarnation—gospel-bedrock—is the foundation of all rejoicing. "Behold, I bring you good news of a great joy . . . for to you is born this day . . . , a saviour." The people of God rejoice for one reason: We have been given a saviour, the saviour, that saviour apart from whom any human being is undone.

Christmas is nothing less than a search-and-rescue mission. During my teenage years, I read everything I could about the Battle of Britain. The exploits of the small number of young men who flew against overwhelming odds thrilled me. The tension mounted in their stories whenever one was shot down and had to parachute into the English Channel. Immediately, a search-and-rescue mission was mobilized to seek the downed flier, find him, and recover him lest he be lost to future battles where he would be needed; indeed, lest he be lost. The search-and-rescue mission had to find him, or else the downed flier would soon be a drowned flier. When at last, in the story I was reading, he was pulled into the recovery vessel, my joy was scarcely less than his must have been!

Christmas is important for one reason: The search-and-rescue mission we need has been mobilized on our behalf. Our joy at the news of the rescuer himself is the measure of our awareness of our need and our gratitude for the gift.

Jesus sends out seventy missionaries two by two. They are to speak in his name. The seventy return elated. What spiritual triumphs they have witnessed! Why, they have even expelled evil spirits in the power their Lord has given them! Jesus tames their exuberance as he tells them what should set their joy a-throbbing. "Do not rejoice that the spirits are subject to you; rejoice that your names are written in heaven." Obviously, there is nothing more important, because nothing is more elemental than having one's name written in heaven. Assurance that it is is the basis of our joy.

It is no wonder, then, that when Zacchaeus found himself overwhelmed by mercy and freed to abandon his hiding place in the tree, he took Jesus home joyfully.

It is no wonder, too, that when Philip proclaimed what Luke calls "the good news of Jesus" to the Ethiopian eunuch, the latter fellow "went on his way rejoicing." Because he was black he was the butt of racist slurs, and because he was a eunuch he was the butt of vulgar taunts. Yet, he went on his way rejoicing in spite of it all, for through hearing the good news of the Savior, he had met him whose news it is. This is the bedrock reason for rejoicing in any man or woman.

As we rejoice in our salvation, we find that other joys are added to us. For instance, the psalmist writes, "I will rejoice and be glad for thy steadfast love . . . thou hast taken heed of my adversities." There is no one whose life is not riddled with adversities. All of us are identical in this regard. Where we differ is in what adversity does to us. Does it grind us down like an emery wheel? Does it make us more bitter than lemon juice? Does it suffocate us in the deadly gases of hopelessness and apathy? Or are our adversities (still unpleasant) occasions when God's love soaks us with even greater penetration? Christians become more mature by echoing Jeremiah's conviction. "The steadfast love of the Lord never ceases; his mercies never come to an end; they are new every morning." The philosopher Kierkegaard used to say, "Life has to be lived forwards but it can only be understood backwards." He's right. Life can only be understood backwards. But to say this is to say that the longer we look back, the more obvious it is that the steadfast love of the Lord has never ceased, and his mercies never come to an end. Then life can be lived forwards even more enthusiastically! The one whose love gave up his son for me would never withhold from me what I need now. To know this does not mean that we grin stupidly when adversity next settles upon us. It is, however, to rejoice in the sense of which Martin Niemöller spoke: turbulence on the surface and rejoicing in the depths, for God's love is as steadfast as his mercies are endless.

And then there is the writer of Ecclesiastes. "Enjoy life with the wife whom you love." The same writer urges us, "Go, eat your bread with enjoyment and drink your wine with a merry heart." In other words, it is our foundational rejoicing in Christ that enables us to rejoice in all the creaturely joys that God has given us.

It is commonplace that those who pursue happiness never find it, since happiness is that by-product that surprises us when we are pursuing something else that takes us out of ourselves. People who expect creaturely joy to yield foundational joy always find creaturely joy a disappointment.

Everyone knows that human beings tolerate (in the medical sense of tolerate) any pleasure-giving stimulus. As we tolerate something, it takes more and more of the same stimulus to give us the same pleasure. At the crudest, it takes more and more cocaine to generate the same high. Similarly, it takes a bigger and bigger stereo to keep the buff happy. And what sailboat enthusiast has ever decided he needed a smaller boat? No wonder we have to have more and more to stave off feelings of ho-hum, boredom, and disappointment.

Not so with those who rejoice in the depths. For to be possessed of joy in Christ is to be rendered able to "enjoy life with the wife whom we love," enjoy the simple pleasures of bread and wine. We do not need ever more intense, more costly, or more superficial stimulation to be content. "Because you are Christ's," Paul writes, "all things are yours as well." Indeed, the whole realm of creation is ours richly to enjoy.

Lastly, "we rejoice in our hope of sharing the glory of God." Do you ever wonder how your life will end up? By end up, I do not mean wondering if it is going to be the nursing home or a premature heart attack. I mean what are we finally going to become humanly. What is our ultimate destiny? To Philippian Christians already rejoicing in their restoration in Christ, Paul writes, "He who began a good work in you will bring it to completion at the day of Jesus Christ." True. But what will the completion be? We are going to share the glory of God. The splendor that surrounds God eternally; the magnificence, majesty, and grandeur of God—we are going to be taken up into this and bathed in it so that it spills over us and comes to characterize us. What other destiny could even approach this? No wonder the apostle rejoices in the mere anticipation of it!

My father died at age fifty-nine; one heart attack, no warning whatsoever, two weeks after he had been given a clean bill of health. My father-in-law, on the other hand, is ninety-five years old and will likely see one hundred. What about me? Which is more likely to happen to me? I do not waste two seconds thinking about it. Speculation is pointless. There is point only to reflecting on and rejoicing in our destiny in Christ: We are going to share the glory of God.

Karl Barth, the greatest theologian of the twentieth century, was teaching at the University of Bonn in 1935 when the Gestapo arrived at the classroom door and told him not to bother finishing his paragraph. Barth was going to be deported to his native Switzerland. He had five children, no job, and faced many wartime years of difficulty and discouragement. Yet, it was Barth who wrote in his largest work, "The person who hears and takes to heart the biblical message is not only permitted but plainly forbidden to be anything but merry and cheerful."

The biblical message speaks of our Lord, who is at hand, whose presence forestalls anxiety, and who summons us to rejoice always in him. The joy he lends us the world neither gives nor takes away, since he alone causes hearts to sing.

Suggestions for Worship

Call to Worship (Isa. 12:1-5):

> LEADER: Surely God is my salvation; I will trust and not be afraid.

> PEOPLE: **The LORD is my strength and my song;**

> LEADER: Give thanks to the LORD, call on his name;

> PEOPLE: **Sing to the LORD, for he has done glorious things.**

Act of Praise: Isaiah 12:2-6.

Suggested Hymns: "Lo, How a Rose E're Blooming"; "There's a Song in the Air"; "Joy to the World."

Opening Prayer: Eternal and ever-merciful God, you come among us in the giving of your Son, Christ Jesus our Lord.

As we, your people, now come among each other and come before you, we ask you to come upon us afresh, for we need to be forgiven, we need to be encouraged, we need to be inspired, and we need to rededicate ourselves to you and to the work of your kingdom.

Hear us, we plead, and sensitize us anew, that we might hear you now and heed you forever and ever. Amen.

Pastoral Prayer: Gracious God, as the disciples asked of Jesus, "Teach us to pray," so we make the same request of you, for we want our petitions and thanksgivings to reflect the advent of your kingdom and its expansion in our midst. Then move us to plead with you for the rule of righteousness, that you might ever create faith in those who hear our testimony, that those in whom you quicken faith might overflow in love, that those whose hearts abound in love might ever hope for that day when righteousness will indeed fill the new heaven and new earth that you have fashioned.

As the disciples asked of Jesus, "Increase our faith," so we ask you to increase our faith, for we know it is faith that banishes fear, it is faith that victoriously overcomes the world, and it is faith that allows your mercy to overwhelm us.

As the disciples were rebuked for hindering the approach of children to Jesus, so we ask you to save us from hindering any and all who are drawn to our Lord, especially those who are often slighted: the poor, the unemployed, the deranged, the disreputable. Grant that we might so reflect your compassion that they will say of us, as it was said of Jacob of old, "Your face is transparent to the face of God, with such favour have you received us."

We conclude our pryaers in the spirit of him who will teach us to pray, who will increase our faith, and who will ever use us in calling men and women to himself. Amen.

DECEMBER 18, 1994

☐

Fourth Sunday of Advent

The Magnificat announces the nearness of salvation (the coming of Christmas) to all who are longing and poor.

The Sunday Lessons

Micah 5:2-5a: Micah prophesied that a deliverer would come from Bethlehem. A son of David from the clan of Ephrathah would rule the united kingdom of Israel and Judah. He would feed his flock and all would dwell seure in the stregnth and majesty of God. Micah spoke at a time when his king, Hezekiah, was besieged and belittled (II Kings 18:17).

Hebrews 10:5-10: Contrasting sacrifices of burnt offerings with the obedience of Christ, the epistle describes the relationships of the incarnate Christ to God. God found no pleasure in sin offerings, but rather in the sacrifice of Christ who said, "I have come to do your will, O God" (v. 7).

Luke 1:39-45: In the days of pregnancy, Mary went to visit her kinswoman, Elizabeth, who was also expecting. Those things characteristic of God's presence in human happenings marked their meeting—the Holy Spirit, exclamations of joy, thanksgiving, and blessings. The Magnificat is our thanksgiving, through Mary, for God who exalts those of less degree and satisfies the hungry.

Note: Luke 1:47-55 replaces the psalm for this week.

Reflections

Martin Luther's Christmas book contains a compelling commentary on the Magnificat. Concerning Luke 1:46-48 "he has looked with favor on the lowliness of his servant," he wrote:

> They do Mary wrong who say that she gloried not in her virginity but in her humility. She gloried neither in her virginity nor in her humility, but solely in God's gracious regard . . . Her low estate is not to be praised, but God's regard, as when a prince gives his hand

to a beggar, the meanness of the beggar is not to be praised, but the graciousness and goodness of the prince . . . True humility does not know that it is humble.

Concerning Luke 1:53 "He has filled the hungry with good things." Luther wrote:

You must not only think and speak of lowliness, but come into it, sin in it, utterly helpless, that God alone may save you. Or at any rate, should it not happen, you should at least desire it and not shrink . . . see how purely Mary leaves all to God, and claims for herself no works, honor, or reputations.

A sermon outline from these selected verses could speak of: (1) God's gracious regard, (2) God's powerless servants, (3) God's work alone. (JKB)

MANIFESTO OF THE REAL REVOLUTION

Luke 1:46-55

A SERMON BY VICTOR A. SHEPHERD

It is easy to sympathize with revolutionary movements, since revolutions are spawned by shocking injustices and unendurable oppression. It is easy to see a new day dawning in revolutionary movements, a new day for those who have endured the long night of exploitation and frustration.

Because it is so easy to sympathize with revolutionary movements, we are all the more jarred—if not left feeling hopeless— when at last we admit that the movement that promised human liberation has delivered no such thing. No one knew this better than Robespierre, an architect of the French Revolution with its threefold promise of "Liberty, Equality, Fraternity." Robespierre was executed at the hands of the social transmutation he had engineered. Little wonder he commented, minutes before his death, "Revolutions consume their daughters."

As we watch Latin American countries lurch from fascism to communism, we see it happening all over again. The African nations that threw off colonialism as inhumane have installed a monster whose human rights violations make colonialism appear almost benign. In pre-revolutionary Russia, Czarist rule was deemed insupportable; yet, in the early period of Leninist rule, the state executed one thousand people per month. A revolution that had promised people freedom and human fulfillment (even minimal foodstuffs) had delivered no such thing.

Revolutions founder over one thing: human nature. And in a fallen world, human nature means human depravity. The problem with revolutionary movements is this: They are incapable of being genuinely revolutionary! They merely revolve; that is, turn up and recycle the same fallen human nature. Revolutionary movements cannot get to the heart of the matter simply because they are powerless to deal with the human heart. Political leaders may speak of a "New World Order"; Christians, however, know that the only new world order is the kingdom of God. New orders are merely a case of déjà vu. The only real revolution is the Kingdom of God, fashioned and ruled by the king himself. It alone supplies the new heart, new mind, new spirit of which the prophets spoke, for which everyone longs, and that Jesus Christ alone bestows.

According to Mary, mother of our Lord and spokesperson of his revolution, real revolution begins with the scattering of the proud in the imagination of their hearts. *Heart* is biblical shorthand for the innermost core of a person—the nerve center or control panel. Heart has to do with thinking, willing, feeling, and discerning. In addition, heart means identity, who we really are underneath all cloaks, disguises, and social conventions. The "imagination of our heart" is our fashioning a god of our own making, a god after our own image and likeness, which god we follow zealously. Through the prophet Isaiah God says, "I have held out my hands to an obstinate people, who walk in ways not good, pursuing their own imaginations." Isaiah knows that first we disdain the holy one of Israel and his claim on us; then we fabricate whatever deity will legitimate and satisfy our craving, whether we crave wealth, recognition, or domination.

Isaiah is not alone in his discernment. Ezekiel, fellow-prophet, knows that those who "prophesy out of their own imagination" are always false prophets.

While Mary is customarily depicted as demure and dainty, the picture she paints of human nature is anything but pretty. She tells us of proud people who are victimized by the imagination of their hearts. We are at this moment stumbling down paths that are not good, certainly not godly. All of us are like the fool of whom the psalmist speaks, the fool who "said in his heart, 'There is no God.' " He is a fool just because he maintains that there are no consequences to dismissing the holy one of Israel while preferring and pursuing the imagination of the heart, no consequences to exchanging the god we fancy for the God who claims our faithfulness. Blinded by and in love with the gods of our own making, we are all fools whose folly is fatal.

Yet, Mary remains spokesperson for a revolution that is to be announced as good news, the uniquely good news of Christmas: God has scattered the proud! Our first response to learning that God scatters us vigorously may not be that we have just heard good news. To be told that we have been scattered, at God's hand, suggests that God has hammered us so hard as to fragment us, and then swept away the remains. To be sure, we have been judged and been found wanting; yet, this is not to say that God sweeps us away in his judgment. The Greek verb *diaskorpizo*, meaning to scatter, also means to winnow. To winnow grain is to toss a shovelful so that the wind carries away chaff but leaves behind the kernel, prized and soon to be put to use. In other words, God scatters us, the proud, inasmuch as he longs to save us and intends to use us. In getting rid of chaff, he lays bare the heart that he can then renew in accord with his nature and kingdom, and use ever after.

"Scattering the proud in the imagination of their hearts" is essential if a revolution is to be real and not merely a recycling of human depravity. Mary insists that in the invasion of God's Son, God has scattered us all and will continue to do so, yet not out of petulance, irritability, frustration, or disgust. God scatters us inasmuch as he plans to do for us what we cannot do for ourselves, and use us in ways we cannot anticipate.

Mary maintains that God has done something more; God has "brought down the powerful from their thrones" (v. 52). But has he? In one sense, it appears that God has done no such thing. Caesar Augustus was not put down the day Jesus was born. No mighty ruler has been unseated just because the gospel was upheld. We need think only of Stalin's cynical comment when told that the pope opposed Stalin's mass murders. "The pope," snickered Stalin, "how many troops does the pope have?" Stalin strutted just because he knew that he, and no one else, ruled the USSR.

And yet, at a much deeper level, the advent of Jesus Christ does mean that God has put down the mighty from their thrones. Herod was not paranoid when he raged that the Bethlehem child was a threat to his throne. After all, in the coming of Jesus Christ into our midst, the world's only rightful ruler has appeared. Herod intuited correctly that the Christmas gift would win to himself the loyalty of men and women who would never transfer that loyalty back to Herod. All political manipulators, ideologues, social engineers, and educational programmers—in short, all who want to reshape society, even remake humankind—must know sooner or later that just because the world's rightful ruler has appeared, and is now enthroned, their authority has been exposed as mere postulating and their promises as mere wind. Discerning Christians testify that those who think they can coerce or control have in fact been dethroned. Corrie Ten Boom, as simple a Christian as one could find (she was a fifty-year-old unmarried daughter of a Dutch watchmaker who kept house for her father and sister) the moment Corrie defied Hitler in harboring Jewish fugitives, the moment she refused to acknowledge the rightness of Hitler's rule and refused to conform to it—in that moment Hitler was dethroned. After all, before this unarmed middle-aged woman, Hitler was powerless. Any Christian who refuses to conform anywhere to the blustering and bullying of the mighty just because this Christian acknowledges the rulership of Christ alone, any such Christian testifies that God continues to dethrone.

The revolution of which Mary speaks is unquestionably real. Still, the question can always be asked, "Real as it is, how far does it go? Whom does it finally affect?" It is easy to say that it manifestly affects all the tyrants we do not like in any case and whom we are glad enough to see dethroned. But Mary's revolution is unique, qualitatively different from all social dislodgings and historical upheavals only if the self-important potentate who manipulates me is dethroned as well. I know how easy it is to look askance at the person who is so obviously ruled by chemical substance, psychological habituation, or shameless self-promotion, when all the while I secretly scramble to hide the things that rule me and brazenly try to excuse them when I can no longer hide them. I know how easy it is to speak of a new heart and mind when my reactions, in unguarded moments, suggest a heart still ruled by passions and instincts that serve my self-indulgence, self-preservation, self-advantage, and self-congratulation.

Then I can only cry out to God that I do want the revolution of which Mary speaks to reach me and revolutionize me. And so far from gloating over the fact that God has put down the swaggerers whom I am glad to see put down, I must plead with him to dethrone in me whatever has usurped the rule of Jesus Christ. For only then will the genuine new world order be under way.

It is a singular mark of God's kindness that the work of God's left hand assists the work of his right. To say the same thing differently, a mark of God's kindness that his right hand is stronger than his left, that mercy triumphs over judgment, that whatever wound he inflicts is only surgical repair for the sake of restoration to health. Having put down, God now exalts; he exalts those of low degree, the humble.

The humble, it must be noted, are not those who belittle themselves miserably and otherwise display abysmally weak self-image. (Crippling self-image is not humility; it is illness.) Neither is humility a religious technique whereby we can get ourselves exalted. And, of course, humility could never be the end-result of struggling to make ourselves humble, since the effort of making ourselves humble merely reinforces pride. Humility is self-forgetfulness—the self-forgetfulness that steals over us when we lose ourselves in something or someone who is bigger, richer, deeper.

In the revolution of which Mary speaks, it is these humble self-forgetful people whom God exalts. To be exalted, ultimately, is to be lifted up a child of God. When John speaks of the incarnation, its purpose and its result, he writes, "To all who received him [Jesus Christ], who believed in his name, he gave power to become children of God." In other words, to forget ourselves into Christ is to become sons and daughters of God. To the believers in Thessalonica, Paul writes, "You are all sons of the light and sons of the day. We do not belong to the night or to the darkness.'" What it is to be exalted—lifted up, held up—as a child of God, who no longer belongs to night or darkness, Paul makes clear in his letter to the congregation in Philippi. Those people are "children of God without blemish in the midst of a crooked and perverse generation, among whom you shine as lights in the world, holding fast the word of life."

There is nothing more revolutionary than the person who shines in the midst of a perverse world. No one, believer or unbeliever, has ever doubted that the world can repopulate itself (that is, that a crooked and perverse generation can produce crooked and perverse offspring). Humanists insist that the world does not have to repopulate itself (that is, left to itself the world can produce better and better citizens—this belief is clung to even though the wars of this century alone have slain one hundred million). Christians, however, know that the world has to repopulate itself, can do nothing else except repopulate itself, for the only person who is profoundly different, before God, is the person whom God's grace has rendered self-forgetful, and then rendered God's own child. This person shines like a light bulb in the midst of a crooked and perverse generation. This person is a beacon of hope, because this person is living testimony that at God's hand there is something genuinely different.

Mary gathers up everything about her revolutionary manifesto in her pithy summation: "He has filled the hungry with good things, and sent the rich away empty" (v. 53).

Who are the rich whom God has sent away empty? Bashing the rich is fashionable nowadays. Those who like to bash the rich are quick to tell us who the rich are: The rich are those who have fifty dollars more than the bashers have? Such an attitude bespeaks only someone's envy and resentment. The truth is, those whose riches are a spiritual threat are not those who have money, but rather those who are preoccupied with money—whether they have it or not. The medieval Christians who spoke of the seven deadly sins were correct in naming gluttony as one of them. They were also correct in insisting that gluttony is not a matter of eating too much; gluttony is being preoccupied with food, even if one's preoccupation with food is a preoccupation with avoiding food! (The person obsessed with slenderness is as much food preoccupied—and therefore gluttonous—as the person who can think only of what to eat next.) It is no different with respect to money. Those who do not have it can be as absorbed by it as those who are awash in it.

In those revolutions that remain forever ineffective, those who have money disdain and dismiss those who lack it, while those who lack it hate and envy those who have it. While appearing to be poles apart, those who have it and those who lack it are in fact identical, since both alike are engrossed with it. Only the real revolution gets us beyond this, for only the real revolution makes our preoccupations shrivel as the holy God looms before us in his awesome, all-consuming presence. As this God looms before us, the chaff we have been gorging is simply forgotten, and we become aware of a hunger we never knew.

Our Lord Jesus has promised that all who hunger for God and his righteousness are going to be filled. All who crave the ultimate satisfaction of a relationship with God that cannot be snatched away by psycho-religious intruders or evaporated by the fires of harassment; all who finally hunger for this as they hunger for nothing else, will be given that bread of life that profoundly satisfies yet never satiates. For this bread leaves us seeking none other, yet always seeking more of he who is the way, truth, and life.

The rich who are sent empty away need not remain away forever. For as soon as they recognize their preoccupations as unworthy of someone who is created to be a child of God, they too will hunger, will look to him who alone satisfies, and will be yet another fulfillment of Mary's Christmas cry.

Suggestions for Worship

Call to Worship (Luke 1:47-55):

LEADER: My spirit rejoices in God my Savior,

PEOPLE: For the Mighty One has done great things for me—holy is his name.

LEADER: His mercy extends to those who fear him, from generation to generation.

PEOPLE: He has filled the hungry with good things.

Act of Praise: Luke 1:47-55.

Suggested Hymns: "O Come, All Ye Faithful"; "Hark! the Herald Angels Sing"; "While Shepherds Watched Their Flocks."

Opening Prayer: O saving God, the word that you gave to Mary you intend for us all, for we, too, are called to magnify you and rejoice in you, to fear you and to thank you. Let us also glory in your goodness and might as you

exalt the humble,

fill the hungry,

and assist your servant people whom you have summoned to honor you and obey you.

When this hour of worship ends let us remember you, O God, for you have remembered your promise of mercy from the days of Abraham to the days that we now live before you. And let our remembering you give way to our thanking you, for you have never failed us or forsaken us. Amen.

Pastoral Prayer: Gracious God,

Come to us with a gentle touch that we might be heartened in our discipleship;

Come to us with a forceful shove that we might step ahead where we are afraid;

Come to us with a healing balm, for our hurts are greater than our best friend knows;

Come to us with a saving grip, for we want you to hold us fast forever.

Today we intercede for those who find it difficult to worship on account of their preoccupations: those whose financial hardship hounds them, those whose emotional pain gives them little rest, those whose bodily illness renders them anxious, those whose loneliness leaves them numb. All such people we lift up before you, our God. Alert us to their needs. Move us to open our hearts and hands and homes. Remind us that they and we alike are gathered together by him whose arms encircle us all.

For it is to his care and keeping that we commend each other now and always. Amen.

DECEMBER 25, 1994

□

Christmas Day

"God has . . . spoken to us by a Son, whom he appointed heir to all things, through whom he also created the worlds" (Heb. 1:2).

The Sunday Lessons

Isaiah 52:7-10: This is the conclusion of an extended poem (Isa. 51:1–52:12) expressing what God intends for Jerusalem. For a third time the troubled city is told "Awake, awake . . . O Zion" (v. 1). A messenger will bring good news. "How beautiful upon the mountains are the feet of the messenger who announces peace, who brings good news" (v. 7). The ruins of the war torn Jerusalem are told to "Break forth together into singing" (v. 9). God's salvation will be shown to the ends of the earth.

Hebrews 1:1-4 (5-12): In the past, God spoke through prophets, "but in these last days he has spoken to us by a son" (v. 2). The son is the radiance of God's glory. God is like Jesus Christ reveals God to be. Christ is an "exact imprint" (v. 3). When the son had provided "purification for sins" (v. 3), he sat down at the right hand of God.

John 1:1-14: Matthew's Gospel begins by showing the genealogy of Jesus, and records the visit of the prestigious magi. Luke's Gospel tells of Christ's humble birth—virgin, manger, angels, and the visit of lowly shepherds. John's Gospel begins before time and reaches beyond space. The prologue portrays a cosmic Christ—the Word that was before the beginning, the Word that is larger than light and life, the Word has become flesh and dwells among us. To those who believe, he gives the right to become children of God.

Reflections

There are many majestic buildings in the world that, as the seat of governments, represent power and influence. None is more majestic than the Capitol building in Washington, D.C.

Inscribed within the dome of the Capitol are these words: "One far-off divine event toward which the whole creation moves." When a tour guide was asked what the inscription means, he answered, "It refers to the coming of Christ. Some of the God-fearing fathers of America believed that all of history will end at his feet, so they had these words etched in this place of government. For me, they make the Capitol even more awesome."

The message of Christmas proclaimed by the Gospel of John, tells of a divine event that has interrupted history. Christ has come. His power and might are already evident. All things were made by him.

It also tells of divine presence in terms of eternal destiny. His creation is new creation and it is happening now. To those who believe, he gives power to become children of God. The judgments of his light and truth have eternal consequence. Christ is coming again.

Legend tells of a Danish king named Canute who ruled in the eleventh century. His courtiers and admirers were extravagant in praising his greatness. For more than twenty years he ruled with power, and his flatterers called him invincible. Then one day he ordered that a throne chair be set near the ocean's shore. As the tide began to come in, the king ordered the waves to stop their advance and not get him wet. Yet, in due time the tide claimed his throne. The king hung his crown on a crucifix and never wore it again.

The Christmas card was dark blue accented with radiant silver. The only image on it was that of the thorn-crowned Christ. Inside the card were the words of John. "And the life was the light of all people" (John 1:4). The card was one of our favorites that year. That was because other words from John's Gospel were written in our friend's own hand: "From the fullness of his grace we have all received one blessing after another." (JKB)

THE LIGHT THAT NEVER FAILS

John 1:10-18

A SERMON BY WALLACE E. FISHER

Christmas Day, 1994, "Joy to the world, the Lord has come." The four Gospels provide details and emphases on Jesus' birth.

Matthew begins with Jesus' Jewish genealogy: son of Abraham, son of David, son of Mary and her intended husband, Joseph. Mark begins his account with Isaiah's prophecy that a herald (John the Baptist) will prepare the way for Jesus' ministry. Luke provides the historical setting of Jesus' birth: Herod was king of Judea; Augustus held sway over the Roman Empire; Judea was a Roman province. All three Gospels provide synopses of Jesus' birth.

The Gospel of John is substantively different. Its author, writing toward the close of the first Christian century (perhaps editing and enlarging an earlier Gospel account), provides testimony to Jesus' birth. He also sets forth the *universal* (came to save the world) and *cosmic* (in the beginning the Word was with God) context of Jesus' birth. Using the thought patterns of the Greek world, his account interprets the purpose and meaning of Jesus' coming as God's activity to save the world. John's thesis is historical, universal, cosmic: Jesus was with God "in the beginning" (v. 2). Jesus came into the world and the world in general did not receive him. To the few who did receive him, he gave "power to become children of God" (v. 12). That, John emphasizes, is why the Word (Jesus) became flesh. Jesus came into the world to save those who accept his offer to save all who believe in him. All four evangelists testify to Jesus' birth as a historical event.

John, like Paul, is a towering theologian. Both men, reflecting on Jesus' birth, life, teachings, miracles, death, and resurrection, tell us what the Christ-Event means. The two men are the Christian church's first theologians. Indeed, they are its two most influential theologians. Origen, Tertullian, Augustine, Aquinas, Luther, Calvin, and the host of theologians since ground their theologies in the theologies of John and Paul.

John, having established the cosmic (in the beginning when all things were made) and universal (all the peoples on earth, and the earth itself) significance of the Jesus-Event, proceeds in the Gospel for Christmas Day (John 1:10-18) to describe the two basic human responses to Bethlehem's child—some reject him as Savior (vv. 10, 11); some accept him as Savior (vv. 12-14). In this realistic handling of human history (rejection and acceptance), John testifies to God's absolute respect for his creation's freedom to say no or yes to the Christ. The God of Christians wants sons and daughters, not slaves or robots. God yearns to be loved, but even God cannot coerce love. He can and does love us in Christ. We humans can accept God's love and love him in return because he first loves us. That is the essence of Christ's coming. We can also turn our backs on his deed in Christ and go on loving self and this present world. That is the either/or nature of the Cross.

We humans can exhaust the love of our parents, mates, children, and friends. But as long as we live, God loves us with a love that does not give up on any one of us. To be sure, his love is structured by his righteousness. We come home through repentance (turning away *from* self to God) and accept his unearned love, as the prodigal son did, or we refuse his reconciling hand, as the prodigal's brother did, and live in darkness. Listen to John as he gets deeper into his reflections on Jesus: "God so loved the world that he gave his only Son, so that everyone who believes in him may not perish but may have eternal life" (John 3:16). Luther called John's soaring claim "the gospel in miniature." And so it is! "The gospel in a nutshell," as we would put it.

It is in this context of John's thinking—the cosmic, universal, inexhaustible love of God—that we reflect on human beings' rejection and acceptance of Christ.

John states plainly (vv. 10-11) that Christ met rejection in the world God and he created. All Gospels testify to that tragic reality. At the outset of Jesus' ministry, great crowds swirled around him. Hungry for forgiveness, thirsty for assurances of hope, eager to be healed physically and emotionally, they called him Lord. But when he spelled out the personal costs of being his disciples—service, sacrifice, and obedience to his way of life—the crowds melted away. By the time of his crucifixion, he was not only rejected, but also despised, mocked, spat upon. On Golgotha, he was alone, except for God. After his resurrection, his followers were maligned, imprisoned, murdered. Stephen was the first in a long line of martyrs to die for Christ.

During the first three centuries of Christian witness, the world rejected Christ on three levels of culture. (1) The Jewish religious leaders saw Jesus to be a stumbling block. To them, he was neither God's son nor the last of Israel's great prophets. He was a usurper of God's place in their religion and a false prophet. They rejected Christ. (2) The intellectuals of that day (Greeks) considered Christ's cross to be sheer foolishness. The gods they knew were superhumans who did not humble themselves by becoming mere humans. They rejected Christ. (3) The political-social hierarchy of the Roman world had no taste for divinity, except in their emperor. They rejected Christ. At the religious, intellectual, and social-political levels of society during the early centuries of Christianity, Jesus was rejected.

So it has gone over the centuries, the world rejecting the lordship of Christ. It is not different in our era. Everywhere Christ is rejected. Devotees of other world religions consider his divinity a stumbling block; they will not accept a God who became flesh. Most intellectuals reject Christ because they consider it irrational to believe in a supernatural being who squanders himself in caring for the dregs of society and the elites of society alike. To follow that God is foolishness. Thoroughgoing secularists simply have no space for a spiritual being; materialists to the core, they believe only in the things they can see, hear, touch, taste, and smell.

It is the shame of the church that many of its members reject Christ. That has been true since the first century. Among the original disciples, Judas betrayed Christ to the Jewish religious leaders; Peter, in a cowardly effort to protect his person, denied Christ; the other ten declined to intervene in his trial before Pilate. Ananias and Sapphira, first-generation church members, worshiped Christ publicly while their life-styles denied him privately. One can be in the church without being in Christ. Today, millions of church members reject Christ by refusing to accept the costs of Christian discipleship.

John's Gospel is realistic. People have rejected Christ through the ages. They still do. Loving darkness, they flee from the light of the world.

John reports equally, with joy as well as realism, that some of the people who were attracted initially to Christ accepted, trusted, and obeyed him. Following his resurrection, eleven of the disciples and several hundred others returned to march under his banner. The scattered little bands of Christ followers around the shores of the Mediterranean have become a mighty host of Christophers (Christ bearers) in every corner of this small planet Earth today. Those who pay the personal costs of discipleship are legion.

Never in Christian history have so many Christians been oppressed, imprisoned, persecuted, and murdered for Christ's sake in so many parts of the world as in this twentieth century, a few of them in this nation. And millions more, living in democratic states, have made sacrifices for Christ's sake. Like Paul, these Christ followers believe that nothing—hardship, rejection, suffering, or death itself—can separate them from God in Christ. They count their personal losses for Christ as imperishable gains. And gains they are. Penitent, these Christ followers have their dark thoughts and deeds cleansed and healed by Christ's forgiveness. Believing in him, they receive his gift of power to combat the demonic forces that terrorize them from within and assault them from without. Clothed in his righteousness through faith, they face death unafraid because the Resurrection Christ, their best and dearest friend, is the one who makes them "children of God . . . born . . . of God" (vv. 12-13).

The church's first and foremost theologians, John and Paul, were able to define for all time the solid ground of biblical faith: "The Word became flesh" (v. 14) and "God was in Christ reconciling the world to himself."

So we sing this Christmas Day, 1994, and every day in every year:

> O Light that followest all my way,
> I yield my flickering torch to thee;
> My heart restores its borrowed ray,
> That in thy sunshine's blaze its day
> May brighter, fairer be.
>
> —George Matheson

Suggestions for Worship

Call to Worship (Ps. 96):

LEADER: Sing to the LORD a new song; sing to the LORD, all the earth.

PEOPLE: **Sing to the LORD, praise his name; proclaim his salvation day after day.**

LEADER: Declare his glory among the nations, his marvelous deeds among all peoples.

PEOPLE: **For great is the LORD and most worthy of praise; he is to be feared above all gods.**

LEADER: Let the heavens rejoice, let the earth be glad;

PEOPLE: **For he comes, he comes to judge the earth. He will judge the world in righteousness and the peoples in his truth.**

Act of Praise: Psalm 98.

Suggested Hymns: "Hark! the Herald Angels Sing"; "Infant Holy, Infant Lowly"; "Silent Night, Holy Night."

Opening Prayer: O Blessed Child of Bethlehem in whom the God of righteous love meets the highest aspirations of human beings: Open our eyes to the light that the darkness cannot extinguish, our ears to the power of the truth that error cannot vanquish, and our hearts and minds to the new life you offer to all who believe in you; and hasten that glorious day when every knee shall bow and every tongue confess that you are Lord over all. Amen.

Pastoral Prayer: Almighty God, in whom we live and move and have our being and from whose creative hand has come all that ever has been, is now, or ever will be good: We thank you this day and every day for the inestimable gift of yourself in your only son, Jesus of Nazareth and the Resurrection Christ, apart from whom nothing of lasting good ever happens to, in, or around us; we thank you for the gifts of Christian forebearers, Christian parents, Christian mates, Christian children, Christian friends, and above all for the church whose head is Jesus Christ, our Lord.

To you we confess our sins of commission and omission for which we are heartily sorry, and do now repent. We ask that your forgiveness cleanse and heal us, and that your saving power lead and guide us.

We ask, too, that you sensitize us to all those in our troubled nation and in every nation who have need of you. We ask that you give us the desire and the courage to join Christ in his ongoing ministry to the lost and the lonely, to the oppressed and the oppressors in this demon-ridden world. And we pray that we who are learning to love and live in the light now will not slide into the darkness during some future hour of hardship.

Hear our prayer, O Lord. Amen.

SECTION II

□

SERMON
RESOURCES

LESSON GUIDE
BASED ON THE REVISED COMMON LECTIONARY, CYCLE B

Sunday	First Lesson	O.T. Theme	Second Lesson	Epistle Theme	Gospel Lesson	Gospel Theme	Psalm
1/2/94	Isa. 60:1-6	Your light has come	Eph. 3:1-12	To preach to the Gentiles	Matt. 2:1-12	The visit of the magi	72:1-7, 10-14
1/9/94	Gen. 1:1-5	The beginning	Acts 19:1-7	Baptized in the name of Jesus	Mark 1:4-11	The baptism of Jesus	29
1/16/94	I Sam. 3:1-10 (11-20)	Speak Lord, Your servant hears	I Cor. 6:12-20	Body a temple	John 1:43-51	Andrew and Simon called	139:1-6, 13-18
1/23/94	Jon. 3:1-5, 10	Jonah goes to Nineveh	I Cor. 7:29-31	Present world passing away	Mark 1:14-20	Calling the disciples	62:5-12
1/30/94	Deut. 18:15-20	The Lord will raise up a prophet	I Cor. 8:1-13	Food offered to idols	Mark 1:21-28	An evil spirit rebuked	111
2/6/94	Isa. 40:21-31	God's great power and mighty strength	I Cor. 9:16-23	All things to all men	Mark 1:29-39	After healing many Jesus prays alone	147:1-11, 20c
2/13/94	II Kings 2:1-12	A double portion of your spirit	II Cor. 4:3-6	God's glory in the face of Christ	Mark 9:2-9	The transfiguration	50:1-6
2/20/94	Gen. 9:8-17	The rainbow covenant	I Pet. 3:18-22	Brought to safety through baptism	Mark 1:9-15	The wilderness temptation	25:1-10
2/27/94	Gen. 17:1-7, 15-16	The promise of a son, Isaac	Rom. 4:13-25	The promise depends on faith	Mark 8:31-38	Jesus predicts his suffering and death	22:23-31
3/6/94	Exod. 20:1-17	The ten commandments	I Cor. 1:18-25	The cross a stumbling block	John 2:13-22	Cleansing the temple	19
3/13/94	Num. 21:4-9	Jerusalem conquered, exiles taken away	Eph. 2:1-10	Not because of works	John 3:14-21	God so loved the world	107:1-3, 17-22

Date	Scripture	Title	Scripture	Title	Scripture	Title	Hymn
3/20/94	Jer. 31:31-34	Written on your hearts	Heb. 5:5-10	Christ made perfect thru suffering	John 12:20-33	Christ prays, Glorify thy name	51:1-12
3/27/94	Isa. 50:4-9a	He offered his back to smiters	Phil. 2:5-11	Obedient to death on the cross	Mark 11:1-11	The triumphal entry	118:1-2, 19-29
4/3/94	Acts 10:34-43	The shroud of death destroyed	I Cor 15:1-11	Witnesses of the resurrection	John 20:1-18 or Mark 16:1-8	The empty tomb	118:1-2, 14-24
4/10/94	Acts 4:32-35	Witnesses to the resurrection	I John 1:1-2:2	Proclaiming the Word of life	John 20:19-31	Unless I see nail prints	133
4/17/94	Acts 3:12-19	A lame man healed	I John 3:1-7	In the image of God	Luke 24:36b-48	Jesus appears to disciples in Jerusalem	4
4/24/94	Acts 4:5-12	The stone rejected	I John 3:16-24	Love in deed and truth	John 10:11-18	The good shepherd	23
5/1/94	Acts 8:26-40	Philip and the Ethiopian eunuch	I John 4:7-21	Love born of God	John 15:1-8	I am the vine	22:25031
5/8/94	Acts 10:44-48	Gentiles receive Spirit	I John 5:1-6	The victory that overcomes the world	John 15:9-17	Not servants but friends	98
5/15/94	Acts 1:15-17, 21-26	Matthias chosen for discipleship	I John 5:9-13	He who has the Son has life	John 17:6-19	Jesus' farewell prayer . . . be kept from evil	1
5/22/94	Acts 2:1-21	Tongues, wind, fire	Rom. 8:22-27	First fruits of the Spirit	John 15:26-27, 16:4b-15	Advocate & Spirit of truth	104:24-34, 35b
5/29/94	Isa. 6:1-8	Here am I. Send me.	Rom. 8:12-17	We are God's children	John 3:1-17	Can one be born again?	29
6/5/94	I Sam. 8:4-11 (12-15) 16-20 (11:4-15)		II Cor. 4:13–5:1	Achieving an eternal glory	Mark 3:20-35	Jesus, Beelzebub and blasphemy	138
6/12/94	I Sam 15:34–16:13	Samuel anoints David	II Cor 5:6-10, (11-13), 14-17	A new creation in Christ	Mark 4:26-34	Parables of growing seed and the mustard seed	20 or 72

Sunday	First Lesson	O.T. Theme	Second Lesson	Epistle Theme	Gospel Lesson	Gospel Theme	Psalm
6/19/94	I Sam 17:(1a, 4-11, 19-23) 32-49	David slays the giant	II Cor. 6:1-13	Paul offers himself	Mark 4:35-41	Jesus stills the storm	9:9-20
6/26/94	II Sam. 1:1, 17-27	Saul's death and David's lament	II Cor. 8:7-15	The grace of giving	Mark 5:21-43	A sick woman healed; dead girl raised	133
7/3/94	II Sam. 5:1-5, 9-10	David becomes king over Israel	II Cor. 12:2-10	Paul's vision and his thorn	Mark 6:1-13	A prophet without honor	48
7/10/94	II Sam. 6:1-5, 12b-19	The ark brought to Jerusalem	Eph. 1:3-14	Blessed with every spiritual blessing	Mark 6:14-29	The head of John the Baptist	24
7/17/94	II Sam. 7:1-14a	God's promise to David; he will be my son	Eph. 2:11-22	Made members of God's household	Mark 6:30-34, 53-56	Crowds like sheep without a shepherd	89:20-37
7/24/94	II Sam. 11:1-15	David and Bathsheba	Eph. 3:14-21	To be filled with the fullness of God	John 6:1-21	The feeding of the five thousand	14
7/31/94	II Sam. 11:16-12:13a	Nathan rebukes David; You are the man	Eph. 4:1-16	Unity in the body of Christ	John 6:24-35	The bread of God gives life	51:1-12
8/7/94	II Sam 18:5-9, 15, 31-33	David mourns Absalom; My son, my son!	Eph. 4:25-5:2	Getting rid of bitterness and anger	John 6:35, 41-51	Jesus the bread of life	130
8/14/94	I Kings 2:10-12, 3:3-14	Solomon asks for wisdom	Eph. 5:15-20	How to live when days are evil	John 6:51-58	Feeding on the flesh and blood of Christ	111
8/21/94	I Kings 8:(1, 6, 10-11) 22-30, 41-43	Solomon's prayer of dedication	Eph. 6:10-20	The full armor of God	John 6:56-69	Many disciples desert Jesus	84

Date	OT Reading	OT Title	Epistle	Epistle Title	Gospel	Gospel Title	Psalm
8/28/94	Song of Songs 2:8-13	The season of singing has come	James 1:17-27	Listening and doing; not hearers only	Mark 7:1-8, 14-15, 21-23	The clean and the unclean	45:1-2, 6-9 or 72
9/4/94	Prov. 22:1-2, 8-9, 22-23	A good name is more desirable	James 2:1-10, (11-13) 14-17	Favoring the rich is forbidden	Mark 7:24-37	A Phoenician woman's faith rewarded	125 or 124
9/11/94	Prov. 1:20-33	Warnings against rejecting wisdom	James 3:1-12	Needing to tame the tongue	Mark 8:27-38	Peter's confession, "You are the Christ!"	19
9/18/94	Prov. 31:10-31	A wife of noble character	James 3:13-4:3, 7-8a	Marks of wisdom from above: peace, mercy	Mark 9:30-37	If anyone would be first, be servant of all	1
9/25/94	Esther 7:1-6, 9-10, 9:20-22	Queen Esther gains freedom for her people	James 5:13-20	Prayer of faith for healing	Mark 9:38-50	Warning against causing others to sin	124
10/2/94	Job 1:1, 2:1-10	Job's second test amid sores and ashes	Heb. 1:1-4; 2:5-12	Jesus, lower than angels, crowned with glory	Mark 10:2-16	Is it lawful to divorce?	26 or 25
10/9/94	Job 23:1-9, 16-17	Job, not silenced by the darkness	Heb. 4:12-16	The word; a two-edged sword	Mark 10:17-31	The rich young man	22:1-15
10/16/94	Job 38:1-7 (34-41)	The Lord asks, "Who established the earth?"	Heb. 5:1-10	Christ, made perfect, is the great high priest	Mark 10:35-45	James and John ask for seats of honor	104:1-9, 24, 35c
10/23/94	Job 42:1-6, 10-17	Now my eyes have seen you	Heb. 7:23-28	Christ's sacrifice is once for always	Mark 10:46-52	Blind Bartimaeus receives sight	34:1-8 (19-22)
10/30/94	Ruth 1:1-18	Where you go I will go	Heb. 9:11-14	The cleansing blood of Christ	Mark 12:28-34	The greatest commandment	146
11/6/94	Isa. 25:6-9	The Lord will wipe away all tears	Rev. 21:1-6a	No more death in the new Jerusalem	John 11:32-44	Jesus raises Lazarus from the dead	24
	Ruth 3:1-5, 4:13-17	Ruth became the wife of Boaz	Heb. 9:24-28	Christ entered heaven itself	Mark 12:38-44	The widow's mite	127 o4 42

Sunday	First Lesson	O.T. Theme	Second Lesson	Epistle Theme	Gospel Lesson	Gospel Theme	Psalm
11/13/94	I Sam. 1:4-20	The birth of Samuel	Heb 10:11-14 (15-18) 19-52	A call to persevere	Mark 13:1-8	Signs of the end of the age	I Sam. 2:1-10 or Ps 113
11/20/94	II Sam. 23:1-7	The last words of David	Heb. 12:1-2, 18-24	You have come to the city of God	Rev. 1:4b-8	Every eye will see him	132:1-12
11/27/94 Redemption is	Jer. 33:14-16	A righteous branch 25:1-10 from David's line	I Thess. 3:9-13	Lord comes	Blameless when our	drawing near	Luke 21:25-36

A SCHEDULE OF HYMNS FOR 1994

Sunday	Sunday	Opening Hymn	Second Hymn	Closing Hymn	Psalm
1/2/94	Epiphany	We Three Kings	Go, Tell It on the Mountain	Lead, Kindly Light	72:1-7, 10-14
1/9/94	1st After Epiphany	Love Divine, All Loves Excelling	Hope of the World	Nothing But the Blood	29
1/16/94	2nd After Epiphany	We've a Story to Tell to the Nations	Behold a Broken World	Dear Jesus, in Whose Life I See	139:1-6, 13-18
1/23/94	3rd After Epiphany	All Praise to Thee, For Thou, O King, Divine	Jesus Calls Us	Ye Servants of God	62:5-12
1/30/94	4th After Epiphany	The Battle Hymn of the Republic	Blessed Assurance	Pass Me Not, O Gentle Savior	111
2/6/94	5th Sunday After Epiphany	God of Love, and God of Power	Jesus! the Name High over All	Only Trust Him	147:1-11, 20c
2/13/94	Transfiguration Sunday	Immortal, Invisible God Only Wise	We Would See Jesus	Be Thou My Vision	50:1-6
2/20/94	Lent 1	Guide Me, O Thou Great Jehovah	I Am Thine, O Lord	It Is Well with My Soul	25:1-10
2/27/94	Lent 2	The Old Rugged Cross	Are Ye Able	When I Survey the Wondrous Cross	22:23-31
3/6/94	Lent 3	Trust and Obey	For the Healing of the Nations	O Master, Let Me Walk with Thee	19
3/13/94	Lent 4	Come, Thou Fount of Every Blessing	My Faith Looks Up to Thee	How Firm a Foundation	107:1-3, 17-22

Sunday	Sunday	Opening Hymn	Second Hymn	Closing Hymn	Psalm
3/20/94	Lent 5	Lift High the Cross	Jesus, Keep Me Near the Cross	To Mock Your Reign, O Dearest Lord	51:1-12
3/27/94	Lent 6 Passion	Ask Ye What Great Thing I Know	O Sacred Head, Now Wounded	Alas! and Did My Saviour Bleed	31:9-16
4/3/94	Lent 6 Palms	All Glory Laud and Honor	Were You There	Go To Dark Gethsemane	118:1-2, 19-29
	Easter Sunday	Christ The Lord Is Risen Today	Up from the Grave He Arose	The Day of Resurrection	118:1-2, 14-24
4/10/94	Second Sunday of Easter	God of The Ages	Christ Is Alive	Come, Sinners, to the Gospel Feast	133
4/17/94	Easter 3	All Hail the Power of Jesus' Name	Fairest Lord Jesus	O Young and Fearless Prophet	4
4/24/94	Easter 4	Crown Him with Many Crowns	Jesus Loves Me; He Is Lord	The Lord's My Shepherd, I'll Not Want	23
5/1/94	Easter 5	Jesus! the Name High over All	I Need Thee Every Hour	Close to Thee	22:25-31
5/8/94	Easter 6	Come, We That Love the Lord	What A Friend We Have in Jesus	My Jesus, I Love Thee	98
5/15/94	Easter 7	For the Beauty of the Earth	Happy the Home When God Is There	Children of the Heavenly Father	1
5/22/94	Pentecost Sunday	Spirit of God, Descend upon My Heart	Spirit of Faith, Come Down	Breathe on Me Breath of God	104:24-34, 35b
5/29/94	Trinity Sunday	Holy, Holy, Holy! Lord God Almighty	All Creatures of Our God and King	Spirit Song	29
6/5/94	Pentecost 2	How Firm a Foundation	O God in Heaven	Be Thou My Vision	138
6/12/94	Pentecost 3	Sing Praise to God Who Reigns Above	Nobody Knows the Trouble I See	Precious Name	20 or 72

Date					
6/19/94	Pentecost 4	How Great Thou Art	To God Be the Glory	Many Gifts, One Spirit	9:9-20
6/26/94	Pentecost 5	All Hail the Power of Jesus' Name	Jesus, Savior, Pilot Me	Lonely the Boat	133
7/3/94	Pentecost 6	Now Thank We All Our God	O How I Love Jesus	Precious Lord, Take My Hand	48
7/10/94	Pentecost 7	He Leadeth Me: O Blessed Thought	Morning Has Broken	Dear Lord and Father of Mankind	24
7/17/94	Pentecost 8	Come Ye Disconsolate	O Happy Day, That Fixed My Choice	Let Us Break Bread Together	89:20-37
7/24/94	Pentecost 9	I Need Thee Every Hour	I Want a Principle Within	Make Me a Captive, Lord	14
7/31/94	Pentecost 10	I Love to Tell the Story	Pass It On	A Charge to Keep I Have	51:1-12
8/7/94	Pentecost 11	Guide Me, O Thou Great Jehovah	Savior, Like a Shepherd Lead Us	Amazing Grace	130
8/14/94	Pentecost 12	I'll Praise My Maker While I've Breath	God of the Sparrow, God of the Whale	What Wondrous Love Is This	111
8/21/94	Pentecost 13	Stand Up, Stand Up for Jesus	Tis So Sweet to Trust in Jesus	God of Grace and God of Glory	84
8/28/94	Pentecost 14	Let All the World in Every Corner Sing	Leave It There	More Love to Thee, O Christ	45:1-2, 6-9 or 72
9/4/94	Pentecost 15	From All That Dwell Below the Skies	Sweet Hour of Prayer	Soldiers of Christ, Arise	125 or 124
9/11/94	Pentecost 16	O For a Thousand Tongues to Sing	Open My Eyes, That I May See	Where He Leads Me	19
9/18/94	Pentecost 17	Or All the Spirit's Gifts to Me	There's a Wideness in God's Mercy	Ask Ye What Great Thing I Know	1
9/25/94	Pentecost 18	Come Christians, Join to Sing	Take Time to Be Holy	I Am Thine, O Lord	124
10/2/94	Pentecost 19	Joyful, Joyful, We Adore Thee	Spirit of God, Descend upon My Heart	Spirit of the Living God	26 or 25
10/9/94	Pentecost 20	Maker, in Whom We Live	O Master Let Me Walk with Thee	Take My Life, and Let It Be	22:1-15

Sunday	Opening Hymn	Second Hymn	Closing Hymn	Psalm
10/16/94 Pentecost 21	Praise to the Lord, the Almighty	Jesus Is All the World to Me	Close to Thee	104:1-9, 24, 35c
10/23/94 Pentecost 22	All Creatures of Our God and King	Heal Me, Hands of Jesus	Open My Eyes, That I May See	34:1-8, 19-22
10/30/94 Pentecost 23	Holy God, We Praise Thy Name	Jesus, Thine All-Victorious Love	Where He Leads Me	146
11/6/94 All Saints' Day	For All The Saints	Great Is Thy Faithfulness	O Zion, Haste	24
Pentecost 24	We Thy People Praise Thee	More Love to Thee, O Christ	Jesus Is All the World to Me	127 o4 42
11/13/94 Pentecost 25	All Praise to Thee, for Thou, O King	My Hope Is Built	Leaning on the Everlasting Arms	I Sam. 2:1-10 or Ps. 113
11/20/94 Christ The King	Come, Thou Almighty King	We Gather Together	Lead On, O King Eternal	132:1-12
11/24/94 Thanksgiving Day	To God Be the Gory	Now Thank We All Our God	America the Beautiful	126
11/27/94 Advent 1	O Come, O Come, Emmanuel	Come, Thou Long-Expected Jesus	Jesus Shall Reign	25:1-10
12/4/94 Advent 2	Angels from the Realms of Glory	Hail to the Lord's Anointed	Lift Up Your Heads, Ye Mighty Gates	Luke 1:68-79 (UMH 208)
12/11/94 Advent 3	Lo, How a Rose E're Blooming	There's a Song in the Air	Joy to the World	Isa. 12:2-6
12/18/94 Advent 4	O Come, All Ye Faithful	Hark! The Herald Angels Sing	While Shepherds Watched Their Flocks	Luke 1:47-55 (UMH 199)
12/24/94 Christmas Eve	Hark! the Herald Angels Sing	Angels Sing Infant Holy, Infant Lowly	Silent Night, Holy Night	96
12/25/94 Christmas Day	Angels We Have Heard on High	The First Noel	O Little Town of Bethlehem	98

THE HOLY WEEK SCRIPTURES WITH CHILDREN

□

Stations of the Cross

by Hope Vickers

The Background

The story of Christ's death and resurrection are often approached in a gingerly manner with younger children—and perhaps skirted altogether by many with the very young. We often go from Palm Sunday to Easter Sunday telling the story of "Jesus Triumphantly Riding into Jerusalem" then follow it with "Jesus Rose from the Dead" with nothing said of the events that happened in between. Children need to know "Jesus-The-Dying" in context of "Jesus-The-Living" for the Easter story to fit their conceptual skill levels and to enable them to share in our Christian faith and worship. Careful preparation geared to the understandings of the children can make all the difference for them.

Our preparation for Easter begins many weeks earlier as we talk about the life and ministry of Jesus as God's Son. The children hear the stories and build an understanding of Jesus healing the sick, and lovingly teaching people how to be kind and caring for one another and how to be worshipful toward God. We share with them that sometimes people became angry with Jesus because they did not like what he said. Some people felt ashamed and angry with themselves, and that made them angrier when Jesus saw those things in them, too.

In this context, we can discuss similar feelings that children encounter—being angry when they have to share, pick up their toys, and so forth. We can talk about the ways Jesus would want us to respond to our friends and family. We can talk about what Jesus said, and the stories Jesus told to show us how to be loving and kind. We tell the children these stories, and the story of some people being so very angry with Jesus because of their own bad feelings, before we begin our Stations of the Cross walk.

The Stations of the Cross Walk proceeds from the story of Jesus' life and ministry even for the youngest members of our church family. This event takes place on Good Friday. A session is done for our preschool children in the morning, and another session is done in the afternoon for older children and adults. The youngest group to go on our walk is our two-year-olds class. The walk is a series of settings, or stations, telling the events leading from Palm Sunday lessons of the Triumphal Ride into Jerusalem.

The Settings

The settings are an experience designed to appeal to all of the senses. We want the children to see and feel something close to each of the events, to hear the events that took place, to imagine how Jesus felt and what he might have thought, and to be able to walk through all of the events through the eyes of Jesus' followers. They should gain a viewpoint similar to that which they would have had if they had walked along witnessing the actual events. The settings are recreated telling the stories of the Triumphal Ride, the Last Supper, the Garden of Gethsemane, the Court of Pontius Pilate, the Crucifixion, the Resurrection, and the Empty Tomb. These stations need to be out of view and earshot of one another so that several small groups can take the walk and have a more vivid experience than would be accomplished in one large group. (Scripts follow for the storytellers at each setting.)

The Triumphant Ride into Jerusalem

We begin with a processional into our Narthex where the children encounter a woman in biblical costume who tells about Jesus coming to Jerusalem. The children carry palms and sing as they arrive. The mood is festive and upbeat. The children are invited to imagine how exciting it would have been to be there and see Jesus.

Storyteller: "When we celebrate Palm Sunday, we know the story Jesus told his disciples. They were getting ready to go into Jerusalem and he said to go find a donkey. He told them where to go and he said: 'If anybody gives you any trouble and asks why you are taking the donkey, just tell them that the Lord has need of the donkey.' The disciples left and found the donkey—one that had never been ridden before. The owner came out and asked why they were taking his donkey and the disciples explained, 'The Lord has need of this donkey.' They took the donkey to Jesus and he got up and sat on the donkey. The donkey didn't buck him off at all. The donkey was very, very good and allowed Jesus to ride him all the way into Jerusalem. As they entered the gates of the city of Jerusalem, all the people—mommies and daddies, boys and girls, were very, very happy and excited. They waved their palm branches and sang "Hosanna," which means "Oh Save Us." They were so happy to see Jesus. They had heard so many wonderful stories about Jesus healing sick people, loving the children, and teaching everyone how to be good. They had heard all these wonderful things about him being God's Son, and now he had come to their town where they were.

"Let's pretend that we are in that crowd of people that welcomed Jesus to Jerusalem. Let's sing our song "Sing Hosanna" and wave our palm branches. Just sing as happy as you can and pretend that you were there seeing Jesus on that first Palm Sunday. Let's walk to the sanctuary to find out what happened next."

The Last Supper

The children move from Jerusalem to the next setting, which is the station of the Last Supper. Our setting is on the floor in the chancel area. The children come in to find a table created by a large rectangle of burlap on the floor with carpet squares around as seats. In the center of the table is a chalice and a tray with a fresh loaf of bread. (Look to your local bakery for a whole loaf that is braided or shaped in a way that lends authenticity to the setting—or bake it yourself.) To the side of the table is a small stand or table holding a pitcher of water and a basin and towel. (These props are effectively done with pottery but any old looking items will work.) The storyteller is dressed in biblical costume and invites everyone to join together at the seats around the table.

Storyteller: "After Jesus came into Jerusalem, he spent a few days working very hard. So many people wanted to see him. They wanted to hear his stories, touch him, get him to heal their illnesses, to forgive them for their mistakes, and to learn how to be good. There were so many people who wanted Jesus to help them. He had so much to do and so much to tell the people because he knew that he didn't have much more time to be a man on earth. One thing about being the Son of God was that Jesus knew exactly what God wanted him to do, and what was going to happen. Jesus knew that the soldiers were going to arrest him and that he was going to die and eventually go back to be with God. Before he was arrested though, Jesus got his very best friends, the disciples, together and they went to the upstairs room in a house. Jesus wanted to have dinner with them. Having dinner with your friends is a great way to be close to one another. In Jesus' time, friends would get together for dinner and sometimes just eat bread and drink wine for dinner. Jesus took this bread and said a special prayer over it. Then he said, 'This is something I want you to always do and remember me when you do it.' Christians are the only ones who do this special ceremony to remember Jesus. Jesus took the bread and ate some of it. They passed it around to all of the disciples, who also took some and ate it. Then Jesus took a drink from the cup and passed it around and they all drank some. Jesus told us to remember his blood and his body when we drank and ate at this special ceremony so that this food would represent these elements for us, and he would live in us and through us. After Jesus had this special meal with his friends, he wanted to take a walk and if you will go to the Garden of Gethsemane you will find out what happened next."

Garden of Gethsemane

The garden needs to be a restful, quiet setting. Find a relatively dark area where you can bring in plants, rocks (real or artificial props can be used for both), and perhaps a round pool filled with water. A string of white Christmas lights might be woven into some bushes to give the effect of starlight. We always work a new setting each year and no two are alike. You might want to have a person costumed as Jesus, kneeling in the shadows with his back to the participants.

Storyteller: "After their meal together, Jesus needed some time to be alone. Have you ever felt like you just need some time to be by yourself? That's how Jesus felt. He went to a special place called the Garden of Gethsemane. It might be like one of our quiet, beautiful parks. It was nighttime and dark like it is in here right now. All over that garden were trees called olive trees. There were some big rocks and maybe a quiet pool of water running and making a soothing sound. Jesus chose this place late at night when it was cool so that he could go and talk to God. He took three of his disciples along with him and asked them to wait and watch by the big rock while he went over and prayed.

"Jesus told God how sad he was feeling. He told God how afraid he was feeling. He told God everything that was in his heart that night. He soon went back to his friends, but do you know what he found when he got to the rock? His three friends had fallen asleep. He said, 'Can't you stay awake for just a little while?' Again, he went back to pray. He prayed hard to God and then he went back to his three friends. Do you know what they had done? That's right—they went to sleep again. He said, 'Stay awake and pray with me.' Jesus went to pray again, but for a third time, his friends fell asleep. This time though, a crowd of people came up. They were carrying torches to light their way and they made lots of noise in the quiet garden. In the front leading them was Judas. Judas went up to Jesus and kissed him on the cheek. Kissing him was a secret signal to the soldiers that Jesus was the one they were to arrest. The soldiers GRABBED Jesus by the arms and tied him up. They took him off all alone to his trial. The disciples were afraid and ran the other way.

"Now, if you will go to the next room, you will hear the story about the trial Jesus was taken to in front of Pontius Pilate."

Court of Pontius Pilate

The court of Pontius Pilate needs to be regal enough to enable you to clearly draw a contrast between the simplicity of Jesus and the wealth and pomp of a Roman Court. This is an implied aspect of the story and not an aspect that is pointed out for the children. In addition to the storyteller, who should have on a robe or biblical costume, there will be a regally costumed Pontius Pilate to actually bring this aspect of the story to life as he pours the water and washes his hands of the matter.

Storyteller: "When the soldiers arrested Jesus at the Garden of Gethsemane, they tied him up very tightly with a rope. Then they took Jesus to a judge. Lots of people were coming and yelling at Jesus. These were the people who had been angry with Jesus. They had sticks that they were waving and they were shouting mean things at him. When they got to the place where the judge was he said, 'Why did you wake me up to make me come see this man? What did this man do?' Do you know what the people said? They said Jesus was wanting to be the king of the whole world. They said that Jesus wanted to be king instead of the king they had.

"The judge looked at Jesus and asked him if this was true. Jesus didn't say anything. The judge asked Jesus again. Jesus said his kingdom was not of this world. Now do you know what a king wears on his head? Kings wear gold crowns. Well, Jesus was crowned, too, only it wasn't with a gold crown. They put a crown of thorns on his head. You know when you touch a bush with stickers and they stick you? They made a crown out of those things and jammed it onto Jesus' head. It hurt Jesus and made him bleed.

"The soldiers made fun of Jesus and teased him. They hit him and put a purple robe on him and waved palm branches in his face. They said, 'Hail king!' but they were doing it to make fun of him. Jesus was not a bad man. He was a very, very good man. In that town, though, there was a bad man named Barabbas, who was a murderer. He had killed some people. The judge didn't know what else to do with Jesus and wanted to let him go because of the special Jewish holiday that was coming. He said, 'I can let a prisoner go free because of your special holiday. I don't want to crucify Jesus. I don't want to nail his hands to a cross and make him die. I will give you people a choice, surely you would rather Jesus go free than this awful murderer, Barabbas.'

"The judge gave the people a choice then, between Jesus, who had been kind and loving to them, and Barabbas, who had murdered innocent people. I wish those people would have chosen Jesus, but they didn't."

Pontius Pilate: "After the people chose to release Barabbas and insisted that Jesus be crucified, I wanted nothing more to do with the whole business. I told them it was their decision and out of my hands. I washed my hands of the whole thing." [Act out by pouring a pitcher of water into a basin and wash your hands.]

The Crucifixion

The setting for the Crucifixion needs to be empty except for a box of nails and a supply of wooden crosses about 18 to 24 inches tall. The storyteller should be in a robe or biblical costume. The starkness of this setting helps to create that sense of aloneness and abandonment facing Jesus at his death. We do our portion of this story at the end of an empty hallway.

Storyteller: "Jesus was very sad. He was hurting from the thorns on his head and all the places they had hit him. They made him carry a cross—only it was too heavy and he had to have a friend help him carry it. Everyone went outside of town and up on a hill. When they got there, they took Jesus and laid him down on the cross. Then they took nails and put them through his hands and into the wood. You know that would hurt. Then they took a nail and nailed his feet to the cross. This is probably what it looked like when they stood the cross up in a hole in the ground. [Show a crucifix or picture of Jesus on the cross.]

"Jesus was there hanging on that cross for six hours. His body hurt badly and he was bleeding. After a while, he looked around and saw his mother. He told one of his friends to take care of her after he was gone. A little while later, he looked around and saw his friends there. He saw the people who had been angry with him. He saw the soldiers and other people. Do you know what he did? He prayed. He prayed a prayer to God asking God to forgive these people. It's hard for us to believe that he would ask God to forgive these people when he was hurting so badly, but Jesus did. Then after about six hours Jesus couldn't live any longer, and so he finally died.

"But that isn't the end of the story! To know the end of the story you need to go to the next station."

The Resurrection and Empty Tomb

The setting for the last station needs to be vivid enough to make a lasting impression, focusing on the empty tomb. In our own setting, we complete a circle through our church, crossing the narthex where the participants first began their walk, and moving to a room off the narthex where sheets have been draped and a long bench has been covered to create the empty tomb. Use something to create a giant boulder (perhaps a large cardboard panel painted to look like a rock.) and have it rolled over to the side from the entrance to the tomb. Within the space of the tomb, walls leave an opening for the angel to step out. We use the sound of chimes just before the angel steps out. The storyteller should be dressed in biblical costume.

Storyteller: "After Jesus died on the cross, two of his friends, Arimathaea and Nicodemus, took his body off the cross. That's why our cross in our church is empty because he is not there anymore. They wrapped up his body in a white cloth and took it to a tomb in a cave. They laid it in there all wrapped up in this white cloth and then they got a great big stone and rolled it in front of the tomb so no one could get in. Then they left. A couple of days later, some of the ladies, Mary and Mary Magdalene and Salome, came and wanted to anoint Jesus' body with spices and oils the way it should have been done when he was buried. They were really worried about how they were going to get that big rock rolled away because it was really heavy. When they got to the tomb though, they found that the rock was already rolled away. They went up and looked in. Do you know what they saw? Nothing! It was empty! Jesus wasn't there. There was an angel in there instead." [Chimes Ring]

Angel: "Don't be afraid. You are looking for Jesus and he is not here anymore. He is risen! He is alive! Go and tell his disciples."

Storyteller: "The ladies started off to tell the disciples the good news. This is the good news for us, too! It shows us that God loved us so much that he sent his only Son, Jesus Christ, to die for us. He died for us so that we could have eternal life if we believe in him. That's our good news! Jesus is alive today! Let's go tell everyone! Do you know the song 'Go Tell It on the Mountain'? Let's sing it as we leave."

THE CHRISTMAS LESSONS WITH CHILDREN

□

A Christmas Journey: *No Room in the Inn*

by Hope Vickers

The Background

The Christmas story is usually told as a historical event. At best, we usually view it as though we were travelers looking back on what happened. Sometimes we find a way to hear the story through the eyes of those that were present that day.

Children can learn and understand the story of Jesus' birth at a very early age if we find just the right way to make the story come to life for them. We know that young children learn best by experiential learning where they are actively involved in the activity of the story. Our goal then is to create a setting where the children can be a part of the events around Jesus' birth. By traveling to Bethlehem through the eyes of Mary and Joseph, being weary of the trip, hunting and hunting for a place to stay, feeling the rejection of gruff innkeepers, and finally finding a place to rest in a stable, the children gain a vivid experience of the first Christmas.

Take your youngest children on the Christmas Journey. Even two-year-olds gain some perspective from the experience. Older children and even adults come to see Christ's birth in a new light when they experience the smell of the stable, the presence of animals, and their own view through the eyes of Mary and Joseph.

The Setting

The goal is to provide a truly realistic experience of the stable in which the birth of Jesus could have taken place. To achieve this feeling of realism, the sights, sounds, smells, and textures all

413

work together. Pick a location that is not normally visited by the children. It can be a side entrance to the church sanctuary as we use, or a storage area, or basement hallway. Cover the floor with straw, creating a six-to-ten inch base. Cover the walls with burlap, old sheets, brown paper, or other covering to create the rustic appearance of a barn. Turn the lights to low or screen them to a low level. Props can be used such as farm implements, pieces of split rail fences, additional bales of straw. In this setting create a corner area for Mary, Joseph, and Baby Jesus to sit and for the shepherd and wise man to visit.

You will need a place for the angel to enter. This may be another doorway or a screened area for the angel to step out from at her appointed time.

The use of farm animals adds a wonderful feeling of authenticity to the table. If your setting allows a corral area, or even a sheep or two on a leash, their presence make the event much more real for the children. The goal is realism!

The Characters

Mary, Joseph, and Baby Jesus do not have speaking parts. A real infant also lends a lot to the experience, if one is available, and the child's mother might be the best one to play the part of Mary.

The speaking is done by the Innkeeper, one Shepherd, one Wise Man, one Angel, and the leader who brings the children on the journey. A crowd of extra shepherds, angels, and wise men do not contribute to the story and may cause some young children to be intimidated by so many costumed characters. One of each character provides a simple basis for the story and keeps the children focused on the event itself.

The following script is written for classroom teachers to know the way the journey will progress from the time of leaving their classroom. It can easily be followed by those who are participating as characters in the story as well.

The Script: "No Room in the Inn"
Characters:

Leader	Wise Man
Innkeeper	Angel
Shepherd	

The journey begins at the door of your room. The children will pretend that they are Joseph and Mary and they are ready for the long journey to Bethlehem. [Please tell them the Christmas story several times prior to the journey. You might want to make headpieces for them to put over their heads; one color for girls and another for boys.]

The children pretend to be Mary and Joseph and travel with the leader from room to room looking for a place to stay after their long journey. The leader will sing their song with them at each room [listed below].

Each time they are only answered with a gruff *no* or "Stop bothering us, we're busy," or just a shake of the head.

Finally, they come to an inn [minister's office] and knock. They sing their song again:

> Is there any room here in your inn, we pray?
> Is there any room here in your inn?
> We've come such a very long way, Oh friend,
> Is there any room here in your inn?

The Innkeeper looks at them and sadly shakes his head. He tells them that he is so sorry, but his inn is already full. They start to leave when he says, "No, wait, I don't have any room in my inn, but I could at least give you a place to sleep out of the night air. . . . Here, come with me."

The innkeeper leads them to the stable explaining that it is the only place he can think of, and at least they can get out of the night air. The leader comments that they are just so tired and have come such a long way and anything will do if they can just lie down and get some rest somewhere.

At the stable, the children come in and sit down [after seeing the animals] and see where Baby Jesus was born. The leader will point out to the the Baby Jesus and tell them what has happened.

There is a knock at the door and a shepherd enters. He kneels down in front of the manger to worship the Christ Child. He tells how he was watching his sheep out in the fields when an angel came to him and all the skies filled with angels singing about the birth of Baby Jesus. "Now I have found Him!"

There is another knock at the door. The Wise Man enters.

"We have traveled a long way following the star and looking for the Son of God. We bring him these gifts. Where is the Baby Jesus?" [The children will all point to the manger.] The Wise Man will take his gift and place it in front of the manger, kneeling as he does so.

There is a sound of heavenly chimes and an angel enters.

"Do not be afraid! God loves you. He sent his Son to you. Jesus was born here in Bethlehem. He has come to bring love and peace to the world. He brings us great joy!"

The leader will say: "Now, boys and girls, you can leave your gift and go and tell everyone that Jesus Christ is born!"

The angel begins singing and everyone joins in, "Go Tell It on the Mountain."

The children will leave a gift for Baby Jesus and return to their class. (Gifts could be class-made or actual gifts for a baby, which will be sent to a needy family this Christmas.)

Offertory Sentences

□

New International Version

Luke 6:38: "Give, and it will be given to you. A good measure, pressed down, shaken together and running over, will be poured into your lap. For with the measure you use, it will be measured to you."

Luke 12:33: "Sell your possessions and give to the poor. Provide purses for yourselves that will not wear out, a treasure in heaven that will not be exhausted, where no thief comes near and no moth destroys."

Luke 20:25: " 'Caesar's,' they replied. He said to them, 'Then give to Caesar what is Caesar's, and to God what is God's.' "

Luke 21:4: "All these people gave their gifts out of their wealth; but she out of her poverty put in all she had to live on."

John 3:16: "For God so loved the world that he gave his one and only Son, that whoever believes in him shall not perish but have eternal life."

John 6:27: "Do not work for food that spoils, but for food that endures to eternal life which the Son of Man will give you. On him God the Father has placed his seal of approval."

John 13:34: "A new command I give you: Love one another. As I have loved you, so you must love one another."

John 1:16: "From the fullness of his grace we have all received one blessing after another."

Romans 12:11: "Never be lacking in zeal, but keep your spiritual fervor, serving the Lord."

II Corinthians 8:7: "But just as you excel in everything—in faith, in speech, in knowledge, in complete earnestness and in your love for us—see that you also excel in this grace of giving."

II Corinthians 8:9: "For you know the grace of our Lord Jesus Christ, that though he was rich, yet for your sakes he became poor, so that you through his poverty might become rich."

II Corinthians 9:8: "And God is able to make all grace abound to you, so that in all things at all times, having all that you need, you will abound in every good work."

Galatians 5:22: "But the fruit of the Spirit is love, joy, peace, patience, kindness, goodness, faithfulness, gentleness and self-control. Against such things there is no law."

II Thessalonians 2:16-17: "May our Lord Jesus Christ himself and God our Father, who loved us and by his grace gave us eternal encouragement and good hope, encourage your hearts and strengthen you in every good deed and word."

I Peter 4:10: "Each one should use whatever gift he has received to serve others, faithfully administering God's grace in its various forms."

BENEDICTIONS

□

New International Version

Jude 1:24-25: "To him who is able to keep you from falling and to present you before his glorious presence without fault and with great joy—to the only God our Savior be glory, majesty, power and authority, through Jesus Christ our Lord, before all ages, now and forevermore! Amen."

Romans 15:13: "May the God of hope fill you with all joy and peace as you trust in him, so that you may overflow with hope by the power of the Holy Spirit."

Romans 15:33: "The God of peace be with you all. Amen."

I Corinthians 1:3: "Grace and peace to you from God our Father and the Lord Jesus Christ."

II Corinthians 13:14: "May the grace of the Lord Jesus Christ, and the love of God, and the fellowship of the Holy Spirit be with you all."

Philippians 4:7: "And the peace of God, which transcends all understanding, will guard your hearts and your minds in Christ Jesus."

Colossians 3:15: "Let the peace of Christ rule in your hearts, since as members of one body you were called to peace. And be thankful."

II Thessalonians 3:16: "Now may the Lord of peace himself give you peace at all times and in every way. The Lord be with all of you."

Hebrews 13:20-21: "May the God of peace, who through the blood of the eternal covenant brought back from the dead our

Lord Jesus, that great Shepherd of the sheep, equip you with everything good for doing his will, and may he work in us what is pleasing to him, through Jesus Christ, to whom be glory forever and ever. Amen."

Mark 5:34: "He said to her, 'Daughter, your faith has healed you. Go in peace and be freed from your suffering.'"

John 1:14: "The Word became flesh and made his dwelling among us. We have seen his glory, the glory of the One and Only, who came from the Father, full of grace and truth."

Romans 5:1: "Therefore, since we have been justified through faith, we have peace with God through our Lord Jesus Christ, through whom we have gained access by faith into this grace in which we now stand. And we rejoice in the hope of the glory of God."

Ephesians 2:4: "But because of his great love for us, God, who is rich in mercy, made us alive with Christ even when we were dead in transgressions—it is by grace you have been saved."

II Peter 3:18: "But grow in the grace and knowledge of our Lord and Savior Jesus Christ. To him be glory both now and forever! Amen."

Jude 1:2: "Mercy, peace and love be yours in abundance."

Revelation 1:4: "Grace and peace to you from him who is, and who was, and who is to come, and from the seven spirits before his throne."

Revelation 22:21: "The grace of the Lord Jesus be with God's people. Amen."

I Corinthians 1:8: "He will keep you strong to the end, so that you will be blameless on the day of our Lord Jesus Christ."

I Corinthians 5:8: "Therefore let us keep the Festival, not with the old yeast, the yeast of malice and wickedness, but with bread without yeast, the bread of sincerity and truth."

Ephesians 1:17: "I keep asking that the God of our Lord Jesus Christ, the glorious Father, may give you the Spirit of wisdom and revelation, so that you may know him better."

Ephesians 4:3: "Make every effort to keep the unity of the Spirit through the bond of peace."

Jude 1:21: "Keep yourselves in God's love as you wait for the mercy of our Lord Jesus Christ to bring you to eternal life."

ABINGDON PREACHER'S ANNUAL 1994
SERMON CONTRIBUTORS

Dr. Michael B. Brown	Sr. Pastor Central UMC	Asheville	NC
Rev. Kenneth W. Chalker	Sr. Pastor Cleveland First UMC	Cleveland	OH
Dr. David W. Richardson	Sr. Pastor Dexter United Methodist Ch.	Dexter	MO
Dr. Gayle Carlton Felton	Asst. Prof. Duke Divinity School	Durham	NC
Bishop Joseph B. Bethea	Bishop Columbia Area UMC	Columbia	SC
Rev. Charles M. Cook	Pastor Gardners UMC	Fayetteville	NC
Dr. Norman M. Pritchard	Sr. Pastor The Scot's Church (Presb)	Melbourne	AUST.
Colonel Bernard H. Lieving, Jr.	Commandant, US Army Chaplain School	Fort Bragg	NC
Dr. Heather Murray-Elkins	Assoc. Prof. of Worship Drew University	Madison	NJ
Bishop Robert E. Fannin	Bishop Birmingham Area UMC	Birmingham	AL
Dr. David Z. Ring III	Pastor Paradise Hills United Meth. Ch.	Albuquerque	NM
Dr. Ralph C. Wood	J. Allen Easley Prof. Wake Forest Univ.	Winston Salem	NC
Dr. Ronald H. Love	Pastor Summit UMC	Erie	PA
Rev. Judith A. Olin	Council on Ministries Director E. Ohio	North Canton	OH
Lt. Col. Milford Oxendine	Native American Chaplain, US Navy	New Bern	NC
Rev. Michael T. McEwen	University of Central Oklahoma	Edmond	OK
Dr. John K. Bergland	Sr. Pastor Haymount United Meth. Ch.	Fayetteville	NC
Rev. Edith L. Gleaves	Assoc. Director Council on Ministries NC	Raleigh	NC
Rev. Robert Eric Bergland	Pastor Trinity United Methodist Ch.	Elizabethtown	NC
Dr. Scott J. Jones	Pastor First United Methodist Church	Howe	TX
Dr. R. Benjamin Garrison	Retired United Methodist Pastor	Park Falls	WS
Dr. Richard Andersen	Sr. Pastor St. Timothy's Lutheran Ch.	San Jose	CA
Dr. Jerry L. Mercer	Prof. of Homiletics Asbury Theol. Sem.	Wilmore	KY

Dr. Jaime Potter-Miller	Pastor Bethel United Methodist Ch.	Lower Burrell	PA
Dr. Reginald W. Ponder	Ex. Sec. Administrative Council SE Juris	Lake Junaluska	NC
Rev. Louise Stowe Johns	Pastor Tuskegee-Armstrong Charge UMC	Tuskegee	AL
Dr. Craig M. Watts	Sr. Pastor First Christian Church	Louisville	KY
Rev. Camille Yorkey-Edwards	Pastor Seaside United Methodist Ch.	South Brunswick	NC
Dr. Victor A. Shepherd	Streetsville United Church of Canada	Mississauga, Ont.	CD
Dr. Wallace E. Fisher	Pastor Emeritus Trinity Lutheran Ch.	Pinehurst	NC
Hope Vickers	Student Duke Divinity School	Durham	NC

INDEX

□

OLD TESTAMENT

NEW TESTAMENT

Acts

Romans

I Corinthians

INDEX